THE
PANTROPHEON

THE
PANTROPHEON

OR

A HISTORY OF FOOD
AND ITS PREPARATION
IN ANCIENT TIMES

EMBELLISHED WITH
FORTY-ONE ENGRAVINGS ILLUSTRATING THE GREATEST
GASTRONOMIC MARVELS OF ANTIQUITY

BY

ALEXIS SOYER

PADDINGTON
PRESS LTD
NEW YORK & LONDON

Library of Congress Cataloging in Publication Data

Soyer, Alexis, 1809-1858.
    Pantropheon.

    Reprint of the 1853 ed. published by Simpkin, Marshall, London.
      1. Food. 2. Gastronomy. 3. Cookery. I. Title.
TX353.S73   1977   641.3'009'01   76-53623
ISBN 0-448-22976-5

Printed in England by Balding & Mansell Ltd., Wisbech, Cambs.

IN THE UNITED STATES
PADDINGTON PRESS LTD.
Distributed by
GROSSET & DUNLAP

IN THE UNITED KINGDOM
PADDINGTON PRESS LTD.

IN CANADA
Distributed by
RANDOM HOUSE OF CANADA LTD.

IN AUSTRALIA
Distributed by
ANGUS & ROBERTSON PTY. LTD.

PUBLISHER'S NOTE

Alexis Soyer (1809-1859), hailed by a contemporary as that "high authority in the science of living," was, from all reports, a talented, dashing, flamboyant, French egocentric whose gastronomic genius was the rage and envy of mid-nineteenth-century England. Between 1821 and 1837 he served as cook to various French and English notables: among them M. Douix, the famous French restaurateur of the Boulevard des Italiens, Prince Polignac of the French Foreign Office, the Duke of Cambridge, the Duke of Sutherland, the Marquis of Waterford, and William Lloyd of Aston Hall, Oswestry.

Soyer is most widely known, however, for his triumphant tenure as master chef of the London Reform Club, a post he accepted in 1837. A year later, on June 28, 1838, the day of Queen Victoria's coronation, Soyer executed one of the greatest culinary extravaganzas of all time: a breakfast for two thousand people at Gwydyr House, where the club was temporarily housed. His dinner for Ibraham Pasha on July 3, 1846, a *banquet de luxe* for 150 guests, has also become a culinary legend.

Soyer further consolidated his reputation by writing some of the most ambitious, authoritative, and useful books on the history and art of preparing food ever written. Among his works are the highly acclaimed and successful *The Gastronomic Regenerator: A Simplified and New System of Cookery* (1846) and *The Modern Housewife, or Ménagère* (1849). Also to his credit are *Soyer's Charitable Cookery, or the Poor Man's Regenerator* (c.1848) and *A Shilling Cookery Book for the People* (1855), two volumes which readily display that his interests and talents went well beyond his ability to tickle the palates of the well-to-do.

Indeed, Soyer devoted his vast energies to both the rich and the poor. There was Soyer, proprietor and chef of the effete gourmet establishment, The Gastronomic Symposium of All Nations, and Soyer, the inventor of new-fangled gadgetry: a Tendon Separator, for example, a not very successful carving aid; and his famous Magic Stove, a portable unit with which a Marquis once cooked dinner for himself atop one of the Great Pyramids. But more significantly, there was Soyer the humanitarian—the Soyer who organized soup kitchens for the poor during the Irish famine of the late 1840s and the Soyer who, during the Crimean War, provided soldiers with nourishing foods on the battlefields and, in collaboration with Florence Nightingale and her medical staff in Balaklava, reorganized food provisioning in hospital kitchens.

It is with a similar blend of lofty purpose and high frivolity that Soyer wrote his *Pantropheon* in 1853. "What cooks! what a table! what guests! in that Eden of paganism," cries the elated chef-cum-historian in his opening chapter. Addressing himself to the major peoples of the ancient world—Greeks, Romans, Assyrians, Egyptians and Jews— he beckons them to reveal themselves and the business of their daily lives, their ways of eating and drinking, the prose of life:

> "Tell me what thou eatest, and I will tell thee who thou art."

The publisher salutes M. Soyer and delights in making this witty cornucopia of classical food lore available to the public for the first time in many years. *Amateurs* of history and food alike are bound to rejoice with the republication of his charming study of antiquity's larder.

Contents.

———

CONTENTS.

IX.

X.

XXI.

CONTENTS.

List of Illustrations.

———

PANTROPHEON.

"I did feast with Cæsar."

SHAKSPERE.—"Julius Cæsar," Act iii., Sc. 3.

" Dis-moi ce que tu manges,
Je te dirai ce que tu es."

BRILLAT-SAVARIN.—" Physiologie du Goût."

THANKS to the impressions received in boyhood, Rome and Athens always present themselves to our minds accompanied by the din of arms, shouts of victory, or the clamours of plebeians crowded round the popular tribune. "And yet," said we, "nations, like individuals, have two modes of existence distinctly marked—one intellectual and moral, the other sensual and physical; and both continue to interest through the lapse of ages."

What, for instance, calls forth our sympathies more surely than to follow from the cradle that city of Romulus—at first so weak, so obscure, and so despised—through its prodigious developments, until, having become the sovereign mistress of the world, it seems, like Alexander, to lament that the limits of the globe restrict within so narrow a compass its ungovernable ardour for conquest, its insatiable thirst of *opima spolia* and tyrannical oppression. In like manner, a mighty river, accounted as nothing at its source, where a child can step across, receives in its meandrous descent the tribute of waters, which roll on with increasing violence, and rush at last from their too narrow bed to inundate distant plains, and spread desolation and terror.

History has not failed to record, one by one, the battles, victories, and defeats of nations which no longer exist; it has described their public life,—their life in open air,—the tumultuous assemblies of the forum,—the fury of the populace,—the revolts of the camps,—the barbarous spectacles of those amphiteatres, where the whole pagan universe engaged in bloody conflict, where gladiators were condemned to slaughter one another for the pastime of the over-pampered inhabitants of the Eternal City—sanguinary spectacles, which often consigned twenty or thirty thousand men to the jaws of death in the space of thirty days!

But, after all, neither heroes, soldiers, nor people, can be always at war; they cannot be incessantly at daggers drawn on account of some open-air election; the applause bestowed on a skilful and courageous *bestiarius* is not eternal; captives may be poignarded in the Circus by way of amusement, but only for a time. Independently of all these things, there is the home, the fire-side, the prose of life, if you will; nay, let us say it at once, the business of life—eating and drinking.

It is to that we have devoted our vigils, and, in order to arrive at our aim, we have given an historical sketch of the vegetable and animal alimentation of man from the earliest ages; therefore it will be easily understood why we have taken the liberty of saying to the austere Jew, the voluptuous Athenian, the obsequious or vain-glorious senator of imperial Rome, and even to the fantastical, prodigal, and cruel Cæsars: " Tell me what thou eatest, and I will tell thee who thou art."

But, it must be confessed that our task was surrounded with difficulties, and required much laborious patience and obstinate perseverance. It is easy to penetrate into the temples, the baths, and the theatres of the ancients; not so to rummage their cellars, pantries, and kitchens, and study the delicate magnificence of their dining-rooms. Now it was there, and there alone, that we sought to obtain access.

With that view we have had recourse to the only possible means :

we have interrogated those old memoirs of an extinct civilisation which connect the present with the past; poets, orators, historians, philosophers, epistolographers, writers on husbandry, and even those who are the most frivolous or the most obscure—we have consulted all, examined all, neglected nothing. Our respectful curiosity has often emboldened us to peep into the sacred treasure of the annals of the people of God; and sometimes the doctors of the Primitive Church have furnished us with interesting traits of manners and customs, together with chance indications of domestic usages, disseminated, and, as it were, lost in the midst of grave moral instruction.

The fatigue of these unwonted researches appeared to us to be fully compensated by the joy we experienced on finding our hopes satisfied by some new discovery. Like the botanist, who forgets his lassitude at the unexpected sight of a desired plant, we no longer remembered the dust of fatidical volumes, nor the numberless leaves we had turned over, when by a happy chance our gastronomic enthusiasm espied a curious and rare dish.

Thus it is that this work—essay, we ought to call it—has been slowly and gradually augmented with the spoils of numerous writers of antiquity, both religious and profane.

We have avoided, as much as possible, giving to this book a didactic and magisterial character, which would have ill-accorded with the apparent lightness of the subject, and might have rendered it tedious to most readers. We know not whether these researches will be considered instructive, but we hope they will amuse.

When we compare the cookery of the ancients with our own—and the parallel naturally presents itself to the mind—it often betrays strange anomalies, monstrous differences, singular perversions of taste, and incomprehensible amalgamations, which baffle every attempt at justification. Apicius himself, or perhaps the Cœlius of the 3rd century, to whom we owe the celebrated treatise " *De Opsoniis*," would run great risk—if he were now to rise from his tomb, and attempted to give vogue to his ten books of recipes—either of passing for a poisoner or of being put under restraint as a subject decidedly insane. It follows, then, that although we have borrowed his curious lucubrations, we leave to the Roman epicurean and to his times the entire responsibility of his work.

The reader will also remark, in the course of this volume, asserted facts of a striking oddity, certain valuations which appear to be exaggerated, some descriptions he will pronounce fabulous or impossible. Now, we have never failed to give our authorities, but we are far from being willing to add our personal guarantee ; so that we leave all those antique frauds—if any—to be placed to the account of the writers who have traitorously furnished them.

We think, however, that most persons will peruse with some interest (and, let us hope, a little indulgence) these studies on an art which, like all arts invented by necessity or inspired by pleasure, has kept pace with the genius of nations, and became more refined and more perfect in proportion as they themselves became more polite.

It appears that the luxury and enchantments of the table were first appreciated by the Assyrians and Persians, those voluptuous Asiatics, who, by reason of the enervating mildness of the climate, were powerless to resist sensual seductions.

Greece—"beloved daughter of the gods"—speedily embellished the culinary art with all the exquisite delicacy of her poetic genius. "The people of Athens," says an amiable writer, whom we regret to quote from memory, "took delight in exercising their creative power, in giving existence to new arts, in enlarging the aureola of civilisation. At their voice, the gods hastened to inhabit the antique oak ; they disported in the fountains and the streams ; they dispersed themselves in gamesome groups on the tops of the mountains and in the shade of the valleys, while their songs and their balmy breath mingled with the harmonious whisperings of the gentle breeze."

What cooks ! what a table ! what guests ! in that Eden of paganism— that land of intoxicating perfumes, of generous wines, and inexhaustible laughter ! The Lacedæmonians alone, those cynics of Greece, threw a saddening shade over the delicious picture of present happiness undisturbed by any thought of to-morrow.

Let us not forget that an Athenian, not less witty than nice, and, moreover, a man of good company, has left us this profound aphorism : *" La viande la plus délicate est celle qui est le moins viande ; le poisson le plus exquis est celui qui est le moins poisson."*

Rome was long renowned for her austere frugality, and it is remarked that, during more than five centuries, the art of making bread was there unknown, which says little for her civilisation and intelligence. Subsequently, the conquest of Greece, the spoils of the subjugated world, the prodigious refinements of the Syracusans, gave to the conquered nations, says Juvenal, a complete revenge on their conquerors. The unheard-of excesses of the table swallowed up patrimonies which seemed to be inexhaustible, and illustrious dissipators obtained a durable but sad renown.

The Romans had whimsical tastes, since they dared serve the flesh of asses and dogs, and ruined themselves to fatten snails. But, after all, the caprices of fashion, rather than the refinement of sensuality, compelled them to adopt these strange aliments. Paulus Æmilius, no doubt a good judge in such matters, formed a high opinion of the elegance displayed by his compatriots in the entertainments ; and he compared a skilful cook, at the moment when he is planning and arranging a repast, to a great general.

We were very anxious to enrich our " PANTROPHEON" with a greater number of *Bills of Fare,* or details of banquets; but we have become persuaded that it is very difficult, at the present day, to procure a complete and accurate account of the arrangement of feasts at which were seated guests who died two or three thousand years ago. Save and except the indications—more or less satisfactory, but always somewhat vague—which we gather on this subject from Petronius, Athenæus, Apuleius, Macrobius, Suetonius, and some other writers, we can do little more than establish analogies, make deductions, and reconstruct the entire edifice of an antique banquet by the help of a few data, valuable, without doubt, but almost always incomplete.

One single passage in Macrobius—a curious monument of Roman cookery—will supply the place of multiplied researches : it is the description of a supper given by the Pontiff Lentulus on the day of his reception. We present it to the amateurs of the magiric art :

" The first course (*ante-cœna*) was composed of sea-hedgehogs, raw oysters in abundance, all sorts of shell-fish, and asparagus. The second service comprised a fine fatted pullet, a fresh dish of oysters, and other shell-fish, different kinds of dates, univalvular shell-fish (as whelks, conchs, &c.), more oysters, but of different kinds, sea-nettles, beccaficoes, chines of roe-buck and wild boar, fowls covered with a perfumed paste, a second dish of shell-fish, and purples—a very costly kind of crustacea. The third and last course presented several *hors-d'œuvre,* a wild boar's head, fish, a second set of *hors-d'œuvre,* ducks, potted river fish, leverets, roast fowls, and cakes from the marshes of Ancona."

All these delicacies would very much surprise an epicurean of the

present day, particularly if they were offered to him in the order indicated by Macrobius. The text of that writer, as it is handed down
to us, may be imperfect or mutilated; again, he may have described the
supper of Lentulus from memory, regardless of the order prescribed for
those punctilious and learned transitions to which a feast owes all its value.

Let us, we would say, in addressing our culinary colleagues, avoid
those deplorable *lacunes;* let us preserve for future generations, who
may be curious concerning our gastronomic pomp, the minutiæ of our
memorable magiric meetings, prompted, almost without exception, by
some highly civilising idea—a love of the arts, the commercial propa-
gandism, or a feeling of philanthropy. The Greeks and Romans—
egotists, if there ever were any—supped for themselves, and lived only
to sup; our pleasures are ennobled by views more useful and more
elevated. We often dine for the poor, and we sometimes dance for the
afflicted, the widow, and the orphan.

Moreover, a most important ethnographical consideration seems to
give a serious interest to the diet of a people, if it be true, as we are
convinced it is, and as we shall probably one day endeavour to demonstrate, that the manners of individuals, their idiosyncrasies, inclinations,
and intellectual habits, are modified, to a certain extent, as taste, climate,
and circumstances may determine the nature of their food; an assertion
which might be supported by irrefragable proofs, and would show the
justness of the aphorism: "Tell me what thou eatest, and I will tell
thee who thou art."

Alfred Johnson del.

Edward & Insell sc.

A. Sayer del.

VICTUA

OR

THE GODDESS OF GASTRONOMY

I.

AGRICULTURE.

EVERY nation has attributed the origin of agriculture to some beneficent Deity. The Egyptians bestowed this honour on Osiris, the Greeks
on Ceres and Triptolemus, the Latins on Saturn, or on their king
Janus, whom, in gratitude, they placed among the gods. All nations,
however, agree that, whoever introduced among them this happy and
beneficial discovery, has been most useful to man by elevating his mind
to a state of sociability and civilization.[1]

Many learned men have made laborious researches in order to discover, not only the name of the inventor of agriculture, but the country
and the century in which he lived ; some, however, have failed in their
inquiry. And why ? Because they have forgotten, in their investigation, the only book which could give them positive information on the
birth of society, and the first development of human industry. We
read in the Book of Genesis that : " The Lord God took the man, and
put him into the garden of Eden, to dress it and to keep it." [2] And,
after having related his fatal disobedience, the sacred historian adds:
" Therefore the Lord God sent him forth from the garden of Eden,
to till the ground from whence he was taken." [3]

Would it be possible to adduce a more ancient and sublime
authority ?

If it be asked why we take Moses as our guide, instead of dating the
origin of human society from those remote periods which are lost in the
night of ages, we invoke one of the most worthy masters of human
science—the illustrious Cuvier—who says :—

" No western nation can produce an uninterrupted chronology of more than three thousand years. Not one of them has any record of connected facts which bears the stamp of probability anterior to that time, nor even for two or three centuries after. The Greeks acknowledge that they learned the art of writing from the Phœnicians thirty or thirty-four centuries ago; and for a long time after that period their history is filled with fables, in which they only go back three hundred years to establish the cradle of their existence as a nation. Of the history of western Asia we have only a few contradictory extracts, which embrace, in an unconnected form, about twenty centuries. The first profane historian with whom we are acquainted by works extant is Herodotus, and his antiquity does not reach *two thousand three hundred years*. The historians consulted by him had written less than *a century* previous; and we are enabled to judge what kind of historians they were by the extravagances handed down to us as extracts from Aristæus, Proconesus, and some others. Before them they had only poets; and Homer, the master and eternal model of the west, lived only *two thousand seven hundred*, or *two thousand eight hundred, years ago*. One single nation has transmitted to us annals, written in prose, before the time of Cyrus: it is the Jewish nation. That part of the Old Testament called the *Pentateuch* has existed in its present form at least ever since the schism of Jeroboam, as the Samaritans receive it equally with the Jews, that is to say, that it has assuredly existed more than *two thousand eight hundred* years. There is no reason for not attributing the Book of Genesis to Moses, which would carry us back *five hundred* years more, or *thirty-three centuries;* and it is only necessary to read it in order to perceive that it is, in part, a compilation of fragments from antecedent works: wherefore, no one can have the least doubt of its being the oldest book now possessed by the western nations."[4]

The descendants of our first parents—and, first of all, the Hebrew people, who, as a nation historically considered, must occupy our foremost attention—devoted all their energy to agricultural labour.

The chief of the tribe of Judah as well as the youngest son of the tribe of Benjamin followed the plough, and gathered corn in the fields. Gideon was thrashing and winnowing his corn, when an angel revealed to him that he should be the deliverer of Israel;[5] Ruth was gleaning when Boaz saw her for the first time;[6] King Saul was driving his team of oxen in the ploughed field, when some of his court came and apprized him that the city of Jabesh was in danger;[7] and Elisha was called away to prophesy while at work with one of his father's ploughs.[8] We could multiply these incidents without end, to prove what extraordinary interest the Jews took in agricultural occupations.

Moses regarded agriculture as the first of all arts, and he enjoined the Hebrews to apply themselves to it in preference to any other: it was to the free and pure air of the fields, to the strengthening, healthy, and laborious country life, that he called their first attention. The sages of Greece and Rome held the same opinion: in those republics the tradesman was but an obscure individual, while the tiller of the soil was considered as a distinguished citizen. The urban tribes yielded precedence to the rustics, and this latter class supplied the nation with its generals and its magistrates.[9] Our present ideas on this point have materially changed with the times, and our modern Cincinnati very seldom return to the field to terminate the furrow they have commenced. The Israelites did not possess this excessive delicacy: they preserved the taste for agriculture with which their great legislator, Moses, had inspired them, and which the distribution of land naturally tended to strengthen. No one, in fact, was allowed to possess enough ground to tempt him to neglect the smallest portion; nor had any one the right to dispossess the Hebrew of his father's field,—even he himself was forbidden to alienate for ever land from his family.[10] This wise disposition did not escape the notice of an ancient heathen author,[11] and various states of Greece adopted the same plan; amongst others, the Locrians, Athenians, and Spartans, who did not allow their fathers' inheritance to be sold.[12]

The plan which we have adopted for our guidance in this work hardly justifies us in casting more than a glance at the Mosaic legislation; we shall, therefore, pass over all those prescriptions, all those memorable prohibitions, which the reader must have so often admired in the Books of Leviticus and Deuteronomy, and content ourselves with observing that Moses knew how to find in agriculture an infallible means of developing the industry of his people, and that, by imposing the necessity of giving rest to the land every seventh year,[13] he obliged them, by the generality of this repose, to have stores in reserve; and consequently to employ every means of preserving portions of the grain, fruit, wines, and oil which they had gathered in the course of the six years preceding.

Ancient casuists of this nation enter into the most minute details on tillage and sowing, and also on the gathering of olives, on the tithes which were paid to the priests, and the portion set aside for the poor. They also mention some species of excellent wheat, barley, rice, figs, dates, &c., which were gathered in Judea.[14]

The soil of this delicious country was astonishingly fertile,[15] the operation of tillage was easy, and the cattle here supplied a greater abundance of milk than anywhere else;[16] we will just remark that even the names of several localities indicate some of these advantages. For instance, Capernaum signified a beautiful country town; Gennesareth, the garden of the groves; Bethsaida, the house of plenty; Nain was indebted for its sweet name to the beauty of its situation; and Magdela, on the borders of the sea of Galilee, to its site, and the happy life of its inhabitants.

Next to the Hebrews, in agriculture, came the Egyptians, a strange and fantastical people, who raised the imperishable pyramids, the statue of Memnon, and the lighthouse of Alexandria, and who yet prayed religiously every morning to their goddess—a *radish*, or their gods—*leek* and *onion*.[17] Whatever there may be of folly and rare industry in this mixture, we cannot but agree that the art of agriculture was very ancient in Egypt, as the father of the faithful—Abraham—retired into that country at a time of famine;[18] and, later, the sons of Jacob went there also to purchase corn.[19]

We know that the Romans called this province the granary of the empire, and that they drew from it every year twenty million bushels of corn.[20] If we are to believe the Egyptians, Osiris, son of Jupiter (and hence a demi-god of good family), taught them the art of tilling the ground by aid of the plough.[21] This instrument, we may easily believe, was much less complicated than ours of the present day; there is no doubt that in the beginning, and for a great length of time afterwards,

---

DESCRIPTION OF PLATE No. I.

No. 1. Represents an Egyptian labourer tilling the ground with a pickaxe of a simple form; drawn at Thebes, by Mons. Nectoul, member of the commission of the French expedition in Egypt, from paintings in the subterranean vaults of Minich.

No. 2. Is a sketch of the plough, which a great number of Egyptian figures hold as an attribute; this was taken from the subterranean vault of Eileithya; it represents the plough guided by a labourer, and drawn by oxen tied by the horns, and whipped by a second labourer, whilst a third, placed by the side of the oxen, throws before them the seeds which are to be covered by the ploughed earth.

No. 3. A basket to carry the seeds. On the tombs of the kings of Thebes is seen painted a sower, with a basket like this, an attribute which is seen hanging on the back of the divinity Osiris.

No. 4. Represents an Egyptian with a sickle, much like in shape to a scythe; and Denon, of the French expedition, proved that corn was also cut with a scythe.

Pl. I.

WINE CASK ORIGINALLY FROM THE ALPS.

it was nothing but a long piece of wood without joint, and bent in such manner that one end went into the ground, whilst the other served to yoke the oxen;[22] for it was always these animals which drew the plough, although Homer seems to give the preference to mules.[23]

The Greeks, clever imitators of the Egyptians, pretended that Ceres taught them the art of sowing, reaping, and grinding corn; they made her goddess of harvest, and applied themselves to the labour of agriculture with that rare and persevering ability which always characterised these people, and consequently was often the cause of many things being attributed to them which they only borrowed from other nations.[24]

The Romans, future rulers of the world, understood from the first that the earth claimed their nursing care; and Romulus instituted an order of priesthood for no other object than the advancement of this useful art. It was composed of the twelve sons of his nurse, all invested with a sacerdotal character, who were commanded to offer to Heaven vows and sacrifices in order to obtain an abundant harvest. They were called *Arvales* brothers;[25] one of them dying, the king took his place, and continued to fulfil his duty for the rest of his life.[26]

In the palmy days of the republic, the conquerors of the universe passed from the army or the senate to their fields;[27] Seranus was sowing when called to command the Roman troops, and Quintus Cincinnatus was ploughing when a deputation came and informed him that he was appointed dictator.

Everything in the conduct of the Romans gives evidence of their great veneration for agriculture. They called the rich, *locupletes*, that is, persons who were possessors of a farm or country seat (*locus*); their first money was stamped with a sheep or an ox, the symbol of abundance: they called it *pecunia*, from *pecus* (flock). The public treasure was designated *pascua*, because the Roman domain consisted, at the beginning, only of pasturage.

After the taking of Carthage, the books of the libraries were distributed to the allied princes of the republic, but the senate reserved the twenty-eight books of Mago on agriculture.[28]

We shall briefly point out the principal processes of this art in use among the Greeks and Romans, or at least those which appear to us most deserving of interest. Like us, the ancients divided the land in furrows, whose legal length (if we may so term it) was one hundred and thirty feet.[29]   Oxen were never allowed to stop while tracing a furrow, but on arriving at the end they rested a short time; and when their task was over they were cleaned with the greatest care, and their mouths washed with wine.[30]   The ground being well prepared and fit to receive the seed, the grain was spread on the even surface of the furrows, and then covered over.[31]

The primitive plough, already mentioned, was of extreme simplicity. It had no wheels, but was merely furnished with a handle, to enable the ploughman to direct it according to his judgment; neither was there any iron or other metal in its construction.   They afterwards made a plough of two pieces, one of a certain length to put the oxen to, and the other was shorter to go in the ground; it was similar, in shape, to an anchor. Such was the style of plough which the Greeks used.[32]   They also very often employed a sort of fork, with three or four prongs, for the same purpose.[33]   Pliny gives credit to the Gauls for the invention of the plough mounted on wheels. The Anglo-Norman plough had no wheels;[34] the ploughman guided it with one hand, and carried a stick in the other to break the clods.

The Greeks and Romans had not, perhaps, the celebrated guano of our days, though we would not positively assert it; but they knew of a great variety of manures, all well adapted to the various soils they wished to improve.   Sometimes they made use of marl, a sort of fat clay;[35] and frequently manure from pigeons, blackbirds, and thrushes, which were fattened in aviaries[36] for the benefit of Roman epicures.   Certain plants, they thought, required a light layer of ashes, which they obtained from roots and brushwood;[37] others succeeded best, according to their dictum, on land where sheep, goats, &c., had grazed for a long time.[38]

When the harvest season arrived, they joyfully prepared to cut the corn, with instruments varying in form according to the locality or the fancy of the master.   In one place they adopted the plain sickle,[39] in another that with teeth.[40]   Sometimes they mowed the corn, as they did the meadows, with a scythe;[41] or else they plucked off the ears with a kind of fork, armed with five teeth.[42]   A short time after the harvest, the operation of thrashing generally began. Heavy chariots, armed with

DESCRIPTION OF PLATE No. II.

Nos. 1 & 2. Greek and Roman plough, made of several pieces; the first taken from the " Miscel-an. Erudit." of Spon, the second from an engraved stone in the gallery of Florence.

No. 3. Plough, made of one crooked piece of wood, turned once or twice.

No. 4. Plough, as used by the Gauls, furnished with wheels.

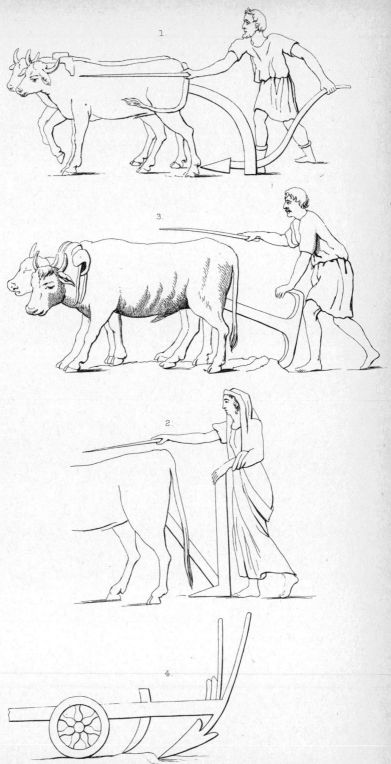

Pl. 2.

1.

3.

2.

4.

F. T. Z. Volant, del.

Saddler & Chant, scul.

pointed teeth, crushed the ears: Varro calls this machine the "Car-thaginian chariot."[43] Strabo asserts that the ancient Britons carried the corn into a large covered area, or barn, where they thrashed it; adding that, without this precaution, the rain and damp would have spoiled the grain.[44] At all events, this kind of thrashing in barns, with flails and sticks, was not unknown to other countries; Pliny speaks of it,[45] and Columella describes it;[46] we may add that the Egyptians were also very probably acquainted with this method, since the Jews, who had sub-mitted to their power, employed it themselves.[47] When the corn had been thrashed, winnowed, and put into baskets very similar to our own of the present day,[48] they immediately studied the best means of pre-serving it: some preferred granaries exposed to a mild temperature, others had extensive edifices with thick brick walls without openings, except one hole only, in the roof, to admit light and air.

The Spaniards, Africans, and Cappadocians, dug deep ditches, from which they excluded all moisture; they covered the bottom and lined the sides with straw, then put in the grain, and covered it up. The ancients were of opinion that corn in the ear could, by this means, be preserved a great number of years.[49]

If it is desirable to keep corn for any length of time, choose the finest and best grown. After having worked it, make a pile as high as the ceiling will permit. Cover with a layer of quicklime, powdered, of about three inches thick; then, with a watering-pot, moisten this lime, which forms a crust with the corn The outside seeds bud, and shoot forth a stalk, which perishes in winter. This corn is only to be touched when necessity requires it. At Sedan, a warehouse has been seen, hewed out of the rock and tolerably damp, in which there had been a consider-able pile of corn for the last hundred and ten years. It was covered with a crust a foot thick, on which persons might walk without bending or breaking it in the slightest degree.

Marshal Vauban proposed eating corn in soup, without being ground; it was boiled during two or three hours in water, and when the grains had burst, a little salt, butter, or milk, was added. This food is very nice, not unwholesome, and might be employed when flour is scarce, heated, or half-rotten.—DUTOUR.

The Chinese instituted a ceremony which had for its base to honour the profession of agriculture: every year, at the time of ploughing the fields, the emperor with all his court paid a visit to his country residence near Pekin, and then marked out several furrows with his plough.

In 1793, the National Convention of France instituted also a similar fête; and the president of the local administration of his county was to mark out a furrow.

In 1848 a grand republican procession took place through Paris, to the Champ de Mars, wherein agriculture played a prominent part.

The first treatise on agriculture was printed in 1538; and its importance has been so much felt from that period, that there are now in France more than one hundred and twenty societies of agriculture, who distribute prizes to encourage discoveries for the improvement of this science.

We have, in our days, the Royal Agricultural Society of England, which also awards prizes;* and through such institutions all information can be obtained on the successive progresses made in that indispensable art, which may be said to have arrived to such a degree·of perfection, that future generations may find some difficulty in improving upon it. One great evidence of which is, the immense number of samples of agricultural produce, machines, and implements of husbandry, which great and the glorious Exhibition of 1851 has ushered to the world.

Previous to the arrival of the Romans, the ancient Britons paid but little attention to agriculture. Their intestine discords left them scarcely any leisure to cultivate their fields, or apply themselves to the improvement of an art which flourishes only in peaceful times. They reared a great number of cattle; but their chief corn was barley, of which they made their favourite drink. They put the grain in the ear into barns, and beat it out as they wanted it. Those inhabitants of the island who were the least civilized subsisted solely on milk and the flesh of animals,

---

* A grand banquet was held by the Royal Agricultural Society, at Exeter, on July 20th, 1850, for description of which see end of volume.

DESCRIPTION OF PLATE No. III.

No. 1. Is the plain sickle. No. 2. Another, with teeth.

No. 3. A scythe, very similar to those now in use.

No. 4. A spade; its handle is supplied with a double crossbar, fixed at a little distance off the spade, to support the foot; it is still so used in Italy and the southern parts of France.

No. 5. A pickaxe, as it was found engraved on the various sarcophagi; the pick end was sometimes flattened, and then called pick-axe.

Nos. 6 and 7. The mattocks; the first was drawn from an engraved stone in the " Monuments Antiq." of Winckelman.

No. 2 A. Represents a plough, composed according to the " Georgics" of Virgil.

Pl. 3.

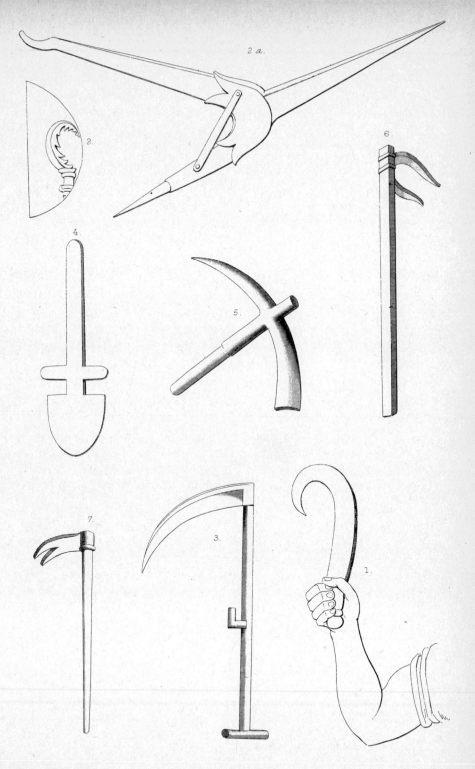

which they had learned to master by their skill.[50] But the people of this nation, for which Heaven had in reserve such a brilliant destiny, knew how to endure hunger, cold, and fatigue, without a murmur. A Briton passed entire days immersed to the neck in the stagnant waters of a marsh; a few roots sufficed for his nourishment, and, if we are to believe Dio, his frugal habits enabled him to appease the craving of his stomach with an aliment composed of ingredients no longer known, and of which he took each time, at long intervals, a quantity not exceeding in size that of a bean.[51]

Let us add that the art of gardening was known rather early in Great Britain, and that marl was employed to manure the land.[52]

The Anglo-Saxons employed themselves diligently in the cultivation of the soil; they established farms, sowed grain, and reared cattle. The fleece of their sheep furnished them with precious wool, which they spun, and then converted into sumptuous clothing.[53]

Strutt gives us a curious detail of rural occupations at that epoch. We will cite the original text :

" January exhibits the husbandman in the fields at plough, while his attendant, diligently following, is sowing the grain.

" February. The grain being put into the earth, the next care was to prune their trees, crop their vines, and place them in order.

" March. Then we follow them into the garden, where the industrious labourer is digging up the ground, and sowing the vegetables for the ensuing season.

" April. Now, taking leave of the laborious husbandman, we see the nobleman regaling with his friends, and passing the pleasant month in carousings, banquetings, and music.

" May brings the lord into the field to examine his flock, and superintend the shearing of the sheep.

" June. With this month comes the gladsome time of harvest. Here are some cutting down the corn, while it is, by others, bound up in sheaves and laid into the carts, to be conveyed to the barns and granaries; in the meantime they are spirited up to their labours by the shrill sound of the enlivening horn.

" July. Here we find them employed in lopping the trees and felling of timber, &c.

" August. In this month they cut down the barley with which they made their old and best beloved drink (ale).

"September. Here we find the lord, attended by his huntsmen, pursuing and chasing the wild boars in the woods and forests.

"October. And here he is amusing himself with the exercise of that old and noble pastime, hawking.

"November. This month returns us again to the labourers, who are here heating and preparing their utensils.

"December. In this last month we find them thrashing out the grain, while some winnow or rather sift it, to free it from the chaff, and others carry it out in large baskets to the granaries. In the meantime, the steward keeps an account of the quantity, by means of an indented or notched stick."[54]

Agriculture was always protected with paternal solicitude by a prince, whose name will ever remind us of the sanguinary day of Saint Bartholomew. Here is a textual passage from the edict issued by Charles IX., the 18th October, 1571.

"We have commanded and ordained, and do hereby command and ordain, that no man engaged in the cultivation of land, by himself, his servants, and his family, with intent to raise grain and fruit necessary for the sustenance of men and beasts, shall be liable to the process of execution for debt, nor on any account whatsoever, neither in his own person, nor his bed, horses, mares, mules, asses, oxen, cows, pigs, goats, sheep, poultry, ploughs, carts, waggons, harrows, barrows, nor any other species or kind of cattle or goods serving in the said tillage and occupation. * * * The said husbandmen being under our protection and safeguard, seeing that we have so placed them and do place them by these presents."[55]

II.

CEREALS.

THE nomenclature which the Romans have left us of their various kinds of corn is so obscure and uncertain, that some modern writers are continually contradicting each other, and, by these means, have raised doubts which render our task more difficult, instead of enlightening us on the subject.

We shall do all in our power to avoid the censure which we take the liberty of passing upon them.

" *Triticum*," wheat, or corn ; " *Blé*," from the ancient Latin word " *Bladus*," which signifies fruit or seed. The botanist Michaux has discovered in Persia, on a mountain four days' journey from Hamadan, the place where wheat (a species known as *spelt*, from the Latin *spelta*) is indigenous to the soil, from which we may presume that wheat has its origin in that country, or some part of Asia not far from Persia. This grain was more cultivated formerly than it is now ; nevertheless, it is still gathered in Italy, Switzerland, Alsace, in the Limousin and in Picardy, to make bread, with spelt, a greater quantity of leaven, and, above all, a little salt. This bread is white, light, savoury, and keeps moist for several days.—PARMENTIER.

Robus, a variety of corn heavier than triticum, and remarkable for its brilliant polish.

Every year, on the 25th of April, an appeal was made to the god Robigus, to prevent the mildew from corrupting this fine specimen of corn. This festival was founded by the great king, Numa Pompilius.[1]

Siligo, a beautiful quality of wheat, of great whiteness, but lighter in weight than the preceding kind.[2]

Trimestre, a kind of siligo, sown in Spring, and which was ready for reaping three months afterwards.

Granea, the grain merely deprived of its husk: it was boiled in water, to which milk was added.[3]

Hordeum, barley.[4] The flour of this corn was the food of the Jewish soldiers.[5] It was, with the Athenians, a favourite dish, but among the Romans an ignominious food. Augustus threatened the cohorts that, should they not fight bravely, he would punish every tenth man with death, and give the remainder barley for food.[6] This corn was certainly in use among the Egyptians in the time of Moses, since one of the plagues which afflicted that people was the loss of the barley in the ear before it came to maturity.[7]

Panicum, panic grass.[8] Certain inhabitants of Thrace and of the borders of the Euxine, or Black Sea, preferred this to all other food.[9]

Millium, millet, was used for making excellent cakes.[10]

Secale, rye.[11] Pliny thinks this grain detestable, and only good to appease extreme hunger.[12]

Avena, oats.[13] Virgil had but very little esteem for this grain.[14] The Romans cut it in the spring for the cattle to eat green; and the Germans, in the time of Pliny, took great care in its cultivation, and made a pulp of it which they thought excellent.[15]

Oryza, rice. Pliny[16] and Dioscorides[17] class it with the wheats; whereas Galen, on the contrary, places it among vegetables.

Rice was rather scarce in Greece at the time when Theophrastus lived: it had lately been brought from India, 286 years before Christ.

The ancients considered it most nutritious and fattening.[18]

Zea, spelt, or rice wheat,[19] equally esteemed by Greeks and Latins.[20]

Sesamum, sesame. Pliny classes this among the seeds sown in March,[21] and Columella places it among the vegetables.[22] The Romans knew how to prepare this corn in a manner at once wholesome and agreeable. They made it into very dainty cakes, which were served at dessert,[23] whence sprang the saying *sesame cakes*, which was applied to those sweet and flattering expressions called honied words (in French, *paroles sucrées*).[24]

A people so restless and unmanageable as were the Greeks and Romans, when pressed by hunger, required that the greatest care should be exercised for the supply of corn, and the easy sale of this precious provision. Hence nothing could be wiser than their regulations on this subject.

One of the laws of the twelve tables punished with death the individual who had premeditatedly set fire to his neighbour's corn; and inflicted a fine or the whip on any one who caused so great a calamity by his imprudence.[25]

In Greece, a special magistrate, the " *Sitocome*," was charged with the inspection of the corn; and various officers, such as the *sitones*, the *sitophylaces*, and the *sitologes*, were appointed to watch over its purchase.

And lastly, public distributors, under the names of *siturches* and *sitometres*, were exclusively occupied with the allotment of corn;[26] they prevented any one from purchasing a greater quantity than was actually necessary for his wants. The law forbad the delivery of more than fifty measures to one individual.[27] The Roman government was so convinced that abundance of bread was one of the best means of maintaining public tranquillity,[28] that Julius Cæsar created two prætors, and two ediles or magistrates, to preside over the purchase, conveyance, storing, and gratuitous distribution of wheat.[29] For we know that this people of kings, powerful but frivolous, and careless of the morrow, submitted to the incredible follies of their rulers on the sole condition of being well fed and amused by them.[30] In the time of Demosthenes the common price of wheat in Greece was about 3s. 11d. the four bushels.[31] In Rome, during the republic, wheat was distributed to 60,000 persons.[32] Julius Cæsar desired that 320,000 plebeians should enjoy this bounty; but this number was afterwards reduced to 150,000,[33] or perhaps, according to Cassius, to 160,000.[34] Augustus fed, at first, 200,000 citizens, then only 120,000.[35] Nero, who always went to extremes either in good or evil, gave corn throughout the empire to 220,000 idle people, including the soldiers of the prætorian guard.[36] Adrian added to this list all the children of the poor: the boys to the age of 18, and the girls to that of 14. Finally, this liberality, more politic than generous, and so foreign to our present manners, was carried, under the Emperor Severus, to 75,000 bushels per day.[37] The bushel weighed twenty pounds of twelve ounces each.[38]

The Greeks esteemed highly the corn of Bœotia, Thrace, and Pontus. The Romans preferred that of Lombardy, the present duchy of Spoletta, Sicily, Sardinia, and a part of Gaul. Sardinia, Sicily, and Corsica, supplied them every year with 800,000 bushels of twenty-one pounds weight, which made them call those islands " the sweet nurses of Rome."[39]

Africa furnished 40,000,000 of bushels; Egypt 20,000,000, and the remainder came from Greece, Asia, Syria, Gaul, and Spain.[40]

The erudite are not agreed as to the aboriginal country of corn: some say it is Egypt, others Tartary, and the learned Bailly, as well as the traveller Pallas, affirm that it grows spontaneously in Siberia. Be that as it may, the Phocians brought it to Marseilles before the Romans had penetrated into Gaul. The Gauls ate the corn cooked, or bruised in a mortar; they did not know for a long time how to make fermented bread.

The Chinese attribute to Chin-Nong, the second of the nine emperors of China who preceded the establishment of the dynasties (more than 2,207 years B.C.), the discovery of corn, rice, and other cereals.

We find in the Black Book of the Exchequer, that in the reign of Henry I., when they reduced the victuals (for the king's household) to the estimate of money, a measure of wheat to make bread for the service of one hundred men, one day, was valued only at one shilling.[41]

But in the reign of Henry III., about the 43rd year, the price was mounted up to fifteen and twenty shillings a quarter.[42]

The ancients, as well as the moderns, caused wheat to undergo certain preparations to enable it to be transformed into bread, we shall enumerate in the following chapter the different processes by which they obtained flour, the essential foundation of the food of man.

Cereals.—This name has been given to all plants of the gramineous family, the fundamental base of the food of man. The *cereals*, properly speaking, are limited to wheat, rye, barley, and oats; however, there are others, such as canary grass, Indian corn, millet, rice, &c., &c. The immediate and most abundant principle of all these plants is the *fécule*, or flour, and the vegeto-animal matter of which bread is made, and other preparations for food, and fermented liquors; these cereals are given green or dry to cattle as forage; their straw covers houses, and serves as litter and manure.

Cereals was also the name given to a feast in honour of Ceres, instituted at Rome by the edile Mumonius, and celebrated every year on the 7th of April. The ladies of Rome appeared clothed in white, and holding torches in remembrance of the travels of that divinity. Cakes sprinkled with salt and grains of incense, honey, milk, and wine, were offered to that goddess. Pigs were sacrificed to her. The *cereals* of the Romans were the *thesmophories* with the Greeks.

III.

GRINDING OF CORN.

AT a very distant period, when gods, not over edifying in their conduct, descended at times from the heights of Olympus to enliven their immortality amongst mortals, we are told that a divine aliment charmed the palate of Jupiter and that of his quarrelsome wife; nay, of all those who inhabited the celestial abode. We are ignorant of the hour at which the table of the god of thunder was laid; but we know well that he breakfasted, dined, and supped on a delicious ambrosia—a liquid substance, it may be presumed, since it flowed for the first time from one of the horns of the goat Amalthæa, and of rather an insipid taste, if we are to believe Ibicus,[1] who describes it as nine times sweeter than honey. The gods have disappeared; we would forgive them for leaving us, had they left behind them the recipe of this marvellous substance; but its composition and essence remain unknown, and man, not skilful enough to appropriate to his use the inexhaustible treasures of culinary science, began his hard gastrophagic apprenticeship by devouring acorns which grew in the forests.[2] This is assuredly very mortifying to our feelings; but you may believe it on the authority of a poet, for we well know that a poet never tells an untruth.[3] Besides, fabulous antiquity adds new weight to the fact, by informing us that the Arcadian Pelasgus[4] deserved that altars should be erected to his memory, for having taught the Greeks to choose in preference the beech-nut, as the most delicate of this class of comestibles, according to the tender Virgil, who, however, only judged of it by hearsay.[5]

There is a great degree of probability in the supposition that the different races of the north, each inhabiting a country covered with immense forests, lived for a long time on the fruit of these different kinds of oak which they possessed in such abundance. The great respect they had for the tree, the pompous ceremony with which the high priest of the Druids came every year to cut away the parasitical plant which clings to it, the very name of the Druids—derived from a celtic word signifying *oak*—all seem to point out the first food of our ancestors. The oak furnished the primitive aliment of almost every nation, in their original state of barbarism. Some of them had even preserved a taste for the acorn after they became civilized. Among the Arcadians and the Spaniards, the acorn was regarded as a delicious article of food. We read in Pliny that, in his time, these latter had them served on their tables at dessert, after they had been roasted in the wood-ashes to soften them. According to Champier, this custom still subsisted in Spain in the 16th century.

The regulation made by Chrodegand, Bishop of Metz, about the end of the 8th century, for the canons, says expressly[6] that if, in an unfavorable year, the acorn or flour should fail, it will be the duty of the bishop to provide it.

When, animated by the most praiseworthy zeal and courage, Du Bellay, Bishop of Mans, came, in 1546, to represent to Francis I. the frightful misery of the provinces, and that of his diocese in particular, he assured the king that in many localities the people had nothing to eat but bread made of acorns.

But mankind, who soon get tired of every thing, even of acorns and beech-nuts, began to dislike this wholesome and abundant food, when Ceres, the ancient Queen of Sicily, came just *à propos* to give a few lessons in the art of sowing the earth.[7] Corn once brought into fashion acquired a surprising repute, and the ancient food was given up to the animal which it fattens; and if this last were eaten, it was no doubt in gratitude for the fruit mankind had formerly so much loved.

The good Ceres did not stop there; it was very well to have corn, but to know how to grind it was also requisite; and the human race was then so lamentably backward, that one might have gone round the world without meeting a miller, or even the shadow of the meanest little mill.

The Queen of Sicily then invented grinding-stones,[8] but, as the most useful discoveries require time to be known and improved upon, the way of grinding corn with stones did not become uniform everywhere. The inhabitants of Etruria (now called Tuscany) pounded the grain in

ALCINOUS'S HAND MILL.

F. T. Z. Volant. del.

Chant & Saddiler. scud.

mortars.[9] The early Romans adopted the same means, and gave the name of *Pistores,* grinders, to those persons who followed this occupation.[10] Pliny relates that one of the ancient families of Rome took the surname of *Piso,* having descended, as they believed, from the inventor of the art of bruising wheat with pestles.[11]

Down to the latest days of the Roman republic the corn was bruised after being roasted. The pestle used for this purpose was somewhat pointed, and suspended by the aid of a ring to the extremity of a flexible lever, supported by an axle.[12]

From the time of Moses the Hebrews used grinding-stones: several passages of the Holy Scripture clearly indicate this. Among others: " No man shall take the nether or the upper millstone to pledge ; for he taketh a man's life to pledge."[13] Another text shows that the Egyptians used grinding-stones with handles, at about the same period.[14] The Israelites, when in the Desert, employed the same means to pound manna,[15] and after their settlement in the Promised Land, these utensils served to grind corn.

The Greeks, following faithfully the system from which they had but slightly deviated, have honoured King Miletus as the inventor of grinding-stones;[16] the upper part was of wood, and armed with heads of iron nails. A passage of Homer would seem to lead us to believe that the gráin was first crushed with rollers on stone slabs, which operation would naturally lead to the crushing of it between grinding-stones.[17] However this may be, these last were no doubt still scarce in the heroic times, since the same poet does not fail to inform us that one was to be seen in the gardens of Alcinous, chief of the Phæacians.[18] This kind of decoration would but very little please the taste of our modern horticulturists.

Nearly two centuries before our era, in the year of Rome 562, the Romans, victorious in Asia, brought with them handmills.[19] This conquest of industry soon made an immense stride, and to the labour of man succeeded by degrees the obedient aid of horses and asses. Hence the two kind of mills so often mentioned—by hand, *manuales ;* by animal, *iumentariæ.*[20]

Delighted with a discovery which supplied an important necessity of life, the Romans invented a divinity to whom they might show their gratitude, and Olympus was honoured with a new inmate : the goddess Mola, protectress and patroness of mills and millstones.[21]

Now Mola was one of a large family; she had several charming
sisters, like herself, who could not endure living among the commoners,
while Ganymede served ambrosia to their elder sister, or poured out for
her the nectar of the gods. Besides, it cost so little to be made a
goddess! A few grains of incense, more or less, who would grudge
such a trifle? The Flamine of Jupiter, whom they consulted, was at
first rather refractory. He feared the crowding of Olympus; he doubted
whether polite intercourse could ever be established between gods of
high birth and little divinities covered with flour; but when at last the
high priest had ceased speaking, the deputation removed all scruples by
a reasonable bribe, and the sisters of Mola were forthwith enrolled in the
list of immortals, under the designation of well-beloved daughters of the
god of war.[22] Mars was rather ungentlemanly on the occasion, but the
high priest undertook to bring him to reason.

This took place about the end of May, and the Romans resolved to
celebrate, from the 9th of the following June, the festival of the patroness
of Roman millers, and of her sisters, the newly elected divinities; the
ceremony was worthy of those for whose apotheosis it was instituted,
and every year, on the same day, new rejoicings consecrated this great
event.[23]

The mills ceased to turn and to grind, a profound silence reigned in
the mills; the asses, patient and indefatigable movers of an incessant
rotation, took a lively part, whether or no, in the festivals of which they
became the principal actors. These honest creatures' heads[24] were
crowned with roses, and necklaces of little leaves encircled their necks
and fell gracefully on their chests;[25] we need not add that, on this day,
the thick bandages which generally covered the eyes of these useful
labourers were removed.[26]

Independently of this annual solemnity, the asses, turners of the
mills, had sometimes their windfalls,—that is to say, hours of holiday,
during which they could freely graze on the neighbouring thistles. This
happened when an awkward slave performed badly the duties of fanning
his master, or spilt carelessly a few drops of Falernian wine when filling
his cup. The unfortunate creature was immediately condemned to
work at the mill;[27] he was deprived of his name, and received in lieu that
of the quadruped he replaced—*Asinus*;[28] and the instrument of his
sufferings, by a refinement of strange irony, was called his manger.[29]

It sometimes happened that a free man, reduced to extreme indi-

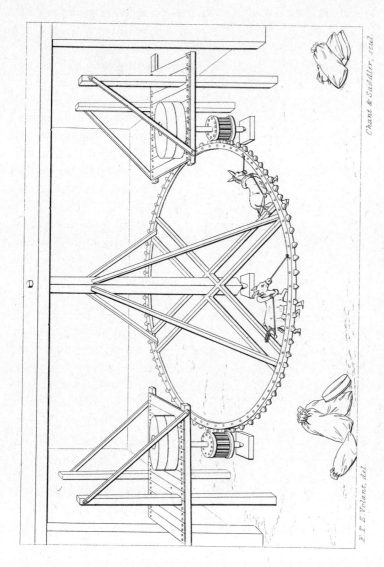

Fig. 3.

F. T. Z. Volant, del.

Chant & Saddler, sculp.

ASINUS OR JUMENTARIÆ MILL.

Pl. 6.

F. T. Z. Volant, del.   Saddler & Chant, scul.

PLAUTUS'S MILL.

gence, had recourse to this hard occupation, in order to earn a living. Plautus was obliged to work at it, and we know that he wrote some of his comedies during the short moments of leisure allowed him by his master the miller.[30]

An important modification was subsequently made in the mechanism of mills: we mean hydraulic mills, whose introduction into Italy is of uncertain date, although Pomponius Sabinus asserts (but without proof), that this discovery took place in the reign of Julius Cæsar. They were known in Rome at the time of the Emperor Augustus, and Vitruvius mentions them.[31] More than sixty years afterwards, Pliny speaks of them as rare and extraordinary machines.[32]

Some writers have thought that *hydraulæ*, or *hydromilæ*, watermills, were invented by Vitruvius, and that this celebrated architect made experiments with them, which were forgotten or neglected after his death.[33] Curious readers, who are not afraid of the venerable dust with which time has covered many useful though despised books, will consult with benefit the learned treatise of Goetzius on the mills of the ancients, printed in the year 1730.[34]

Strabo, who flourished under the Emperor Augustus, tells us a watermill was to be seen near the town of Cabire and the palace of Mithridates.[35]

Nevertheless, this useful invention, which we could not now dispense with, made so little progress during four centuries that princes thought it a duty to protect, by several laws, those establishments, still rare, but which people began to appreciate. Honorius and Arcadius decreed, in 398, that any person who turned the water from mills for his own profit, should be punished by a fine of five pounds weight in gold; and that any magistrate encouraging such an act should pay a like sum.[36] The Emperor Zeno[37] maintained this law, and rendered it still more stringent by adding, that the edifices or land into which the water had been turned should be confiscated.[38]

It is to be regretted that the precise origin of the miller's profession cannot be traced; but, alas! in almost all the arts which tend to preserve life, we discover the same uncertainty: we are ignorant of the period of their discovery, and it frequently happens that but few traces of their development remain. On the contrary, the dates of battles, or scourges which have decimated the human race, are certain enough: the stain of blood leaves an impression which can never be effaced.

In the midst of the conflicting opinions of the writers of antiquity, what appears most probable is, that watermills were invented in Asia Minor, and that they were not really used in Rome till the reign of Honorius and Arcadius.

Under the rule of the Emperor Justinian, when the Goths besieged the Roman city,[39] the celebrated Belisarius thought of constructing some on the Tiber. The means which he employed were simple and ingenious. Two boats firmly fixed, at two feet distance from each other, caused the stream to give a rapid motion to the hydraulic wheel, suspended by its axle between these lateral points of support; and this wheel turned the mills.[40] This system differed but little from that of Vitruvius, which he described more than five centuries before, and is explained in a few words. A little wheel, fixed to the axle of the hydraulic wheel, turned a third wheel, adhering to the axle of the upper grindstone, and the corn fell between the two stones in passing from the hopper placed above.[41]

These grindstones were made of a kind of porous lava, which retained its roughness, or rather, its roughness was renewed, by the continual friction.[42]

The introduction of watermills, however, did not prevent the use of those worked by hand, which habit, cheapness, and facility of removal recommended: these antique mills of the Hebrews, the Egyptians, and the Greeks of the heroic times, were only five feet high. Each family was supplied with as many as they might require. In the residence of Ulysses, that great king of little Ithaca, there were as many as twelve. Women turned the mills, and were obliged to deliver a certain quantity of flour before leaving the task imposed on them.[43]

Corn was at first ground in a portative hand mill; by the Britons, women and young girls were employed in this kind of labour.[44]

It is, however, probable that watermills were known at a very early period in England. Strutt cites a passage from a charter by Ulfere, in 664, which warrants the supposition.[45]

It would be difficult to point out the precise date of the first employment of mills; nevertheless, Somner informs us, in his " Antiquities of Canterbury,"[46] that the Anglo-Normans of that place ground their corn. " There was," says he, " sometime a windmill standing neare the nonnery without Ridingate, which the hospitall held by the grant of the nonnes there: the conditions mutually agreed upon, at the time of the grant, were that the nonnes, bearing the fourth part of the charge of the mill, should reap the fourth part of the profit of it, &c. * * * and this about the reign of King John."

The bran was separated from the flour by means of a sieve; the dough was made, and sent to the bakers to be baked. The poor contented themselves with cakes baked under the ashes.[47]

Something remains to be said of windmills. We will say but little on the subject: this aerial mechanism—which the knight-errant, Don Quixote, of imperishable memory, thought it necessary to fight with sword and lance—was unknown before the Christian era in any nation whose writers have transmitted to us the least traces of their civilisation; but nothing proves that windmills were unknown to others. This opinion seems to be well-founded, from a passage of the chronicler Winceslaus, who relates, in his "History of Bohemia," that the first watermill raised in that country was in the year of Christ 718, and that no other was in use before (antea) but mills built on the summit of mountains, which were put in motion by the wind.[48] It appears, then, that there is some untruth in the assertion, that this sort of mill was introduced into Europe, about the year 1040, by the first Crusaders, on their return from the East.[49] At all events this question is no doubt very deserving the laborious search of the learned; it has but a secondary interest for the gastrophilist. It matters little to him whether he owes the grinding of his corn to the breath of a zephyr or to the slimy source of a river; all he requires is good flour, because it enters into a great number of culinary preparations—and, first of all, bread is made from it.

IV

MANIPULATION OF FLOUR.

M<small>AN</small> has not always eaten fine wheaten bread, biscuits, or sponge cakes; and, for many centuries, the inexperience of his palate prevented his imagining or understanding those magiric combinations, that science of good living,[1] which requires time and serious study. Nature makes us hungry; art creates, modifies, and directs the appetite—these are incontestable truths, which this work will serve to unfold, and, if necessary, to prove, should any of our readers unfortunately not be already convinced of the depth of these wise axioms.

Let us go no further back than the year 2000 before the Christian era, and enter together the tent of the father of nations—*Abraham.* We might lead you to the fire-side of each of the nineteen patriarchs who preceded him, but that would take us too far.

In the interior of this nomad dwelling, Sarah, the venerable companion of the Pastor-King, has just prepared, with flour and water, round pieces of flattened paste, which she places on the hearth, and covers afterwards with hot ashes.[2] It was thus that princes and servants made bread in the East. The Jewish people who inhabited the Desert ate no other kind;[3] and the Prophet Elijah, reposing under the shade of a juniper tree, appeased his hunger with this simple and primitive food.[4] Sometimes, however, at certain periods of solemnity, the Hebrews used a gridiron, placed on the coals, or a frying-pan, into which they put the paste;[5] but these various modes of cooking produced a kind of cake, dry, thin, and brittle,[6] somewhat like the Jewish Passover cake, which was broken by the hand without the aid of a knife;[7] they were called *lechem*, choice and chief food,[8] and the mother of the family generally renewed them each day.[9] The inhabitants of the East thought so much of bread, that it was considered a special mark of regard and hospitality to the person to whom it was offered.[10] Boaz says to Ruth: " At meal time come thou hither and eat of the bread, and dip thy morsel in the vinegar." [11]

Although the use of bread without leaven and baked under the ashes was common among the Jews,[12] it is nevertheless evident that they knew and employed, at an early period, some substance to raise the dough, which they designated by the name of *seor*. It was, perhaps, flour diluted with water left to get sour. Pliny assures us that of all means employed by the ancients to render bread savoury and light, this is the most simple and easy.[13]

It appears not unlikely that the Hebrews learned from the Egyptians how to prepare the leaven they made use of. The period at which an allusion is made to it for the first time, in the Bible, renders this supposition likely. It is when the people of God were about to escape from the slavery of the Egyptians, and are preparing to celebrate the Passover, on the eve of their setting out for the Desert.[14] The Israelites, therefore, knew how to make bread more digestive and of better taste than is generally believed—not so good, perhaps, as our delicate fancy bread, but better than the clumsy lumps of paste baked under the ashes, in the frying-pan, or on the gridiron.[15] They had also ovens at a very distant period of their history—some four thousand years ago.[16] These ovens were made with bricks or clay; afterwards they used iron and brass;[17] but nothing in the Holy Writings shows us that any one exercised among them the trade of a baker, at least at this early period, nor, indeed, very much later.

The chief baker or butler, whose punishment and death Joseph foretold, when he interpreted that officer's dream, was an Egyptian, and belonged to King Pharaoh.[18]

Hitherto an infallible book has been our guide; let us now dive into the dark and almost boundless regions of fabulous antiquity.

The most frightful god of which the fevered imagination of man could possibly form an idea—a god with the face and legs of a goat, the horrible Pan!—according to some credulous writers, taught mortals the art of making and baking bread. The name even of this food, they say, furnishes an incontestable proof of this assertion.[19] You are mistaken, reply more sensible writers; it is in the Greek word *pan*, signifying *all*, that we must seek the etymology of this nutritious substance, which accompanies all other aliments, takes their place if needful, and agrees equally with all mankind.[20]

This, one would think, is conclusive; but the learned, the philologist, and every Procrustes of literature, protests against a halt with so fair a field before him. It is from the word *pascere*,[21] proudly exclaims another interpreter, that the substantive, bread, is derived.[22] This word has been rather disfigured on its way: think of the length of time it has been travelling down to us.

Ceres taught the Greeks how to cultivate corn; they learned from Megalarte and Megalomaze how to knead flour and bake it in ovens.[23] The gratitude of the Bœotians erected statues and altars to their memories, and shortly after, Greece could boast of having obtained the most skilful bakers in the world. The bread of Athens and Megara had a well deserved reputation: its whiteness dazzled the eye, and its taste was exquisite.[24] This voluptuous and fickle nation very soon began to tire of so intelligent and simple a manipulation, and must needs mix with the paste a host of ingredients which greatly altered its flavour: and seventy-two different sorts of bread[25] took birth from the scientific association of milk, oil, honey, cheese, and wine with the best flour.[26] All these varieties were called by the generic name of *artos*, bread; to which was added an epithet which prevented the mistaking of one kind for another.

The bread-market at Athens was very amusing; women (for the fair sex busied themselves with this trade) waited, seated, by the side of their baskets until Mercury should send them customers, and woe to those who came late, or whose evil genius led them to find fault with either the quality, quantity, or price of the goods. Have you ever heard the ladies of Billingsgate playing off their pleasant jokes on a timid countryman, or a foreigner, whose accent had betrayed him? It is a running fire of puns and crude picturesque expressions which nothing can resist; our Greek market-women would have been more than a match for them—can we bestow upon them greater praise?[27]

Some of them sold *azumos*, a delicate sort of biscuit, but rather tasteless, prepared without leaven;[28] others—irresistible syrens—invited children to taste of the relishing *artolaganos*, in which a renowned baker had the talent of introducing wine, pepper, oil, and milk.[29]

Here the sparkling eyes of a rich epicurean were on the look out for some *escarites*, a very light paste, seasoned with new sweet wine and honey,[30] and which was relished even by fatigued appetites at the close of a repast.[31] The poorer people made their choice among heaps of *dolyres*, or *typhes*: they were coarse compounds of rye and barley;[32] the ladies of fashion (*petites maitresses*) preferred the puff cakes called *placites*,[33] or the sweet *melitutes*, whose exquisite and perfumed flour was delicately kneaded with the precious honey of Mount Hymettus.[34] Lastly, the robust workman of the Pyræus bought the *tyrontes*, bread mixed with cheese,[35] which the higher classes of society in Athens abhorred, and which even the middling classes excluded from their tables.

Let us add to this imperfect enumeration, that the Greeks baked their bread in several different manners: some in ovens, others under ashes, over charcoal, or between two pieces of iron, similar to our *gauffre* moulds, and under a bell, or cover of some metal with a rim round the top, and fire over it.[36] For making a batch of bread, they employed nine pounds six ounces of leaven to twelve bushels of flour.[37] With regard to their ovens, in the construction of which they excelled, they always took particular care to place them near a hand-mill,[38] in order that the various processes that the wheat had to undergo should take place with ease and promptitude.

The Romans were for a long time *Pultiphagists*, or eaters of gruel, &c.;[39] and it would be difficult to ascertain with accuracy the precise period at which they gave a preference to bread; they no doubt knew of it before the year 365 of Rome, for, at the siege of the Capitol by the Gauls, Jupiter, who protected the besieged, thought of nothing better to get them out of their difficulties than to appear at night to their general, Manlius, and to give him the following advice: "Make," said he, " bread with all the flour you have left in store, and throw it to the enemy to show them that Rome has no apprehension of being reduced by famine." This stratagem, worthy of a Merry-Andrew, pleased Manlius so much, that he immediately put it into execution. The Gauls fled, Master Jupiter was highly delighted with the trick he had played, and thereby the Romans got rid of this swarm of barbarians.[40]

Whether this little story be true or not, the people of Romulus had a decided taste for gruel; it was a national dish, and was only discontinued to be given to the soldiers, defenders of the republic, when it was perceived that their laborious duties required more substantial food.[41] The Romans made their gruel of all kinds of flour.

King Numa (1715 B.C.), guided by the advice of the nymph, Egeria, taught his subjects the art of parching corn, of converting it into flour by means of mortars, and of making that gruel with which he liked to regale himself.

This good prince was rather fond of interfering in what did not concern him, and the royal compound was afterwards cooked in the public bakehouses, which the piety of the sovereign placed under the protection of the powerful Fornax, a goddess unknown till then, and who soon became the object of general and fervent worship.[42]

There is but one step from gruel to bread: the Romans perceived it. Thus this favourite dish lost its reputation, and the worship of Fornax somewhat cooled. But, on the other hand, there was still the smell of cakes on all sides; cooking on the hearth, on the coals, in small bell-stoves, and in large baking pans, until ultimately they became acquainted with the use of ovens.[43]

At last, Rome began to have them built, under the reign of Tarquinius Superbus, about 630 years before the Christian era. They were solid constructions, immoveable, and very like those of the present day.[44] Men were employed to keep up the necessary degree of heat; and their useful profession (thanks to the strange caprices which so tyrannically rule the social hierarchy) became one of the vilest and most sordid occupations in the capital of the world.[45] These ovens were ordered to be built far away from all edifices, in order to prevent accidents by fire;[46] an excellent precaution, where so many incautious and merry old gossips came daily to bake their bread.

Once there, those worthy plebeians amused themselves by giving full scope to their noisy fun, slandering their neighbours freely and charitably, telling each other all the little scandal they had picked up here and there, among the good souls in their neighbourhood. Hence these public places of labour and incessant babbling were called the "gossip bakehouses."[47]

These joyous meetings continued until the arrival of Greek bakers, 170 years B.C., who followed the victorious armies of the republic on their return from Macedonia.[48] These new operatives effected a complete revolution in the art of making bread: they reformed the taste of their masters, and, by degrees, the proverbial frugality of the conquerors of the universe gave way to the exquisite researches and wonderful delicacies of those whom they had subdued.

The Romans perceived the importance of perpetuating the talent of these strangers, and converting it eventually into a national industry. With these views, they gave them Roman colleagues, and subsequently they were formed into a college, or sort of association, which no member could quit on any pretext whatever. The son followed his father's profession, and he who married the daughter of a baker became one himself.[49] Sometimes one of these privileged artisans was raised to the dignity of senator, as an honour to his colleagues; but in that case he was required to abandon his fortune to the person who took his place; he might, however, decline the dignity, and remain at his kneading-trough.[50] All alliances with gladiators and comedians were interdicted them; and the law decreed that the delinquent guilty of such dishonour should be first scourged, then banished, and that his property should be confiscated for the benefit of the community.[51] Finally, the prodigal baker was assimilated with the dishonest bankrupt, and expelled the college.[52]

The above details on some of the dispositions of the law regarding this interesting corporation, sufficiently prove the importance that the Roman government attached to it, and wished it should always maintain.

The bakers of Rome received from the public granaries whatever they required, at a price fixed by the magistrate. If the officer charged with the distribution of it gave a bad quality, or exacted a bribe to supply good corn, that officer was disgraced, and he became for ever a journeyman baker.[53]

Independently of public bakeries, the number of which reached 329 under the reign of Augustus, there were also, in the houses of the wealthy, slaves whose sole occupation was the making of bread, and these slaves brought an exorbitant price when they excelled in their art.[54] They used portable ovens, made of iron or earthenware, under which they placed red-hot coals. Sometimes they employed a round brass vessel with a cover, which was put under the flames. In the houses where the greatest luxury reigned, they had a kind of silver mould, from which the bread was taken, and served to the guests.[55]

It is absolutely necessary to dive into the private life of the Roman people, and not to neglect any of their domestic customs (accounts of which are scattered here and there, in the writings of the more serious historians, and among the dangerous frivolities of certain poets), if we wish to have a correct idea of the excessive refinement which the opulent classes evinced, even in the most ordinary things.

Modern nations are satisfied with the bread more or less white, and even bear, without much complaint, certain illicit mixtures, in which various heterogeneous substances are sometimes strangely amalgamated; but this was not the case in Rome. The prefect of provisions (*præfectus annonæ*) was scrupulously careful to see that the supply of bread was abundant; that it was of exact weight; that the manipulation of it was excellent; and that it was made of the best flour the public granaries contained.

As we have already observed, that was one of the most serious cares of the government on behalf of a people who only required two things—bread and the circus,[56] and whose ferocity, when pressed by hunger, knew no bounds.[57]

They studied carefully every modification that the art of baking might seem to require: they examined the leaven in use, and experimented with new kinds. The following are the compositions Pliny has transmitted to us:—

The Romans thought much of millet for their leaven; they mixed it with sweet wine, in which they let it ferment a year.

They employed, also, wheat bran, soaked for three days in sweet white wine, and dried in the sun. Of this they diluted a certain quantity at the time of making bread, which was left to ferment in the best wheat flour, and afterwards mixed with the entire mass.

The leavens just mentioned were made during the vintage; the rest of the year they were replaced by the following:—A dish containing two pounds of barley paste was placed on red-hot coals, and heated until ebullition commenced. It was put into vessels till it became sour.

Very often leaven was procured from dough just made. A piece was taken from the mass previous to salt being added; it was then left to turn sour, and might be used the next day.

The celebrated naturalist who supplies these details, tells us that, in his time, the Gauls and Spaniards, after having made a drink from wheat, saved the scum to raise the dough, and that their bread was the lightest of all.[58]

It would be difficult to form an idea of the prodigious luxury which Rome introduced into an aliment so common, and of such universal use as bread. Its name, its form, and flavour indicated the various ranks of society to which it belonged.[59] There was the senator's bread, that of the knights, of the citizens, of the people, and that of the peasants.[60]

Let us go together under the vast galleries supported by those magnificent arcades.[61] The *ediles* have preceded us; they are visiting the shops;[62] it is the *Forum Pistrinum*, or bread-market. The year is good: a *septier* (five bushels) of wheat is only twenty-five shillings,[63] and provisions of all kinds abound in Rome. Foreigners, also, are here, attracted by curiosity; for Vespasian is preparing to deposit with solemnity the spoils of Jerusalem in the temple of Peace.[64]

In the middle of the inclosure you see the statue of Vesta, the goddess worshipped by bakers.[65] In the front, and round the gallery, those open stalls are loaded with a number of round loaves of the same form and weight: they are all five inches in thickness; the top is divided by eight notches—that is to say, they are first divided across, and the four parts are again subdivided.[66] These lines are made in the dough, so that they may be more easily broken.

The Roman gentry and shopkeepers give the preference to this sort of household bread, simply composed of flour, water, and salt.[67]

You perceive, here and there, several baskets, full of heavy biscuits; they are called *autopyron*; it is a coarse, black food, composed of bran mixed with a little flour, and made expressly for the dogs and slaves.[68]

Do you see that colossal-looking man, with enormous limbs, who is walking about with an air of stupidity, and whose small head is covered with scars? The dealers know his profession, and one of them offers him the *athletæ's* bread; it is kneaded, without leaven, with soft, white curd cheese, and is a coarse, heavy food, which that class of people seem to partake of with great delight.[69] That stout baker before us occupies two of the most spacious shops in the market, on the left of the statue; he is one of the richest members of the corporation, and is the principal purveyor for the camp and army. Those large sacks, placed before him with so much symmetry, contain the *buccellatum* biscuit, or dried bread for the troops.[70]

His neighbour (called the Greek), was born at Athens; he is the fashionable purveyor to the princes, senators, and sybarites of Rome. No one understands so well as himself the art of mixing salt, oil, and milk with the best wheaten flour; an exquisite combination, which produces the celebrated bread of Cappadocia, served only on the tables of the wealthy.[71] With the *artoplites*, a light bread, made with the best wheaten flour, and baked in a mould, it is the only kind of which refined persons can partake.[72] If we were not afraid of tiring you, we could point out many other sorts of bread which abound in the *Forum Pistrinum*, for there is some for all tastes and classes, from the *artopticii*, baked in moulds,[73] a most nutritious and digestive bread, down to the *furfuraceus*, a mass of indigestible bran that the wildest savages among the Scythians could not have swallowed with impunity.

We should have spoken to you of the *astrologicus* bread, the paste of which is similar to that we use in our days to make fritters, commonly called batter.

Also of the *cacabaceus*, which is indebted for its agreeable and spicy flavour to the water, which is previously boiled in a kind of bronzed stewpan; and the *siligineus* bread, made of the best flour. Its manipulation is difficult and tedious; no matter—the epicurean prefers it, when, by chance, he happens to be hungry.[74]

Neither ought we to forget the *panis madidus*, a species of paste made of milk and flour, with which the fashionable ladies and effeminate dandies covered their faces before going to bed, to preserve the freshness and beauty of their complexion.[75]

But this enumeration may appear to you idle and endless; let us, therefore, leave the market and assist at the distribution of bread *civilis* among the people, of which thirteen ounces is given to each person;[76] we will then give a rapid glance at the various other *cereals* besides wheat, which, in some shape or other, are converted into food.

The customs of the middle ages cannot be better illustrated than by adding the following curious notes:

The Norman kings subjected the bakers to very severe laws with

---

DESCRIPTION OF PLATE No. VII.

BREAD.—No. 1. In Herculaneum there were found two entire loaves of the same dimension, being 13½ inches in diameter, and 3½ inches thick. Each had eight divisions cut on the top, that is to say,—a cross was first marked, and between each, another division was made; some had stamps on the top.

No. 2. At Pompeii, in a shop near the Pantheon, were discovered bronze moulds for pastry and bread.

No. 3. The Cappadocia bread, made in a mould, found at Pompeii.

No. 4. The mould for the above.

Pl. 7.

1.

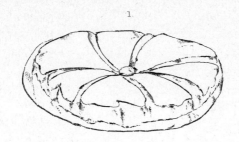

2.

3.

4.

respect to the weight and price of bread. The first offence was punished by the confiscation of their bread; the second by a fine; and the third by the pillory.[77]

Saint Louis made statutes for the bakers of Paris. He forbade them to bake on Sunday or any festival day, under pain of a fine of eighteen sous (about eight pence), and a certain quantity of bread. But he gave them permission to open their shops and *sell* every day of the year without exception.[78]

In the 17th century, a new regulation was made concerning bakers; they were to bake " daily, and have always on sale three kinds of bread, viz., that known as *pain de chalis*, of twelve ounces; *pain de chapitre*, of ten ounces; and brownish household bread, of sixteen ounces. The price of each to be *douze deniers* (a halfpenny), marked by the baker with his own particular mark." They were also permitted to make " rolls and other sorts," but not to expose them for sale " under pain of being fined four hundred Paris livres (a little more than twelve pounds sterling)." [79]

Master-bakers were admitted at Paris, in the 14th century, in the following manner :—

When a young man had been successively winnower, sifter, kneader, and foreman, he could, by paying a certain amount to the king as legiance money, become an aspirant-baker, and commence business on his own account. Four years after, he was received as master by going through certain formalities. On a given day, he set out from his house, followed by all the bakers of the town, and repaired to the residence of the master of the bakers, to whom he presented a new pot filled with nuts, saying : " Master, I have accomplished my four years ; here is my pot of nuts." Then the master of the bakers asked the secretary of the trade whether that were true, and having received a reply in the affirmative, the master of the bakers returned the pot to the aspirant, who broke it against the wall, and was at once reckoned amongst the masters.

Let us reckon up the different kinds of bread that were in use at that epoch :

The bread made simply with flour, water, salt, and yeast—the common bread ; the best was made at Chailly or Gonesse.

The bread cooked in hot water—*pain échaudé* (in England, we should call it baked dumpling).

The bread made of the finest flour, beaten a long time with two sticks—pounded bread.

The bread made of the very finest and purest flour (biscuit flour) slightly baked—roll bread.

The bread made of fine flour, kneaded with butter, and sprinkled with whole wheat—sheep bread.

The bread made of fine flour, eggs and milk—Christmas bread.

And lastly, rye bread, kneaded with spice, honey, or sugar—ginger-bread.[80]

V.

FRUMENTA.

Do not be alarmed, fair readers, at the Latin noun which heads this chapter : tolerate it in consideration of our promise seldom to solicit a like favour. It meant, among the Latins, all the plants which produce ears of corn,[1] the seeds of which can be converted into flour.[2] Clearly there never was a more innocent expression.

Barley seems to claim the first place among cereals of the second order ; the Greeks looked upon it as the happy symbol of fertility,[3] and the ancient inhabitants of Italy gave it a name (*hordeum*) which, perhaps, recalled to their mind the use mankind made of it before wheat was known (*exordium*).[4]

The Jews had a great esteem for barley, and sacred history generally assimilates it to wheat, when the fruits of the earth are mentioned. Thus a beloved spot produces both these plants :[5] Shobi offered to David wheat and barley ;[6] and Solomon promises twenty thousand sacks of wheat and as much barley to the workmen charged with cutting down the cedars of Lebanon.[7]

The Greeks and Romans did not carry their love for this grain so far as the Hebrews. In Rome it was the food of the flocks and cowards.[8] In Lacedæmon and at Athens the gladiators and common people had no other aliment ;[9] they made it into barley-gruel (*alphiton*), the composition of which was very simple, and would not probably tempt a modern Lucullus. Here is the recipe of this ancient and national dish :—

Dry, near the fire or in the oven, twenty pounds of barley flour, then parch it. Add three pounds of linseed meal, half a pound of coriander

D

seed, two ounces of salt, and the quantity of water necessary.[10] To this
mixture of ingredients the Italian epicureans added a little millet, so as
to give the paste more cohesion and delicacy.[11]

This culinary preparation must appear rather unworthy of those
nations who so completely eclipsed all the gastronomic glories of the
universe ; wherefore let us hasten to reinstate them as men of taste and
exquisite intelligence, by citing a more learned combination, which obtained the judicious patronage of the Archestrates and Apicii : —

Take pearl barley, pound it in a mortar, make use of the flour only,
and put it in a saucepan ; pour on it by degrees some of the best oil ;
with that certainty which science alone gives to the hand, and stir it
carefully, whilst a slow, equal fire performs the great work of cookery.
Be, above all, attentive to enrich it, at proper intervals, with a delicate
gravy extracted from a young fat chicken or from a succulent lamb.
Unceasingly watch, lest the ebullition, by going on too rapidly, force
this delightful mixture to overflow the side of the vessel ; and when your
practised palate informs you that it is worthy of your guests, present it
to their impatient sensuality.[12]

So it appears the ancients were acquainted with pearl barley, and
barley water ; the latter took the name of diet drink (*ptisana*), which
we only associate with melancholy reminiscences.[13] Hippocrates was
not only in raptures with the virtues and properties of this aliment,[14]
but he also conferred the highest praise on that sweet and insipid drink,
which our doctors order their patients, as did the oracle of Cos, and
which at that time was called " barley broth."[15]

Oats occupied an honourable place after barley. Pliny fancied these
two plants so analogous, that the owner of a field who had sown barley
might find oats at the time of harvest, whilst precisely the reverse might
happen to his neighbour.[16] Nature, in our days, is not subject to such
frolics ; and our farmers are tolerably certain that, by care, labour, and
God's assistance, they will gather from the soil what they have sown.

" In order to develop a strong flavour of vanille in black oats,
wash this seed, boil it a moment in water, and employ the decoction as
you would potato flour, and it will form excellent creams.

" In Normandy and Lower Britany they make with flour of oats a
delicious soup. The following is the manner they obtain it. They take
white oats and put them in the oven ; when sufficiently dried, they are
fanned, cleaned, and carried to a mill, the grinders of which are freshly

sharpened. The miller takes care to hold them a little way off, in order that they may not crush the grain, and that this last may preserve the shape of rice; by this means they remove the whole of the pellicle."— PARMENTIER.

The Greeks and Romans knew how to appreciate oatmeal:[17] they used it to make a kind of gruel, such as we have already described, and also a substantial thick milk, which they prepared as we do.[18]

Rice was also held in great esteem by them: they considered it as a food very beneficial to the chest; therefore it was recommended in cases of consumption, and to persons subject to spitting of blood.[19]

Millet, so called from the multiplicity of its seeds,[20] abounded more particularly in Gaul, in the time of Strabo.[21] Pliny pretends that no grain swells so much in cooking, and he assures us that sixty pounds of bread was obtained from a single bushel of millet, weighing only twenty pounds.[22] This naturalist also speaks of another kind of millet, coming originally from India, and which had only been in cultivation ten years in Italy. The stalk resembled that of the reed, and often attained the height of ten feet; its fecundity was such that a single grain produced innumerable ears of corn;[23] therefore, if so prolific, and capable of making good and economical food, why should it not be, in 1853, cultivated largely wherever the climate may allow it?

Some writers place *Panic Grass* among the wheats, because certain nations made bread of it.[24] The higher classes of Rome and Athens always resisted this bad taste. They preferred spelt, or red wheat, a super-excellent grain,[25] which was much honoured by the Latins, if we can credit the charming letter, written by Pliny the younger, to Septilius Clarus, on the occasion of a dinner, where the latter failed to join the guests. Among other delicate dishes with which he desired to treat his friend, he had ordered a spelt cake to be made.[26] This same flour was the base of the Carthaginian pudding; which the reader may taste if he will, here is the recipe:—

CARTHAGINIAN PUDDING.—Put a pound of red wheat flour into water; when it has soaked some time, place it in a wooden bowl, add three pounds of cream cheese, half a pound of honey, and one egg; beat this mixture well together, and cook it on a slow fire in a stew-pan.[27] Should this dish not be sufficiently delicate, try the following:—

When you have sifted some spelt flour, put it in a wooden vessel, with some water, which you must renew twice a day for ten days. At the end of that time squeeze out all the water, and place the paste in another vessel; reduce it to the consistence of thick lees, pass it through a piece of new linen, and repeat this last operation; dry it in the sun, and then boil it in milk.[28]

As regards the exact seasoning of this exquisite Roman dish, it is your own genius which must inspire you with the proportions.

Let us not omit to notice the *Erupmon* of the Greeks, the *Irion* of the Latins, the *Indian Wheat* of the moderns. This plant produces a wholesome and easily digestible food; it was well known in Italy in the time of Pliny,[29] at which period the peasants used to make a crisp sort of heavy bread, probably somewhat similar to that which is still used in the south of France.

Since the famine of 1847 great attention has been paid to this flour; much was imported into England from America, where it is used in domestic economy; when green, its milky pulp is an excellent food: the various advantages of this flour, however, are not sufficiently developed to give all the benefit of its goodness to the world; habit and prejudice assist materially to prevent its being generally employed.

The Romans also ate it as hasty-pudding, parched or roasted, with a little salt. A writer equally remarkable for his elegant and easy style, as well as for the justness of his observations, informs us that, in our days, the Indian inhabitants of the unfruitful plains of Marwar never dress Indian corn in any other way.[30]

Such are the principal *graminea* which the ancients thought worthy of their attention, or allowed to appear on their tables, with more or less honour according to the degree of esteem in which they were held. It is probable that the cooks in the great gastronomic period of Rome and Athens, who knew so well the capricious nature of their masters' palates,[31] had to borrow from magiric chemistry, then so flourishing, some wonderful means of giving to various kinds of cereals a culinary value they now no longer possess—what might we not expect from a Thimbron,[32] a Mithoecus,[33] a Soterides?[34] This latter performed a feat which does him too much honour to be unnoticed here.

The King of Bithynia, Nicomedes, was taken with a strange, invincible, and imperious longing which admitted of no delay; he ordered his cook, Soterides, to be sent for, and commanded him to prepare instantly a dish of loaches. "Loaches, Sire!" cried the skilful, yet terrified cook; "by all the gods, protectors of the kingdom, where can I procure these fish

at this late hour of the night?" Kings ill brook resistance to their will.[35]
Nicomedes was not celebrated for patience when pressed by hunger.
" Give me loaches, I say," replied he, with a hollow and terrible voice;
" or else——" and his clear, fearful, pantomimic expression made the
unfortunate cook understand too well that he must either obey or immediately deliver up his head to the provost of the palace. The alternative
was embarrassing; nevertheless, Soterides thought how to get out of the
scrape. He shut himself up in his laboratory, peeled some long
radishes, and with extraordinary address gave them the form of the
fatal fish, seasoning them with oil, salt, black pepper, and doubtless
several other ingredients, the secret of which the illustrious *chef* has
not handed down to posterity. Then, holding in his hand a dish of
irreproachable-looking fried fish, he boldly presented himself before the
prince, who was walking up and down with hasty strides awaiting his
arrival. The King of the Bithynians ate up the whole, and the next
day he condescended to inform his court that he never had loaches
served he so much liked.[36] This digression, which the reader will kindly
pardon, sufficiently shows to what height the art of ancient cookery was
carried, and of which this work will furnish new and abundant proofs.

The cereals having had so much of our attention, we have now to
consider those grains or seeds which serve as the bases or necessary
adjuncts to different dishes.

VI.

GRAINS: SEEDS.

ONE of the most important was *Mustard* seed. Pythagoras maintains (and no one has contradicted his assertion) that this seed occupied the first rank amongst alimentary substances which exercise a prompt influence on the brain.[1] Indeed the ancients attributed to it the same qualities that we do at the present day.

Mustard, according to their opinion, excites the appetite, gives piquancy to meat, strengthens the stomach, and facilitates digestion. It is better suited, say they, to bilious constitutions than to lymphatic persons; and they recommended its use in summer, rather than in winter.[2]

The good Pliny, always disposed to adopt, without much examination, any stories, provided they were but slightly exaggerated, was convinced, and affirms, with his accustomed good humour, that this plant is a sovereign remedy against the bite of the most venomous serpents: it is only necessary to apply it to the wound. And, again, if taken inwardly, there is nothing to fear from the poisonous effects of certain mushrooms.[3] The doctors of the 19th century are, apparently, little inclined to adopt the method recommended by the worthy naturalist.

Mustard seed is only mentioned in the Bible as a term of comparison; its alimentary qualities are nowhere indicated.[4]

The Romans, and other nations after them, fermented this seed in new sweet wine. It is from this, perhaps, we must seek for the origin of the word mustard, "*mustum ardens*" (burning wine)[5]; some gastronomic writers give it another derivation, not generally adopted. This condiment, say they, was formerly called *sauve* or *senevé*. It was only towards the close of the 14th century that this name was changed. Philip the Bold, Duke of Burgundy, marching against the inhabitants of Ghent, who had revolted from him, and the city of Dijon having supplied him for this expedition with a thousand men-at-arms, the prince, in gratitude, granted to that city, amongst other privileges, that of bearing his arms, with his motto, "*Moult me tarde.*" The whole of this was carved on the principal gate of Dijon, but an accident having destroyed the middle word, the two others *moult tarde* caused many a smile at the expense of the Dijonnais; and as they traded in *senevé* (mustard), this grain was called in derision *moutarde*, when it came from Dijon, a name it has preserved ever since.[6] If this etymology is not true, at least it is ingenious.

Coriander, amongst the Romans, appears to have possessed the same property as mustard, that is to say, they considered it was strengthening and digestive.[7] They employed it also in a very useful manner during the great heat of summer: they mixed it with vinegar, after it had been well bruised or pounded, and laid it over any kind of meat, which this coating preserved in a perfect state of freshness.[8]

Pliny classifies the bitter seed of the *Lupin* as a grain pertaining to that of wheat;[9] and if you soak it, he says, in boiling water, it becomes so mild that it can be eaten.[10] Zeno, of Citium, was of the same opinion. This philosopher, with all his wisdom, could not help showing his bad temper, even towards his best friends at times, but was very affable after he had quaffed several cups of delicious wine. One day he was asked for an explanation of this contrast in his temper. "That is very simple," he replied; "I am of the same nature as the lupins: their bitterness is insupportable before they are soaked, but they are of an exquisite mildness when they have been well steeped."[11]

We strongly doubt, nevertheless, whether this plant has ever been honoured by the patronage of connoisseurs and people of delicate taste; a very high authority in cookery—Lycophon, of Chalcis—used to say, with a kind of disdain, that this despicable plant was hardly good enough for the common fare of the mob, or to feast the guests at a beggar's table.[12]

It was principally used as food for cattle, and not without reason, if it be true that twenty pounds of lupins are sufficient to fatten an ox.[13]

The lovers of etymology, who may be classified in the family of readers of logogriphs, were in raptures at finding the following : " The Latin name of *Lupinus* has been given to this grain because the lupin wears out and destroys the land nearly as the wolf destroys and devours the flocks ; whereupon they exclaimed, with pride, ' *Lupinus à lupo !* ' "[14]

At the period when the gods did not exact much, but were contented with humble offerings, men placed on the altars loaves made of *Linseed* meal; a treat the immortals gratefully accepted, though certainly it would not much tempt us[15] of the present day.

The Asiatics afterwards thought of pounding the linseed, frying it, and mixing it with honey ; these cakes seemed to them too good for their divinities, so they ate them themselves.[16]

In the time of Pliny, the Lombards and Piedmontese ate this miserable bread of the gods, and even found in it a most agreeable flavour :[17] these nations have since improved their taste.

Shall we mention *Hempseed*, the *Cannabis* of the ancients, which was served fried for dessert ? [18] That hemp should be spun and made into ropes, well and good ; but to regale one's-self with it after dinner, —when the stomach is overloaded with food, and hardly moved from its lethargic quietude by the appearance of the most provoking viands that art can invent—what depravity ! What strange perversion of the most simple elements of gastronomy !

The Arabs, that wandering nation, who are not yet acquainted with the roasting-spit, nor the voluptuousness of a delicious repast, formerly intoxicated themselves with a beverage extracted from linseed ;[19] we, who are in possession of generous wine, let us deplore such excesses, and not imitate them.

VII.

VEGETABLES.

ALL nations have sown vegetables, and judged them worthy of their particular attention; sometimes they have even confounded many of these plants with the cereals, because they were converted into flour and bread,[1] especially in time of famine.[2]

After the Deluge, when God made a covenant with Noah he said, with respect to the food of man:—"Even as the green herb have I given you all things;[3]" and, subsequently to that epoch, the holy writers frequently demonstrate, in their simple and interesting style, the various uses which the Hebrews made of vegetables. Esau, pressed by hunger, sold his birth-right to Jacob for a dish of lentils.[4]

Among the presents which David received from Shobi, were beans, lentils, and parched pulse.[5]

The four Hebrew children were fed with vegetables, at the court of Nebuchadnezzar, King of Babylon.[6] It is sufficient, we think, to indicate these passages, without uselessly increasing the number.

The heroes of Homer, those men covered with iron and brass, whose terrible blows dealt death and desolation, reposed after their exploits, partaking of a dish of beans or a plate of peas.[7] Happy simplicity of the Homeric ages! Patrocles peeled onions! Achilles washed cabbages! and the wise Ulysses roasted, with his own hands, a sirloin of beef!

One day the son of Thetis received under his tent a deputation sent by the Greeks, to entreat him to be friends with Agamemnon. The young hero, who could only be accused of a little pride and passion, invited these worthy personages to dinner, and, with the assistance of his friend, gave them a magnificent banquet, in which vegetables occupied a most conspicuous place.[8]

Sixteen Greek authors have devoted their vigils to profound researches concerning the qualities of these useful plants; their works have not been transmitted to us, but their names are to be found inscribed in the gastronomic treasure which Athenæus—that grammarian, philosopher, and epicurean—has bequeathed to the meditations of posterity.[9]

But it is principally with the Romans that this interesting branch of the magiric art flourished. They have told us that this great family of herbs took the name of vegetables (*legumina*), because they were chosen and picked by the hand;[10] and their most celebrated horticulturists have prided themselves on the preparation of the ground to which they were confided, on the attention which they claimed, and on the Hygeian virtues which experience attributed to them. Heathen theology, too, consecrated several of them to the solemnities of their religion, and some nations even considered them worthy of their homage and the fumes of incense.[11]

Virgil himself seems to regret his inability to sing of gardens and vegetables. Perhaps a rapid sketch of what the great poet says on this subject, may not be misplaced here.

> " Si mon vaisseau long-temps égaré loin du bord,
> Ne se hâtait enfin de regagner le port,
> Peut-être je peindrais les Ciens chéris de Flore ;
> Le Narcisse en mes vers s'empresserait d'éclore,
> Les roses m'ouvriraient leurs calices brillants,
> Le tortueux concombre arrondirait ses flancs ;
> Du persil toujours vert, des pâles chicorées
> Ma muse abreuverait les tiges altérées,
> Je courberais le lierre et l'acanthe en berceau,
> Et du myrthe amoureux j'ombragerais les eaux."[12]

One more fact will serve to show to what extent the Romans carried their enthusiastic affection for leguminous plants: we know that illustrious families did not disdain to borrow their names from them. The appellations, Fabius, Cicero, and Lentulus, thus enhanced the humble renown of beans (*faba*), peas (*cicer arietinum*), and lentils (*lenticula*).[13] The eminent orator we have just named gave the preference one day to a dish of beet-root, instead of oysters and lampreys, of which he was passionately fond.[14] It is true that, since the promulgation of the Licinian law,[15] which allowed but little meat and plenty of vegetables, the voluptuaries of Rome invented most astonishing ragouts of mushrooms and pot-herbs. So true is it that the genius of man develops itself more particularly under difficult circumstances, and that the art of cookery owes, perhaps, the perfection and glory which it has attained to the impediments with which its formidable enemy, frugality, seems always ready to surround it.

Apicius, that profound culinary chemist, who nobly expended immense treasures in inventing new dishes, and who killed himself [16] because the remainder of his fortune was not sufficient for him (though to another it would have seemed magnificent)—Apicius shows us what he believed to be the most suitable manner of preserving vegetables. "Choose them," he says, "before they are perfectly ripe, put them in a vessel coated with pitch, and cover it hermetically." [17]

The reader will decide for himself between this process and those which science has since discovered.

The capitulars (or statutes) of Charlemagne enter, on the subject of vegetables, into some instructive details. They inform us that lettuces, cresses, endive, parsley, chervil, carrots, leeks, turnips, onions, garlic, scallions, and eschalots, were nowhere to be found, except in the emperor's kitchen-gardens. Charlemagne had all those vegetables sold, and derived from them a very considerable revenue.[18]

Anderson makes an observation (under the date 1548), which deserves to be noticed here, were it only on account of its singularity. "The English," says he, "cultivated scarcely any vegetable before the last two centuries. At the commencement of the reign of Henry VIII., neither salad, nor carrots, nor cabbages, nor radishes, nor any other comestibles of a like nature, were grown in any part of the kingdom; they came from Holland and Flanders."

According to the author of a project, printed in London in 1723, in 8vo., "for the relief of the poor, and the payment of old debts, without the creation of new taxes," Queen Catherine herself could not procure a salad for her dinner. The king was obliged to send over to Holland for a gardener to cultivate those pot-herbs, with which England is, perhaps, better furnished now than any other country in Europe.

Anderson asserts (1660) that cauliflowers were not known in England until about the time of the Restoration. And, lastly, the author of the "State of England," printed in 1768, remarks that asparagus and artichokes were only introduced a few years antecedent to that date.

VIII.

DRIED VEGETABLES.

———

BEANS.

This innocent vegetable, which with us certainly awakens no lugubrious thoughts, was formerly consecrated to the dead. It was offered in sacrifices to the infernal gods, and its mysterious virtues evoked by night, spirits, and shadows.[1] The Flamen of Jupiter could not eat it, and he was forbidden to touch a bean, or even to pronounce its name ;[2] for the fatal plant contains a little black spot, which is no other than a noxious character—a type of death.[3]

Pythagoras and his followers carefully avoided this dismal food, in the fear of submitting a father, sister, or beloved wife to the danger of a cruel mastication ;[4] for who knew where wandering souls might rest during the course of their numerous transmigrations.

Grave writers say the cause of this abstinence is, that beans are difficult of digestion ; that they stupify those who make use of them as food ; and that hens who eat them cease to lay eggs.[5] What more shall we say? Hippocrates, wise as he certainly was, had some of these strange fears, and he trembled for his patients when beans were in blossom.[6]

In spite of such ridiculous prejudices, this plant had numerous and enlightened defenders. When green, it was served on tables renowned for delicacies ; and, when fully ripe, it frequently replaced both wheat and other corn.[7] One of the festivals of Apollo—the *Pyanepsia*—owed its origin and pomp to the bean. This vegetable then obtained pre-eminence over all that were boiled in the saucepan, and offered to the God of Day and the Fine Arts.[8] Is it possible to imagine a more brilliant rehabilitation?

If we are to believe Isidorus, this plant was the first culinary vegetable of which man made use;[9] he was, therefore, bound to preserve a grateful remembrance of it.

King David did not deem it unworthy of him,[10] and the Prophet Ezekiel was commanded to mix it with the different grains of which he made his bread.[11]

We possess few certain indications proving the different culinary combinations to which beans gave rise among the ancients. All we know is, that they ate them boiled,[12] perhaps with bacon; raw,[13] with salt, we should imagine; or fried[14] with fat, butter, or oil.

Two kinds especially attracted the attention of true connoisseurs of that class of *gourmets* elect, whose palate is ever testing, and whose sure taste detects and appreciates shades, of almost imperceptible tenuity —first, the bean of Egypt, recommended for its rich, nutritious, and wholesome pulp; this bean was also cultivated in Syria and Cilicia:[15] and secondly, the Greek bean, which passed at Rome for a most delicious dish.[16] Certain gastronomists, however, preferred another vegetable of which we are going to speak.

Ever since the middle ages the bean has played a very important part in the famous "Twelfth-night cake," almost all over Europe. The ephemeral royalty it bestowed was often sung by the poets, and consecrated in chronicles. Thomas Randolph informs us that Lady Flemyng was queen of the bean in 1563.[17] Some days after the Duke of Guise was assassinated by Poltrot. History has its puerilities as well as its great tragedies.

The Spaniards had also their Twelfth-night cake. When John, Duke of Braganza, had obtained the crown of Portugal (1640), Philip IV. of Spain informed Count Olivares of the event, and added, as if it were a consolation for the loss of a kingdom, that this new sovereign was nothing more than a "king of the bean."[18] Philip was mistaken.

These cakes were made in former days nearly in the same manner that we make them now. Sometimes they contained honey, flour, ginger, and pepper. One portion was for God, another for the Holy Virgin, and three others for the Magi; that is to say, they gave all these portions to the poor.[19]

In England the cake was often full of raisins, among which one bean and one pea were introduced.

"Cut the cake," says Meliboeus to Nisa; "who hath the beane shal be kinge; and where the peaze is, shal be queene."[20]

"At the present day the bean is one of the vegetables most cultivated in Egypt and Italy. At Naples, as in Egypt, they are eaten raw when young, and the large ones cooked and grilled in the oven. They are publicly sold already cooked."—LEMAN.

———

HARICOTS.

It is well known that Alexander the Great was fond of travelling, and that he was generally accompanied in his peregrinations by a certain number of soldiers, who occasionally took for him, on his route, cities, provinces, and sometimes kingdoms. It happened, one day, that as the Macedonian prince—worthy pupil of Aristotle—was herbalizing in India, his eyes fell upon a field of haricots, which appeared to him very inviting. It was the first time that he had seen this plant, and he immediately ordered his cook to prepare a dish of them—we do not know with what sauce; but he thought them good, and, thanks to this great conqueror, Europe was enriched with a new vegetable.[21]

Virgil was doubtless ignorant of this noble origin, when he decried haricots severely, by qualifying them so disgracefully.[22] It is true that the lower classes of people, who were very fond of them, did great injury to their reputation; for things the most exquisite soon lose their value when they fall within the reach of the vulgar. It is thus with a pleasing melody—when given up to the barbarous and melancholy street organs it ceases to charm the ears of drawing-room fashionables. The same again with a plaintive ballad—it loses its attraction the moment a street Orpheus begins to murder it with his Stentorian bawl.

Let it not be thought, however, that the plant of which we speak was exclusively reserved for the vulgar appetite. Oh, no! the Greeks and Latins had too much good taste for that. The former allowed it a distinguished place on their tables, together with figs, and other side dishes. They only required that haricots should be young, tender, and green.[23]

In Rome they were preserved with vinegar and garum; and, prepared in this manner, they excited the appetites of the guests at the beginning of the repast.[24] Moreover, it was admitted that this vegetable was much more wholesome than beans, that the stomach was less fatigued by it, and that persons of delicate constitutions might partake of it without fear. Certain amateurs even pretended that no vegetable was to be compared to haricots;[25] but others differed from them on this point; and the latter, right or wrong, pronounced in favour of peas.

PEAS.

Green peas, we are sorry to say, were not appreciated as they deserved to be by the Romans.[26] It was reserved principally for our century to discover their value, to cultivate them with care, and to force nature to give them to us before the appointed time. This plant was hardly known in 1550. Since that period, the gardener, Michaux, undertook to bring it into repute. For some time in France it was called only by the name of this worthy man.[27]

Before that it was an unappreciated vegetable; it came forth, blossomed, and disappeared, without utility and without renown.

It was not thus with grey peas (*pois chiche*), which flourished at a very remote period, and are mentioned in the sacred writings.[28] The common people of Rome and Greece made them their ordinary food. They ate them boiled or fried; a rather disagreeable dish, according to the caustic Martial,[29] who, however, speaks with disdain of every kind of peas, in whatsoever manner they may be prepared.

Nevertheless, the satirical humour of this celebrated poet did not prevent this vegetable from being universally sold: and men, women, and children regaled, and even gorged, themselves, with fried grey peas,[30] or ram peas (*cicer arietinum*), a singular name, for which they were indebted to the slight asperity remarkable in each of the grains.[31]

At the Circus, and in the theatres, they were sold at a low price to the spectators, whom it seemed impossible to satiate with this delicacy,

although it has so little attraction for us.[32]   In short, the nation of
kings had so decided a taste for grey peas, that those who coveted public employment did not fail to distribute them gratuitously to the people,
in order to obtain their suffrages.[33]   We must acknowledge that in
those days votes were obtained at a very cheap rate.

LENTILS.

The Egyptians, whose ideas were sometimes most eccentric, imagined it was sufficient to feed children with lentils to enlighten their
minds, open their hearts, and render them cheerful. That people, therefore, consumed an immense quantity of this vegetable, which from
infancy had been their principal food.[34]

The Greeks also highly esteemed this aliment, and their ancient
philosophers regaled themselves with lentils. Zeno would not trust to
any one the cooking of them; it is true that the stoics had for their
maxim: "A wise man acts always with reason, and prepares his lentils
himself."[35] We must confess that the great wit of these words escapes
us, although we are willing to believe there is some in them.

However it may be, lentils were abundant in Greece and in the
East; and many persons, otherwise very sensible, maintained, with the
most serious countenance in the world, that they softened the temper and
disposed the mind to study.[36]

It is hardly necessary to observe that this plant was well known to
the Hebrews. The red pottage of lentils for which Esau sold his birth-
right,[37] the present of Shobi to David,[38] the victory of Shammah in the
field of lentils,[39] and, lastly, the bread of Ezekiel,[40] sufficiently prove that
the Jews numbered this vegetable as one of those in ordinary use
among them.

The Romans had not the same esteem for it as the nations we have
mentioned. According to them, the moisture in lentils could only cause
heaviness to the mind, and render men reserved, indolent, and lazy.
The name of this vegetable pretty well shows, they said, the bad effect it
produces. Lentil derives its origin from the word *lentus* (slow),[41] "*Lens
a lente.*"

And, as if enough had not been alleged to disgrace this unfortunate

E

plant, and to give the finish to the ill-fame it had acquired, it was placed amongst funereal and ill-omened foods. Thus Marcus Crassus, waging war against the Parthians, was convinced that his army would be defeated, because his corn was exhausted, and his men were obliged to have recourse to lentils.[42]

How was it possible to resist such attacks! The humble plant gave way in spite of the few flattering words of the poetic Virgil,[43] and the assurance of Pliny that this food produced two uncommon virtues—mildness and moderation.[44]

IX.

KITCHEN GARDEN.

THE art of gardening, which may be called the luxury of agriculture,[1] was known at the most remote periods.[2] In the same inclosure was to be found the kitchen garden, orchard, and flower garden,[3] at a short distance from the habitation of the rich.[4] Royal hands did not disdain to embellish those spots which afforded a pleasing retreat, solitude, and repose.

Thus Attalus resigned the cares of his crown to cultivate his little garden, and sow in it the seeds of his favourite plant.[5]

Babylon, the renowned city of antiquity, was celebrated amongst other wonders for her gardens suspended in the air; they were partly in existence sixteen centuries after their erection, and astonished Alexander the Great[6] by the sublime grandeur of their prodigious boldness and the rare beauty of their workmanship.

Homer has left us the description of Alcinous's garden,[7] from which can be traced the birth of the art of gardening; its luxury consisted in the order and symmetry of its form, in the richness of its soil, the fertility of the trees, and in the two fountains which ornamented it. It was not so with the Romans. Those conquerors of the world displayed every where pomp and ostentation: Lucullus, Crassus, Pompey, and Cæsar, filled their gardens with the riches of Asia and the spoils of the universe.[8]

The serious horticulturist, who wanted a garden for enjoyment, and not for show, carefully laboured, to see it bring forth fine fruits and excellent vegetables[9] Water was properly distributed for irrigation by means of aqueducts[10] of tiles, wood, or lead pipes,[11] and everywhere the plants received the necessary moisture; and clever experienced gardeners were constantly occupied in improvements suggested by an attentive and skilful master.[12]

The kitchen garden of the ancients contained mostly the vegetables, herbs, and roots, of which we still make use; but they also cultivated certain other kinds, which modern cookery has either put aside or rarely employs. We shall describe all those which appear most worthy of notice.

CABBAGE.

This plant has experienced the fate of a host of human things that have not been able to bear the weight of a too brilliant reputation. Time has done justice to the extraordinary qualities attributed to it, and the cabbage now remains, what it ought always to have been, an estimable vegetable and nothing more.

The Egyptians adored it, and raised altars to it. They afterwards made of this strange god the first dish of their repasts, and were imitated in this particular by the Greeks and Romans, who ascribed to it the happy quality of preserving from drunkenness.[13] It was more particularly the red cabbage that obtained these honours and prerogatives. From Italy the victorious legions introduced it among the Gauls, as well as the green cabbage; the white species appears to belong originally to southern countries.

Hippocrates had a peculiar affection for this vegetable. Should one of his patients be seized with a violent cholic, he at once prescribed a dish of boiled cabbage with salt.[14] Erasistratus looked upon it as a sovereign remedy against paralysis. Pythagoras, and several other learned philosophers, composed books in which they celebrated the marvellous virtues of the cabbage.[15]

A writer, not less serious than those we have just quoted, the wise Cato, affirms that this plant infallibly cures all diseases; and pretends to have used this panacea to preserve his family from the plague, which, otherwise, would not have failed to reach them. It is to the use the Romans made of it, he adds, that they were able during six hundred years to do without the assistance of physicians, whom they had expelled from their territories.[16] This bold assertion deserved a little retaliation on the part of the faculty; so they deposed the cabbage from the rank occupied by it in medicine, and banished it to the kitchen.

The Athenian ladies formerly partook of the general enthusiasm in favour of this wholesome vegetable, which was always served to them when a new-born infant required their maternal love and care.[17]

The ancients were acquainted with three principal kinds of cabbage: the silken-leaved, the curled, and the hard, round, white cabbage.[18]

Apicius does not busy himself with any one of these varieties in particular in the various preparations he points out, and which we submit to the appreciation of connoisseurs:

1st. Take only the most delicate and tender part of the cabbage, which boil, and then pour off the water; season it with cummin seed,[19] salt, old wine, oil, pepper, alisander, mint, rue, coriander seed, gravy, and oil.

2nd. Prepare the cabbage in the manner just mentioned, and make a seasoning of coriander seed, onion, cummin seed, pepper, a small quantity of oil, and wine made of sun raisins.[20]

3rd. When you have boiled the cabbages in water, put them into a saucepan and stew them with gravy, oil, wine, cummin seed, pepper, leeks, and green coriander.[21]

4th. Add to the preceding ingredients flour of almonds, and raisins dried in the sun.[22]

5th. Prepare them again in the above manner, and cook them with green olives.[23]

Who will question the service rendered to the culinary art by resuscitating these antique dishes, in which the cabbage admits of such a variety of combinations, and which we owe to the learning and experience of a man of taste? Whatever may be the opinion of our modern Trimalcions, we must not forget that this vegetable, prepared according to the recipe of Apicius, was the delight of the *gourmets* of Rome more than eighteen centuries ago.

The Romans brought the red cabbage into Gaul, and the green cabbage also. White cabbages came from the north, and the art of making them headed was unknown in the time of Charlemagne.[24]

"In some countries cauliflowers are dried, and the white headed cabbages are preserved. The first, stripped of their leaves, are cut in slices, and boiled two minutes in water slightly salted.   They are shortly after withdrawn, and put to drain on hurdles, which are afterwards exposed to the sun during two or three days.   At the expiration of that time the cauliflowers are placed in an oven half-warm, and are kept there till the stalks are dry; they are then wrapped in paper to preserve them from damp.   To keep the headed cabbages, divide them in six or eight pieces, according to size, throw them for an instant in boiling water, then withdraw and plunge them in vinegar, which from time to time must be changed, especially at the beginning, taking care to add always a little salt."—DUTOUR.

———

BEET.

Columella pretends that this plant owes its name (*beta*) to its resemblance to the letter B.[25] We shall leave to the professional etymologist the trouble of examining whether Columella made a mistake or not.

The Greeks had two distinct sorts of beet—the black and the pale; they preferred the latter,[26] especially when it came from Ascrea in Bœotia.[27] They called this species Sicilian beet; and the physician Diphilus—who joined to his knowledge of botany that sort of gastrophagic intuition, that culinary *mens divinior*, whose inspiration never leads astray—placed it far above the cabbage, notwithstanding the estimable qualities of this latter vegetable.[28] He recommended it to be eaten boiled, with mustard, and considers this food as a very excellent vermifuge.[29]

The beet has not found favour with Martial, who, always caustic and severe, calls it an insipid dish.[30] This injurious, and perhaps unjust, epithet would doubtless have exercised a fatal influence upon the destiny of this most inoffensive of vegetables, if an opponent of greater weight had not entered the lists against the atrabilarious poet.

We read in Apicius: "Boil, over a slow fire, some very tender white beet; add leeks, which have been taken from their native soil some days previous; when all this is cooked put it into a saucepan with pepper, gravy, and raisin wine; take care that the ebullition be regular, and serve.[31]

" Or, if you prefer : tie in bundles the beet you have carefully chosen, wash it, throw in some nitre, and boil it with water; then put it into a saucepan with sun-raisin wine, pepper, cummin, and a little oil; at the moment of ebullition add a mixture of gravy and coarsely chopped walnuts; cover the saucepan for an instant, uncover, and serve."[32]

The skilful artist is pleased for the third time to mention this culinary herb; and this is the new preparation which he gives :—

" When you have boiled beet in water until it is tender, add a pulp of leeks, some coriander, and cummin seed, carefully combined with flour and sun-made wine; place these different ingredients in a saucepan, and add gravy, oil, and vinegar."[33]

By tasting one of these dishes you will be convinced that Martial did not understand them; or, perhaps, he composed his epigram after dinner.

One species of beet is well known in its two principal varieties, under the name of beet-root and white-beet. The southern parts of Europe appear to be the native countries of the beet. It serves as food for both man and cattle. Sugar is extracted from the root, and potash from the stalks and leaves.

Beet-root is preserved, after stripping it completely of its leaves, and the earth which remains on them, in greenhouses, in dry cellars, and even in trenches covered with earth, in layers, lengthwise, with sand. They are thus preserved until the following May.

" Beet-root is eaten cooked in ashes or in water, and seasoned in various ways; they are excellent in salad, either by themselves, or mixed with endives or dandelion, &c."—Bosc.

SPINACH.

It does not appear that spinach was known to the Greeks and Romans. Some authors think that it might be the *chrysolacanon* of the Greeks,[34] but it is probable that this was no other than the *orach ;*[35] Beckmann[36] thinks, with several botanists, that this plant came from Spain; and, indeed, it has been often called the *Spanish vegetable.*[37]

We only speak of this plant by way of memento, and regret that our first masters in cookery have not been able to transmit to us the results of their studies and experience in the preparation of spinach, whose precocity must always render it valuable to amateurs of vegetable food.

MALLOWS.

The ancients ate mallows, and recognised in them soothing and softening qualities.[38] Diphilus of Siphne says that their juice lubricates the windpipe, nourishes, and is easily digested.[39] Horace praises this aliment;[40] and Martial, for once just, recommends its use.[41]

It is true that a passage of Cicero would seem to indicate we know not what deception, which appeared all at once when eating or after partaking of mallows;[42] but the Roman orator, perhaps, knew little of the properties of the plant, which were only described much later by Pliny the naturalist. The curious may consult on this subject the twenty-first chapter of the twentieth book of his great work.

At all events mallows were in high renown; they occupied one of the first ranks among pickles, those famous *acetaria* which had so powerful an effect in quickening the appetites of the Greeks, and preparing their stomachs for great gastronomic struggles.[43] They were served as a salad. The large-leaved mallow was mixed with œnogarum, pepper, gravy, and sun-made wine.[44]

The small-leaved mallows were also prepared with œnogarum and gravy; but instead of pepper and wine, oil and vinegar were added.[45]

ASPARAGUS.

"*Quiconque ne voit guère n'a guère à dire aussi.*"[46] But travellers, those daring pioneers of science, have sometimes, in their travels, the strange good fortune to behold wonders invisible to other eyes. Thus some skilful explorers of Africa saw, about the middle of the second century of the Christian era, in Getulia, asparagus of excellent quality and of very beautiful growth, being no less than twelve feet high! It is needless to add that the Libyan vendors rarely sold them in bundles. But these veridical travellers, on quitting the plain to ascend the mountains, found something still more wonderful; the land there seemed to suit these plants still better, for they acquired the height of twenty cubits.[47] After this, what shall we say of our European asparagus, so shrivelled and diminutive in comparison with that of Getulia?

The Greeks, not having any better, contented themselves with the ordinary sort, such as we have at the present day. They considered it very useful in the treatment of internal diseases.[48] Diphilus, who was very fond of it, regrets that this vegetable should be so hurtful to the sight:[49] is it because we eat asparagus that spectacles have become necessary at nearly all periods of life?

The Romans cultivated this plant with extreme care,[50] and obtained the most extraordinary results. At Ravenna, they raised asparagus each stem of which weighed three pounds.[51]

Then, as in our days, they were allowed but a short time to boil; hence the favourite expression of Augustus, who, to intimate his wish that any affair might be concluded without delay, was accustomed to say: "Let that be done quicker than you would cook asparagus."[52]

The cooks of Rome had a method which appears to have been subsequently too much neglected; they chose the finest heads of asparagus, and dried them. When wanted for the table, they put them into hot water, and then boiled them a few minutes.[53] Thanks to this simple process the plant swelled considerably, and passed as being very tender and fine flavoured.

The Apicii, Luculli, and other connoisseurs of renown, had this vegetable brought from the environs of Nesis, a city of Campania.[54]

It is asserted that Asia is its native soil, and that it was originally brought to us from that part of the world. Nevertheless, wild asparagus grows naturally in certain sandy soils, as, for instance, in the islands of the Rhône and the Loire.[55]

"When it is found impossible to eat all the asparagus you have cut, and which has arrived at a convenient maturity, place them by the thick ends in a vessel containing about two inches of water; or else, bury them half-way up in fresh sand. By means of these precautions asparagus may be preserved several days."—PARMENTIER.

GOURD.

This vegetable, which the wise *gourmet* is too discreet to despise, and to which the whimsical fancy of Roman gardeners gave the most grotesque forms,[56] appears to be the very image of those soft and easy dispositions who yield to and obey every one, and whose unintelligent mildness is only repaid with sarcasm or disdain. Observe this creeping vegetable, left free to grow to its full size, which would sometimes attain the length of nine feet,[57] and which the will of man was able to reduce to the slender and tortuous shape of a hideous dragon.[58] When hardly ripe, it was cut and served on the tables of the most dainty, where it was eaten with vinegar and mustard, or seasoned with fine herbs :[59] and whilst the ungrateful guests savoured the stomachic and nourishing flesh of the gourd,[60] they did not cease to amuse themselves at the expense of its round and almost empty body[61]—the proverbial image of a head not over well-provided with brains.[62]

To the present day even, more than one popular joke continues to pursue this plant, although its culinary qualities are appreciated as formerly.

We are indebted to India for the seed of the gourd,[63] which the Greeks designated, according to the species, by the names of Indian and common gourd. The latter kind was either boiled or roasted ; the former was generally boiled in water.[64] Antioch furnished the finest specimens to the markets of Athens.[65]

The ancients were acquainted with the manner of preserving this vegetable in such a state of freshness as to enable them to eat it with pleasure in the month of January :[66] the method is as follows,—the gourds were cut in pieces of a moderate size ; these pieces, strung like beads, where first dried in the open air, and then smoked ; when winter arrived, each piece was well washed before putting it into the stewpan, with the various culinary herbs which the season produced ; to this was added endive, curled cabbage, and dried mushrooms.[67] The rest of the operation is easily understood. The Romans prepared this vegetable in different ways : a few of the principal ones will suffice.

1st. Boil the gourd in water, squeeze it out carefully, place it in a saucepan, and mix some pepper, a little cummin seed, rue, gravy, vinegar, and a small quantity of wine, reduced to one-half by boiling. Let the whole stew, and then sprinkle it lightly with pepper, and serve.[68]

2nd. Boil and carefully squeeze them to extract the water, then put the gourds into a saucepan with vinegar and gravy; when it begins to simmer, thicken with fine flour, sprinkle lightly with pepper, and serve.[69]

3rd. Throw some salt on the gourd after it has been boiled, and the water pressed out of it; put it into a saucepan, with a mixture of pepper, cummin seed, coriander, green mint, and the root of benzoin; add some vinegar; then chop some dates and almonds; a little later, more vinegar, honey, gravy, sun-made wine, and oil; sprinkle lightly with pepper, and serve.[70]

4th. Put into a stewpan a fowl, with a gourd; add some apricots, truffles, pepper, cummin, sylphium, mint, parsley, coriander, penny-royal, and calamint; moisten with wine, gravy, oil, vinegar, and honey.[71]

These four recipes are sufficient to prove that this vegetable stood very high in the estimation of the Romans.

TURNIPS.

The epicureans of Athens preferred turnips brought from Thebes;[72] Roman gastronomists placed those of Amitermes in the first rank, and those of Nursia in the second. The kitchen-gardeners of Rome furnished them with a third variety, to which they had recourse when they could not procure any other.[73] They were eaten boiled, thus:—after the water had been extracted from them, they were seasoned with cummin, rue, and benzoin, pounded in a mortar, adding to it afterwards honey, vinegar, gravy, boiled grapes, and a little oil. The whole was left to simmer, and then served.[74]

CARROTS.

The Greeks and Romans planted or sowed them in the beginning of the spring, or autumn.[75] They distinguished two kinds, the wild and the cultivated.[76]

This much esteemed root received the honour of being prepared in many ways. Sometimes it was eaten as a salad, with salt, oil, and vinegar.[77]

It was also stewed, and mixed afterwards with œnogarum.[78] Again, they boiled it in a stewpan, over a slow fire, with some cummin and a little oil, and just before serving it was sprinkled with ground cummin seeds.[79]

BLIT

(A SORT OF BEET).

Blit is one of the family of *atriplices,* which grows in Europe, and in the temperate regions of Asia; it owes its ancient reputation entirely to the insipidity of its flavour, from which it derives its Greek name, synonymous with stupidity and insignificance.[80] Blit was eaten boiled, when nothing better was to be had. In fact, it was a last resource— and nothing more.

PURSLAINE.

This vegetable, the aspect of which would lead us to suppose it possessed savoury qualities (though experience proves the contrary), was formerly mixed in different salads, and still enjoys some esteem when associated with a leg of mutton.[81]

In default of esculent qualities (which it certainly does not possess), the ancients recognised in purslaine many admirable virtues,[82] which are not acknowledged in the present day. The internal use of this plant, also its external application, cured the bite of serpents, wounds inflicted by poisoned arrows, and infallibly neutralized the effects of poisonous drinks.[83] But, alas! purslaine is not now what it was formerly; for it is hardly permitted to appear by the side of one of our fresh white lettuces.

SORREL.

Sorrel is a polygenous plant, and grows throughout Europe amidst the grass fields. The Romans cultivated it in order to give it more vigour,[84] and ate it sometimes stewed with mustard, and seasoned with a little oil and vinegar.[85]

BROCOLI.

Drusus, son of Tiberius, was so passionately fond of the brocoli, which Apicius induced him to eat, that he was more than once severely reprimanded by his father on the subject.[86] It is true that the celebrated Roman epicurean displayed so much art, and gave such delicious flavour to it, that this dish alone would have been enough to establish his reputation. In fact, brocoli has always been appreciated by connoisseurs; and Glaucias, who passed his life in meditating seriously on the perfectibility of culinary ingredients, said: "That nothing could be better than this vegetable, boiled and suitably seasoned." [87]

This was the method of preparing it at Rome: they used only the most tender and delicate parts of the brocoli, which were boiled with that extreme care the artist always devotes to this first operation; and, afterwards, when the water had been well drained off, they added some cummin seed, pepper, chopped onions, and coriander seed—all bruised together, not forgetting, before serving up, to add a little oil and sun-made wine.[88]

ARTICHOKE.

A young and unfortunate beauty had the ill-luck to displease a vindictive and irascible god, who instantly metamorphosed her into an artichoke.[89] This poor girl's name was Cinara. Although she had become a bitter plant she preserved this sweet name, which the moderns have strangely modified. Our readers, who eat artichokes with so much indifference, will, perhaps, sometimes lament this poor victim of a blind resentment.

This plant was well known to the ancients; the hilly regions of Greece, Asia, and Egypt were covered with it;[90] but the inhabitants made no use of it as an aliment, and it remained uncultivated.[91]

It would be rather difficult to trace the precise period when it was first introduced into Italy. All we know is, that it grew there more than half a century before the Christian era, in the time of Dioscorides, who mentioned it.[92] It appears, nevertheless, that hardly any one troubled himself about artichokes, or their esculent qualities, up to that time; but the wealthy, about a century after, began to appreciate them, and Pliny, in one of his jesting whims, reproaches the rich with having deprived the lower classes and *asses* of a food which nature seemed to have destined for them.[93]

This vegetable was then very dear,[94] for it did not succeed, and was subsequently given up. It was so far forgotten that in the year 1473 it appeared as a novelty at Venice;[95] and towards the year 1465 it was brought from Naples to Florence, whence it passed into France in the sixteenth century.[96]

Galen[97] looked upon the artichoke as a bad food.[98] Columella sung its praise in his verses; he recommended it to the disciples of Bacchus, and forbid the use of it to those who were anxious to preserve a sweet and pure voice [99]

This plant, whatever may be in other respects its estimable qualities, does not please every one equally well; its bitterness and unpleasant odour keep it at a distance from numerous palates—perhaps because too many allow themselves to be prejudiced by deceitful appearances. Here are two very ingenious methods by means of which a trial might be made to overcome, or lessen, the defects it undoubtedly has, and which we can but deplore :—

Artichokes will become mild by taking care to steep the seed in a mixture of honey and milk.[100] They will then exhale the most agreeable perfume, particularly when this seed has passed three days in the juice of bay leaves, lilies, or roses.[101]

Having quoted the authority, we give the recipe for what it is worth.

Until the result of this experiment is known, artichokes may be eaten raw, with a seasoning of hard eggs chopped in very small pieces, garum, and oil.[102]

If you prefer a sharper sauce, mix well some green mint with rue, Greek fennel,[103] and coriander; add, afterwards, some pepper, alisander, honey, garum, and oil.[104] They are also eaten boiled, with cummin, pepper, gravy, and oil.[105]

"It is well known under what form artichokes, either raw or cooked, appear on our tables. The best way to preserve them is to half cook them, separate the leaves from the fur, and preserve the fleshy part, called *the bottom*, and throw them, still warm, in cold water, to make them firm. That operation is called *blanchir*. They are laid afterwards on hurdles, and put four different times in the oven, as soon as the bread is taken out. They become then very thin, hard, and transparent, like horn, and return to their original form in hot water. They must be kept free from damp."—Parmentier.

POMPION.

Like the gourd, the good and creeping pompion has served more than once as a term of comparison, and that in a style most humiliating. Should any one happen to be thick-headed, or not very intelligent,[106] he was immediately compared to a pompion (popularly, pumpkin—whence bumpkin). The insult went still further: it was said of a pusillanimous man, "That he had a pompion where his heart ought to have been."[107]

The obesity of this vegetable, and its inelegant shape, have doubtless given rise to these injurious remarks.

It was, however, acknowledged that it possessed many estimable qualities, which ought to have compensated for its outward defects. It was thought to be very refreshing, and was employed with success in the treatment of diseases of the eyes.[108]

We might undertake (if permitted) a long dissertation, in order to prove that the Hebrews, weary of being in the Desert, murmured because they were deprived of the pompion of Egypt,[109] and not the melon, as translators have rendered it; but we should be accused of egregious presumption; the learned would frown, critics would not spare us, and our pompions would, nevertheless, pass as melons.

This plant occupies a prominent place in the precious catalogue of Roman dainties which we offer for the meditation of judges. Here are some of the ancient modes of preparing this vegetable:

1st. Boil some pompions, put them in a stewpan with cummin and a little oil; place them for a short time over a slow fire, and serve.[110]

2nd. When you have well boiled, reduce them to a pulp, then put them on a dish with pepper, alisander, cummin, wild marjoram, onion, wine, garum, and oil; thicken with flour, and serve.[111]

3rd. When the pompion has boiled in water, it is then seasoned with wild fennel, sylphium,[112] dried mint, vinegar, and garum.[113]

———•———

CUCUMBER.

When the Israelites were in the Desert they regretted much the cucumbers of Egypt, which were sold to them at a very trifling price when under the yoke of Pharaoh.[114] We may thence infer that this vegetable was very plentiful, and chiefly in great demand by the lower order of people; for as the Jews were in a state of servitude, they were necessarily assimilated with the most abject of the Egyptians.

We see that this *cucurbitacea* has been long known, and that, after the lapse of many centuries, it is held in the same degree of estimation it enjoyed among the Eastern nations.

The Greeks thought much of the cucumber, particularly of that kind which came from the environs of Antioch.[115] They attributed to this plant marvellous properties, which modern scepticism has completely thrown aside.   We think it good in salad, with vinegar, oil, pepper, and salt, and that is all

It is, we imagine, the only good quality our farmers ascribe to it at the present day.   Formerly, in Greece, the same class of persons, being clearer-sighted, or more credulous, were convinced that this vegetable protected all kinds of seeds against the voracity of insects.   To obtain this result it was only necessary to steep the seed in the juice obtained from the root of the cucumber, before it was sown.[116]

We freely offer this preservative to those who may wish to give it a trial, and sincerely hope they may profit by this revival of the Greek process.

The Romans conceived that this cold and somewhat insipid vegetable (we beg pardon of its admirers) required a seasoning to heighten its flavour.   No sooner had they transplanted it from Asia into Rome,[117] than they busied themselves in rendering it worthy of their tables by various preparations, which may, perhaps, interest the curious.

1st. Scrape the cucumbers, and eat them with œnogarum.[118] *

2nd. Scrape the cucumbers, and boil them with parsley, seed, gravy, and oil; thicken, and sprinkle pepper over the dish before serving.[121]

3rd. Again, they may be seasoned with pepper, pennyroyal, honey, or sun-made wine, gravy, vinegar, and a little sylphium.[122]

4th. You will obtain a most delicate dish by boiling the cucumbers with brains, already cooked; adding afterwards some cummin, and a little honey.[123]

The cucumber, although but little nutritious, does not agree with cold stomachs.   In the north an astonishing quantity are consumed. The Poles ate them at every repast with boiled meat.

"Cucumbers are preserved in a very simple manner.   The essential point is to obtain good wine-vinegar.   After having well washed and wiped them, put them into either white or red vinegar (the colour is better preserved by using the white); add salt; cover simply the vessel containing them with a board.   The vinegar must always be an inch higher than the cucumbers, and must be entirely renewed at the end of a month."—PARMENTIER.

* Apicius composed the œnogarum (or rather eleogarum, for wine is not mentioned in his recipe) in the following manner : bruise, in a mortar, pepper, alisander, coriander, and rue ; then add some garum, honey, and a little oil.[119]

Or, prepare the condiment with thyme, wild mint, pepper, and alisander ; to which add, as before, garum, oil, and honey.[120]

F

LETTUCE.

From time immemorial the lettuce has occupied a most distinguished place in the kitchen garden. The Hebrews ate it, without preparation, with the Paschal lamb.[124] The opulent Greeks were very fond of the lettuces of Smyrna,[125] which appeared on their tables at the end of a repast;[126] the Romans, who at first imitated them, decided, under Domitian, that this favourite dish should be served in the first course with eggs,[127] purposely to excite their indomitable appetites, which three courses (and such courses, ye gods! when compared with ours of the present day) would hardly satisfy.

The bitter lettuce was sufficient for the frugal Hebrews,[128] but the delicate epicureans of Athens and Rome were much more particular; they valued them only when a mild and sweet savour invited the most rebellious palate, and awakened the slumbering desires of a fatigued stomach. And what care, what attention, did they not bestow on the growth and maturity of this cherished plant!

Aristoxenus, a philosopher by profession, an epicurean by taste, had in his garden a species of lettuce which was the envy of his surrounding neighbours. The worthy man, rendered happy by their jealous admiration, went every evening, without fail, to contemplate the small square of ground which contained his treasure, and sprinkled it carefully with water, doubtless from a limpid stream. Tush! Water, to moisten the lettuces of Aristoxenus! No: the philosopher kept in reserve a sweet and excellent wine to quench the thirst of his plants, and to communicate to them that delicate perfume and exquisite taste, the mysterious cause of which baffled the neighbouring gastronomists.

The day after, the arch old man would say, with a roguish smile, that he was going to gather some relishing green cakes, which the earth prepared expressly for him,[129] and the simple countrymen were wonderstruck without understanding the cause.

The lettuce—favourite plant of the beautiful Adonis[130]—possesses a narcotic virtue, of which ancient physicians have taken notice. Galen mentions that, in his old age, he had not found a better remedy against the wakefulness he was troubled with.[131] The biographer of

Augustus informs us that this Emperor, being attacked with hypo-chondria, recovered only by the use of lettuces, recommended by Musa, his first physician;[132] nothing, therefore, is wanting in praise of this useful plant—literally nothing, · since the king of cooks, Cœlius Apicius, judged it worthy of an honourable place in the immortal book he has bequeathed to the amateurs of the Archeologico-culinary science of all ages and all countries.

" Take," says he, " the leaves of lettuces, let them be boiled with onions, in water wherein you have put some nitre; take them out, squeeze out the water, and cut them in small pieces; mix well some pepper, alisander,[133] parsley seed, dried mint, and onions; put this mixture to the lettuce, and add to the whole some gravy, oil. and wine."[134]

Lettuces may also be eaten with a dressing of gravy and pickles.[135]

Our ancestors served salads with roasted meat, roasted poultry, &c. They had a great many which are now no longer in vogue. They ate leeks, cooked in the wood-ashes, and seasoned with salt and honey; borage, mint, and parsley, with salt and oil; lettuce, fennel, mint, chervil, parsley, and elder-flowers mixed together. They also classed among their salads an agglomeration of feet, heads, cocks' combs, and fowls' livers, cooked, and seasoned with parsley, mint, vinegar, pepper, and cinnamon. Nettles, and the twigs of rosemary, formed delicious salads for our forefathers; and to these they sometimes added pickled gherkins.[136]

ENDIVE.

Pliny assures us that the juice of this plant, mixed with vinegar and oil of roses, is an excellent remedy for the head-ache:[137] we leave to the proper judges a pharmaceutical mixture which does not belong to our province, and which we only quote *en passant*.

Virgil thought endive bitter,[138] but he did not speak ill of it. Columella recommended this salad to fastidious and satiated palates;[139] this is praising it. The Egyptians appreciated its merits,[140] which the Greeks had too much sense and good taste to disdain; and the Romans ate it prepared in the following manner:—

Choose some fine endive; wash it well; drain off all the water; add a little gravy and oil; then chop some onions very small; strew them over the endive, and add honey and vinegar.[141]

It is understood that the sweet savour of the honey corrects the bitterness of the plant; but a judicious attention must preside over the quantity of that substance, for too much or too little might easily spoil this salad of Apicius.

ONIONS.

Whoever wishes to preserve his health must eat every morning, before breakfast, young onions, with honey.[142] Such a treat is assuredly not very tempting: besides, this rather strong vegetable leaves after it a most unpleasant perfume, which long reminds us of its presence; wherefore this recipe has not met with favour, and, indeed, it is much to be doubted whether it will ever become fashionable.

Alexander the Great found the onion in Egypt, where the Hebrews had learned to like it.[143] He brought it into Greece, where it was given as food to the troops, whose martial ardour[144] it was thought to excite.

Pliny assures us that Gaul produced a small kind, which the Romans called Gallic onions, and which they thought more delicate than those of Italy.[145] At any rate, it was a dish given up to plebeians and the poor. Horace opposed to it fish—the luxurious nourishment of rich and dainty Romans.[146] In spite of this reprobation on the part of the elegant poet, Apicius does not fear to introduce the plant in his *Olus Molle*, a kind of *Julienne*, not devoid of merit.

Take onions, rather dry, and mix pepper, alisander, and winter-savory, to season a variety of vegetables previously boiled in water and nitre, the which, when very fine, thicken with cullis, oil, and wine.[147]

LEEKS.

This vegetable—a powerful divinity, dreaded among the Egyptians,[148] and a food bewailed by the Israelites in their journey through the Desert [149]—cured the Greeks of numerous diseases, which in our days it is to be feared would resist its medicinal properties.[150] Everything changes in this sublunary world, and the leek no doubt follows the common law.

The authors of a compilation rather indigestible at times, but often very curious, assert that this vegetable attains an extraordinary size, by putting as many of the seeds as one can take up with three fingers into a piece of linen, which is then to be tied-up, covered with manure, and watered with care. All these seeds—so they say—will at last form themselves into one single seed, which will produce a monstrous leek.[151]

This process, which is revealed to us by the geoponics, would have had an enthusiastic reception from those fervent pagans who vied in zeal with each other, to see who could offer Latona, on the day of the Theoxenias, the most magnificent leek.[152]

The mother of Apollo received this plant with pleasure, although presented to her quite raw; but she would probably have preferred it dressed in the following manner :—

Take leeks, the mildest it is possible to procure ; boil them in water and oil, with a handful of salt, and put them into a dish, with gravy, oil, and wine.[153]

Or, cover the leeks with young cabbage leaves ; cook them under the hot embers, and season afterwards as above.[154]

MELON.

This *cucurbitacea*, the most delicate vegetable belonging to this numerous family, has always been the delight of the inhabitants of the

East and of Europe. It came originally from the most temperate regions of Asia; the chivalric Baber made it known to his Hindoo subjects;[155] and the Romans introduced it into the west, at the time of their first expedition against the Persians. Melons had a prodigious success at Rome, and soon became a necessity with which the wealthy could not dispense. The Emperor Tiberius, that cruel and covetous prince,[156] liked them so much that they were served to him every day throughout the year.

The Greeks, whose ingenious and lively imagination mingled with everything the sweet perfume of flowers, contrived to place the seeds of melons in vessels full of rose leaves, with which they were afterwards sown. They maintained that, when at maturity, this cool and refreshing vegetable was impregnated with sweet emanations, and that its flavour called to mind its sweet and delicious abode with the queen of flowers.[157]

Sometimes also they macerated the seeds in milk and honey. Not only melons, but all the *cucurbitaceæ* were treated in this manner, when it was wished to communicate to them a milder flavour.[158]

In pointing out these processes in use among the ancient horticulturists, we do not at all pledge ourselves for their efficacy. However, it must be acknowledged that they exhibit a singularly praiseworthy emulation, which has perhaps prepared the way for the wonders with which our modern gardeners have made us familiar.

Independently of its exquisite flavour, the melon passed, among the Greeks and Romans, as being very beneficial to the stomach and head.[159] It is possible that they may have gone a little too far; but then man is so ready to give imaginary qualities to what he loves, that we cannot wonder at their praises of this delicious plant, which we generally eat in the most simple manner, without any other seasoning than a little sugar, sometimes with salt and pepper. Not so with the Romans; their practised palates required a more exquisite combination; they, therefore, added to it a sharp savoury sauce—a compound of pepper, pennyroyal, honey, or sun-made wine, garum, vinegar, and sylphium.[160]

Melons were not known in central or northern Europe until the reign of Charles VIII., King of France, who brought them from Italy.[161]

RADISH.

Amongst other singularities which abound in the Talmud, the curious can but have remarked the following:

Judea formerly produced kitchen garden plants so large, that a fox bethought himself to hollow a radish, and make it his residence. After he had removed, this new kind of lair was discovered; it was put into a scale, and found to weigh nearly one hundred pounds.[162]

It is a pity that no one preserved the seed of so remarkable a vegetable, which no doubt was only to be found in Judea.

The Greeks had very fine radishes, but they were not of such a surprising size. They procured them from the territory of Mantinea.[163] Mount Algidea also furnished the Romans with an excellent kind,[164] but which they esteemed less highly than those of Nursia,[165] in the country of the Sabines. These latter cost about threepence a pound in the time of Pliny; they were sold for double that sum when the crop was not abundant.[166]

Writers of antiquity notice three distinct kinds of radishes: the large, short, and thick; the round; and the wild.[167] They fancied that, at the end of three years, the seed of this plant produced very good cabbages,[168] which must have been rather vexatious, at times, to honest gardeners who might have preferred radishes.

In times of popular tumult this root was often transformed into an ignominious projectile, with which the mob pursued persons whose political opinions rendered them obnoxious to *the majority*, as we might say in the present day.[169] As soon as calm was re-established, the insulting vegetable was placed in the pot to boil, and afterwards eaten with oil and a little vinegar.[170]

The Romans preserved radishes very well, by covering them with a paste composed of honey, vinegar, and salt.[171]

HORSE-RADISH.

" By Apollo !" cried, mournfully, a philanthropic and gastronomic Greek, " one must be completely mad to buy horse-radish, when fish can be found in the market."[172] So thought the philosopher Amphis. And at Rome, as in Greece, this reviled and despised root hardly found a place on the table of the poor, when anything else could be had.

There were several serious causes for this fatal proscription : this plant was found to be bitter, stringy, and of difficult digestion ;[173] it was looked upon as a very common food ;[174] the lowest class alone dared to feed upon it; the opulent were therefore compelled to exclude it from the number of their dishes. And again, certain strange customs, authorised by the Roman law, contributed greatly to make the horse-radish an object of horror and detestation ; so true it is, that the manner in which objects are associated with our ideas determines almost invariably our love or hatred for them.

Nevertheless, all the species of this vegetable (and there were five in number, distinctly mentioned by Theophrastus[175]) ought not to have been condemned so severely. The Corinthian, the Leiothasian, the Cleonian, the Amorean, and the Bœotian, were so many distinct and separate species, each of which possessed its own peculiar property and quality.[176] The last-named, with its large and silky leaves, was tender, and had a sweet, agreeable taste.[177] The others, not so good, perhaps, were wholesome and nourishing, and their natural bitterness never failed to disappear, when the seeds were allowed to soak for some time in sweet or raisin wine before they were sown.[178]

Shall we now mention the properties the horse-radish possessed, and which ought to have been sufficient to establish its reputation, if prejudice were not both deaf and blind ?

Take, fasting, some pieces of this beneficent and despised root, and the most inveterate poisons will be changed for you into inoffensive drinks.[179]

Would you have the power to handle and play with those dangerous reptiles whose active venom causes a speedy and sure death? Wash your hands in the juice of horse-radish.[180]

Do you seek an efficacious remedy for the numerous evils which besiege us unceasingly? Take horse-radish,—nothing but horse-radish.[181]

It is true that this incomparable root attacks the enamel of the teeth, and, indeed, soon spoils them;[182] but why should we be so particular when so many marvellous properties are in question?

As to its culinary preparation, Apicius recommends us to serve it mixed with pepper and garum.[183]

———•———

GARLIC.

Garlic was known in the most remote ages. It was a god in Egypt.[184] The Greeks held it in horror. It was part of their military food—hence came the proverb, "Eat neither garlic nor beans;" that is to say, abstain from war and law.[185] There was a belief that this plant excited the courage of warriors; therefore, it was given to cocks to incite them to fight. The Greek and Roman sailors made as great a use of it as the soldiers,[186] and an ample provision was always made when they set out on any maritime expedition.[187] It was a prevailing opinion that the effects of foul air were neutralized by garlic; and it was, no doubt, this idea which made reapers and peasants use it so lavishly.[188]

However, the taste for this vegetable was not always confined to the people, in the southern countries of Europe; it gained, at times, the high regions of the court. It is reported that, in 1368, Alphonso, King of Castile, who had an extreme repugnance to garlic, instituted an order of knighthood; and one of the statutes was, that any knight who had eaten of this plant, could not appear before the sovereign for at least one month.[189]

The priests of Cybele interdicted the entry of the temple of this goddess to persons who had made use of garlic. Stilphon, troubling himself very little about this interdiction, fell asleep on the steps of the altar. The mother of the gods appeared to him in his dream, and reproached him with the little respect his breath disclosed for her. "If you wish me to abstain from garlic," replied Stilphon, "give me something else to eat."[190]

The ancients, great lovers of the marvellous, believed that this despised vegetable possessed a sovereign virtue against the greater number of diseases,[191] and that it was easy to deprive it of its penetrating odour by sowing and gathering it when the moon was below the horizon.[192]

The Greek and Roman cooks used it but very seldom, and it was only employed as a second or third-rate ingredient in some preparations of Apicius which we shall hereafter mention.

"Garlic is called the physic of the peasantry, especially in warm countries, where it is eaten before going to work, in order to guarantee them from the pernicious effects of foul air. It would be too long were we to relate all that has been written in favour of this vegetable; let it suffice to say that it is employed in numerous pharmaceutical preparations, and among others in vinegar, celebrated by the name of *aromatic vinegar*."—Bosc.

ESCHALOTS.

Alexander the Great found the eschalot in Phœnicia, and introduced it into Greece. Its Latin name, *Ascalonica*, indicates the place of its origin, Ascalon, a city of Idumea.[193] Its affinity with garlic set the ancients against its culinary qualities, and this useful plant, too much neglected, only obtained credit in modern times.

PARSLEY.

Hercules, the conqueror of the Nemæan lion, crowned himself with parsley; a rather modest adornment for so great a hero, when others, for exploits much less worthy, were decked with laurels. A similar crown became, subsequently, the prize of the Nemæan[194] and Isthmian Games.[195]

Anacreon, that amiable and frivolous poet, who consecrated all his moments to pleasure, celebrates parsley as the emblem of joy and festivity;[196] and Horace, a philosophic sensualist of the same stamp, commanded his banquetting hall to be ornamented with roses and parsley.[197]

Perhaps it was thought that the strong, penetrating odour of parsley possessed the property of exciting the brain to agreeable imaginations; if so, it explains the fact of its being worn by guests, placed round their heads.

Fable has made it the food of Juno's coursers.[198] In battle, the warriors of Homer fed their chargers with it;[199] and Melancholy, taking it for the symbol of mourning, admitted it at the dismal repasts of obsequies.[200]

Let us seek to discover in this plant qualities less poetic and less brilliant, but, assuredly, more real and positive. In the first place:—

Wash some parsley with the roots adhering; dry it well in the sun; boil it in water, and leave it awhile on one side; then put into a saucepan some garlic and leeks, which must boil together a long time, and very slowly, until reduced to two-thirds—that done, pound some pepper, mix it with gravy and a little honey, strain the water in which the parsley was boiled, and pour it over the parsley and the whole of the other ingredients. Put the stewpan once more on the fire, and serve.[201]

The following recipe is much less complicated and more expeditious:—

Boil the parsley in water, with nitre; press out all the water; cut it very fine; then mix, with care, some pepper, alisander, marjoram and onions; add some wine, gravy, and oil; stew the whole, with the parsley, in an earthen pot or stewpan.[202]

If the illustrious pupil of Chiron, the warlike Achilles, had known the culinary properties of parsley as well as he knew its medicinal virtues, he no doubt would have been less prodigal with it for his horses;[203] and the conquerors of Troy would have comforted themselves, during the tediousness of a long siege, by cooking this aromatic plant, and enjoying a new dish.

Parsley, according to some writers, was of Egyptian origin; but it is not known who brought it into Sardinia, where it was found by the Carthaginians, who afterwards made it known to the inhabitants of Marseilles.

CHERVIL.

This plant, which Columella has described,[204] furnished a relishing dish, prepared with gravy, oil, and wine; or served with fried fish.[205] At the present day it is highly commendable in salad.

———•———

WATER-CRESSES.

The water-cress, the sight alone of which made the learned Scaliger shudder with terror, is supposed to be a native of Crete. It was, doubtless, the cresses of Alen (Suabia), which are cultivated in our gardens, and not those commonly found in brooks and springs.

The Persians were in the habit of eating them with bread:[206] they made, in this manner, so delicious a meal, that the splendour of a Syracusan table would not have tempted them.[207] This is one of those examples of sobriety which may be admired, but are seldom followed.

Plutarch did not share the opinion of the Persians, but scornfully ranked cresses amongst the lowest aliments of the people.[208] Nevertheless, the Romans, as well as the Greeks, granted to this cruciform plant a host of beneficent qualities, and among others, a singularly refreshing property. Refreshing! to say the truth, it refreshes much in the same way that mustard and pepper do.[209] Boiled in goat's milk, it cured thoracic affections;[210] introduced into the ears, it relieved the toothache:[211] and finally, persons who made it their habitual food found their wits sharpened and their intelligence more active and ingenious.[212]

However, it does not appear that cresses ever enjoyed, in Rome or Athens, a culinary vogue equal to their officinal reputation; it was said that its acrid taste twisted the nose,[213] and this coarse jest naturally did it harm to a certain degree with the rich and delicate. Be that as it may, those who dared, ate it dressed it in the following manner:—

With garum, or oil and vinegar ;[214] or with pepper, cummin-seed, and lentiscus (leaves of the mastic-tree).[215]

The water-cress *par excellence* grows in springs, rivulets, and ditches, in Europe. Its piquant taste is rather agreeable; it is eaten as a salad or seasoning, with poultry and other roasted meat. This plant increases the appetite, fortifies the stomach, and possesses anti-scorbutic qualities.

A great consumption is made of it in certain countries. It is cultivated in running waters, either in gardens, or sown in the shade, where it is watered abundantly. The less it sees the sun, the softer it is.—Bosc.

PLANTS USED IN SEASONING.

WE will point out, as briefly as possible, those plants mostly used in the kitchens of the ancients to heighten the flavour of their dishes, or to give them a particular taste, according as the dish or fancy might require it. In them especially lies the secret of those *irritamenta gulæ*, or excitements of the palate, which Apicius brought so much into fashion.

———•———

POPPY.

The seed of this plant was offered, fried, at the beginning of the second course, and eaten with honey.[1] Sometimes it was sprinkled on the crust of a kind of household bread, covered with white of eggs.[2] Some of it was also put into the panada, or pap, intended for children[3]— perhaps to make them sleep the sooner.

———•———

SESAME.

This seed was used in nearly the same manner as the poppy, and it occupied a distinguished rank among the numerous dainties served at dessert.[4] Certain round and light cakes were covered with this seed.[5] The Romans brought sesame from Egypt.[6]

SOW-THISTLE.

This plant furnished a kind of milk, which was sometimes drunk : sometimes various kinds of meat were seasoned with it.[7] It was afterwards given up to rabbits, and there is every probability that they will retain undisputed possession of it.

ORACH.

Few vegetables have been more exposed to injurious accusations. Pythagoras reproaches it with causing a livid paleness, dropsy, and the scrofula, in those persons who eat it.[8] Nevertheless, a greedy curiosity introduced it into the catalogue of culinary preparations, and the guests of Apicius tasted more than once the fatal orach without knowing its pernicious properties. History does not say that they suffered any pernicious effects from it.

This plant is also eaten like spinach, and mixed with sorrel to soften its acidity.—Bosc.

ROCKET.

Persons about to undergo the punishment of the whip were recommended to swallow a cup of wine, in which rocket had been steeped. It was asserted that this draught rendered pain supportable.[9] And again, that this plant, taken with honey, removed the freckles which sometimes appear on the face.[10]

Whatever may be the degree of credence accorded to these two recipes, this vegetable enjoyed some reputation among the ancients, who mixed the wild and the garden rocket together, so as to temper the heat of the one by the coldness of the other.[11]

FENNEL.

It was employed but seldom in the preparation of dishes or pastry; but it was believed that the juice of its stalk had the property of restoring or strengthening the sight.[12]

DILL.

This plant, which, according to the ancients, weakened the eyes,[13] was much renowned for its exquisite odour,[14] and its stomachic qualities.[15]   A much-admired perfume[16] was made from it; it produced an agreeable sort of wine or liqueur;[17] and a small number of choice dishes, for the enjoyment of connoisseurs, owed to it the reputation they had acquired.[18]

ANISE-SEED.

The production of an umbelliferous plant, which grows wild in Egypt, in Syria, and other eastern countries. Pliny recommends it to be taken in the morning, with honey and myrrh in wine:[19] and Pythagoras attributes to it eminent Hygeian properties, whether eaten raw or cooked.[20]

HYSSOP.

The Greeks, the Romans—and before them, the nations of the east[21] —believed that hyssop renews and purifies the blood. This plant, mixed with an equal quantity of salt, formed a remedy much extolled by Columella.[22]   It was crushed with oil to make a liniment, used as a

remedy for cutaneous eruptions.[23]   An excellent liqueur was obtained
from it, known under the name of hyssop wine;[24] and lastly, this plant
was used in a number of dishes, which it rendered more wholesome and
refreshing.

WILD MARJORAM.

Nearly the same qualities were attributed to this herb as to hyssop;[25]
and it was employed still more frequently in the composition of the
most delicate condiments.   Dioscorides[26] and Cato[27] make copious remarks on a much-esteemed liqueur, which they called wild marjoram
wine.

SAVORY.

An odoriferous herb, which entered into the seasoning of nearly
every dish.[28]

THYME.

Besides the various culinary purposes for which the ancients used
this plant, they, like ourselves, extracted from thyme aromatic liqueurs,[29]
the preparation of which will be given in another part of this work.

WILD THYME.

We find it rarely spoken of by magiric writers.   Pliny believes it to
be most efficacious against the bite of serpents.[30]

SWEET MARJORAM.[31]

Was much employed in the Isle of Cyprus; very little, if at all, in
Rome, where they knew little more of sweet marjoram than the oil
extracted from it.[32]

G

PENNYROYAL.

The ancients entwined their wine cups with pennyroyal,[33] and made crowns of it, which were placed on their heads during their repasts, by the aid of which they hoped to escape the troublesome consequences of too copious libations.[34]   On leaving the table, a small quantity of this plant was taken, to facilitate digestion.[35]

Pennyroyal occupied, also, an important place in high gastronomic combinations.

RUE.

The territory of Myra, a city of Lycia, produced excellent rue.[36] Mithridates looked upon this vegetable as a powerful counter-poison ;[37] and the inhabitants of Heraclea, suspicious—and with reason—of the villany of their tyrant, Clearchus, never stirred from their dwellings without having previously eaten plentifully of rue.[38]   This plant cured also the ear-ache ;[39] and to all these advantages, it joined that of being welcomed with honour on all festive occasions.[40]

MINT.

There was formerly—no matter where or when—a beautiful young girl, who was changed into this plant through the jealous vengeance of Proserpine.[41]   Thus transformed, she excited the appetite of the guests, and awakened their slumbering gaiety.[42]   Mint prevented milk from curdling, even when rennet was put into it.[43]

SPANISH CAMOMILE.

The Romans sometimes mixed with their drink the burning root of the Spanish camomile ;[44] and we are astonished at meeting with the name of this formidable plant among the ingredients of some of their dishes.

CUMMIN.

The condiments prepared with cummin had a very great reputation; and culinary authors frequently mention this vegetable, which the Greeks and Romans invariably used.[45]

ALISANDER.

The same might be said of alisander, which, in the time of Pliny, passed as an universal remedy,[46] and which Apicius honours by naming in many of his dishes.

CAPERS.

Young buds of the caper tree, a shrub—native of Asia, where the species are in great varieties. It was but little thought of at the tables of the higher classes, and therefore was left to the people.[47]

The buds of the caper are gathered, and thrown into barrels filled with vinegar, to which a little salt is added; then, by means of several large sieves made of a copper plate, rather hollow, and pierced with holes of different sizes, the different qualities are separated, and classed under different numbers. The vinegar is renewed, and the capers are replaced in the barrel, ready for exportation.

ASAFŒTIDA.

This plant, which we have excluded from our kitchens, and whose nauseous smell is far from exciting the appetite, reigned almost as the chief ingredient in the seasoning of the ancients. Perhaps they cultivated a kind which in no way resembled that of modern times. If it were the same, how are we to explain the extreme partiality which Apicius shows for it? and which he says must be dissolved in luke-warm water, and afterwards served with vinegar and garum.[48]

It is certain that the resin drawn by incision from the root of this plant is still much esteemed by the inhabitants of Persia and of India; they chew it constantly, finding the odour and taste exquisite.

"The neck of the root is cleared of the earth it is covered with, and replaced by a handful of herbs. At the end of forty days the summit of the root is cut transversely; then a small bundle of herbs is laid over, so as not to touch it. A whitish liquor exudes from the cut, and every other day it is gathered; the cut is renewed until the root is quite exhausted. The result of this crop is laid on leaves, and dried in the sun."—Bosc.

SUMACH.

The Romans made use of the seed to flavour several kinds of dishes.[49]

GINGER.

This root was known at Rome under the Emperors, and many persons have confounded ginger with pepper, although they in no way resemble each other. Pliny refutes this error, and represents it as a native of Arabia.[50] It was used with other condiments.[51]

"The Indians grate this root in their broth or *ragoût*; they make a paste which they believe is good against the scurvy. The inhabitants of Madagascar eat it green, in salad, cut in small pieces, and mixed with other herbs, which they season with salt, oil, and vinegar. In other places ginger is taken infused as a drink; it fortifies the chest, and awakens the appetite. It is preserved in sugar after it has been stripped of its bark, and soaked in vinegar. Delicious preserves are made of it with much perfume, and which keep a very long time."—Dutour.

WORMWOOD.

The Egyptians had a great respect for the wormwood of Taposiris,—no doubt on account of the medicinal properties which physicians attributed to it.

Heliogabalus often regaled the populace with wormwood wine,[52] and the Romans gave it to the victorious charioteers. Pliny thinks this plant so salutary that nothing more precious could have been presented to them.[53] This explanation appears to have had but little plausibility, and it has been more rationally supposed that this liquor prevented or counteracted any giddiness they might feel. " You can cure yourself of dizziness," says Strabo, "with the bitter leaf of wormwood."[54]

The Roman wormwood wine was composed in the following manner :

They bruised one ounce of this vegetable, and mixed it with three scruples of gum, as much spikenard, six of balm, and three scruples of saffron ; to which was added eighteen *setiers*, or 180 gallons English, of old wine. This mixture was left to stand some time, but was not heated or subjected to any other process.[55]

In pharmacy, wine is made of wormwood; also a syrup, a preserve, an extract, oil by infusion, an essential oil, and wormwood salt. It is supposed that several brewers on the Continent substitute the leaves and flowers of this plant for hops, in the manufacture of beer. It is, perhaps, a calumny, and we only repeat it in a whisper.

" The leaves of wormwood are used in salad to make it more digestible and heighten the flavour. They are preserved in vinegar, and to season dishes. Lastly, they are considered by some persons as a remedy, and the frequent use of them to be indispensable for the preservation of their existence."—Bosc.

In concluding this chapter, it will be necessary to anticipate a question which naturally presents itself : did the Romans know the art of forcing fruits, and of procuring, at one season, the various vegetables or plants which belong to another period of the year ?

Some verses from Martial will leave no doubt on the subject :—

" Whoever has seen the orchards of the King of Corcyrus (Alcinous), dear Entellus, must have preferred thy rural habitation. Thou knowest how to preserve from the rigours of winter the purple grapes of thy vine bower, and prevent the cold frost from devouring the gifts of Bacchus. Thy grapes live enclosed under a transparent crystal, which covers without concealing them.

" What can avaricious nature refuse to the industry of man ? Sterile winter is constrained to give up the fruits of autumn."[56]

This curious passage gives us to understand that the Romans had hot-houses and, no doubt, glass bells in their orchards and gardens, to bring sooner to maturity some of those productions of the earth which, by their delicate flavour and perfume, raised the insatiable desires of a people, decidedly the greatest epicureans ever known in the history of gastronomy to the present day.

XI.

FRUITS.

WHEN the Creator placed the first man in the Garden of Eden, he commanded him to nourish himself with the fruit it contained;[1] and, from that epoch, the most ancient which the sacred work records, this kind of aliment is incessantly mentioned in the history of all nations, and at every period of their history.

The great Hebrew legislator seems to have considered fruit trees worthy of his especial care, for he forbad the Jews to cut them down, even on their enemies' lands;[2] and, in order to teach his people how to preserve them in all their vigour, he declares the fruits of the first three years impure, and consecrates to the Lord those of the fourth.[3] He even goes further; he exempts from military service any one who has planted a vineyard, and all fruit trees conferred the same privilege until the first vintage.[4]

Heathen nations also understood the importance of this branch of agriculture, and invented protective divinities—such as Pomona,[5] Vertumnus,[6] Priapus[7]—whose sole care consisted in protecting orchards from the inclemency of the seasons, and dispelling insects and robbers, who would damage and plunder the crops.

Each kind had, moreover, a benevolent patron, who could not honestly refuse to be useful to it: thus the olive tree grew under the auspices of Minerva;[8] the Muses cherished the palm tree;[9] the pine and its cone were consecrated to the great Cybele;[10] Bacchus complacently ripened the perfumed pulp of the fig[11] and the rosy grape,[12] which placed him on a level with the gods.

Among the Greeks, fruits appeared on table at the second course;[13] and were eaten either cooked, raw, or in the form of preserves.

The Romans sometimes breakfasted on a small quantity of dried fruits;[14] but the third course of their *cæna*, or principal repast, offered an incredible profusion of the productions of their own orchards, and of those of three parts of the world.[15]

Rich patricians, after they had exhausted all the immense resources of an incredible luxury—in their garments, habitations, and banquets—contrived to plant fruit trees on the summit of high towers, and on the house tops;[16] thus suspending forests over their heads,[17] as well as vast reservoirs, to keep alive the most exquisite fish.[18]

At Rome they had an expensive, but, as they thought, effective process of preparing pears, apples, plums, figs, cherries, &c., &c., and which was as follows:—

The fruit was chosen with great care, and put, with the stalks attached, into honey, leaving to each one sufficient space to prevent their touching each other.[19]

Our housewives of the 19th century may, perhaps, be curious to try this Roman experiment, if the quantity of honey which it requires does not frighten them.

XII.

STONE FRUIT.

OLIVE TREE.

THROUGHOUT antiquity we find the olive tree acknowledged as something venerable and holy, and taking precedence of all other trees, even the most useful on account of their nourishing fruits, or the refreshing drink they furnished. The wise Minerva gave it birth;[1] and its foliage, which adorned the brows of the goddess,[2] served, thenceforth, to crown victory,[3] or to give rise to the sweet hopes of peace.[4] A green bough of olive rendered the suppliant inviolable.[5] The deadly arrows of Hercules were made of its wood.[6] From it princes borrowed their sceptre,[7] and the shepherd his crook.[8]

If, abandoning mythological fictions which surround the olive with a charming but false poetry, we interrogate history for more certain information concerning this revered tree, we shall find that Diodorus, of Sicily, informs us Minerva discovered and made known to the Athenians its useful qualities.[9] And a writer, in whose possession the most ancient records in the world were found—Moses—who has recounted the birth of vegetation,[10] tells us also of a patriarch pouring purified oil on a stone altar,[11] before the olive tree was known in Athens—nay, before Athens existed.

Profane historians honour Aristeus, son of Apollo, and King of Arcadia, with the invention of oil mills, and the manner of procuring the precious fluid,[12] the abundance of which was such, in the East, that it was used in lamps,[13] in anointing,[14] in seasoning of dishes,[15] and in numerous other instances too long to enumerate.[16]

Thus the most important culture among the Jews was that of the olive tree. There were large plantations of it in all the provinces: Galilea, Samaria, and Judea, were full of them.[17] It must not, however, be thought the Hebrews used olives only to make oil ; they knew how to preserve them in brine, to be eaten at table, and for sale to strangers. Pliny particularly extols those of Decapolis, a province of the Holy Land : " They are very small," he says, " not larger than capers ; but are much esteemed."[18]

Among the Greeks, the oil of Samos was considered to be the purest and finest :[19] next to it they gave preference to that of Caria or of Thurium.[20]

As regards olives, the *Colymbades*, or floating kinds were more esteemed than any other, on account of their size and taste ;[21] they had an exquisite flavour imparted to them by being placed with different herbs in pots of oil :[22] the *Halmade* olives were preserved in brine.[23]

The cultivation of the olive tree was carried to a great extent in Greece ; a host of poets sang in honour of this tree,[24] which produced so sweet a fruit ; and Theophrastus speaks of it very frequently in his celebrated treatise on plants.[25]

The Romans were not acquainted with it until later ; and even in the year 249 B.C., they possessed so few olive trees that a pound of oil sold for twelve *As*, or three shillings ; less than two centuries after (74 B.C.), ten pounds of it only cost one *As ;* but Italy had so far increased its plantations at the end of a few years (52 B.C.) that it was able to furnish olive trees to the neighbouring countries.[26] Its olives and oil were thought excellent ; however, those of Grenada and Andalusia were preferred to them, even in the time of Pliny,[27] on account of their sweetness and delicate flavour. That illustrious naturalist has transmitted to us particulars of the highest interest on the cultivation of the olive tree, and the various preparations which its fruit requires, or rather, to which it is necessarily subjected for the luxury of the table.[28] Those who are curious on this subject may also consult Cato (the first among the Romans who has written on this tree),[29] Varro,[30] and Columella,[31] concerning the art of raising the plants, of gathering the olives, of extracting the oil, and of preserving the olives themselves. This latter operation was performed as follows :—

They took twenty-five pounds of olives, six pounds of quick-lime, broken very small and dissolved in water, to which twelve pounds of oak ashes and water in proportion were added. The olives were left to soak for eight or ten hours in this lye; then taken out, washed with care, and immersed for eight days in very clear soft water, which was changed several times. They then took hot water in which some stems of fennel had been infused; this plant was taken out, and the same water saturated with salt until an egg would float. When it was quite cold, the olives were put into this pickle.[32]

As regards the large olives, or *colymbades*, they were sometimes crushed after the first operation, that the brine might penetrate more easily; and odoriferous herbs were added to give them a better flavour. This was the way they prepared those from the marshes of Ancona—the only ones admitted at the tables of *gourmets*.[33]

At Rome, olives made their appearance in the first course, at the beginning of the repast; but sometimes, after their introduction, the gluttony of the guests caused them to be served again with the dessert: so that they opened and closed the banquet.[34]

The distributions of oil, to which Latin authors often allude, were somewhat rare for a long period. The people looked upon this fluid more as an object of luxury than a necessary of life, and it was only on extraordinary occasions that they were gratified with it. Thus, when Scipio Africanus began his curule edileship, each citizen received a measure of oil.[35] After his example, Agrippa made similar distributions, in the reign of Augustus. They became more frequent under the Emperors; and Severus ordered that an immense quantity should be brought into Rome.[36]

Venafra, a town of Campania, supplied excellent oil.[37] Pliny says that it surpassed that of all the rest of Italy.[38] However in those days, as at present, much was consumed of a very bad quality: for instance, that which was served by a clumsy Amphytrion to Julius Cæsar, and with which this prince seemed perfectly satisfied—a proof that the celebrated warrior was either a man of exquisite politeness or an epicure of very scanty ability.[39]

Independently of the culinary preparations in which oil was abundantly used, the ancients also employed much of it for anointing themselves; and, when at the bath, a slave always carried some in a vase,[40] with which they were rubbed. It was believed that the vital heat was thus concentrated, the strength increased, and health preserved.

Augustus inquiring one day of Pollio what ought to be done to preserve health in extreme old age: "Very little," was his answer; "drink wine, and rub yourself with oil."[41]

We shall conclude this article by transcribing the recipe of an odoriferous oil for which the Liburnians were celebrated, and which Apicius considered worthy of his attention.

Pound some alder and cyperus (sedges) with green laurel leaves till they are reduced to a very fine powder—put this powder into Spanish oil, add a condiment of salt,[42] and stir this mixture with great care for three days or more, then let it remain for some time.[43]

Olive oil was little known in France under the two first races of her kings. In the reign of Charlemagne it was drawn from the east and Africa, and was so rare that the Council of Aix-la-chapelle (817) allowed the monks to make use of the oil from bacon. In 1491 the Pope allowed Queen Anne (of Bretagne), then afterwards the whole province, and successively the other French provinces, the use of butter in seasoning on fast days.

PALM TREE.

The poet Pontanus has related, in beautiful Latin verses, the history of two palm trees cultivated in the kingdom of Naples. For a long time there had been a fine one growing in the environs of Otranto, loaded every year with flowers, and yet producing no fruit, in spite of the vigour of the tree and the heat of the climate. But one summer every one was much surprised at seeing this same tree produce a quantity of excellent and very ripe fruit. Astonishment changed into admiration when it was discovered that another palm tree, cultivated at Brindes (fifteen leagues distant), had that same year blossomed for the first time. From that period the palm tree of Otranto continued to yield fruit every year, notwithstanding the distance between it and the one at Brindes.[44]

The palm tree, which mythologic ages consecrated to the Muses,[45] was very common with the Hebrews,[46] to whom it supplied an exhilarating beverage called *sechar*, which is often mentioned with wine of the grape.[47]

Moreover, everything was useful in this tree.

The wood was employed for constructing buildings and for fuel; the leaves were used to make ropes, mats, and baskets; and the fruit served as food for man and cattle.[48]   From the dates a great quantity of honey was extracted, but very little inferior to ordinary honey;[49] and those which were not consumed were sent abroad with so much the more ease that they keep well.[50]

According to Pliny, this fruit was in reputation in Greece and Rome; and he names several excellent species which came from Judea, and principally from Jericho and the valleys of Archelais, Livias, and Phasaelis.[51]

Two Greek writers[52] inform us that the favourite of Herod, Nicolas of Damascus, a poet, philosopher, and historian, much liked by Augustus, sent to the Roman Emperor every year a peculiar kind of date from Palestine; and that the monarch, who became very partial to them, gave them the name of his friend.   Bread and cakes were also made with them.

We shall often have occasion to remark that dates were frequently introduced in the composition of the most exquisite dishes of the Romans.

Dates not quite ripe, if exposed to the sun, become in the first place soft, then pulpy, and lastly acquire a consistency similar to that of French plums; they can then be preserved, and sent to foreign markets.

Riper dates are squeezed to draw out a sweet juice, very pleasant, and which is put, together with the other part, in large vessels, and kept in that state, or buried in the earth.   These are the ones commonly used by the rich as food; the others are given up to the poorer class.

Dates are eaten either with or without preparation, or mixed with different kinds of viands.   Their syrup is used as a sauce to various dishes.

They are also completely dried for exportation; when reduced into flour, the caravans in the Desert employ them as food.   By crushing them in soft water wine is made, which produces a strong spirit, very agreeable.

The best dates are yellowish, semi-transparent, odoriferous, and sweet.

CHERRY TREE.

When on a very hot summer day some inviting cherries deliciously quench our burning thirst, we very little think of offering to Mithridates a souvenir of affection and gratitude. Such is man : he enjoys his wealth, and cares very little for the benefactor who has procured it for him. This ancient King of Pontus, of toxologic memory, and better known by physicians than gardeners, did not, however, pass the whole of his life in composing poisons and their antidotes; for his royal hands planted, and sometimes grafted, and it is to this useful pastime that we are indebted[53] for the sweet fruit, the name of which recalls to mind the city or country which was its birth-place.

Ancient authors have told us, it is true, that Europe is indebted for its cherries to Lucullus,[54] and that he made use of the cherry tree to ornament his triumphal car; honour is therefore due to the Roman general, but on condition that Mithridates shall lose nothing of his glory, or be eclipsed by the renown of this great conqueror.

The researches of several naturalists lead us to believe that cherry trees already existed at that period in Gaul. This tree delights in cold climates ; and the wildest forests of France contain almost the whole of its varieties. Perhaps at Rome they knew no other than the wild cherry tree, which on that account was very little sought after, and Lucullus probably brought it to notice by bringing some grafts or fruits from Cerasus. In this manner the passage of Pliny[55] and that of Virgil[56] can very well be explained, which present the cherry tree as a new guest.

Moreover, the Milesian, Xenophanes, and the physician, Diphilus of Siphne, have spoken of cherries long before Lucullus was in existence. Diphilus praises them in the strongest terms ; he says they are stomachic, and have a delicious flavour.[57] This certainly cannot apply to the sour wild fruit which is to be met with in the woods, and with which the most inexperienced palate is never twice caught.

At all events the authority of Theophrastus would be sufficient to remove all doubts, if any still remained. He informs us that, in his time, the good cherries of Mithridates passed from Lower Asia into

Greece,[58] where they were gladly received as in all other nations, on account of their form, taste, and qualities. This happy gastrologic event was accomplished 300 years before the Christian era, whereas the introduction of cherry trees by Lucullus took place 228 years later.

The capital of the world knew not, at first, how to appreciate this present as it deserved : the cherry tree was propagated so slowly in Italy, that more than a century after its introduction it was far from being generally cultivated.[59]

The Romans distinguished three principal species of cherries : the *Apronian,* of a bright red, with a firm and delicate pulp ; the *Lutatian,* very black and sweet; the *Cæcilian,* round and stubby, and much esteemed.[60]

This fruit embellished the third course in Rome, and the second at Athens.

" The fruit of the cherry tree is eaten raw, cooked, preserved with sugar, and in brandy ; it is also preserved dry, or made into ratafia. By fermentation, the juice of cherries, with the kernel, by adding sugar, makes a very agreeable liquor, which is called cherry wine ; a brandy is produced with fermented cherries drawn by the alembic, very powerful ; that named *kirschen wasser,* in the province of German-Lorraine, is a spirituous liquor, obtained by the distillation of various species of wild cherries."—Bosc.

APRICOT TREE.

The apricot tree was called by the Romans *Armeniaca,* the tree of Armenia, where it originated. It must be looked upon as a useful monument of the valour of the masters of the world, if it be true that, after their conquest, they brought it from that province into Rome.[61]

The Latins also named the apricot *præcocia* (precocious), because it ripens at the beginning of summer (in June) before other fruits.[62]

At the time when Pliny wrote (A.D. 72) the apricot tree had only been known at Rome for 30 years ; and apricots, still very rare, cost one *denarius,* or sevenpence halfpenny each :[63] they were only to be found in the first-rate shops of the fruit market or emporium of the third region, near the *Metasudante,* which was only open every ninth day; or near the Naval Camp, outside the Trigemina Gate. Some years later the agriculturists of the Roman suburbs brought into the city some excellent ones at a very low price; but the fashion and the taste for them had gone by.

"The green apricot is preserved before the stone becomes hard; when ripe it is eaten raw, cooked, or stewed in marmalade; preserves are made of it, as well as a dried paste, which keeps a long time; they are also preserved in brandy. The stone as it is, or broken, is used in ratafia of Noyau. Lastly, the kernel produces oil."—DUTOUR.

<hr/>

PEACH TREE.

This fruit tree, originally from Persia, was first transplanted into Greece,[64] where it existed a long time before it passed into Italy. It was still quite a novelty in Rome towards the middle of the 1st century of the Christian era, and the rich alone could eat peaches, for they cost no less than £11 13s. 4d. the dozen, or 18s. 9d. each.[65] This is rather dear fruit, however good it may be. But the bill of fare of certain banquets will show us, by-and-by, whether the Roman gastronomics knew how to spend their gold profusely, when they wished to satisfy a caprice or enjoy some dainty curiosity.

It was believed in Rome that the peach contained a deadly poison when gathered in Persia;[66] but that, once transplanted to another soil, it lost its injurious properties. This singular opinion, still held by many persons in the present day, has been refuted by Pliny, who treats it as a ridiculous idea;[67] at any rate, Galen[68] and Dioscorides[69] assert that this fruit is indigestible, unwholesome, and that it often causes fevers.

The high price of peaches, and the short duration of their freshness, caused amateurs to seek the means of preserving them for the longest possible time. The following is the recipe given by Apicius:—

"Choose the finest of this fruit, and place them in water, saturated with salt. The next day take them out, dry them with the greatest care, and then put them into a vessel with savory, vinegar, and salt."[70]

PLUM TREE.

Plum trees were known in Africa from time immemorial; and Theophrastus speaks of the great number of these trees which were to be found at Thebes, Memphis, and especially at Damascus.[71] Athenæus, also, praises the excellent plums of this last-named city;[72] and we know that time has not lessened their ancient reputation.

Asia and Egypt sent a great quantity to Europe; and, in order that they might keep better during this long voyage, a part of them were dried, and the rest were preserved—that is to say, the best—in honey and sweet wine.[73] These were the only kind known in Rome in the time of Cato (150 years B.C.), but the Romans, then novices in the art of good living, would have but ill-appreciated the delicate and perfumed pulp of Damascus plums, at the moment when, hardly plucked from the tree, their fresh and velvet-like bloom delights the eye and tempts the palate of epicures. Two centuries later the science of good living made incredible progress. A magiric atmosphere enveloped the capital of the universe with its delicious fragrance, and the joyous free livers of Italy cultivated in their gardens plums of the most beautiful purple and gold,[74] far superior to the much-extolled fruit from Damascus and Memphis. The fields everywhere offered such luxuriance of plum trees that Pliny, the opposition man, or *juste milieu* of that time, complained of their number,[75] and grieved at what he fancied a useless and expensive profusion of them.

The ancient Counts of Anjou transplanted the plums of Damascus into their province; and the good King René of Sicily, Duke of Anjou and Count of Provence, introduced them into southern Europe.[76]

The plums of *Monsieur* are thus named because Monsieur, the brother of Louis XIV., was very fond of them.[77]

The plums of *Reine Claude* owe their name to the first consort of Francis I., daughter of Louis XII.[78]

The plums of *Mirabelle* were brought from Provence into Lorraine by King René.[79]

H

XIII.

PIP FRUIT.

QUINCE TREE.

THIS tree appears to have been a native of Cydon, a city of Crete; from hence it passed into Greece,[1] and soon became the delight of its voluptuous inhabitants. The environs of Corinth, above all, were noted for the sweetness and beauty of their quinces,[2] which the enlightened luxury of Attica preferred to all others.

Rome did not fail to enrich itself with a fruit[3] to which the ingenuity of culinary art was to give a new flavour. Young plants were first imported from abroad, and put in boxes;[4] but the Romans knew not how to rear them, and were obliged for a long time to content themselves with excellent quinces preserved in honey, and sent from Iberia and Syria to the great capital.[5]

At last they learned how to cultivate the quince tree,[6] and subsequently introduced it into Gaul, where it succeeded admirably. They, too, could then enjoy, with a certain pride, preserves nothing inferior to those of Spain,[7] and which the confectioners in the "market of dainties,"[8] kept in reserve with quince wine[9] for the tables of the patricians; and also the stomachic exhilarating liqueur extracted from the fruit of sweet Cydoneum,[10] which even a *petite maîtresse* would not have disdained at a light morning repast.

At any rate, the faculty this time agreed with culinary chemistry in recommending to epicures those delicious preparations. It was asserted, besides, that the quince possessed the most beneficial qualities,[11] first, as an aliment, and next, as a counter-poison:[12] *gourmandise* made the mind docile, and none doubted its marvellous virtues.

This fruit, so much extolled, was preserved by placing it with its branches and leaves in a vessel, afterwards filled with honey or sweet wine, which was reduced to half the quantity by ebullition.[13]

---•---

PEAR TREE.

Many countries have disputed the honour of having given birth to the pear tree. According to some it was a native of Mount Ida, so renowned for its refreshing fountains; others said Alexandria; and in the opinion of some writers it came from different parts of Greece. Let us add to this enumeration Palestine, where this tree grew at a very remote period.[14]

It results from these different allegations that the ancients were acquainted with the pear tree; that they cultivated and were fond of pears, which is not at all surprising, as they are an excellent fruit. Theophrastus was very fond of them; he speaks of them very often,[15] and always with praise. The same thing may be affirmed of Pliny,[16] and more particularly of Galen, whose medical authority was formerly of so much weight. The learned physician of Pergamo is pleased to recognise in the pear strengthening qualities which benefit the stomach, and an astringent virtue which the apple does not possess in the same degree.[17]

Like us, the Greeks and Romans distinguished several kinds of this fruit, whose names indicated their taste and forms. It is not certain whether they possessed the *Bon Chrétien*, which honours our tables in winter, either raw or cooked. This name reminds us of its origin, which we will relate.

Louis XI., King of France, had ent for Saint François de Paule from the lower part of Calabria, in the hopes of recovering his health through his intercession. The saint brought with him the seeds of this pear, and as he was called at court *Le Bon Chrétien,* this fruit received the name of him to whom France owed its introduction.[18]

APPLE TREE.

A very ancient tradition—for it is six thousand years old—represents the apple as being, from the beginning of the world, the inauspicious fruit to which may be traced all the miseries of mankind. We crave permission to defend it from this accusation, merely by these few words, "That it is nowhere written."

The holy books rarely speak of the apple tree. If we are not mistaken, it is only mentioned in five passages[19] of the sacred writings, and at periods very distant from the first offence of man. Therefore, nothing indicates aversion or contempt on the part of the inspired writers for this tree, which on one occasion serves even as a graceful term of comparison ;[20] from which it might be concluded that the inhabitants of the east thought as much of it as other nations.

There is one (and perhaps only one) example of a singular and excessive repugnance to apples. It is said that Uladislas, King of Poland, no sooner perceived them than he became so confused and terrified that he immediately fled. It certainly required very little to disturb this poor prince !

Greece produced very beautiful apple trees, and their fruit was so excellent, that it was the favourite dessert of Philip of Macedon, and of his son, Alexander the Great, who caused them to be served at all their meals.[21] Probably they were obtained purposely for them from the island of Euboea, which enjoyed an extraordinary reputation for apples.[22]

The Athenian legislator—the wise Solon—almost succeeded in throwing discredit on this aliment, so much liked by his fellow-citizens, by a sumptuary law which he thought it necessary to establish.

The inhabitants of Attica were fond of good living ; and when one of them took a wife he spared no expense to give splendour to the nuptial banquet—a very excusable pride on such an occasion. Solon was in the habit of interfering rather too much in the affairs of others. Every one has his failing, and this was *his :* he imagined that his fellow citizens fared too sumptuously on their wedding-day ; and, in order to curtail an expense contrary to his ideas of economy, he ordered that the bridegroom should be content with a single apple, while his guests were regaling themselves at his expense. Who would believe it? This law was religiously observed by the Greeks, and the Persians thought it so original that they, in their turn, adopted it.[23]

The Latins gave a favourable reception to the apple tree, and cultivated it with care. Eminent citizens of Rome did not disdain to give their names and patronage to different kinds procured by themselves, or which they had improved in their orchards. The Manlian apples were so called after Manlius; the Claudian after Claudius, their patron; the Appian owed their name to Appius. Some others preserved that of their native country: such were the Sidonians, the Greeks, and the Epirotes.

After the conquest of Gaul, the Romans introduced all these fruits;[24] and as the climate was more favourable to apple trees than that of Italy, they soon multiplied to a surprising extent. France ought to be grateful to those proud warriors for a present that enriched that province of the empire, and which perhaps still contributes to its prosperity.

LEMON TREE.

Among the richest productions of Media, Virgil mentions a tree, to whose fruit he attributes the greatest virtues against all poisons. The description he gives of it seems to belong to the lemon tree.[25] However this may be, its origin, and even its identity, have given rise to the most animated disputations.

Many have asserted that Juba, King of Mauritania (50 years B.C.), spoke of the lemon tree, and that he looked upon it as being very ancient. They add, that the Lybians gave to its fruit the name of "Hesperide apples," that Hercules stole, and which, on account of their colour, were called "golden apples" by the Greeks, who were indebted to that hero for their introduction.[26]

Others maintain that no one has spoken of them before Theophrastus,[27] who called them "Median apples," after the place of their origin; and that consequently those persons were wrong who confounded them with the apples taken from the garden of the Hesperides.[28]

These difficulties will probably disappear, if we remember that the ancients have given to the lemon tree various names[29] which belong to other trees. The truth is, that the Athenians received it from the Persians, who were neighbours of the Medes, and from Attica it spread all over Greece.[30]

Lemons were only known to the Romans at a very late period, and at first were used only to keep the moths from their garments. The acidity of this fruit was unpleasant to them, and Apicius makes no use of it: those who wish to satisfy their curiosity on the subject may read the remarks of Lister, the celebrated physician of Queen Anne, and editor of the works of this famous *gourmet*.[31]

In the time of Pliny, the lemon was hardly known otherwise than as an excellent counter-poison.[32]

Fifty years after that, Palladius reared the plants which he had received from Media,[33] and at last this tree was slowly naturalized in the south of Europe.

A considerable number of anecdotes have been told of the anti-venomous properties of the lemon. Athenæus speaks of two men who did not feel pain from the bite of dangerous serpents, because they had previously eaten of this fruit.[34] Either this story is false, or men and things have strangely altered.

Apicius preserves lemons by putting each of them into a separate vessel, which is hermetically sealed with plaster, and afterwards suspended from the ceiling.[35]

In another place we shall speak of the tables and beds made of the lemon tree, so fashionable amongst the Romans, and for which they spent prodigious sums.

One thing remains to be noticed; and that is, that preserved lemon peel was considered as one of the best digestives, and that doctors recommend it to weak and delicate persons.[36]

ORANGE TREE.

If confidence is to be placed in some authors, the native land of the orange tree would appear to be the gardens of the Hesperides, so remarkable in mythologic ages, and it was found also in Western Africa, Mauritania, and the Fortunate Islands; to which they add those mountains of Atlas so little known in a botanical point of view, notwithstanding the daring excursions of several learned men.

According to other observers, it originally came from the southern countries of China,[37] from the islands of the Indian Archipelago, or even from that portion of the globe called Oceania.

One incontestable fact is, that writers of antiquity were completely ignorant of the existence of this superb tree. Had they known it, its majestic height, the dark green of its foliage, the suavity of its flowers, its fruit, so fine, bright, and so flattering to the taste, could not have failed to inspire them with brilliant pages. Theophrastus, and the Latin geoponics, never would have neglected to speak of the luxury and fecundity it displays, even in the season of hoary frost. Besides, the name of *Portughan*, which is given to the orange by the Arabs— a name foreign to their language, but which is again heard among the Italians, Spaniards, and even in the southern provinces of France—is it not an indication that the introduction of this tree has some connection with the Portuguese voyages to India, particularly those of Juan de Castro in the year 1520?

It is the Portuguese who have planted the orange tree in the Canaries, at Madeira, where it was supposed to be indigenous on account of the vigorous vegetation it there displays: it is the Portuguese who have introduced this tree into all countries washed by the Mediterranean: and it is still the Portuguese who have furnished the parent suckers, whence the Spaniards have been enabled to form their immense groves in Andalusia and Algarvia.[38]

From the foregoing recital we may conclude that the grand poliphagic triumvirate of antiquity—Archestratus, Vitellius, and Apicius— never tasted this fruit, which Heaven reserved for the appreciation of modern times. Blessed shades! if, attracted sometimes by the exquisite vapours of our stoves, you should wander again round those succulent dishes which a more experienced chemistry enables us to elaborate: if fruitless gastronomic reminiscences should lead you into the delightful retreat of some one of your disciples, who by his enlightened skill is there preparing the treasures of the dessert: oh! turn away your eyes from those enticing fruits which display their golden rays, and rise in pyramids upon a porcelain pedestal. Here are oranges, the nectar and ambrosia of the Olympian ages, which you doubtless regret, and we have again discovered. These wonders of sweetness existed perhaps in China, but you knew it not, for China did not become a Roman province. But console yourselves, giants of cookery! we have not yet attained the high pinnacle of your art; your wild boar *à la Troyenne*, your peacocks' brains, and your phenicopters' tongues, secure for you a triumph which posterity will dispute in vain!

The orange known under the name of "Portugal orange" comes from China. Not more than two centuries ago the Portuguese brought thence the first scion, which has multiplied so prodigiously that we now see entire forests of orange trees in Portugal.[39]

It appears to have been the custom formerly, in England, to make new-year's presents of oranges stuck full with cloves. We read in one of Ben Jonson's pieces, the "Christmas Masque," "He has an orange and rosemary, but not a clove to stick in it."[40]

At the present day we can dispense with this embellishment.

The first orange tree cultivated in the centre of France was to be seen a few years ago at Fontainebleau. It was called *Le Connétable* (the Constable), because it had belonged to the Connétable de Bourbon, and had been confiscated, together with all property belonging to that prince, after his revolt against his sovereign.[41]

FIG TREE.

Antiquity, sacred and profane, has not left us, on any other tree, facts so clear and certain as upon the fig tree; it is the only tree of Eden of which the sacred books have preserved to us any mention.[42] In the East there were immense plantations of it; Egypt had some also;[43] and the land of Canaan produced figs, which enabled Moses to judge of its fertility.[44]

The Scriptures, in order to give us an idea of the happiness and tranquillity the Jews enjoyed under the reign of Solomon, tell us that, "in Judea and in Israel all dwelt safely, every man under his vine and under his fig tree."[45]

And the fruit of this tree was no doubt very dear to the Hebrews, since Rubshakeh, the general of the Assyrian army, thought to seduce them from their obedience to Hezekiah, King of Judea, by saying to them : " Come out to me, and then eat ye every man of his own vine, and every one of his fig tree."[46]

Thus the trade carried on with figs in Jerusalem had become so considerable and active, that Esdras was obliged to interdict it on the Sabbath day. It appears that figs were arranged in small masses, to which they give the form of loaves or cakes, either round or square, which were sold nearly in the same way as at the present day.[47]

From the East the fig tree passed into Greece, then into Italy, Gaul, Spain, and throughout Europe.

The Athenians pretended that this tree was a native of their soil, and this people never wanted mythologic facts to support their asser-tions ; they imagined, and would have others believe, that the grateful Ceres rewarded the Athenian, Phytalus, for his hospitality by giving him a fig tree, which served for all the plantations of Attica.[48]

Whatever may be the way it came to them, they received it with transports of joy ; it was planted with great pomp in the centre of the public square at Athens : from that time this spot was sacred to them.[49]

Ere long the fame of the figs of Attica spread far and wide : they were the best in Greece ; and the magistrates strictly prohibited their exportation.[50] This law was afterwards modified, that is, the exportation of figs was allowed on payment of a very heavy duty.

They then appointed inspectors, whose duty it was to discover con-traventions, and report them : thence arose the name of Sycophant,[51] taken by those informers—a vile and dispised set of men, whose denunciations were often false, and with whom the infamous authors of a base calumny were eventually assimilated.[52]

In Greece every one feasted on figs : it was a sort of regular gastro-nomic *furore*, which knew no bounds, and the wise Plato himself ceased to be a philosopher when presented with a basket of that fruit. As an aliment it was considered so wholesome and strengthening, that on the first introduction of them they constituted the food of the athletæ, whose patron, Hercules, had also fed on them in his youth.

The superiority of the Greek figs was so generally acknowledged that the kings of Persia even had a predilection for them : dried ones were served on the tables of these ostentatious princes.[53]

The Romans believed, according to an antique tradition, that their first princes, Romulus and Remus, were found under a fig tree on the shore of the Tiber ; they therefore rendered signal honours to this tree when it was brought into Italy : they planted it in the Forum ; and it was under its shade that a sacrifice was offered every year to the shepherdess who had suckled their founder.[54]

It may, nevertheless, be affirmed, that no one before Cato had noticed the fig tree,[55] which probably appeared in Rome at the same period as the peach, apricot, and other trees of Asia. Sixty years afterwards Varro speaks of it as a novelty from beyond sea, and points out to us that its various species have retained the names of the countries whence they came.[56]

Those varieties were so numerous, that Pliny counts no less than twenty-nine of them,[57] and the designation of the greater part recalled to mind the illustrious families who had taken them under their patronage.

The people of the north, especially the moderns, cannot well explain the extraordinary infatuation of the ancient southern nations for the fruit of the fig tree. Perhaps we ought to look for the reason in the nourishing, fresh, and sweet qualities of its pulp, and in the numerous plantations of those trees, which sometimes furnished an agreeable food to entire armies, when other provisions failed.[58] That of Philip of Macedon owed its preservation to the figs brought to it by the Magnesians.[59] A long time before, David received with joy, from the hands of Abigail, two hundred baskets of dried figs, for himself and his exhausted men.[60]

More than once the far-famed reputation of some beautiful plantations of fig trees brought long and disastrous wars on an entire country, as steel attracts lightning. Xerxes left Persia, and rushed on Attica, to take possession of those delicious figs, whose renown only had crossed his territory :[61] and it was partly to eat the figs of Rome that the Gauls waged war against Italy :[62] thank Heaven we have now more respect for our neighbours' fig trees.

The best things in the world have had their detractors, and the fig is not an exception. Philotimus and Diphilus looked upon it as bad food ;[63] Galen was unwell after partaking of figs, and he recommends us to mix almonds with them ;[64] Hippocrates himself thought them indigestible, and advised to drink plentifully after eating them.[65]

All these great men may have been right, but the Greeks, their contemporaries, acted as if they were wrong : happily we are not called upon to decide between them.

Figs were commonly served on aristocratic tables with salt, pepper, vinegar, and some aromatics ; they were eaten fresh, or dried in the oven, or on hurdles in the sun.

RASPBERRY TREE.

The ancients hardly mention the raspberry tree, which they placed on a level with the bramble. The Latins called it " *Bramble of Ida*," because it was common on that mountain.[66] There can be no doubt, however, that the Romans knew how to appreciate the raspberry tree, so much esteemed in our days.

CURRANT TREE.

The moderns have attempted to ennoble our two kinds of currants by decorating them with Latin names, which recall their antiquity.[67] Vain effort! To all appearance the Greeks and people of Italy were not acquainted with the currant tree,[68] although they well deserved to possess this delicious fruit.

STRAWBERRY PLANT.

Among the Greeks the name of the strawberry indicated its tenuity, this fruit forming hardly a mouthful. With the Latins the name reminded one of the delicious perfume of this plant. Both nations were equally fond of it, and applied the same care to its cultivation. Virgil appears to place it in the same rank with flowers,[69] and Ovid gives it a tender epithet,[70] which delicate palates would not disavow. Neither does this luxurious poet forget the wild strawberry,[71] which disappears beneath its modest foliage, but whose presence the scented air reveals. Transported to the tables of the Luculli, by the side of its more brilliant and more beautiful sister, a flattering murmur often bore testimony to its merit, and nature triumphed in the midst of ingenious guests, soliciting of art what they repudiated in nature.

MULBERRY TREE.

The ancient mulberry tree was considered the wisest and most prudent of trees, because it took care, they said, not to let the smallest of its buds come to light before the cold had entirely disappeared, not to return. Then, however, it hastened to repair lost time, and a single night was sufficient to see it display its beautiful flowers, which the next morning brightly opened at the rising of Aurora.[72]

The voluptuous Romans, reposing late on their soft couches the day after the fatigues of a banquet worthy of Vitellius, did not trouble themselves much about this interesting phenomenon, which occurred, if Pliny does not mistake, in the gardens of their villas. But they knew that mulberries agree with the stomach, that they afford hardly any nourishment, and easily digest :[73] therefore, no sooner had they opened their heavy eyelids than an Egyptian boy—attentive living bell—at a sign disappeared, and quickly returned, bearing a small crystal vase, filled with mulberry juice and wine reduced by boiling. This beneficent fruit preserved in this mixture all its sweet flavour,[74] and enabled the rich patrician to await until evening the hour for new excesses.

It is quite evident that this luscious fruit was a native of Canaan, for the high road by which the tribes of Israel went up to the feasts at Jerusalem lay through the valley of *Baka*, or Mulberry Tree ;[75] and the whole tract of country from Ekron to Gaza abounded in these trees.

XIV.

SHELL FRUIT.

·—·

ALMOND TREE.

THIS tree, whose fruit was called at one time "Greek Nut," and, at another, "Thasian Nut,"[1] is a native of Paphlagonia, according to Hermippus.[2] The nations of the east thought much of almonds, and Jacob found them worthy of appearing among the presents he designed for Joseph.[3] The almond tree of Naxos supplied the markets of Athens.[4] The Romans, in their turn, sought them, and believed, like the physician spoken of by Plutarch, that it was only necessary to eat five or six almonds to acquire the ability of drinking astonishingly.[5]

Besides, this fruit had not always so mean a destination: the disciples of Apicius made of it one of the most delicate of dishes. Here it is, as taught to them by their master :—

Take almonds that have been pounded in a mortar, and mix them with honey, pepper, garum, milk, eggs, and a little oil ; submit the whole to the action of a slow fire.[6]

The ancients were acquainted with the oil of almonds,[7] of which they made nearly the same use as we do ourselves ; but they possessed, in addition, an infallible means of augmenting the fertility of the almond tree. It was very simple :—A hole was made in the tree, a stone was introduced into it,[8] and, thanks to the virtue of this new manure, the branches soon bent under the weight of almonds.

The good almonds come from Barbary and the south of France.

When young, they are preserved like green apricots. They are eaten at table, fresh or dry; in comfits, pastry, &c.: they are also used to make orgeat and refreshing emulsions. The oil extracted from almonds, even bitter ones, is very sweet; it is best extracted cold, by pressure. The pulp is employed, under the name of almond paste, for several purposes, one of which is to render the skin soft and flexible.[9]

WALNUT TREE.

Asia, the cradle of most fruit trees, gave birth also to the walnut tree. It is believed to be a native of Persia,[10] and its pleasing foliage already adorned, in Biblical times, the orchards of the east. One of the most ancient of the sacred books informs us that it was known to the Jews,[11] and it may be inferred from a passage in the Song of Solomon that they possessed numerous plantations of this tree.[12]

Among the Persians, walnuts were not lavished on the first comer, as with us; the sovereign reserved them for his dessert, and the people were obliged to abstain from them. But perhaps it may be said that, however fond this prince may have been of walnuts, he could not eat all that were produced in his states. The objection is embarrassing, we own, and chroniclers are silent on this point. But let us suppose that this generous potentate distributed to his favourites the walnuts from which his satiated appetite was compelled to abstain; and, indeed, we find that a king of Persia sent some to the Greeks, who called them "Royal Persian nuts,"[13] in gratitude and remembrance of the august gift.

They did still better; the king of Olympus had a great liking for this fruit, so they hastened to consecrate it to him,[14] and the "nuts of Jupiter" were cultivated with honour in the whole of Greece.[15]

Italy received the walnut tree from Attica, and, by degrees, the conquerors of the world introduced it to the different countries of Europe.

The Romans, imitators of the piety of the Greeks, placed this tree also under the protection of the most powerful of their gods. One of their most whimsical customs, perhaps, owed its origin to this consecration, which will serve to explain it :—

After the wedding feast the bridegroom strewed in the nuptial chamber, at night, several baskets of walnuts, which children hastened to pick up.[16]   This was, they said, a kind of offering to Jupiter, and thus he was entreated to grant his supreme patronage to the husband, and to adorn the wife with the virtues of Juno.[17]   The god could not have failed to smile at this part of the request of blind mortals, and it is asserted that, at times, he condescended not to grant it.

Others have given a different interpretation.   According to them, the walnut, being covered with a double envelope when fresh, became a presage of abundance and prosperity.[18]

It would be too tedious to relate all the singular opinions to which this ceremony gave rise.   The most reasonable appears to be that adopted by certain commentators :—Walnuts, say they, served as playthings for children, and, by throwing them on the ground the day of his wedding, the bridegroom made it understood that he and his companion renounced the frivolities of youth, henceforth to devote themselves to the serious exigencies of a family.[19]

This fruit was considered astringent,[20] stomachic, and proper to facilitate digestion.[21]   It was made into preserve, and eaten in small quantity, mixed with figs.   In this manner paralysis of the tongue was avoided—an effect to which it was believed those who partook of them to excess were exposed.[22]   Green walnuts were much esteemed ; they were served at dessert,[23] notwithstanding the opinion of Heraclides, of Tarentum, who looked upon them as a stimulant to the appetite, and advised a trial of them at the beginning of a repast.[24]

When Pompey had made himself master of the palace of Mithridates, he had search made everywhere for the recipe of the famous antidote against poison used by that king.   At length it was found ; it was very simple : however, we offer it to the curious :—

Pound, with care, two walnuts, two dried figs, twenty leaves of rue, and a grain of salt.[25]   Swallow this mixture — precipitate it by the assistance of a little wine, and you have nothing to fear from the most active poison for the space of twenty-four hours.

NUT TREE.

The Greeks gave hazel nuts the name of "Pontic Nuts," and Theophrastus calls them "Nuts of Heraclea," because the territory of that capital of the kingdom of Pontus produced the best.[26]

The Latins, at first, retained the same designation for this fruit, but afterwards, the environs of Præneste and Avellinum supplying them with a great quantity of excellent nuts, they gave them the name of those two cities.[27] They employed also a diminitive[28] to indicate those which came from the first of these localities. The French *Aveline* (filbert), and *Noisette* (hazel nuts), are evidently borrowed from the Roman vocabulary.

The inhabitants of Præneste raised the nut tree to a sort of religious worship. This tree had preserved them from famine during the time Hannibal beseiged their city,[29] and since that memorable epoch it had enriched them, for the ancients preferred hazel nuts to all other shell fruit, as possessing most wholesome and nourishing qualities.[30]

It was the custom in France, some centuries ago, at the time of the summer solstice (Midsummer eve), to take all the kitchen utensils and make the most frightful clatter by knocking them one against another. The simpletons of those times imagined that there were no better means of preventing the rain, which, in their opinion, was detrimental to filberts and hazel nuts.[31] Hospinian, who relates this ridiculous custom, does not tell us what results they obtained by all their racket.

PISTACHIO TREE.

This tree, esteemed by the Romans,[32] is a native of India.[33] Lucius Vitellius brought some plants of it from Syria to Rome, under the reign of Tiberius; a little time subsequently, a knight, named Flaccus Pompeius, introduced it also into Spain.[34]

Galen doubted whether pistachio nuts were good for the stomach.[35] Avicenna proved the contrary ;[36] and several centuries before the Arabian physician, Roman epicures had courageously demonstrated that this fruit never does harm in whatever form it may be presented, whether raw or roasted, alone or accompanied with garum and salt.

CHESNUT TREE.

According to some writers the chesnut tree owes its name to the city of Castana, in Thessaly, where they maintained it originated. On the contrary, it comes from Sardis, in Lydia, if we are to believe the physician, Diphilus, who calls chesnuts, acorns of Sardis, and says they are nourishing, but indigestible.[37]

Amaryllis was fond of this fruit ;[38] but Amaryllis was only a shepherdess, and her beauty did not prevent her from having rather rustic tastes. The Roman ladies abandoned the chesnut to that low class of citizens whose palates, incapable of improvement, remain always stationary in the midst of the incessant progress of cookery ; sad example of invincible frugality, which the most exciting *fumets* fail to arouse.

Nevertheless, there was a soft and tender species of chesnut, *Castaneæ molles*,[39] which were allowed on some of the tables of the higher class of citizens, and recommended themselves by their delicate pulp to the attention of the guests ;[40] perhaps oil of chesnuts was obtained from this particular kind.[41]

To render the chesnuts more agreeable and wholesome they must be pealed of their skins, which is very tough ; put into boiling water, it penetrates and softens the bitter pellicle (the tan) covering them, and facilitates its removal from the floury substance. When the chesnuts can be easily stripped of this pellicle by the pressure of the fingers, take the jar from the fire ; shake them well on all sides. The tan will soon detach itself from their surface, and be altogether removed ; then take them out, and after they have been shaken in a sieve made purposely, they are washed in cold water, to take away, with what remains of the tan, the bitter water they may have preserved ; they are then cooked without water, in a well-covered vessel, and upon a moderate fire.

"To eat chesnuts green all the year, boil them in water for fifteen or twenty minutes; put them afterwards in a common oven, one hour after the bread has been taken out. By this double operation the chesnuts acquire a degree of cooking and desiccation, by which they can be preserved a very long time, provided they are kept in a dry place. They can be used afterwards by putting them to warm in a *bain-marie.*" —DUTOUR.

POMEGRANATE.

Ceres, disconsolate on account of the loss of her daughter, to whom Pluto destined the sceptre of Hell, implored the ruler of Olympus to restore Proserpine. Jupiter promised that the favour should be granted, provided that she had not partaken of anything in the infernal regions. Now, she had eaten some grains of a pomegranate; very few indeed; some serious authors have said three; others, quite as respectable, say nine. The fact is, however, Proserpine had broken her fast; therefore she might think herself fortunate in being allowed to pass six months on earth and six months in the abode of darkness.[42]

This little mythologic story informs us that the pomegranate tree was known to antiquity, and that the garden of the Elysian fields contained most excellent fruit for the use of its melancholy inhabitants.

The pomegranate, whose acidulated flavour is so pleasing to the inhabitants of hot climates, was first cultivated in the east, then in Africa, but especially in the environs of Carthage, from whence the Romans brought it into Italy, where it was commonly called the Carthaginian apple;[43] it was also named *Granatum,* on account of the number of its seeds.[44]

Pliny distinguishes five different species of promegranate;[45] Columella teaches the way to rear this tree;[46] and Apicius treats of the preservation of its fruit, to do which it is only necessary to plunge it in boiling water, take it out immediately, and suspend it from the ceiling.[47]

The Greeks were very fond of pomegranates. The finest came from Attica, so celebrated by the genius of its inhabitants; and from Bœotia,[48] that privileged soil, where agriculture and stupidity flourished together.[49]

XV.

ANIMAL FOOD.

Bread, vegetables, and fruit for a long time provided man with a sufficient and easy alimentation.[1] Wandering with his flocks in search of cool pasture, he only exacted their wool wherewith to make the clothing requisite for his migratory life;[2] their services to assist him in hollowing a difficult furrow;[3] and their first-born as a most agreeable offering to the all-powerful master of heaven and earth.[4] We may also suppose that, in the pastoral ages, the wandering tribes of Asia added to their vegetable food the milk of their ewes, goats, or cows, although it is not mentioned in the Book of Genesis[5] at a very early period, it is true, but which forms a nourishment nature seems to point out as proper to infancy and old age ;[6] mankind, therefore, abstained from animal food during many centuries.[7] Ecclesiastical and profane writers seem to agree on this point.[8] Habit had not yet produced disgust, and curiosity, the fatal mother of experience and sensuality. To eat was for them the most natural and simple action of life. The art of cookery tries, makes choice, and improves: that art did not exist.

The frightful cataclysm which overthrew the world, and of which the history of every nation gives proofs more or less confused, came to modify this state of things. "Men were obliged to be fed with more substantial food,"[9] and our forefathers were allowed to add to vegetables and the herbs of the country, "animated beings, and all that which had life and motion."[10]

The magiric science, therefore, began in the year of the world 1656.

From that period, indeed, the cooking of meat, however little complicated it may have been, required an attention, care, and study, which prepared the development of that marvellous faculty to which no possible limit can be assigned—the last to disappear, and to which, in fact, are related nearly all the actions of human life—*the sense of taste.*

Heathen authors, guided by the lights of reason, some gleams of tradition, and perhaps not absolutely strangers to the writings of Moses, agree pretty well on the diet of the Golden Age;[11] that age of innocence, acorns, and happiness,[12] when everywhere were seen streams of milk, and nectar, and honey, flowing from the hollow oaks and other trees of the forests.[13]

But when the question is to point out the time at which the use of animal food was introduced, ideas become clouded, and highly intelligent minds, bewildered by the obscurity which envelops the subject, have frequently appealed to absurd legends and ridiculous fables, invoking the aid of their false and contested authority.

Xenocrates pretends that Triptolemus forbad the Athenians to eat animals.[14] Man must, then, have been still frugivorous for four centuries after the Deluge.

This opinion found contradictors, who maintained that man contented himself with fruit only because fire was wanting to cook meat; but Prometheus came, and taught him how to draw the useful element from the flint which concealed it, and was the first to venture on the sacrifice of an ox.[15] This happened in the year of the world 2412.[16]

All this is a mistake, say other and very sensible writers; here is the truth on this difficult point: The goddess Ceres had sown a field, and the wheat came up as desired, when a pig entered, tumbled about, and caused considerable damage, which so irritated the lady that she punished him with death. Now, as a pig is good for nothing except to eat, this one was eaten; and from that day, so fatal to the swinish race, mankind learnt to appreciate the flesh of animals.[17]

At the same time, Bacchus killed a goat he found nibbling at the tendrils of his darling vines;[18] and Hyberbius, son of Mars, and a slasher, like his father, amused himself by killing another, in order to become familiar thus early with scenes of combat.[19] These goats were roasted; and as experience had as yet furnished no rule of comparison, and formed no taste—that exquisite sentiment of the beautiful in the plastic arts, and of the good in the culinary science—it was decided that this dish was very tolerable.

Hitherto the bovine race had only lost one individual: its sad destiny began in the year 1506, before our era, under the reign of the fourth king of Athens, Erichtonius, on a day of great solemnity, when an ox, pressed probably by hunger, came near the altar, and devoured one of the sacred cakes which heathen piety had dedicated to Jupiter. The zealous Diomus rushed forward, and pierced the heart of the sacrilegious quadruped.

It might be supposed that the anger of the god was immediately appeased; but no! the terrible Jupiter knitted his brows; Olympus was in great agitation; and pestilence came, and spread its ravages amongst the Athenians.

"All did not die, but all were struck;"[20] and, to propitiate the implacable scourge, they thought of nothing better than to institute the Buphonic Feast, which happily re-established their health, and which they continued to celebrate every year. They sacrificed an ox,[21] offered a piece to Jupiter, and the faithful divided the rest among themselves.

At Tyre, in Phœnicia, meat was consumed on the altar, but the gods had the profit of it, and nobody else. Some fruit and a few vegetables were sufficient for the frugality of people enjoying innocent and primitive customs. But it happened, in the time of Pygmalion,[22] that a young sacrificer having perceived that a piece of the victim had fallen, hastened to pick it up and replace it carefully on the fire of the altar. In the performance of this operation he burned his fingers, and instantly put them into his mouth, to lessen the pain. As he could not help tasting the fat with which they were covered, the greedy young man experienced a new sensation, which tempted him to swallow a mouthful—then a second—a portion of the victim was eaten; he put another piece under his cloak, and, with his wife, made the finest supper in his life. All went on very well until the prince, being informed of this profanation, loaded them with reproaches, and condemned both to the punishment of death.

Gluttony, however, is rash: other sacrificers ate—at first in secret—of this forbidden food; then they were imitated; and, at last, by degrees meat passed from the altar of the gods, who did not taste it, to the tables of mortals, who feasted upon it.[23] People may or may not believe this anecdote, which informs us in so satisfactory a manner of the epoch at which man, from being frugivorous, became carnivorous; but one thing is certain, that in the time of Homer (there is only eighty years between him and Pygmalion), the flesh of animals was then much

in fashion, for we read of his giving to his heroes, as their principal
food, a whole hog, three years old, and oxen roasted—not even jointed.[24]

Some ideologists and dreamers have risen against the use of meat;
their declamations, often very eloquent, have been read; but, from
Pythagoras, a sublime and honest enthusiast, down to the whimsical
J. J. Rousseau—who, by-the-by, was very fond of mutton chops and
bœuf à la mode, although he exclaimed against the cruelty of mankind,
whose hands were stained with the blood of animals—no nation has yet
determined to adopt the patriarchal diet of the first ages of the world.

Plutarch was a vegetarian; and we possess one of his treatises, in
which he endeavours to prove that flesh is not the natural food of man.[25]
As a conclusive answer—meat was eaten. So, when an ancient philosopher one day denied the movement of matter, a person reduced him
to silence by walking.

But, if animal diet has, from time to time, met with a small number
of detractors, what an immense crowd of apologists and adepts has it
not also found! It would signify nothing to name individuals; let us
point out whole nations. Who is not acquainted with the delicacy and
luxury of the Assyrians and Persians? Who is not aware that the
genius of the Greeks improved the culinary art, and that their cooks
were famous in history? What of the Syracusans, whose dainty and
curious ideas passed as a proverb; and of the Athenians, who were so
passionately fond of the pleasures of the table; or of Naples, Tarentum,
and Sybaris, so celebrated for their good cheer? The Romans surpassed even these refinements and sumptuous repasts: theirs is the
honour of the pontiffs' feasts, the excesses of Capreæ, the profusions of
Vitellius, of Galba, Nero, and Caligula. They have the honour of the
banquet of Geta, which lasted three days, and ended by exhausting the
alphabetic list of all the dishes that the universe could supply.

May heaven preserve us from imitating such prodigies of intemperance and gluttonous folly; but let us, at least, be allowed to use with
moderation the good that Providence has granted us, and which it has
not forbidden us to make agreeable and savoury. The inhabitants of
the air, earth, and water, entered within our domains, as well as the
fruits of the fields, on the day when the Creator condescended to say to
his creature:

"Every moving thing that liveth shall be meat for you; even as the
green herb have I given you all things."[26]

REARING OF CATTLE.

All ancient legislators have bestowed the most serious attention to the rearing and preservation of cattle. The Mosaic law, in this respect, enters into details which reveal the most profound wisdom, a delicate and minute research which cannot be too much admired.

More attentive to propagate useful animals than to flatter the sensuality of nations, this law forbids their being mutilated;[27] it requires the Hebrews to treat with generosity the companions of their labour;[28] that they shall interest themselves in the preservation of their brother's, and even of their enemies' oxen;[29] that different species of unequal strength shall not be yoked together to the plough;[30] and, in order that the cattle may not suffer from an excess of hard and constant labour, Moses assures to them at least one day of rest in a week.[31]

It is well known with what care the patriarchs surrounded their flocks; for them they wandered from region to region, and only stopped where pasture was abundant.[32] In imitation of those fathers of nations, the princes of the East, and the Grecian chiefs, were at first shepherds;[33] and were, perhaps, indebted to the innocent occupations of the fields for the sweet and sacred title of pastors of man.[34]

The founder of Rome did not forget the flocks and herds, in those famous laws which were to assure the prosperity of his rising city;[35] one of them allowed the possessor of an estate to take up the acorns which might fall into his field from his neighbour's property,[36] and to divide them among the cattle he is rearing.

Under the republic, it was severely forbidden to ill-use beasts of burthen and others. By the Licinian law, each farmer was required to proportion the number of his sheep and oxen to the extent of his land;[37] the Thorian law contains very wise regulations relative to the quality and keeping up of pasture.[38] Moreover, it is to be remarked, that the Romans never fixed the limits of a rural property, nor formed a new colony, without giving their first care to the spots appointed to feed their flocks,[39] the quiet possession of which was assured by the Emperors. Adrian, among others, did not encourage thieves. This prince ordered that whoever carried away cattle grazing in meadows should be con-

demned to work in the mines; that those who should have been convicted of robbery several times should be beheaded; and that thieves
found with arms in their hands should become the prey of wild beasts.[40]

Illustrious families by birth often added to their name a sort of
epithet, originating either from bulls, goats, or sheep, which were brought
up on the land of their villas.   This singular custom proves the extraordinary attachment which the Romans had for their flocks.   One of
these enthusiasts, Tremellius Scrofa,[41] had written a treatise on the art of
assorting and feeding cattle.[42]   Greek and Latin geoponics have also
transmitted to us some details full of interest, and which often contain
most useful information upon the various species of animals which the
ancients preferred, and the particular care they took in the preservation
and development of various breeds.[43]   Pagan theology reckoned among
its thirty thousand gods[44] some few protective divinities of flocks.   The
shepherds invoked Pales[45] and Anna Perenna;[46] dealers of oxen offered
sacrifices to Bubona,[47] whose special care it was to see that they were fat
and healthy.

The animals chosen to be fattened were put under the protection of
this deity, and were fed in the following manner:

The first day they had given to them cabbages, soaked in vinegar;
then, for five days, straw, mixed with wheat bran; from the seventh day
they had nothing but bruised barley, which was gradually and judiciously increased till the twelfth day.   These oxen were fed at midnight,
at break of day, at twelve o'clock, and at three in the afternoon.   They
were allowed to drink only twice—that is, after the third and fourth
meal.[48]   On the thirteenth day they were led to market.

MARKETS.

The Hebrews held their cattle market at the gates of their cities;
and from this circumstance, perhaps, is derived those expressions so frequent in the sacred writings: "The gates of the flocks," "The sheep's
gate," &c.,[49] which no doubt designated the different quarters of Jerusalem where shepherds and cattle dealers were accustomed to congregate.

Among the Greeks, vast, airy, public places, used to receive, under the orders, and with the authorisation of the *Epimeletes*, or curators, the animals and meat necessary for the subsistence of the citizens.

At Rome, the horned cattle market was situated in the eighth region, behind the Capitoline Mount.[50] It was a magnificent place, surrounded with beautiful galleries, in the midst of which stood on its pedestal, a gigantic brazen bull, at a little distance from the temple of Hercules—a round, mean edifice[51]—where dealers and their customers went to adore this god, the patron of butchers.

The way to reach the pig market was by going round the Quirinal Mount, near the bronze horses of Tyridates, in the seventh region of the town.[52] This market was the most important of all, on account of the immense consumption of pork by the Romans.

As soon as the officer of the Roman præfect appeared, the principal butchers gathered round him; he examined the cattle, regulated the sale, and fixed a price on the meat, from which they were not allowed to deviate,[53] and then only was the market open.

BUTCHERS.

Nothing among the Greeks indicates that they had butchers in the heroic ages. The warriors of Homer had no want of them, so great was their skill in cutting up the enormous pieces placed before them.[54] Ulysses acquired a reputation by his dexterity in this art; and it is more than probable that his martial companions also distinguished themselves by this kind of merit.

As soon as luxury had introduced into Greece that effeminate kind of existence which only permits certain men to be engaged in the painful or repulsive details of every-day life, *bouthutes*, or bullock slaughterers, became indispensable; and of them the meat was bought by the pound—weighed in the scale as now.[55]

The Romans had, at first, butchers who dealt in the same way, and who continued to do so for a long time; but they afterwards employed the following most extravagant method. The buyer shut one of his hands; the seller did the same; each of them suddenly opened the whole or a few of his fingers. If the fingers were even on each side, the seller had the price he pleased; if they were odd, the buyer gave his own price. This was called *micare*.[36] The mication was suppressed in the year 360, by a decree of Apronianus, which is worth quoting, because it points out in a clear and precise manner the attributions of the Roman butcher, and the system of sale since followed :—

" Reason and experience have proved to us, that it is of public utility to suppress the practice of mication for the sale of cattle, and that it is more advisable to sell by weight than to trust to a game with the fingers. We, therefore, ordain that, after the weight of the animal is ascertained, the head, feet, and tallow, shall belong to the butcher who has killed, prepared, and cut it up : this shall be his wages. The skin, flesh, and entrails, shall belong to the master-butcher who is to retail it. In this manner, the buyer and seller will know the weight of the meat on sale, and each will find this method to his advantage. * * * We will and decree that this ordinance be executed for ever, under pain of death."[57]

There were at first, in Rome, two corporations or colleges of butchers : one had to take care that the city was always sufficiently supplied with oxen, calves, and sheep :[53] the other was to provide that immense capital with the quantity of hogs necessary ;[59] and it would be difficult to form an idea of the number consumed by the Romans. Every day a distribution was made to the people, by Valentinian's order, of 24,086 pounds and eight ounces of pork ; to this amount, already considerable, must be added the truly prodigious daily sale ; for the entire population, from the highest to the lowest, were all passionately fond of this kind of food.[60]

The obligations and privileges of these two corporate bodies were nearly the same as those of the bakers.[61] The children could not, under any pretext whatsoever, abandon the trade of their fathers, without

---

DESCRIPTION OF PLATE No. VIII.

Scales and Weights.—The ancients had several species of scales. No. 1. A common scale, with two basins, and a movable weight, which is made in the form of a head, covered with the pileus, because Mercury had the weights and measures under his superintendence. This ornamented scale is engraved on a stone in the gallery of Florence.

No. 2. The Roman scale, beautifully made, with one tray, several hooks, and the movable weight, in the shape of a shell.

No. 3. Common heavy weight.

No. 4. The Roman weights had the form of a sphere, partly cut above and below; the greatest number of those which still subsist are of basalt. The number of ounces, or of pounds, is commonly engraved on the top, or inlaid with silver. All round it are inscriptions with the name of the temple where they were preserved after they had been stamped, together with the name of the prince, or the præfect before whom the standard mark was made.

On No. 4, is " D. N. Honori. Aug. Domini nostri Honorii Augusti ;" and on No. 5, " Temp. Opis. Aug.," or the temple of Opis Augusta.

Pl. 8.

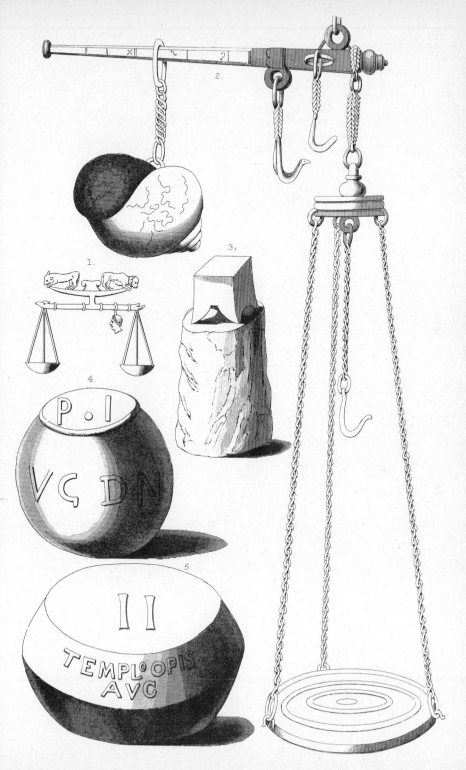

J.T.J. Tolant. del.

Chant & Saddler. sc.t

incurring the entire loss of their share in the common benefit allowed by the college. And, be it remembered, this trade was very lucrative, so much so that those who followed it in Rome always enjoyed a degree of opulence which sometimes caused the people to murmur. They elected from among themselves a chief, who judged their differences; he was, however, subordinate to the præfect of Rome.[62]

The members of the two corporations cut, weighed, and retailed the meat; they had under them working butchers, who killed, skinned, and trimmed the animals, and then brought them each one to the shop of his master.[63]

In the sequel, the two colleges met, and formed one. Subsequently, under the reign of Nero, which seemed at the beginning to promise the most brilliant prospect, the principal market for butchers became an edifice equal in magnificence to the Baths, the Circus, and Amphitheatres.[64] Eventually it was found necessary to erect two new buildings, on account of the increasing extent of the city and its inhabitants.[65] The Roman butchers sold both fresh and salt meat, like our own of the present day. It is not necessary to enter into any explanation respecting the first; as to the second, their method of preparation was somewhat different from the way we manage it now :—The animals they intended to salt were kept from drinking anything on the eve of the day they were to be killed. They boned the meat, and sprinkled it lightly with pounded salt ; then, after having well dried off all dampness, they again sprinkled some more salt, and placed the pieces, so as not to touch each other, in vessels which had been used for oil or vinegar. They poured sweet wine over, covered the whole with straw, and strewed snow all round, in order to make the meat better and more tender.[66]

When the cook wanted to extract the salt, he first boiled the meat well in milk, and afterwards in soft water.[67]

The flesh of various animals was also well preserved without salt. The only thing necessary was to cover each piece with honey, and to place it in a vessel hermetically closed, hung in a cool place. This operation was usually performed in winter, and succeeded equally well with meat, either cooked or raw.[68]

The following are some of the statutes of the pork butchers in France, during the middle ages :—

No one was to cook pork if it was not " *sufficient,* or had not good marrow."

No one could make " sausages of anything but pork."

No one could sell " black puddings, for it is a perilous viand." [69]

The French word *charcutier* (pork butcher) is derived from *caro cocta, chair cuite* (cooked meat).

The numerous regulations concerning the butchers in France during the 14th century rendered it difficult to carry on the trade :—

Prohibition to buy cattle except in the markets.

Prohibition to buy pigs fed by barbers or oil dealers.

Prohibition to kill cattle not a fortnight old.

Prohibition to kill cattle on the eve of fast days.

Prohibition to sell stale meat.

Prohibition to keep meat more than two days in winter, or more than one day and a-half in summer.

Prohibition to sell meat by lamp light or candle light.

The regulations respecting the cleanliness of the slaughter houses and the shambles were very long and very severe.[70]

A butcher in Paris kept but one single kind of meat, in the 14th century. Pork was sold only at Sainte-Geneviève, mutton at Saint-Marceau, veal at Saint-Germain, and beef at the market of the Châtelet.[71]

Philip Augustus gave statutes to the butchers of Paris in the year 1182. He enjoined them to observe the Sabbath, and permitted them to work on the other days, with the exception of the great festivals.[72]

The regulations imposed upon them in the 17th century are to the effect, that they shall not keep the fat from one week to another ; that they shall not mix the different kinds of suet ; and, lastly, that they shall not have more than three shops, and shall not allow the blood to run in the streets.[73]

XVI.

ANIMALS.

—•—

THE PIG.

IF intelligence, strength, or graceful beauty of form were to decide what rank this numerous class of animals—which has contributed its quota to the triumphs of the culinary art—should occupy on our tables, the pig, with its vile and stupid ugliness, its depraved habits, and its waddling obesity, would be banished for ever from the farm-yard and larder in every civilised nation of the world.

But, in refusing to it brilliant external qualities, Nature, by a wise compensation, has conferred on it others much more solid; and this quadruped, so despised during its life-time, does not fail after its death to conciliate the constant favour of rich and poor—of the man indifferent to the attractions of good cheer, and of the Sybarite, ever attentive to enlarge its domain.

Pliny, the naturalist, places the pig one degree below the scale of beings. Apicius, the cook, gives it a marked preference over all meats which passed through his skilful hands. From this, it will easily be understood that the pig presents itself first in this survey of the animal diet of those nations who have transmitted to us an account of their gastrophagic exertions.

History shows us this animal variously appreciated by different countries. Certain people consecrated it, when living, to their divinities most in vogue ; others honoured its image—a symbol, they thought, of the quiet happiness of states ; a small number abhorred it, and the greater part found it excellent eating

The inhabitants of Cyprus abstained from it, in order to offer it to Venus.[1] The Cretans loaded it with acorns and all the comforts of life, because Jupiter was first suckled by a sow in their island.[2] The Egyptian priests never allowed a ham to grace their feasts; they fled at the sight of pigs, unclean beings, whose presence alone defiled them,[3] although respected by the whole nation on account of the services they rendered in turning up the earth, and covering the seeds thrown upon it.[4]

The law of Moses forbad the Jews to eat this quadruped, or to touch it after its death,[5] and more than once they exposed themselves to the most frightful torments rather than be defiled by this proscribed viand.[6]

Tradition, again, strengthened their religious dread, by interdicting the faithful from even pronouncing the name of this animal, from looking at it, or selling it to foreign nations.[7]

The fear of the frightful malady to which the pig was subject in Palestine was, perhaps, the cause of this prohibition. Has not a Jewish doctor observed, that if ten measures of leprosy were to fall in the world, this unhappy animal would take nine parts for his share.[8] However, some theologians of that nation believe that the Messiah whom they expect will allow them the use of this now odious food.[9]

Like the Jews, the Phœnicians[10] and Indians[11] did not eat pork. The followers of Islamism also abstained from it, in consequence of a law of the Koran, which Mahomet borrowed from Moses.[12]

The Greeks and Romans had very different ideas. They knew that their gods showed a particular predilection for those altars on which bacon or swine's flesh smoked;[13] they therefore offered this meat in sacrifice to the Earth, the Lares, to Ceres;[14] and many a time a medal struck at Rome perpetuated the remembrance of this solemnity, in honour of the goddess of harvest.[15]

The pig, emblem of fecundity with these two nations,[16] became, on the banners of Italy, a sign of pardon and peace.[17] Kings and princes immolated two on their wedding-day;[18] and nations subdued by the Roman arms prostrated themselves before the standard, whose image promised them the clemency of their conquerors.[19]

The re-establishment of the succulent quadruped would have been complete, if the cynical carelessness of its rather inelegant habits had not caused it to become a symbol of debauchery and profligacy of manners.[20]

Hitherto the pig has only figured in a point of view purely historical; we have not sought to weaken its faults, nor have we made mention of the qualities attributed to it—for example, that of discovering truffles. Nevertheless, we ought not to lose sight of the fact, that this animal has not passed entirely without renown through the centuries which divide us from the earliest ages of the world. We shall now speak of its flesh, its exquisite flavour, and the place it occupied in feasts: there it reigned with honour; there we must follow it, with all that antiquity has possessed of celebrated men in the science of degustation and good living.

Nature has created the pig for man's palate; he is good only to be eaten; and life appears to have been given to him merely as a sort of salt to prevent his corrupting.[21] It is true that he possesses only a vulgar and purely animal substance; but how good is this substance, and how high does it deserve to be placed on account of its delicacy and flavour?[22]

Such is the praise of which a physician and two philosophers have thought it worthy.

The pig furnishes a strong and somewhat heavy kind of food;[23] wherefore wrestlers were recommended to eat much of it, and Galen advised it to persons who worked hard, or used violent exercise.[24]

But it was not necessary to recommend to the Greeks a meat of which they were so fond. Look over the long work of Athenæus—he everywhere extols it, everywhere speaks of it with fresh complacency, and in pompous terms.[25]

An Athenian, renowned as a man of taste and for the refined elegance of his table, would have thought his reputation lost had he not offered to his guests fat *andouilles*, sausages, pigs' feet, and pork cutlets; above all, he was careful not to forget salted and smoked hams—the honour of the banquet, and the delight of the human race.[26]

The Macedonian, Caranus, invited twenty of his best friends to his wedding, and gave them a feast, of which gastrophagic annals have preserved the remembrance. Each guest received from his munificence a flagon and crown of silver, a crown of gold, and vases of the same precious metal. What shall we say of the dishes displayed at this meeting of learned epicureans? Composed by the art of the most skilful cooks, struck with admiration, they ate and relished, whilst unexpected wonders unceasingly solicited their fatigued, yet not satiated, appetites; when at last appeared an immense silver dish, on which was displayed an entire roasted hog, whose vast sides concealed a multitude of quails and other small birds, *tétines de truie*, relishing yolks of eggs, oysters, and a host of shell fish, prepared with that scientific regard for gastric energy which considerably increases its power.[27]

Macedonia possessed a particular species of pig, greatly envied by the rest of Greece. Certain individuals of this giant race acquired enormous proportions, and King Eumenes used to give as much as sixty-four pounds sterling for one of these animals, provided it measured four feet seven inches in height, and as much in length.[28]

It will be easily understood that the cooks vied with each other, to see who could form unheard-of combinations with the succulent pieces which these enormous pigs furnished. They disguised the taste and form in a thousand different ways, and the most experienced palate was always the dupe of these exquisite deceptions. Thus Titius Quintus, a clever amateur, being enraptured with the number and astonishing variety of dishes which his host caused to be served, at Chalies in Etolia, what was his surprise when the amiable Amphytrion smilingly told him that he had eaten nothing but pork ! [29]

Rome, be it observed, knew how to follow the example of Greece; and, in the hands of its skilful cooks, the flesh of this heavy animal was often transformed into delicate fish, ducks, turtle doves, or capons.[30]

But the masterpiece of these great artists—the *ne plus ultra* of their fertile imagination—was the hog *à la Troyenne,* so named because from the depth of its inside issued battalions of thrushes, myriads of ortolans, and fig-peckers (becaficoes)—an ingenious image of those armed cohorts inclosed in the horse of Troy.[31] Everywhere the sumptuous dish is cited, but nothing is said of the manner in which it was prepared. The curious will perhaps be thankful to find that this omission is here repaired :—

The animal is artistically bled under the shoulder. When all the blood has flowed, the intestines are drawn out by the throat, and washed for a long time with wine, taking care to pass it through them. The pig is then hung up by the feet, and washed also with wine. An excellent gravy must be prepared beforehand, with meat hashed small and well peppered, with which you stuff the intestines, and then force them back into their place by the throat. Pour in at the same time a great quantity of gravy, and fill the animal with small game. Half of the pig is afterwards covered with a thick paste of barley meal, wine, and oil. It is then put into a portable oven, on a small metal

table, where it is roasted by a slow fire. When the skin has assumed
a fine colour it is withdrawn, and boiled on the other side; the paste
covering is then entirely removed, and the pig *à la Troyenne* may be
served.[32] The Romans reared a great number of these animals, and
also procured many from foreign countries, especially from Arcadia,
which produced some of extraordinary size. Varro relates that in this
part of the Peloponnesus he was shown a pig so fat that it was
impossible for the animal to make the least movement; and that
a mouse had settled on its back with her young family, softly
ensconced in the fat, where they fed at the expense of the careless
animal.[33]

Rome adopted, with a kind of gastronomic rage, the preparations
and *ragoûts* celebrated in Greece.[34] The Trojan pig never failed to
appear on tables renowned for their luxury;[35] and sucking pigs were
eaten in such profusion, that the censors were obliged to interdict their
use. Alexander Severus renewed this prohibition.[36] The large pigs
stuffed with game (an expensive delicacy of patrician tables) also called
forth new sumptuary laws,[37] which only provoked disdain, and which
fashion soon rendered obsolete.

We hardly dare mention a strange dish, in great request among the
rich and luxurious, who alone could procure it. The first preparation
consisted in stifling the young before they were littered.[38] Thank
Heaven, this culinary atrocity could not survive an epoch without
parallel, perhaps, in the history of human follies, by we know not what
refinement of incredible gluttony, of frightful depravity, and atrocious
cruelty, which, together, prepared the downfall of the Roman colossus.

Besides this disgusting dish, much was thought at Rome, as well as
at Athens, of pig's head, spare-rib, hams, and bacon. Seven other parts
occupied the second rank—these were the ears, feet, foreloin, fillet,
cheek, intestines, and blood.[39]

Westphalia supplied sumptuous tables with much-esteemed hams;
but those of Sardinia, Catalonia, and Cantabria were, nevertheless,
preferred.[40] They were sometimes served at the beginning of a repast,
in order to excite the appetite; and also often at the close, in order to
re-animate its extinguished ardour, and provoke new libations.[41] One
of the most ancient geoponics teaches how to prepare, salt, and smoke
hams;[42] for the inhabitants of the country, and the lower classes in the
cities, showed a singular taste for this delicate meat, which the Gauls

(great amateurs of pork)[43] sent them at a low price, with an enormous quantity of pickled pork, *andouillettes,* and sausages.[44]

This last preparation, very celebrated in Lucania,[45] served as a means of livelihood to a great number of Roman women, who also employed themselves in making excellent black puddings, in imitation of those eaten in Greece.[46]

Bacon was then of great utility, as in the present day, though oil superseded it in the concoction of a host of dishes. Bacon for a long time served almost as the exclusive food of the Romans,[47] before their unruly luxury had given it up to the soldiers and proletarians.[48] It was also found in all public houses,[49] where the populace habitually gorged themselves with pork, vegetables,[50] and hot water.[51]

The ancients salted the pig, in order to preserve it; but Apicius taught them a very simple process for the use of epicures, which advantageously replaced common brine. You take middling-sized pieces of pork, cover them entirely with a sort of paste, composed of salt, vinegar, and honey, and place them in vessels which you close carefully.[52]

We will now indicate some of the dishes most in vogue prepared with pork—a meat so much esteemed by the Greeks and Romans, and in which they believed themselves to have discovered fifty different flavours,[53] or fifty parts, each possessing a distinct taste from the other.

Apician Pork.—Roast a fine young sucking pig; and whilst a slow fire gently embellishes it with a golden colour, pound, with pepper and alisander, some coriander seed, mint, and rue. Then pour over it some wine, honey, garum, or gravy; mix with care these different ingredients, and pour this seasoning on your roast, as soon as you have taken it from the spit or oven.[54]

Macedonian Pork.—Choose, among a number of large and fine sucking pigs, the one which appears to you the most worthy of the culinary sacrifice. Draw it by the upper part; clean it well, and fill it with chicken sausages chopped small, the flesh of thrushes, ortolans, and pork; add Lucanian sausages, dates without stones, raisins, and afterwards, mallow, beet, leeks, parsley, coriander, whole pepper, and pine nuts; add eggs, and a good quantity of well-peppered gravy. Bake it, having previously scored the back of the animal, so that it may be basted with its own gravy. When a delightful odour shall then warn you that it is done, cover it, before serving, with a relishing mixture of pepper, rue, garum, or gravy, to which you must add wine, honey, and a little oil.[55]

Stuffed Sucking Pig.—The intestines are drawn out by the throat, and an opening made under the skin. You then fill with stuffing a bladder, to the neck of which is securely fixed a long and narrow tube, which will convey to every part the somewhat liquid substance which you will express from the bladder. The opening is then closed with parchment sewn to the skin. It is hardly necessary to say that this operation should be performed in several places.

Let us now see to the inside. Crush pepper, alisander, wild marjoram, and a little benzoin root; mix with this, garum or gravy, cooked brains, raw eggs, flour, and pork gravy; the whole must be boiled on a slow fire, and the pig filled with it, also with little birds, pine nuts, whole pepper, and garum. It now only remains to place it in the oven, watch over the cooking, baste it with gravy, and serve.[56]

Aristoxenic Ham.—Take a fresh ham, salt it, and smoke it two days; then rub it with a mixture of oil and vinegar, and hang it to the ceiling.[57] Some days after you must boil it with a great quantity of figs and three bay leaves; then take off the skin, make incisions in the flesh, and fill them with honey. Finally, prepare a paste of flour and oil, with which cover the ham; put it into the oven, and withdraw it only when this crust is completely done.[58]

Lucullian Ham.—Cook a ham, newly salted, with two pounds of barley and twenty-five figs. Then bone it, and slightly scarify the skin with an iron blade; put it into the oven, taking care to cover it with a little honey. When it begins to colour, put into a saucepan some cooked wine, pepper, wine and a bunch of rue, the half of which is then poured on the ham. The other half of this seasoning serves to humect the quenelles which you have taken beforehand from the ham previous to baking; these must be well soaked with gravy, and then, if you have any remaining, pour it over the ham, which you serve surrounded by the quenelles.[59]

Ventre de Truie à l'Athénienne.—It is boiled with sweet herbs and served with a seasoning of cummin seed, vinegar, and silphium.[60]

Ventre de Truie à la Romaine.—It is cooked in the manner before described, and seasoned with a sauce composed of pepper, parsley seed, dried mint, benzoin-root, honey, vinegar, and garum.[61]

Fillet of Pork à la Bœotienne.—When it has been covered with honey and vinegar, and baked in the oven, it is eaten with a seasoning of pepper, benzoin, and garum.[62]

Tétines de Truie à la Salienne.—Cook them in water; make several incisions; cover them with salt, and place them in the oven, or on the gridiron; prepare a seasoning of pepper and alisander, with garum, wine, and cooked wine; thicken with fine flour; put in the *tétines*, and serve.[63]

Tétines à la Flamine.—Mix the flesh of a sea-hedge hog with carrots and pepper; introduce the mixture into the *tétines;* sew up the opening; cook them in the oven, or on the gridiron, and eat them with brine and mustard.[64]

Olympian Pig's Liver—Take the liver of a pig that has been fed only on figs, bake it, and serve with a seasoning of œnogarum, pepper, thyme, alisander, garum, oil, and a little vinegar.[65]

Capitolian Pig's Liver.—Make incisions in the liver of a pig that has been fed on nothing but figs, and put it into garum with pepper, alisander, and two bay leaves; then wrap it in the caul, cook it on the gridiron, and serve.[66]

Campanian Bacon.—It is cooked by just covering it with water and a good quantity of dill, to which a little oil and salt are afterwards added.[67]

Quenelles of Pig's Liver and Brains.—Roast a pig's liver, and take off all the fibrous parts; sprinkle it with pounded pepper and rue; add some gravy; stir the whole well; then cut it into small slices, each of which you must cover with a bay leaf; hang them over the smoke as long as you think necessary.

When you wish to eat them, roast them afresh; then put them into a mortar, with pepper, alisander, and wild marjoram; stir them, add gravy and dressed sucking pigs' brains, pounded with care; then add five eggs, and dissolve them in such a manner as to make the whole thoroughly compact; pour over it some gravy, and cook in a saucepan; when cooked, throw it on a very clean table, and cut this pulp into small square pieces, which mix in the mortar with pepper, alisander, and wild marjoram. When you have gently stirred all this, it must again be put into a saucepan, and boiled over a slow fire. At the moment of ebullition, pour it on a plate, sprinkle with pepper, and serve.[68]

Lucanian Sausages.—Pound in a mortar some pepper, cummin, and winter savory with bay leaves, and moisten with gravy and garum ; then add to this mixture some pork, chopped small, more garum and pepper, and a good quantity of bacon, with a few pine nuts. When these various ingredients are well incorporated one with another, you stuff the prepared intestines, and hang up the sausages.[69]

Imperial Sausages.—Cut some pork into very small pieces, which must be pounded with the finest bread, well-soaked in wine ; then pound some pepper and decorticated myrtle leaves, and add some gravy. Make some small sausages, and put inside some fir-nuts. When these sausages are finished, you must cook them over a slow fire, with sweet wine, previously reduced to a-third.[70]

The following is the seasoning you must add to it :—

Bone some small chickens, and put them into a saucepan, with leeks, dill, and salt. When this is cooked, add pepper and smallage seed ; then crumble some sesame bread, on which pour some very thick gravy, mix the whole well, and serve with the sausages.[71]

The Gauls had very considerable herds of swine, which they fed exclusively upon acorns. The inhabitants of the towns reared them in their houses. As these animals went frequently out, they caused some obstruction, and we know that Philip, grandson of Louis-le-Gros, lost his life in Paris, in consequence of a furious pig having run between the legs of his horse, and caused him to fall. This accident took place on the 1st October, 1131. The 3rd of the same month a proclamation was issued, forbidding all persons to let their swine ramble through the streets of Paris. A short time after, those which belonged to the Abbaye Saint-Antoine were privileged ; the abbess and the nuns having represented that it would be a want of courtesy to their patron saint not to exempt his hogs from the general rule.[72]

A new proclamation of the 20th January, 1350, interdicted with still greater severity the rearing of swine in the town of Paris, under penalty of a fine of 60 sous (two shillings and four-pence); and the police were authorized to kill them wheresoever they might be found, to take the head as a perquisite for themselves, and to deposit the carcase at the Hôtel-Dieu (the name of an hospital), charging that establishment with the cost incurred for its conveyance [73]

There was nothing more delicate in the 16th century, nothing more odoriferous, than the flesh of young pigs fed on parsnips,[73A] and roasted, with a stuffing of fine herbs.[73B]

THE OX.

A profound sentiment of gratitude has been often the cause of rendering to the ox extraordinary honours, which no animal, perhaps, ever
shared with him. The Egyptians considered this quadruped as the
emblem of agriculture, and of all that serves to support existence;[74] and
incense smoked on its altars at Memphis and Heliopolis.[75]

The Phœnicians religiously abstained from its flesh, and the Phrygians punished with death whosoever dared to slay the labouring ox.[76]

In Greece, during the heroic ages, an ox was the reward adjudged
to the conquering wrestlers and pugilists; a horse was the prize of
racing or the quoits.[77]

At a later period the Athenians decreed that their coins should bear
the image of this useful quadruped;[78] and though they then offered it
to their gods, the ceremonies even of the sacrifice testified the repugnance felt at shedding its blood.

The sacrificer fled with the greatest speed after he had struck it;
he was followed, and, to avoid being arrested, he threw away the axe he
had used, and accused it of causing the death of the innocent ox. The
axe was then seized and tried; some one defended it, and alleged that i
was less guilty than the grinder who had sharpened the blade. The
latter cast the odium of the crime on the grinding stone, so that the
trial was never ended, and the pretended offence remained unpunished.[79]

For a long time the greater part of the ancients considered it a sin
to eat the flesh of the ox, the companion of the agriculturist, whose
patient vigour hollows the furrow which is to be the means of his
support.[80] But the bad example of Proserpine, who prepared one for
Hercules,[81] caused these scruples, one by one, to be hushed, the solemn
prohibition of the legislator of Athens forgotten;[82] and, in spite of the
obstinate resistance of the Pythagorians and the disciples of Empedocles,
every one declared in favour of the doctrines of Zeno and Epicurus.

Moreover, it is certain that the heroes of Homer were not so
scrupulous: Menelaus offered roast-beef to Telemachus; Agamemnon
also presented some to the wise Nestor; and an ox, roasted whole, frequently appeased the robust appetite of the illustrious chiefs of Greece.[83]

If we go back to centuries still more remote, and of which a venerable historian has preserved us an account, we find herds of oxen were possessed by the great patriarchal families.* [84] Abraham cooked a calf and served it to the three angels, in the valley of Mamre;[85] and the flesh of this animal, whether ox or heifer, was evidently much in use in the primitive ages, since no particular proscription exempts them from those beings having "life and motion,[86] and which are to serve us as food.[87] As to Moses, far from interdicting it to the Israelites, he places the ox in the first rank of pure animals,[88] whose flesh was allowed them.

The oracle of ancient medicine, Hippocrates, praises the flesh of the ox, in which he recognises the most nutritious qualities, but nevertheless he believes it to be heavy and indigestible.[89]

Of what material, then, must have been the stomach of Theagenes, of Thasos—he, who devoured a whole bull in one day.[90]

To be sure, the same exploit is attributed to Milo of Crotona, whose ordinary meal consisted of eighteen pounds of meat, as much bread, and fifteen pints of wine.[91] These formidable polyphagists could, without much expense, indulge their fabulous appetites; for, in the time of Demosthenes, 354 B.C., an ox of the first quality cost only eighty drachmas, or about two pounds, eleven shillings, and eightpence.[92]

Magiric writers have left us very few details on the different methods of cooking the flesh of the ox or calf. It appears to have been generally roasted,[93] in which case it was eaten alone; but sometimes it was eaten boiled, with one of the sauces to be hereafter mentioned.

These animals were fed with particular care, in order to render them more worthy of the luxurious tables for which certain choice pieces were destined. The manner of fattening oxen has already been described: it is only necessary to add, that calves, which were to be slaughtered, received no other food than their mothers' milk; and that, frequently, they were not killed before the expiration of a twelvemonth.[94]

Double tripe was reputed as an excellent food. The Asiatics,

---

* The word Ox—*Bos*—is a general term applied equally by sacred and profane writers to the bull, ox, and cow.—VALLA, lib. iv., cap. 42. It would appear that the castration of bulls originated with the Greeks, though they and the Romans, their imitators, saw only in this operation the facility of subduing them, and accustoming them to the yoke.—GEOPONICS, COLUMELLA, PLINY, &c.

Greeks, and Romans were particularly fond of it. It was served at a
sumptuous repast prepared for Achilles; and Homer observes, that
this dish was always honourably received at the banquets of heroes.[95]

Athenæus, describing a feast of the most exquisite elegance, names
double tripe among a host of dishes he enumerates;[96] he also says,
speaking of a state dinner at which Philoxenus, one of the generals
of Alexander the Great, was a guest, that first of all there appeared
large basins containing the intestines of animals, disposed with art around
their heads :[97]   and it is thus, he adds, that even the gods gave themselves up, in the society of their friends, to the pleasures of good
cheer.[98]   To be brief, this artless chronicler of antique gastrophagy,
tells us that after the sacrilegious undertaking of the Titans, the human
race enjoyed such perfect happiness, that men caused to be served
at every one of their repasts delicious double tripe and savoury intestines.[99]

This touching example of felicity and innocent gluttony found few
imitators at Rome among that class of voluptuous men who entertained,
at enormous expense, tasters whose discriminating palates could tell
whether a fish had been caught at the mouth of the Tiber, or further off;
whether a goose's liver had been fattened with fresh figs, or only on
dried ones.[100]   For them tripe could have very little attraction, but this
rather plebeian dish appeared with honour on modest tables, and prole-
tarian epicures sought for it with eagerness.[101]

Beef à l'Ibérienne.—Well boil an excellent piece of beef, and serve
it with the following sauce. Grind and mix pepper, alisander, parsley
seed, wild marjoram, and dried onions; moisten with sun-made raisin
wine; stir, and add honey, vinegar, wine, garum, oil, and sweet wine.[102]

Stewed Beef à la Sarmate.—Carefully choose a piece of beef, which
stew slowly for a long time with leeks, cut small, onions, or beans.
When it is well cooked, pour over a mixture of pepper, benzoin, and a
little oil.[103]

Dish of Veal à la Syracusaine.—Cook a piece of veal, on a slow
fire, with pepper, alisander, carrots, and parsley seed, bruised together in
a mortar; then add honey, vinegar, garum, and oil; thicken the whole
with fine flour, and serve.[104]

Noix de Veau à la Tarantaise.—Take a *noix de veau*, cook it in a
saucepan with pepper, alisander, and fenugreek seed; add, later, some
wild marjoram, pine nuts, and dates; then moisten with a mixture of

honey, vinegar, garum, mustard, and oil. When the cookery of these various substances shall have made an homogeneous whole, serve.[105]

Cisalpine Preserve.—Mince some beef in very small pieces; do the same with a little bacon; add pine nuts, pounded with dates; pour on the whole a mixture of vinegar, garum, mustard, and oil; stir well, and throw on this pulp a powder of strong odoriferous herbs. Stir it a long time, let it rest, compress it strongly in a prepared intestine, close the opening, and put a string round to tighten it still more. This preserve cannot turn bad.[106]

The ox was so precious among the Romans, that mention is made of a certain citizen accused before the people and condemned, because he had killed one of his oxen to satisfy the fancy of a young libertine, who told him he had never eaten any tripe. He was banished, as if he had killed his farmer.[107]

The Brahmin women think to obtain abundance of milk and butter by invoking one particular cow,—the darling cow of the king of heaven; the type, mother, and patroness of all cows. The entire species are treated with the greatest deference; they have lavished upon them every expression of gratitude, and one day of each year is set apart as a solemn festival consecrated to their worship.[108]

Some centuries ago the large pieces of meat were boiled first, and then roasted. Roasted meat was always served with sauce. Animals roasted whole were generally filled with an aromatic stuffing. Sage was the common seasoning for geese, and sucking-pigs were stuffed with chesnuts. Some minutes before these were taken from the spit, they were covered with bread crumbs; and appeared on the table enveloped in a crust composed of bread, sugar, orange juice, and rose water.[109]

Bœuf Gras.—There is a very old custom in the whole of France, and which consists in leading throughout the streets, in the provincial towns, on Shrove Tuesday, a fatted ox, ornamented with flowers and ribbons. This ceremony is considered as a commemorative emblem of the fecundity of the earth. In Paris, the ox chosen for the same purpose has generally obtained beforehand the prize awarded by the Agricultural Society. The horns of the animal are gilded; he is afterwards decorated in a sumptuous manner, and led through the principal thoroughfares of that city, on Shrove Sunday, Monday, and Tuesday, to the Palace of the Tuileries, the ministerial residences, the Hôtel-de-Ville, and the foreign embassies. Troops of butchers, dressed in appropriate fancy costumes, both on horseback and on foot, are preceded by bands of music ; and the heathen divinities, drawn by eight horses in a richly gilt triumphal car, form one of the most splendid and grotesque pageants of modern times.

———•———

THE LAMB.

Formerly, sworn examiners of the clouds, skilful in discovering the storms they concealed, announced to the inhabitants of the country the hail by which their crops were threatened, and every one immediately offered a sacrifice to the inimical cloud, in order that it might carry ruin and desolation elsewhere. The most devout sacrificed a lamb ; the luke-warm worshippers a fowl ; some even contented themselves with pricking their finger with a pin, and throwing towards heaven the drops of blood which came out. The cloud, it is said, satisfied with these pious offerings, soon disappeared never to return.[110]

The lamb, an oblation pure and agreeable in the sight of the gods, reconciled the earth with Olympus. In Egypt, the inhabitants of Sais and Thebes offered it to their divinities.[111] Minerva and Juno also were pleased to see its flesh smoking on the altars which Greece and Italy raised to them.[112]

These practices, no doubt, were an obscure imitation of the religious rites which Moses prescribed to his people,[113] and which heathen nations adopted in their turn, one from the other.[114]

The Hebrew law forbad the killing of the Paschal lamb before it was weaned, and also the cooking of it in its mother's milk. It was to be eaten roasted, with unleavened bread, lettuces, mustard, or bitter herbs : whatever might remain was to be burnt with fire. It was not to be boiled, nor a bone of it broken. It must be chosen of that year, a male, and without fault or blemish.[115]

Many passages of the sacred writings allow us to appreciate the pastoral riches of the first nations of the East ; and an idea may be formed of the number of their flocks, when we are told that Jacob gave the children of Hamor a hundred sheep for the price of a field ;[116] and that the King of Israel received a hundred thousand every year from the

King of Moab, his tributary, and a like number of rams, covered with their fleece.[117]

The delicate flesh of the lamb was the ornament of the tables of the voluptuous inhabitants of Sion and Samaria. The prophet Amos reproaches them with this luxury, and threatens them with the Divine anger[118] on that account. The Greeks carried their love for this meat to such a height, that the magistrates of Athens were obliged to forbid the eating of lamb which had not been shorn.[119] This restriction did not prevent the epicures of Attica from buying one of these animals every day, which cost them ten drachmas[120] (6s. 5d.), and the head of which, prepared with art, heightened the beauty of the first course.[121] Rome and Italy imitated Greece,[122] and the flocks of the fertile Campania hardly sufficed for the exigencies of the capital of the world, especially towards the end of autumn, a period at which lambs afforded, according to the Romans, a more highly flavoured and wholesome meat than in the spring.[123]

Lamb's Head à la Quirinale.—The head is boiled with pepper, garum, and beans, and served with a sauce consisting of garum, pepper, benzoin, and cummin, to which is added a little oil, and small pieces of bread, soaked in sweet wine.[124]

Quarter of Lamb à l'Esquilin.—Place a quarter of lamb in a saucepan with onions and coriander, chopped very small. Then pound pepper, alisander, and cummin; put to it some oil, wine, and garum. Pour the whole on the lamb; cook well, and thicken with fine flour.[125]

Palatine Broil.—Leave a piece of lamb during some time in a mixture of pepper, benzoin, garum, and oil. After having cooked it in oil and garum, put it a little while on the gridiron, sprinkle with pepper, and serve.[126]

Roast Lamb à la Phrygienne.—Bake a lamb and serve it with the following sauce:—Mix well half an ounce of pepper, six scruples of cinnamon, a little ginger, half a pint of excellent garum, and the quarter of that quantity of oil.[127]

Lamb à la Trimalcion.—Draw a lamb at the neck; preserve the intestines entire, and wash them with the greatest care; fill them with force meat and garum; put them back again by the same way; sew up the opening, and place the lamb in the oven. Then mix gravy and milk; add pounded pepper, garum, wine, sweet wine, and oil; let it boil only an instant; thicken with fine flour, and serve it with the lamb.[128]

Blount informs us of a very ancient and rather strange custom. He says :—

" At Kidlington, in Oxfordshire, the custom is, that on Monday after Whitson week, there is a fat, live lamb provided, and the maids of the town, having their thumbs tied behind them, run after it, and she that with her mouth takes and holds the lamb is declared *Lady of the Lamb*, which, being dressed, with the skin hanging on, is carried on a long pole before the Lady and her companions to the Green, attended with music, and a morisco dance of men and another of women, when the rest of the day is spent in dancing, mirth, and merry glee. The next day the lamb is part baked, boiled, and roast, for the Lady's feast, where she sits majestically at the upper end of the table, and her companions with her, with music and other attendants, which ends the solemnity."[129]

THE KID.

The kid was one of the most delicate dishes of the Hebrews : Rebecca prepared some for Isaac, in order to dispose him to give his blessing to Jacob.[130] Moses ordered that, for the Feast of Passover, a lamb or a kid should be slain.[131] Samson carried a kid to his young wife when he wished to be reconciled to her.[132] The brother of the prodigal son complains to his father that he has never given him a kid to make merry with his friends.[133]

The Egyptians, who represented their god Pan with the face and legs of a goat, abstained religiously from killing a kid or eating its flesh.[134] Their veneration for this animal went so far, in some countries, that goat-keepers appeared in their eyes invested with an august and sacred character.[135] The Greeks did not judge it convenient to adopt these strange ideas, although on other points their theology was sufficiently ridiculous. The kid was considered one of the most dainty dishes in state banquets; it was served whole, on a silver basin, to each of the guests at the wedding of the Macedonian, Caranus.[136]

The kids of Attica were especially praised, and a considerable trade was made of them in Athens.[137]   Certain connoisseurs, whose authority had weight, preferred, however, those produced in the Island of Mælos.[138] A great many also came from Sicily : they were in less repute, and sold at a low price.[139]

At Rome, the kid of Italy was much thought of ; the most delicate were fattened at Tivoli,[140] and in different localities of the Roman Campagna.[141]

Kid à la Trans-Tibérienne.—The kid is to be cooked slowly, with a little milk, four ounces of honey, an ounce of pepper, a little salt and benzoin.   After some time, add eight dates crushed in a mortar, a little gravy, garum, a small quantity of excellent wine ; the whole is thickened with fine flour.[142]

Roast Kid à la Janiculum.—Empty and carefully clean a kid ; rub it well with oil and pepper ; sprinkle with salt and a large quantity of coriander seed ; place it in the oven, and bake slowly.[143]

Kid à la Tarpéienne.—Empty the kid ; stuff it, and sew it up ; then entirely cover it with a thick mixture of pepper, rue, winter savory, onions, a small quantity of thyme, and some garum ; then place it in an oven, or on a dish, covered with oil.   When the kid is cooked, you surround it with a sauce of winter savory, onions, rue, dates, mixed with wine, oil, and cooked wine ; sprinkle with pepper, and serve.[144]

Kid à la Tivoli.—Bake the kid ; then pound some pepper, rue, onions, winter savory, and Damascus plums (without their stones), a little benzoin, which you must dilute in wine, garum, and oil ; throw this sauce on the kid as you withdraw it from the oven, and, at the moment of serving, cover it with boiling wine.[145]

Kid à la Mélissienne.—Draw the kid at the neck, and clean the intestines ; then pound some pepper, alisander, benzoin root, two bay leaves, and a little Spanish camomile ; add two or three brains ; mix them well together ; then add some garum and a little salt ; afterwards, a small quantity of milk and honey.   Fill the intestines with this stuffing, and place them round the kid, which you then put into a large basin on the fire.   When half-cooked, you must add a mixture of garum, oil, and wine.   Then bruise some pepper and alisander seed, which moisten with the gravy of the kid, and a little cooked wine ; pour it into the basin, and the moment before serving thicken with fine flour.[146]

THE ASS.

The ass was an impure animal, according to the law of Moses, whose flesh was forbidden because it did not ruminate.[147] However, at the siege of Samaria, the Jews were compelled to eat it for want of other food. The famine was such, that the head of an ass was sold for eighty pieces of silver.[148]

The Roman peasants thought the flesh of the young ass had a very agreeable taste,[149] and regaled themselves with it at their rustic festivals. The celebrated Mecænas one day tasted of this dish at the house of one of his free slaves; he spoke of it with much praise, caused it to be served on his own table, and even succeeded in introducing it on those of the great and rich, who gave up the onager, or wild ass, which they had hitherto preferred, to humour this illustrious favourite. But this new gastronomic conquest had only a short vogue; and was forgotten after the death of Mecænas.[150] Galen tells us that the cooks of Alexandria thought much of the ass,[151] whose flesh, he says, much resembles that of the stag.[152] Still, this great physician disapproves of the use of this food, which he considers unsuited to mankind.[153]

It is asserted, even at the present day, that the flesh of the young ass is a pretty good dish; we have heard, but we hardly can repeat it, that much is consumed in the *guinguettes* round Paris, where the artless customers are far from thinking that anything else but veal can be served to them.

The modern restaurateurs of the Barrières of Paris, have, perhaps, read the biography of Mecænas, and endeavour to render popular the dish so honoured by the celebrated favourite. Who can blame them?

––––—•—––––

THE DOG.

We must beg pardon of the reader for informing him that the dog presented a very relishing dish to many nations advanced in culinary science. To them, one of these animals, young, plump, and delicately prepared, appeared excellent food.[154]

The Greeks, that people so charming by their seductive folly, their love of the arts, their poetic civilization, and the intelligent spirit of research presiding over their dishes—the Greeks (we grieve to say it) ate dogs, and even dared to think them good: the grave Hippocrates himself—the most wise, the least gluttonous, and therefore the most impartial of their physicians—was convinced that this quadruped furnished a wholesome and, at the same time, a light food.[155]

As to the Romans, they also liked it,[156] and no doubt prepared it in the same manner as the hare, which they thought it resembled in taste.[157]

However, it is but right to add, that this dish, which we will not even hear mentioned, was never favourably received by the fashionable portion of Roman society, and that the legislators of ancient gastrophagy even repulsed it with disdain.

There is every reason to believe that the people regaled themselves with a roast or boiled dog, especially once a year, at the period when they celebrated the deliverance of the Capitol from the siege of the Gauls. It is known that, at this solemnity, a goose, laid on a soft cushion, was carried in triumph, followed by an unhappy dog nailed to a cross,[158] whose loud cries greatly amused the populace. In this manner they commemorated the signal service rendered by one animal, and the fatal negligence of the other. The Gauls scaled the Capitol while the dogs slept, and Rome had been lost if the deafening cries of the geese had not given an alarm to the garrison, who, it must be allowed, should have kept better watch.

The quadrupeds last mentioned are the only domestic animals of the kind used as food by the ancients. The chase afforded them several others, which we shall mention, after having just glanced at the poultry —one of the most interesting divisions in natural history for the serious and reflective appreciator of gastronomic productions.

XVII.

POULTRY.

The air is less dense than the earth, said Aristotle; poultry ought, then, to stand higher in estimation than quadrupeds.[1] It is, adds Galen, the lightest and best of all aliments.[2] After this, would any one dare to accuse of sensuality those who, wisely following the diet recommended by these great men, prefer a fat capon or delicate fowl, to heavy, common butcher's meat?

Our masters, the ancients, have left us fine examples on this head. In vain did impertinent sumptuary laws, enemies of progress, strive to repress the luxury of the farm-yards. These precautions on behalf of abstinence against the magiric genius were unceasingly met by a resistance, as energetic as it was truly Roman. Fannius, Archius, Cornelius, could make martyrs; but let us say, with pride, good cheer never had cause to envy them deserters and apostates. One of these tyrannical decrees was just published; a tribune of the people, a man of heart and taste, undertook to have it repealed. He courageously mounted the rostrum, and cried, with an inspired voice: "Romans! you are treated like slaves. By the gods! what can be more strange than the new law? They would force you to sobriety, whether you will or no! They would impose temperance on you! Ah! renounce this pretended liberty, of which you are so jealous, since you are no longer allowed to ruin yourselves, each one according to his fancy, or die of indigestion if you please."

This discourse was received as it deserved to be, and unanimous applause proved to the orator that he was addressing men capable of understanding him. But, alas! this excellent tribune had a dangerous enemy: the censor, Lucius Flaccus, a sort of fanatic teetotaller and carniphobis of that time, had sufficient credit to cause this worthy citizen to be driven from the senate. But Rome revenged him by devouring more poultry than ever.[3]

In the early ages of the Church, poultry in general was regarded as a food for fast days; and this opinion was founded on the text in Genesis, where it is said that birds and fishes were created on the fifth day, whereas quadrupeds were created on the sixth.[4]

St. Benedict, in his rule, does not formally forbid the monks any other flesh than that of quadrupeds; and St. Columbanus, in his, permits the monks the flesh of poultry, in default of fish. The Greek monks ate it down to the 10th century.

THE COCK.

An object of divine worship in Syria,[5] the cock was considered by almost every nation as the emblem of vigilance and courage.[6] Thus, heathen antiquity consecrated it to the god of battles.[7] Themistocles, marching with his army against Xerxes, King of Persia, met with some cocks fighting furiously; he made his troops halt, that they might observe them, and he then addressed a spirited discourse to them on the subject. He conquered, and on his return to Athens, desired that every year a cock-fight should commemorate his victory.[8] These cruel games soon spread throughout Greece, and feathered champions were reared with great care, and obtained at a high price from Rhodes, Bœotia, Mela, and Chalcis.[9]

Italy also wished to enjoy this barbarous pastime. At Pergamus, any spectator might throw a cock into the arena, and a prize was awarded to the lucky possessor of the bird who remained master of the field of battle.[10]

This warlike bird has never enjoyed a high culinary reputation; nevertheless, it was eaten when old, that is to say, at that period of its life when its flesh, hard, fibrous, and tough, possesses neither juice nor flavour—then this wretched food was left to those among the common people who joyously feasted in the drinking-shops of Rome. They,

K

however, always avoided making fricassees of white cocks, because they were consecrated to the month, and proclaimed the hours.[11]

THE CAPON.

The cock being banished from the table of all respectable people, the necessity of dressing hens became evident, for it was necessary to live. Now, you are aware that there are two sorts of hens; one sort consumptive looking and tough, the other tender, plump, and before which an epicure banishes every other thought, and sighs with pleasure. These last were preferred, and, in order to render them more worthy of the voluptuous epicures for whom they were intended, they learned from the inhabitants of the island of Cos the art of fattening them in dark and closed places, with certain wonderful pastes, which increased their delicacy and tempting whiteness.[12]

This ingenious invention belonged to Greece and Asia. Rome possessed herself of it, and even improved it; but soon the constant tyrant of the kitchen, the Consul, C. Fannius, who thought bad what others thought good, and who pretended that in consequence of the immense consumption made of them, the result would be that not a living hen would be left in the empire, ordered that for the future the Romans should dispense with fattening and eating this delicious winged animal.[13]

Fortunately, the law said nothing about young cocks; this silence saved Roman gastronomy, and the capon was invented.[14] It is not necessary to relate with what transports of delight this new creation was greeted; it will be easily understood. Rome was moved; the famous Greek cooks, who consecrated their science to *her*, were on tip-toe. Everywhere, from mouth to mouth, spread the name of the skilful enchanter, who could in such a manner metamorphose the clarion of the farm yard. Fannius, himself, it is said, wished to be assured of the truth of the prodigy : he was served with a roast capon, and the praises he bestowed on it were assuredly the triumph of the bird, of epicures, and of art.[15] From this remarkable epoch, nearly all chickens underwent the ingenious transformation which rendered them so welcome to all Lucullian tables;[16] and it caused such a destruction of birds, that the consul repented, but too late, that he had only named hens in his sumptuary law.

Capon à la Déliaque.—Draw completely a fat capon ; then bruise pepper, alisander, and ginger, which you must mix with sausage-meat and fine flour, and a pig's brains cooked ; add some eggs, then some garum, a little oil, whole pepper, and several pine nuts. Make a stuffing of this mixture, and put it into the capon, which afterwards roast before a slow fire.[17]

THE HEN

The cackling of hens infallibly announced, among the ancients, some dreadful calamity to the person who had the misfortune to hear it.[18] This fatal omen must have rendered a great number of people unfortunate ; for whether she lays eggs, or conducts her young family, a hen generally cackles.

They therefore sought to diminish the number of these birds of ill-omen ; they fattened them for eating, and they did right, since, according to learned physicians, the flesh of these birds is good for weakly persons, as well as those who are convalescent.[19] Healthy individuals also find this food suit them perfectly. In Greece there would have been something wanting at a feast, if fat hens had not been served. They embellished the celebrated wedding repast of Caranus ; and Athenæus often speaks of them when describing a grand banquet.[20]

At Rome, the art of fattening them became a serious occupation, which was long studied, and had its precepts and rules. Marcus Lœlius Strabo, belonging to the order of knights, invented aviaries in which hens were confined ;[21] others sought and discovered the means of giving to their flesh that particular flavour unperceived by uncultivated palates, but which the experienced gastrophilist always appreciates. They patiently gave themselves up to laborious experiments : a warm, narrow, dark spot received these interesting *volatiles* ; the feathers of their wings and tails were plucked, and they were gorged twice a day during three weeks with balls of barley flour mixed with soft water. Great cleanliness was combined with this diet : their heads were well cleansed, and care taken that no insect should enter the aviary.[22]

Afterwards barley flour, kneaded with milk, was preferred : then, instead of milk, water, and honey were employed. Excellent wheaten bread, soaked in good wine and hydromel, was also used with success.[23]

Skilful breeders by these means obtained magnificent hens of an incredibly exquisite flavour, and which weighed no less than sixteen pounds.[24]

The Fannian law unfortunately came, and, as we have before observed, brought impediments to these beautiful results by interdicting aviaries and skilfully prepared pastes. It is true that this law allowed a farm-yard hen to be served at every repast [25]—*mais une poule par jour est-ce contentement?* It became necessary, then, to have recourse to a *mezzo-termine*, which was discovered in the capon. But the favourite dish forbidden by the consular authority was not altogether abandoned : some faithful epicureans always possessed in the shade well-furnished aviaries ; and it was even then, we are assured, that Rome and the universe were enriched with the *poularde*.[26]

Poularde à la Viminale:—Cook a fine hen in its gravy ; pound and mix benzoin, pepper, oil, and garum, a little thyme, fennel seed, cummin, mint, and rue ; stir for a long time ; add some vinegar ; pound some dates, and mix them with honey and a little vinegar. Of all this make a homogeneous seasoning, and pour it on the hen when it is cold.[27]

THE CHICKEN.

It is certainly surprising that a people so serious as the Romans generally were, should make the success of the greatest enterprise depend on the appetite of their famous sacred chickens. They were brought from the Island of Negropont, and were kept shut up in cages ; their guardian was designated by the name of Pullarius.[28]

Publius Claudius, constrained to consult these strange prophets before engaging in a naval combat, ordered them to be fed ; they refused to open their beaks. The incredulous general ordered them at once to be thrown into the sea, and laughingly exclaimed to the dismayed Pullarius : "Since they will not eat—well! then let us make them drink."[29]

Diodorus of Sicily, and some ancient writers, tell us that the Egyptians, from a remote period, hatched chickens in ovens. This process is decidedly of the highest antiquity, and was applied to the eggs of all kinds of poultry.[30] . In the last century, Réaumur tried various experiments, and recovered this art, which was thought to have been lost; others again have followed the steps of this skilful observer, and, at the present day, obtain the most satisfactory results.

Chickens have ever been considered an estimable food, and hardly yielded to the two glories of their family—the fattened hen and the capon.[31] The Greeks served them at all their feasts of ceremony, and the Romans granted them a distinguished place among the dishes of the second course.

Apician Macedonia of Chicken.—Chop small the meat of a chicken, which mix with a kid's breast, and put it into a saucepan with parsley seed, dried pennyroyal, dried mint, ginger, green coriander, and raisins; then add three pieces of the finest oaten bread, some honey, vinegar, oil, and wine; some time after, add some excellent cheese, pine nuts, cucumbers, and dried onions, well chopped. Pour some gravy over the whole, and when it is cooked, surround the dish on all sides with snow, and serve.[32]

Parthian Chicken.—Open the croup dexterously, and put it in the saucepan; then mix some pepper, alisander, a little carrot, garum, and wine; fill the chicken with this seasoning; cook well, and sprinkle with pepper before serving.[33]

Numidian Chicken.—Begin by boiling a chicken for some time; then place it in a stew-pan, after having sprinkled it with benzoin and pepper. Afterwards bruise some pepper, cummin, coriander seed, benzoin root, pine nuts, rue, and dates; add honey, vinegar, garum, and oil; boil, thicken with fine flour, sprinkle with pepper, and serve.[34]

Chicken à la Frontoniènne.—Half cook a chicken, and then put into the saucepan garum, oil, a bunch of dill, some leeks, winter savory, and green coriander. You then sprinkle with pepper, and serve.[35]

Chicken à la Cœlienne.—Cook a chicken with garum, oil, wine, coriander seed, and onion. Then put some milk and a little salt into another saucepan, with honey and a little water, and cook this mixture over a very slow fire. Throw in by degrees some raspings of sweet biscuits, and take care to stir continually. Put the chicken into this sauce, and then serve with a seasoning of pepper, alisander, and wild marjoram, mixed with honey and cooked wine, which must be boiled and thickened with fine flour.[36]

THE DUCK.

The duck swims so well it was thought to be paying a compliment to Neptune by sacrificing it to him.[37] The god of the seas never found fault with this offering.

Attica and the whole of Greece sought the beautiful ducks of Bœotia,[38] and that province was always found to have supplied a larger number than it reared. It is true the poulterers of Athens, banishing all scruples of conscience, rarely failed to satisfy their customers as to the doubtful origin of a white *nêssa* (duck), by taking Neptune to witness that it was a pure Bœotian, a real duck, as they said emphatically, of that species so much appreciated by connoisseurs. Future *quidnuncs* will examine whether the friendly duck of the English and the political and literary *canard* of the French have, or have not, found their way from Greece, after wandering a little on the road.

There were ducks at that prodigious dinner of the opulent Caranus, of whom we have already spoken several times. They were always served at the tables of the rich Greeks ;[39] and Archigenes reckons them among the viands which agree best with the stomach.[40] Cato was of the same opinion ; and, if we are to believe Plutarch, he made them the food of those of his family who were ill, and boasted of maintaining his children, servants, and himself in perfect health, by the aid of this diet alone.[41] It was the same idea that made Mithridates mix the flesh of ducks with all he ate, as an antidote against poison, which he feared.[42]

Hippocrates evinces a contrary opinion. The flesh of this bird seemed to him hard, heavy, and indigestible.[43] Avicenna goes still further : he threatens all who eat it with fever.[44] The Romans were no more frightened than the Greeks at the decision of the father of medicine. Lentulus, one of the high magiric authorities of Rome, ordered that the duck should figure in the most honourable manner at the brilliant feast of which Macrobius has preserved us an account.[45] It must, however, be remembered that polite people, who observed the forms and usages of society, only offered to their guests the breast and head of this biped; the remainder returned to the kitchen.[46]

Ducks' Brains à l'Epicurienne.—Cook some ducks' brains, and mince them very small; then place in a saucepan, with pepper, cummin, benzoin root, garum, sweet wine, and oil; add milk and eggs, and submit the whole to the action of a slow fire, or rather, cook them in a *bain-marie*.[47]

Apicius's Seasoning for a Roast Duck.—Make a mixture of pepper, cummin, alisander, mint, stoned raisins, or Damascus plums; add a little honey and myrtle wine; place it in a saucepan; cook, and then add to these substances vinegar, garum, and oil; afterwards some parsley and savory; serve with the roast duck.[48]

THE GOOSE.

When a flock of geese are obliged to pass Mount Taurus—the dreaded abode of their enemies, the eagles—each of them takes the precaution to hold a stone in its beak, in order that he may keep a profound silence, which, otherwise, his natural loquacity would render impossible.[49] This, if true, would justify Aristotle in attributing foresight to the goose;[50] a quality which Scaliger also claims for this bird.[51]

The ancients highly esteemed its flesh. Homer[52] and Athenæus[53] speak with praise of the fat geese and goslings which the Greeks ate.

The Egyptians served them at their meals every day; it was, with veal, the favourite dish of their monarchs,[54] and they did not forget to offer some to King Agesilaus, when he was travelling through the country.[55]

Some eastern nations were impressed with such deep veneration for this bird that they swore by nothing else.[56] The Britons honoured it, and forbad all persons to do it the least harm.[57] It remained for Queen Elizabeth to prove, at her joyous dinners of the 29th September, that tastes and usages are modified by time.[58] And moreover, many centuries before, her ancestors had been greatly wanting in respect towards a particular kind of goose, which they roasted without any ceremony.[59] A well-deserved sentiment of gratitude rendered them dear to the Romans: their noisy clamour had formerly saved the Capitol.[60] They became for them, as for the Egyptians,[61] a symbol of safety, and were reared, both in town and country, to guard the houses.[62]

Those which were kept, out of gratitude, in the Capitol, were consecrated to Juno, Isis, Mars, and Priapus,[63] and every year one of them was chosen for the brilliant and solemn ceremony we have already mentioned.[64]

But, alas! time obscures and effaces all the glories of this world; and that of the Roman geese, no doubt, had to submit to this sad fate,[65] for they were eaten at least a century before the time of Pliny. Unfortunate bird! Yes, a perfidious art fed them delicately in the shade, in convenient aviaries, where nothing was wanting for their comfort, and at the end of a few days the poor victims made but one step from this dangerous retreat to the place of execution.[66] The Emperor Alexander Severus became so fond of this dish, that on his great festival days they served him with a goose and a pheasant.[67] Nothing, in his estimation, could equal the exquisite flavour of these two birds.

The luxurious Romans, however, neglected the entire animal, and thought only of the liver. They invented the art of fattening this viscera, and of increasing its size to such an extent that it often weighed two pounds. To obtain this result, they simply fed their victims of sensuality, during twenty days, with a paste of dried figs and water.[68] As soon as the goose was killed, the liver was put to soak in milk and honey.

It is not known exactly to whom we are to attribute this gastronomic discovery. Scipio, Metellus, and Marcus Sejus disputed the glory of the invention.[69] At all events, it is certain that the same method was used in Greece as in Italy; that white geese were chosen in preference,[70] and that the fat livers were served roasted, or fried in the frying-pan, and enveloped in the *omentum*, a membrane which we term the caul.[71] Pliny assures us that Apicius found means to increase livers to a monstrous size,[72] which almost equalled in weight the whole body of the animal.[73]

The wings and neck of the goose also acquired some favour; the feet were added, when Messalinus had taught how to peel them by passing them rapidly over the fire, and then preparing them with cocks' combs. The remainder was only good for the common people.[74]

Stuffed goslings also enjoyed a reputation among the Greeks,[75] who fattened them by giving them, three times a day, during a month, a mixture of bran and flour, moistened with hot water (two parts of flour and four parts of bran); but, if Palladius is to be believed, it is much better to feed them solely with millet, and as much water as they may require.[76]

Sejus Seasoning.—Bruise pepper, alisander, coriander, mint, and rue; mix with it garum and a little oil; pour it over the roast goose, and serve.[77]

Apician Seasoning for a Roast Goose's Liver.—Crush in a mortar, and then well mix, pepper, carrots, cummin, parsley-seed, thyme, onions, benzoin root, and fried pine nuts; add honey, vinegar, garum, and oil, and serve with the roast liver in the omentum.[78]

Boiled Goose à la Gauloise.—Boil a goose with garum, oil, wine, a bunch of leeks, coriander, and savory; then crush pepper and pine nuts, to which put a little water. Then take the leeks, coriander, and savory out of the saucepan; put in their place the mixture mentioned, add some milk, boil it, thicken with whites of eggs, and serve.[79]

In the sixteenth century they had dark cages, in which they fattened poultry with ground tares, wheaten flour, and barley meal. Capons fattened in hutches, where they could not turn, nor even stir, were esteemed delicious. They fed pigeons on the crumb of bread, steeped in wine; peacocks on the sediment from cider.

On Michaelmas Day, the 29th of September, many persons in England eat roast goose for their dinner. It is said that this custom dates from the time of Queen Elizabeth, who was being served with a piece of goose on Michaelmas Day, at the very moment when news was brought of the defeat of the famous Armada. Some persons affirm that the Queen expressed a desire that this dish might, each year, serve to perpetuate the remembrance of so signal a victory. Would it not be more simple to suppose that Elizabeth herself already conformed to a custom which had existed before her time?[80]

At Mans, instead of letting the poultry eat freely, they are shut up in a dark place, and made to swallow pellets of about two inches long and one thick, composed of two parts of barley flour, and one of maize, made with sufficient quantity of milk.

"In the time when the French had a decided taste for spices and aromatics, they imagined to vary at will the flavour and perfume of the flesh of fowls. With the paste used to fatten them was mixed musk, anise-seed, and comfits, with other aromatic drugs. A Queen was known to spend 1,500 francs (£60) in fattening three geese, whose livers she wished to render more delicate."—PARMENTIER.

———•———

THE PIGEON.

The dove, a bird so dear to Venus,[81] served ambrosia to Jupiter,[82] and became the interpreter of Dodona's oracles.[83] Several nations consecrated it to their gods.[84] The Jews discovered in it the image of the sweetest virtues,[85] of beauty, innocence, and purity;[86] and they sacrificed it to the Almighty, as a burnt offering agreeable to His unspeakable holiness.[87]

This was because the dove or pigeon (begging pardon, here, for mixing varieties) is to the hawk, according to an expression of a father of the Church, what the lamb is to the wolf,[88]—a symbol of good by the side of evil, or of a calm and peaceful conscience, as opposed to the sad and agitated criminal. But, alas! the ancient prerogatives of this tender bird, its candour and innocence, could not even preserve it from the fate common to almost everything which breathes. Its delicate flesh— fatal gift of Heaven!—recommended it to the epicure; not for its poetical qualities, but for its delicate flavour; and, after many songs of praise, it was condemned to be roasted.

From the beginning of the heroic ages, pigeons were caught with snares and nets,[89] in order to feed them, and be able to procure some at once, if required to be served at a repast; for they formed a dainty dish upon the tables of the most fastidious.[90] Of course they figured in the joyous wedding feast of that opulent Caranus who entertained his guests so sumptuously.[91]

The Greeks, therefore, used to bring up an immense number of pigeons, and built for them, in the most open situations, charming pigeon-houses, in the form of small towers, models of elegance and cleanliness, where those timid birds found at night a retreat, always fatal to some one amongst them.[92]

The Romans introduced in these sorts of edifices the most unusual luxury.[93] Each kind of pigeon had a particular home[94]—a foolish and expensive taste, which they continually attempted to embellish. It was,

however, a profitable speculation for those who knew how to be satisfied
with pigeon-houses of more simple appearance. A brace of rather ordinary pigeons did not cost less than 16s.: the finest were sold at £4
a pair. It is even known that L. Axius, a Roman knight, demanded
and obtained £6 8s. for two young pigeons intended for a patrician's
table.[95]

Physicians of that period greatly praised the flesh of these birds;
they recommended it to the sick and convalescent.[96]

Roast Pigeon, with Servilian Seasoning.—Bruise some dill seeds,
dried mint, and the root of benzoin; add some vinegar, dates, garum,
a little mustard, and oil; stir well; then mix with it some wine reduced
to half, and pour the whole on the roasted pigeon.[97]

THE GUINEA HEN.

This bird, called by the ancients the "Hen of Numidia," comes originally from many burning regions of Africa. In Greece, and especially
in Rome, vanity alone gave it a price which was willingly granted, more
on account of its scarcity than for its taste.[98] The Guinea hen appeared
at great banquets, when the Amphytrion was more anxious to show his
opulence than to demonstrate the delicacy of his dishes. Martial,[99] and
Pliny,[100] the naturalist, raised great objections against this ostentatious
and useless rarity.

Guinea Hen à la Numide.—Cook it; then put it in a saucepan with
some honey and garum; make several incisions in the bird; baste it
with its own gravy, and sprinkle with pepper previously to its being
served.[101]

THE TURKEY HEN.

"There must be two to eat a truffled turkey," said a gastronomist of
the 18th century, to one of his friends—a noted *gourmand*—who had just
come to pay him a visit. "Two!" replied the visitor, with a smile of sen-

suality. "Yes, two," answered the first; "I never do otherwise: for instance, I have a turkey to-day, and of course we must be two." The friend, looking earnestly at the other, said: "You, and who else?" "Why," answered the gastronomist, "I and the turkey."

In Greece, more than one stomach would have been capable of challenging nobly the voracity of this modern polyphagus: witness the insatiable greediness of the well-known glutton who complained that nature ought to have given him a neck as long as the stork, that he might enjoy for a longer period his eating and drinking.[102]

But for a long time the Greeks were quite ignorant of the culinary value of the turkey; it was looked upon as an uncommon curiosity, and not condemned to the spit. Sophocles, the first who spoke of it, pretended that those marvellous birds came purposely from some distant climate beyond the Indies, to bewail the death of Meleager, who took possession of the throne of Macedonia (279 years B. C.), and who was soon driven from it.[103] This Prince, it is reported, carried them away from barbarous regions, that they might enjoy the charms of Greek civilization; and hence could there be anything more natural than to find those compassionate volatiles shedding tears for their benefactor, in one of Sophocles' tragedies? They have been called since, Meleagrides, and this name perpetuated "misfortune, favour, and gratitude."

Aristotle hardly supplies us with any details upon turkey hens: he merely says that their eggs are distinguished by little specks from those of the common hens, which are white;[104] but Clytus of Miletus, his disciple, gives an exact description of them, by which no mistake can be made.[105]

Egypt also possessed some of these birds; but there they were still more rare than in Greece, and formed one of the principal ornaments in the triumphal pomp of Ptolemy Philadelphus, when he entered Alexandria. Large cages, containing meleagrides, were carried before the monarch, and on that day the people knew not which to admire most—the prince or the turkey.[106]

They were introduced into Rome about the year 115 before our era; but, for a long time, they were objects of uncommon curiosity: and Varro, the first of the Latins who speaks of them, confounds these birds with the guinea hens, or hens of Numidia.[107]

A century later, turkeys greatly multiplied, and vast numbers were reared in the Roman farms. Caligula, who had the good sense to make his own apotheosis during his life-time, through fear lest it might be refused after his death, ordered a sacrifice of peacocks, guinea hens, and turkeys to be made daily before his statue.[108]

It appears, however, that the breed of turkeys soon began to diminish in Europe; very few were reared, and that only as a curiosity: in the citadel of Athens, towards the year 540 of the Christian era;[109] and in 1510, two were exhibited in Rome, which belonged to the Cardinal of Saint Clement.[110] Jacques Cœur brought some meleagrides from India, in 1450; they were the first ever seen in France, and it was not till fifty-four years afterwards that Americus Vespucius made them known to the Portuguese. In our days these ancient inhabitants of Asia or America[111] have become naturalized among us, and let us hope that the day is yet distant when they will be absentees from our farm-yards and our tables. We admire them less perhaps than Charles IX. did when a turkey was served to him for the first time,[112] but we shall always receive with cheerfulness the majestic dish upon which appears a well-fed turkey, truffled, and smoking hot.

Turkey à l'Africaine. — Roast a turkey; bruise some pepper, alisander, and benzoin; mix it with wine and garum. Pour this seasoning on the turkey, sprinkle with pepper, and serve.[113]

The historian of Provence, Bouche, will have it that the French are indebted for the turkey to King René, who died in 1480. Other writers assure us that this volatile was introduced during the reign of Francis I. by Admiral Chabert. La-Bruyère-Champier speaks of it as a recent acquisition, and Beckmann refutes those who date its existence in France previous to the 16th century. He says that this bird, which was wild in the forests of America, became domesticated in Europe.

It is also said that we owe the importation of it to the Jesuits. According to Hurtaut, it was not until about the time of Charles IX. that turkeys appeared in France.[114] It is asserted, adds this author, that at the wedding-dinner of that Prince the first turkey was served, and that it was admired as a very extraordinary thing. The English tasted this new dish in 1525, the fifteenth year of the reign of Henry VIII.

To fatten turkeys—every morning, for a month, give them mashed potatoes, mixed with buck-wheat flour, Indian corn, barley, or beans; a paste is made of it which they are left to eat as they please. Every evening what remains must be taken away. One month after, you add to this food, when they go to roost, half a dozen balls composed of barley flour, which they are made to swallow for eight days successively; at the end of that time turkeys, thus fed, become excessively fat, delicious, and weigh from twenty to twenty-five pounds.

In Provence, walnuts are given to them whole, which they are compelled to swallow by slipping them one by one with the hand along the neck until they have all past the œsophagus; they begin with one walnut, and increase by degrees to forty. This kind of food gives an oily taste to the flesh.

Turkey eggs are good boiled, and are preferred to those of hens for pastry; mixing them with the common eggs makes an omelette more delicate.

"To obtain all the advantages possible from turkeys, they must be killed at the same time as pigs; then cut the turkeys in quarters, and put them in earthen pots covered over with the fat of the pork, and by this means they may be eaten all the year round."—PARMENTIER.

———

THE PEACOCK.

The peacock comes originally from India: it was there that Alexander the Great saw it for the first time. He was so struck with its magnificent plumage that he forbad all persons, under pain of death, to kill any.[115]

Oriental princes kept the peacocks which travellers brought them, from time to time, in their aviaries.[116] It was thus[117] that a certain king of Egypt received one, of which he thought Jupiter alone worthy; wherefore he sent it in great pomp to the temple of that god.[118]

These birds were thus known over various parts of the world. Samos, which seems to have been provided one of the first, ornamented its money with their image.[119] Their reputation soon spread far and wide;[120] and Athenian speculators sent to that island for peacocks, which were shown to the curious once a month.[121]

This variety became afterwards an article of commerce, and all wealthy people became desirous to have them. A male and female cost £8 sterling.[122] But what was that, when delighted eyes could contemplate the charming and lovely colours of the haughty favourite of Juno!

At Rome, the peacock had a prodigious success.[123] When alive, the

Romans praised its beauty; when dead, it appeared on the tables of its enthusiastic admirers.

Quintus Hortensius, the orator, was the first who had them served in a banquet given by him on the occasion of being created an augur.[124] This gastronomic novelty made an extraordinary sensation at Rome—as might be expected—and the peacock became so much in fashion, that no banquet could possibly be given unless it was embellished by its presence.[125]

Marcus Aufidius Livio was the first to contrive a sure way to fatten them;[126] and he succeeded so well that he made prodigious sums every year by the sale of those birds.*

Horace preferred them to the finest poultry,[127] and distinguished amateurs thought that it was not paying much for a young peacock if they could get it for two pounds and three shillings.[128]

The ridiculous consumption which was made of these birds did not allow of their becoming very common. Tiberius reared some in his gardens; and he condemned to capital punishment a soldier of his guards who had the misfortune to kill one.[129]

Ultimately, more savoury or more rare dishes took the place of peacocks' flesh, which then began to be thought hard, unwholesome, and of difficult digestion.[130] However, it re-appeared in the middle ages at the nuptial festivities of the rich, where one of these birds was served, as if alive, with the beak and claws gilded. To do that well, it was necessary to skin the bird very carefully, and then cook it with aromatics, such as cinnamon, cloves, &c. It was then covered with its skin and feathers, and served without any appearance of having been stripped. This luxury was to gratify the sight: nobody touched it. The peacock was thus preserved for several years without being damaged—a property believed to be peculiar to its flesh,[131] but which was owing, no doubt, to the aromatics just mentioned.

Peacock of Samos.—Mix some pepper, alisander, parsley, dill flowers, dried mint, and filberts, or fried almonds; bruise them with green smallage† and pennyroyal, and mix the whole with wine, honey, vinegar, and garum. Make incisions in the bird, and cover it with this seasoning.[132]

---

* No less than £52,000, if Pliny really means the grand sesterce, which everything leads us to believe.

† Smallage, a species of parsley, known by the name of celery, is diuretic and aperitive. The celery, as cultivated now, is derived from the smallage.

XVIII.

MILK, BUTTER, CHEESE, AND EGGS.

———·———

MILK.

It would, probably, be impossible to trace the epoch at which man began to make use of milk as food. Abraham presented some to the three angels who appeared to him in the valley of Mamre;[1] and it is likely, that long before that patriarch, the eastern nations had recourse to an aliment so easily acquired, and which their numerous flocks produced in such abundance.

Among the Jews, milk was always considered as an emblem of the wealth of a country and the fertility of its soil; so much so, that the sacred books almost invariably speak of a happy region, as one "flowing with milk and honey."[2] This metaphorical expression testifies sufficiently to the taste of the Hebrews for this aliment, which their King Solomon recommended to them in these terms: "and thou shalt have goat's milk enough for thy food, for the food of thy household, and for the maintenance of thy maidens."[3]

Profane antiquity agrees on this point with our holy chroniclers. It represents to us the first men, free from passions and fears, surrounded by streams of milk and nectar, from which they drew health and life.[4] Happy time! ere milk-maids existed to practise those deceptions they have now imbibed from the deceitful arts of chemistry.

The greater part of the wandering tribes, such as the Getes and Scythians, were galactophagists,[5] or drinkers of milk;[6] the Gauls[7] and

Germans [8] made it also their principal food. In Greece and Italy, the shepherds decorated the vessels in which they had just milked their flocks with crowns of flowers; and, in honour of the rural divinities, they scattered about a small quantity of this sweet liquid.[9] The reapers offered it to Ceres;[10] and in one of the sections of Rome, Mercury was presented with milk instead of wine.

The ancients attributed to milk from cows, ewes, and goats, various Hygeian qualities.[11] Hippocrates forbade it in cases of head-ache, fevers, and bilious attacks;[12] but he sometimes ordered asses' milk,[13] which was considered as an excellent remedy, and a most wholesome aliment.[14]

The voluptuous people of Rome rubbed their faces and skins with bread soaked in asses' milk, to make them fairer and prevent the beard from growing too fast.

Suetonius[15] and Martial[16] speak of these refinements of luxurious delicacies. The satirical Juvenal informs us that bread was made into a kind of plaster or mask, with which they covered the face.[17] Poppæia, wife of Nero, was the first, or one of the first, to bring this recipe into fashion, being fully persuaded that she would thus preserve the white ness and delicacy of her skin. Five hundred asses used to supply daily the necessary quantity of milk to make the cosmetic and bath[18] of the coquettish empress.

This high patronage did not prevent asses' milk from losing by degrees—and very unjustly, no doubt—the reputation it acquired.[19]

Fashion—capricious and all-powerful deity—undertook to re-instate its virtues, after several centuries of profound forgetfulness. The success was complete. This is how the affair took place :—

Francis I., finding himself weak and languishing, the physicians, after a long consultation on the monarch's illness, advised remedies which did not cure the royal patient. However, the King of France was getting worse every day, and his state gave serious apprehensions. Some one mentioning to his Majesty that a Jew of Constantinople was noted as one of the cleverest doctors in the world, Francis imme-diately ordered his ambassador in Turkey to send him this Israelitish doctor, whatever might be the cost. The Jew arrived, and prescribed no other remedy than asses' milk. The king found himself much better, and the courtiers and ladies of the court eagerly followed the same diet, even for the slightest imaginary indisposition.

A patient, cured by the use of this wholesome and restorative food, thought of expressing his gratitude by the following stanza :—

> " Par sa bonté, par sa substance
> D'une ânesse le lait m'a rendu la santé ;
> Et je dois plus en cette circonstance,
> 　Aux ânes qu'à la faculté."

Macédoine Germanique of Milk.—Pound dry almonds, and put them into a stewpan with the following ingredients :—the most delicate parts of mallows only, and white-beet, some leeks, parsley, and other leguminous herbs, previously cooked, a fowl boiled and minced small, the brains of poultry or sucking pigs, also boiled, and lastly, some hard eggs cut in two. Put all these together, as mentioned before ; some little time after that, add sausage meat, fowls' livers, fresh cod fish, and oysters—the whole reduced into pulp—some fresh cheese, pine nuts, and whole pepper. Whilst this is boiling on a very slow fire, prepare the following seasoning : pound some pepper, alisander, parsley seeds, and silphium ; stew separately with gravy ; mix raw eggs with a great quantity of milk ; add it to the preceding seasoning ; pour it over the contents of the stewpan, then pepper, and serve.[20]

——•——

BUTTER.

A learned writer [21] has maintained that the ancient inhabitants of the east did not know of butter, and that by this word must be understood, when it occurs in the holy writings, *sour milk* or *cream*. Whatever may be the respect due to the grave authority of Beckmann, we beg leave to adhere to the opinion of various translators of the Bible, and believe with them that the Jews knew how to prepare butter. Independently of the signification of *chemack*, to which a profound philosopher gives the same sense,[22] and which appears very naturally to offer this acceptation, we could still fortify our opinion by the passage where Job, recalling with sorrow the happy days of his youth, says, that he used to wash his " feet in butter."[23] We agree that these words are understood in a figurative sense, and that the man of God wished to show by it that he was the possessor of a great number of flocks.

But it is nevertheless true, that this metaphorical locution recalls also one of the uses made of that fat substance, which was for a long while employed, like oil, to soften and refresh the limbs.

Indulgent reader, excuse this episode upon a ground which we ought not to touch, and let us re-enter the kitchen.

The Greeks, who understood many things, and knew them so well, passed over several centuries without once thinking that the milk of their ewes and cows contained a food already well-known by several barbarous nations. Aristotle mentions the serous part of milk, and cheese;[24] but he hardly suspects the existence of butter, which he describes but very imperfectly as a liquid oil.[25] Antecedent to him, Hippocrates never thought of it, except as a foreign remedy which Asia supplied to Greece.[26]

It was only fifty years after Aristotle that it began to be noticed as an aliment. The Greeks, in imitation of the Parthians and Scythians, who used to send it to them, had it served upon their tables, and called it at first " oil of milk,"[27] and later, bouturos, " cow cheese," probably on account of the quantity made from the milk of that animal.[28]

The Germans, according to Beckmann, taught the Romans how to make butter, but they never employed it otherwise than as a remedy in Italy.

It is certain that in the time of Pliny it had hardly been heard of at Rome,[29] and that, according to this writer, the barbarians only—that is to say, those who were unfortunate enough not to be either Greeks or Romans—made their food of it.[30] Towards the year 175 of the Christian era, Galen then placed butter only among the therapeutic agents useful in medicine.[31] However, more than a century before him, Dioscorides wished it to be noticed that fresh butter made of ewes' or goats' milk was served at meals instead of oil, and that it took the place of fat in making pastry.[32]

Herodotus has preserved some interesting details on the manipulation of butter among the Scythians. They received the milk in large pails, and beat it for a long time to separate the most delicate part, and appointed for this labour those enemies whom the fortune of war delivered into their hands. These unhappy creatures were deprived of sight, which prevented their escape.[33]

The Romans set about making butter as we do. Pliny says: " Butter is made from milk, and this aliment, so much sought after by barbarous nations, distinguished the rich from the common people. It is obtained principally from cows' milk; that from ewes is the fattest. Goats also supply some. It is produced by agitating the milk in long vessels with a narrow opening. A little water is added." [34]

Formerly it was required in many countries that the dealer in this article should sell good butter to his customers. In France, for instance, intolerance was carried so far as to forbid " all persons to re-scrape, beat, or work up any butter, either fresh or salted; change, mix, or mingle it, under *pain of being whipped*." [35] Since then the strangeness of such a measure has become palpable, the more so as modern good faith and honesty render it more useless than ever.

During the early ages of the Church, butter was burned in the lamps instead of oil. This practice is still continued in Abyssinia. [36]

The cathedral of Rouen has a tower, called the " Butter Tower." It acquired this name from the fact that George d'Amboise, who was archbishop of that city in 1500, seeing that oil was scarce in his diocese during Lent, authorised the use of butter, on condition that each diocesan should pay *six deniers Tournois* (about a farthing) for the permission. The money obtained by these means served to construct the " Butter Tower." [37]

To obtain butter instantly it is only necessary, in summer, to put new milk into bottles some hours after it has been taken from the cow, and shake it briskly. The clots which form, thrown into a sieve, washed and pressed together, constitute the finest and most delicate butter that can possibly be made.

One of the great means of preserving butter fresh for any length of time is, first to press all the buttermilk completely out, then to keep it under water (renewing the water frequently), and to abstract it from the influence of heat and air by wrapping it in a wet cloth.

When butter has become very rancid, it is melted several times by a moderate heat, with or without the addition of water, and, as soon as it has been malaxated, after the cooling, in order to extract any water it may have retained, it is put into brown freestone pots, sheltered from the contact of the air. Frequently, when it is melted, a piece of toasted bread is put into it, which acts in the same manner as charcoal; that is to say, it attenuates the rancidity. [38]

CHEESE.

A demi-god, Aristæus, the son of Apollo, and King of Arcadia, invented cheese,[39] and the whole of Greece welcomed with gratitude this royal and almost divine present. Sober individuals willingly ate some at their meals;[40] gluttons perceived that it sharpened the appetite; and great drinkers that it provoked copious libations. Thus the aged Nestor, wise as he was, brought wine to Machaon, who had just been wounded in the right arm, and did not fail to add to it goat cheese and an onion, to force him to drink more.[41]

This food was also well known to the Hebrews, and the holy writings sometimes mention it.[42]

Mare's milk, or that of the ass, makes an excellent cheese, but much inferior to that procured from the camel, for which an epicure could not pay too dearly. Cow-milk cheese, although more fat and unctuous, was only considered as third-rate.[43]

The Phrygians made exquisite cheese by artistically mixing the milk of asses and mares. The Scythians only employed the former; the Greeks imitated them.[44] The Sicilians also mixed the milk of goats and ewes.[45]

The Romans smoked their cheeses, to give them a sharp taste; they possessed public places expressly for this use, and subject to police regulations which no one could evade.[46]

In the time of Pliny, little goat cheeses, which were much esteemed, were sent every morning to the market for the sale of dainties, from the environs of Rome.[47] With the addition of a little bread, they formed the breakfast of sober and delicate persons. Asia Minor, Tuscany, the Alps, Gaul, and Nîmes especially, furnished very good ones for the tables of the Romans,[48] who sought in preference certain sweet and soft qualities. The greater part of barbarous nations esteemed only the strong cheese.[49]

The Hebrews, Greeks. and Romans, always kept some of these last for the provision of their armies, and it was among them a military aliment.[50] The Athenians fed their wrestlers with it,[51] and it was the sole treat of the shepherds of Italy.[52]

The lower classes and country people prepared with cheese and various salted substances a dish they thought most relishing, and which epicureans only mentioned with horror. This was called *tyrotarichus*, and Cicero often employs this word to designate a frugal style of cookery.[53]

Besides those countries celebrated for the goodness of cheeses already mentioned, there is Tromelia, in Achaia,[54] and the Island of Cythnus, where they represented their cheeses on their money, an ingenious manner of making them known, which succeeded wonderfully well; and lastly, Salonia, a city of Bithynia, renowned for its rich pastures, where numerous herds of cows were kept, and whose milk furnished an exquisite kind known by the name of Salonite cheese.[55] It appears to have been often served to the Emperor Augustus, who ate it with brown bread, little fish, and fresh figs.[56]

The art of giving a relish to the cheese, by mixing with it odoriferous herbs, is said to be more than nine hundred years old. This operation was designated *persiller*, showing that originally parsley was introduced.[57] We cannot say whether the Romans made use of this plant to give a pungency to their cheese, but it is certain that they often mixed some herbs with it.[58] Thus Columella informs us that sometimes the leaves and small branches of the fig tree were used to communicate an agreeable flavour.[59] The same writer has transmitted to us a very simple process, much in use in his time, for preserving cheese. They first covered it with brine, and then dried it in a thick smoke obtained from straw or green wood.[60]

The following are some of the dishes of which cheese served as the basis :—

Salad of Cheese à la Bithynienne.—Cut some slices of excellent bread ; leave them for some time in vinegar and water ; then make a mixture of this bread with pepper, mint, garlic, and green coriander ; throw on it a good quantity of cow's cheese salted ; add water, oil, and wine.[61]

Dish of Tromelian Cheese.—Take fresh cheese ; mix it well with pepper, alisander, dried mint, pine nuts, sun raisins, and dates ; then add honey, vinegar, and afterwards, garum, oil, wine, and cooked wine.[62]

The celebrated cheese of Rouergue, known under the name of " Roquefort cheese," was made, in the 17th century as follows—we cite from Marcorelle :—

"The curd employed is made from sheep's milk, mixed with a little goat's milk. It is broken as small as possible. When it is taken from the moulds, it is bound with a linen band and taken to the drying room; then to the caves, where it is rubbed with salt on the two flat sides of the surface. The downy substance which subsequently covers the crust is frequently scraped off; after which, it is left to ripen on tablets exposed to currents of air which proceed from the interstices of the rocks in which the caves are formed."

Besides salt, employed as a seasoning and condiment for cheeses, they contain in their composition different substances which give rise to an infinite variety of odours, taste, and colour. In the Vosges, for example, they mix with the cheese of Gerardmer seeds of plants belonging to the family of umbellifers; in the country of Limburg, they incorporate chopped parsley, scallions, and tarragon; the Italians make use of saffron to colour the Parmesan cheese, and the English of roucou for the Cheshire cheese. Others are in the habit of cutting away a portion of the middle of the cheese, and filling the cavity with Malaga or Canary wine.[63]

EGGS.

Orpheus, Pythagoras, and their sectators—good and humane people as ever lived—unceasingly recommended in their discourses to abstain from eggs, in order not to destroy a germ which nature had destined for the production of chicken.[64] Many allowed themselves to be persuaded, and would have believed it an unpardonable crime if they had eaten a tiny *omelette*, or boiled eggs.

Many of the most learned philosophers held eggs in a kind of respect approaching to veneration, because they saw in them the emblem of the world and the four elements. The shell, they said, represented the earth; the white, water; the yolk, fire; and air was found under the shell.[65]

In India and Syria, there was less scruple about swallowing a few eggs; but the hens were devoutly worshipped, because the world is indebted to them for chickens.[66]

The Greeks and Romans, although more reasonable, felt, however, for eggs a trifling weakness not exempt from superstition. They already made use of them in their sacrifices, and carried them with great pomp in the festivals of Ceres.[67] For them it was also a symbol of the universe, and an expiation would not have been complete if some eggs had not been broken on the altar of the irritated gods.[68]

Magicians and sorcerers, who abounded in Rome, established singular fables with regard to eggs. Livia, the happy consort of Nero, being *enceinte*, consulted a sorceress, who said to her, " warm in your bosom a new laid egg until hatched; if a male chicken comes forth, thank the gods, who will grant you a son." The empress followed this advice; a cock chick came, and the princess gave birth to Tiberius.[69] This anecdote circulated in Rome, and all ladies in the same interesting situation, imitating Livia, amused themselves with hatching chickens.

It appears that the egg played also a most important part in dreams. A man having dreamed that he had eaten one, went to consult a sooth-sayer, who told him that the white signified he would soon have silver, and the yolk that he would receive gold. The fortunate dreamer really received very soon afterwards a legacy partly consisting of those two precious metals. He hastened to thank the diviner, and offered him a piece of silver. " This is very well for the white," said the latter, " but is there nought for the yolk ?"[70] It is not known whether the heir was generous enough to understand this *bon mot*.

All these pagan follies are to be accounted for by the doctrine of the poet Orpheus, who first taught the Greeks that a primitive egg had produced all other beings ;[71] a very ancient idea, no doubt, transmitted to them by the Egyptians, who, as well as the Phœnicians, Persians, and Chaldeans, represented the world by that symbol.

It is now time to describe eggs as an aliment.

The shepherds of Egypt had a singular manner of cooking them without the aid of fire: they placed them in a sling, which they turned so rapidly that the friction of the air heated them to the exact point required for use.[72]

In Rome and in Greece, new-laid eggs were served at the beginning of a repast ;[73] and the Roman gourmets asserted that, to maintain oneself in health, " it was necessary to remain at table from the egg to the apple."[74] We have adopted the half of that proverb, and we say every day, this story must be taken up *ab ovo*.

The Romans did not confine themselves to hens' eggs, of which they preferred the long ones;[75] they sought those of the partridge and pheasant, which Galen considered the most delicate.[76] They also thought much of peacocks' eggs. It was Quintus Hortensius who set the example of this luxury,[77] which, however, was discarded by degrees when the precious fecundity of the hens of Adria began to be appreciated.[78]

The ancients appear to have been very partial to soft-boiled eggs, which may be sucked at once. Nicomachus mentions them: "My father," says he, "had left me a poor little estate; in a few months I made it as round as an egg; then, breaking the shell, I made but one gulp of it."[79]

At Rome, this aliment was prepared in twenty different manners; they pickled it,[80] cooked it in water, on hot ashes, on charcoal, and in the fryingpan. Eggs eaten in the shell, however, were thought the most wholesome.[81]

Eggs à la Romaine.—Cook some eggs; cut them, and throw over a seasoning composed in the following manner. Bruise some pepper, alisander, coriander, and rue, to which add garum, honey, and a little oil.[82]

Hard Eggs à l'Athénienne.—Cut each egg in four, and sprinkle over garum, oil, and wine.[83]

Fried Eggs à l'Epænète.—Fry some eggs; place them in a dish, and season with a mixture of pepper, alisander, pine nuts, garum, benzoin, and pepper.[84]

Egyptian Egg Pudding.—Take the yolks of a good number of hard eggs; reduce them to a paste with crushed pine nuts, an onion, a leek, some gravy, and pepper; add a little wine and garum. Stuff an intestine with this pulp, and cook.[85]

Dish of Eggs à la Macédonienne.—Put in a mortar some pepper, mint, parsley, pennyroyal, cheese, and pine nuts; when this is well crushed, add honey, vinegar, fresh water, and garum; then a large number of yolks of eggs; mix well with the rest; throw the whole into a saucepan; add bread soaked in vinegar and water,—which, however, must be well squeezed out—with fresh cow's-milk cheese, cucumbers, almonds, chopped onions, fowls' livers, and garum.[86]

Lesbian Eggs aux Roses.—Pluck the leaves of some roses; take only the whitest part, and put them into a mortar with garum. Stir a long time; add half a small glass of gravy; stir and strain; put into this liquor the brains of four fowls and eight scruples of ground pepper; stir a long time; add to it eight eggs, half a small glass of wine, and as much cooked wine, and, lastly, a little oil. Grease well the inside of a dish, pour the whole into it, and place it over a very slow charcoal fire.   Cook, sprinkle with pepper, and serve.[87]

It was a custom, common to every agricultural population throughout Europe and Asia, to celebrate the new year by eating eggs; and they formed a part of the presents made on that day.   Care was taken to dye them different colours, particularly red—the favourite colour of the ancients, and of the Celts in particular.[88]

It appears that, formerly, people consumed an astonishing number of eggs in England on Easter Sunday.   We find the following article in an account of expenses for the king's household (Edward I.) on the occasion of this festival : —

" For four hundred and a half of eggs, eighteen pence." [89]   At that epoch eggs were not so dear in England as they are now ; nor did kings fail to eat more of them.

In 1533, a bishop of Paris, authorised by a bull from the Pope, Julius III., being disposed to permit the use of eggs during Lent, the parliament took offence, and prevented the execution of the episcopal mandate.   It is this severe abstinence from eggs during Lent which gave rise to the custom of having a great number of them blessed on Easter eve, to be distributed among friends on Easter Sunday ; whence comes the expression, " to give Easter eggs."   Pyramids of them were carried into the king's cabinet after the high mass.   They were gilded, or admirably painted, and the prince made presents of them to his courtiers.[90]

XIX.

HUNTING.

From the first ages of the world man has passionately loved the exercise of hunting; the dangers he then encountered inflamed his courage. It was glorious to struggle with the terrible inhabitants of the forest or the desert; to conquer them; to bring home their bleeding spoils; to furnish an heroic name for the songs of poets, and the admiration of posterity.

The sacred writings have handed down to us the name of the first mighty hunter before the Lord;[1] they inform us that Ishmael, in the solitude of Arabia, became skilful in drawing the bow;[2] and that David, when yet young, dared to fight with lions and bears.[3]

Fable, that veiled light of truth, through which it sometimes glimmers, caused Hercules to be ranked with the gods when he had overthrown the lion of Nemæa, the hydra of Lerna, and the wild boar of Erymanthus.[4]

Diana descended to the earth, and pursued in the forests the timid stag.[5] The Greeks raised altars to her, and the centaur Chiron learned of her the noble art of venery, which he, in his turn, taught to illustrious disciples, among whom are mentioned Æsculapius, Nestor, Theseus, Ulysses, and Achilles.[6]

Pollux trained the first hunting dogs, and Castor accustomed horses to follow the track of wild beasts.[7] From that time, heroes, when resting from real conquests, sought diversion in games nearly as formidable, and imitative of their combats, which often placed their lives in danger. Ulysses, for example, always bore the scar of a wound inflicted by a wild boar.[8]

The most grave philosophers, and the most illustrious poets have
bestowed praises on the chase.

Aristotle advised young men to apply themselves to it early.[9] Plato
finds in it something divine,[10] Horace looks upon it as healthful exercise,
strengthening to the body, and preparing the way for glory;[11] and indeed, this heroic and royal exercise[12] always possessed irresistible attraction for the greatest men of antiquity.

The warriors of Homer,[13] Pelopidas,[14] Alexander of Macedon,[15]
Philopœmen,[16] seemed to derive from it fresh warlike ardour.

The ancients hunted in the open country, in forests, and in parks.
Mounted on fiery steeds, armed with javelins and long cutlasses, or with
swords and lances,[17] they excited their indefatigable hounds, and promised to consecrate to Diana the stag's horns, or the tusks of the boar,[18]
which might become their prey.

The Greeks and Romans reared hunting dogs with extreme care,
and they began to make use of them from the age of eight or ten
months.[19] These animals had names, short, sonorous, and easy to be
pronounced, such as Lance, Flower, Blade, Strength, Ardent, &c.[20]

The strongest and most courageous came from England and Scotland;[21] Crete, Tuscany, and Umbria were the nurseries of the most
expert.[22] The Gallic dogs surpassed all others by their agility and
astonishing swiftness.[23]

Females were generally preferred to the males,[24] either because they
were more docile, or pursued the game with more ardour and persist-
ence. It may be as well to remark, too, in this place, that the Greeks
thought much more of mares than of horses for chariot racing.[25]

The dogs were always chained. Their liberty was only given them
at the moment of starting for the chase.[26] Their fire and ferocity were
then incredible. They dashed off with fury, and when they succeeded
in coming up with their prey, some would suffer their legs to be cut off
rather than loose their hold. The Indian dogs, trained for lion hunting,
often gave this proof of obstinate and implacable rage.[27]

The ancients also took game by means of pits covered over with
brushwood, in snares,[28] with traps,[29] and with nets;[30] moreover, they
often made use of bows and arrows, and understood the art of training
falcons and hawks.[31]

Eastern princes amused themselves by hunting in parks where a
great number of wild beasts were kept.[32] The Romans had too much

taste and money, and too great a desire to spend it, not to imitate this expensive and royal luxury: Fulvius Hirpinus possessed a park of forty acres near Viterbo, in Tuscany. Lucius Lucullus, and Quintus Hortensius hastened to create more beautiful ones, and they did not fail to have a host of imitators.[33]

By the Roman law, hunting was unrestricted :[34] only, no person could pursue game on another's land without the owner's permission.[35]

Besides the pleasure which this amusement afforded, the ancients, like ourselves, discovered profit in it; and the produce of their chase became one of the finest ornaments of their feasts. Isaac ordered his son Esau to go out with his weapons, his quiver and bow, and to prepare for him savoury meat, such as he loved (venison).[36] Solomon had stags, roebucks, and wild oxen served on his table every day.[37]

Cyrus, King of Persia, ordered that venison should never be wanting at his repasts.[38] Is it necessary to add that it was the delight of two nations the most gastronomic in the world?—of the effeminate Greeks, and more especially those Romans for whom the animals of the earth, ocean, and air were only to be valued in proportion to the impossibility of obtaining them in Europe, Asia, and Africa; an immense inheritance, conquered by noble ancestors, and which their degenerated sons ransacked for their satisfaction and insatiable gluttony.[39]

The English have always loved hunting—the favourite pastime of their kings.

Alfred the Great was not twelve years old when he had acquired the reputation of being a skilful and indefatigable hunter.[40]

The noble and the wealthy differed from the serfs by their singular taste for this royal diversion; and, in their pursuit of it, they spared neither pains nor expense in procuring those famous dogs of pure race which the ancient Greeks and Romans prized so highly. When Athelstan, Alfred's grandson, had subdued Constantine, King of Wales, he imposed an annual tribute. The vanquished monarch had to give him gold, silver, cattle, and, which is remarkable, a certain number of hawks, and dogs possessing a quick scent, and capable of unkenneling wild beasts.[41] Edgar, the successor of Athelstan, changed the tribute of money into an annual tribute of three hundred wolves' skins.[42]

Notwithstanding his great piety, and the extreme reserve of his habits, Edward the Confessor took great delight in following the hounds, and exciting their ardour by his cries.[43]

King Harold never appeared anywhere without his favourite hawk on his hand; neither was the approach of the British Nimrod announced otherwise than by the joyous barking of the royal pack.[44]   Indeed, at that epoch, every person of distinction took the prince as his model, and gave himself up, heart and soul, to what people are pleased to call " the noble exercise of hunting."

This aristocratic taste became so extremely prevalent under the domination of the Norman kings, that a writer of the twelfth century has judged it with great severity.   " In our time," he says, " hunting is considered as the most honourable occupation, the most excellent virtue.   Our nobility show more solicitude, sacrifice more money, and make a greater parade in favour of it, than they would if the question were war.   They are more furious in the pursuit of wild beasts, than they would be if they had to conquer the enemies of Great Britain. As a necessary consequence, they no longer retain any sentiment of humanity; they have descended almost to the level of the savage animals they are in the daily habit of tracking and unkenneling." [45]

These uncomplimentary observations of John of Salisbury did not prevent James I. from pursuing the cherished diversion of his predecessors.   That prince being one day at the hunt in the environs of Bury St. Edmunds, remarked, among the persons composing his suite, an opulent citizen magnificently dressed, whose rich costume eclipsed that of the lords the most renowned at court for the elegance of their attire.   The king asked who the hunter was.   Some one replied that it was Lamb.   " Lamb, say you?" rejoined the king, laughing; "I don't know what sort of a lamb that may be; but what I know well is, that he has got a superb fleece on his back." [46]

THE STAG.

Roman ladies of the highest distinction, arrived at that age when, in making an estimate of life, it is found that the largest portion belongs to the past—these ladies, we say, failed not to have the flesh of this animal served on their tables, and to eat as much of it as possible.   Perchance it had but a slight attraction for the worthy matrons, and yet they preferred it to every other, for this reason, that the stag being free from

maladies and infirmities — at least so it was thought—prolongs its existence far beyond the bounds which nature has assigned to other beings.[47]
The noble patrician ladies would not have been sorry to survive their
great-grandchildren, and they took the means which appeared to them
most likely to ensure longevity.[48]

If the celebrated Galen had lived in their time, he would have told
those credulous Roman ladies, that this kind of food could not fail to be
hurtful to them; that this indigestible and heating meat is more likely
to provoke disease than to destroy its germ; and that, consequently,
death finds in it an auxiliary rather than an enemy.[49]

True, the oracle of Pergama wrote nearly all this a century later, and
yet his medical authority was powerless to persuade, although it may
have convinced the obstinate epicureans of his period.

In point of fact, whatever Galen may say, what dreadful accidents
can a piece of stag properly cooked produce? Moses, so attentive to the
health of his people, allows them the use of it;[50] Solomon, the wisest of
men, ate it every day.[51] Do we find that the Jewish monarch and his
people were any the worse for preferring this food?

At Athens, at Rome, and in all Italy, whoever possessed the intelligence of appreciating good cheer, took care to offer to his friends the
shoulder or fillet of stag.[52] Nevertheless, gastronomists by profession,
who so generously devoted their fortunes to the service of the culinary
art, abandoned the whole animal to their slaves, and only reserved for
themselves the most tender shoots of the horns. These were for a long
time boiled, then cut into very small pieces, and this strange dish, seasoned with a mixture of pepper, cummin, savory, rue, parsley, bay
leaves, fat, and pine nuts, sprinkled with vinegar, and fried, passed for
an exquisite and dainty treat, worthy of the most flattering praises.[53]

Quarter of Stag, roast à la Neméenne.—Put into a saucepan
pepper, alisander, carrots, wild marjoram, parsley seed, benzoin root, and
fennel seed; add garum, wine, cooked wine, and a little oil. Boil over
a slow fire, thicken with fine flour, pour on the roast stag, and serve.[54]

Shoulder of Stag à l' Hortensius.—Cook in a saucepan carrots,
alisander, with pepper and parsley seed. Add honey, garum, vinegar,
and luke-warm oil; thicken with fine flour, and pour this sauce on the
shoulder of stag when roasted.[55]

Fillet of Stag à la Persane —Roast it, and at the moment of
placing it on the table, cover it with a seasoning of pepper, alisander,

scallions, wild marjoram, onions, and pine nuts, previously mixed with honey, garum, mustard, vinegar, and oil.[56]

--·--

THE ROEBUCK.

The flesh of the roebuck, according to Galen, has none of the bad qualities which he attributes to that of the stag.[57]   Esculapius and Comus for this once agreed—which very seldom happened—in praising the beneficial properties and the delicious odour of these timid quadrupeds.

The Greeks thought much of the roebuck; they obtained the best from the island of Melos,[58] and served them at their most sumptuous repasts.[59]   They were, perhaps, more rarely seen on Roman tables.

Roebuck with Spikenard.—Pound, in a mortar, pepper, parsley seed, dry onion, and green rue; add spikenard, and then honey, vinegar, garum, dates, cooked wine, and oil; mix well the whole, and cover the roast with it.[60]

Roebuck aux Prunes.—Mix pepper, alisander, and parsley, after having pounded them.   Add to this a good quantity of Damascus plums, which you have soaked in hot water.   Then add honey, wine, vinegar, garum, and a little oil; and, lastly, leeks and savory.   Serve the roebuck with this sauce.[61]

Roebuck aux Amandes de Pin.—Bruise pepper, alisander, parsley, and cummin; mix with it a great quantity of fried pine nuts; and add honey, vinegar, wine, a little oil, and garum.   Pour it over the roebuck.[62]

--·--

THE DEER.

Little need be said with regard to this charming animal, whose slender and graceful form was the admiration of those who visited the parks of Lucullus and Hirpinus.   Its flesh was thought to be less wholesome than that of the roebuck, because it was found to be less succulent.[63] Apicius has consecrated to it four culinary recipes, all very similar.

Deer à la Marcellus.—Put into a saucepan pepper, gravy, rue, and onions; add honey, garum, cooked wine, and a little oil. Boil very slowly, thicken with flour, and pour the whole on the deer when roasted.[64]

THE WILD BOAR.

It was in the year 63 before the Christian era: the consul Marcus Tullius Cicero had just accused and convicted Catilina, and Rome, free from present danger, had forgotten all transitory solicitudes of the past to welcome joyous banquetings.

A worthy citizen, excellent patriot, distinguished gastronomist, and possessor of an immense fortune, of which he made the best use (at least so said several choice epicures, his habitual guests), Survilius Rullus— such was his name—thought of celebrating by an extraordinary banquet the triumph of the illustrious consul, and the deliverance of the country. His cook, a young Sicilian slave of the greatest promise, and whose mode of cooking a dish of sows' paps procured him one day a smile of approbation from Lucullus, succeeded especially in those eminent performances which command the admiration of the guests, and give new strength to their exhausted appetites.

Rullus sent for him, and spoke thus: " Recollect that in three days Cicero will sup here: let the feast be worthy of him who gives it."

The Sicilian even surpassed himself. As soon as the guests had tasted the enticing delicacies of the first course, the hall echoed with an unanimous concert of applause, and the proud Amphitryon, intoxicated with joy, was going to ask that a crown might be presented to his beloved slave,[65] when the cook appeared, followed by four Ethiopians, who gracefully carried a silver vase of prodigious dimensions, in the shape of a large mortar. This extraordinary dish contained a wild boar; baskets of dates were suspended to his tusks, and charming little wild boars, in exquisite pastry, no doubt—for never was there a more tempting culinary exhalation—artistically surrounded the enormous animal.[66] Every voice was hushed; the guests waited in silence the

M

most profound.[67] The tables of the second service were placed round the guests, who raised themselves on the couches with greedy curiosity. The blacks deposited the precious burden before another domestic, a skilful carver, who opened the wild boar with incredible dexterity and precision, and presented to the astonished eyes of Rullus and his friends a second entire animal, and in this a third; then came fresh delicacies, all gradually diminishing in size, until, at length, a delicious little fig-pecker terminated this series of strange viands, of which Rome, wondering and astonished, long preserved the gastronomic remembrance.[68]

Man seldom prescribes to himself reasonable limits in the vast field of vanity and ostentation. At first it was thought an enviable boldness to have dared to serve an entire boar of a large size. Every one did the same thing, and at length it became quite common. It was necessary then to do better. One thought of having three at the same time; another had four; and soon the extravagant—and they were not few—caused eight wild boars à la Troyenne to appear at a single repast.[69] The Macedonian, Caranus, a man of spirit and of merit, placed himself at once on an eminence which baffled rivalry. He invited twenty guests to his wedding, and he had twenty wild boars served.[70]

It must be confessed that such magnificence rather resembles folly; but, alas! has not every nation its failings? Besides, the flesh of the wild boar enjoyed an astonishing reputation in Rome and Greece,[71] and no one could, with credit to himself, receive his friends at his table without presenting them with the fashionable dish,—the animal appointed by nature to appear at banquets.[72]

At length, however, they began to tire of this enormous dish; they divided it into three portions, and the middle piece obtained the preference.[73] Ultimately they served only the fillet and head; the latter of which was more particularly esteemed by the Romans.[74]

The Greeks tried their appetites by tasting the liver, which was served at the first course.[75]

The Romans sought to deprive the wild boar of its terrible ferocity; they raised them on their farms,[76] and sometimes they acquired enormous proportions. These immense beasts weighed no less than a thousand pounds.[77] But delicate connoisseurs had always the wisdom to prefer the dangerous inhabitant of the forest to these bloated victims of enervating domesticity,[78] whose insipid and degenerate flavour hardly betrayed their origin.

The wild boar was generally served surrounded by pyramids of fruits and lettuces.[79]

Wild Boar à la Pompée.—Clean and salt a wild boar, cover it with cummin; let it remain in salt during twenty-four hours; then roast it; sprinkle with pepper, and serve with a seasoning of honey, garum, sweet and cooked wine.[80]

Quarter of Wild Boar à la Thébaine.—Cook it in sea water with bay leaves. When very tender take off the skin, and serve with salt mustard, and vinegar.[81]

Fillet of Wild Boar à la Macédonienne.—Pound pepper, alisander, wild marjoram, skinned myrtle leaves, coriander, and onions; add honey, wine, garum, and a little oil. This seasoning must be submitted to a gentle fire; thicken with flour, and pour the whole over the wild boar as you draw it from the oven.[82]

Wild Boar's Liver à la Grecque.—Fry it, and serve with a seasoning of pepper, cummin, parsley seed, mint, thyme, savory, and roasted pine nuts; to which add honey, wine, garum, vinegar, and a little oil.[83]

Wild Boar's Head à la Cantabre.—Make the seasoning in the following manner: mix well, pepper, alisander, parsley seed, mint, thyme, and roasted pine nuts; add wine, vinegar, garum, and a little oil; afterwards onions and rue; thicken with whites of eggs; boil over a slow fire, and stir gently.[84]

Green Ham of Wild Boar à la Gauloise.—Insert a long and narrow blade at the joint, and carefully separate the skin from the flesh, so that the latter may be well covered with the following seasoning: pound pepper, bay leaves, rue, and benzoin; add to it some excellent gravy, cooked wine, and a little oil. Fill the ham, close the opening, and then cook it in sea water, with some tender shoots of laurel and dill.[85]

Under the Norman kings the wild boar's head was considered a noble dish, worthy of the sovereign's table. This, we are told, was brought to the king's table with the trumpeters sounding their trumpets before it in procession. "For," says Holinshed, "upon the day of coronation (of young Henry), King Henry II., his father, served him at table as sewer, bringing up the bore's head with trumpetes afore it, according to the ancient manner."—STRUTT, "*Manners and Customs,*" Vol ii., p. 19.

"A very small consumption is made of the old wild boar; the flesh is hard, dry, and heavy; the head only is good. The young wild boar is a fine and delicate game, also, when a year old. The ancients submitted those they could take away from their mother to castration, and left them afterwards to run about the woods, where these animals became larger than the others, and acquired a savour and flavour which made them preferable to the pigs we rear."—SONNINI.

THE HARE.

Plutarch contends that the Jews abstained from eating the hare, not because they thought it unclean, but because it resembled the ass, which they revered.[86] This is only a pleasantry on the part of the celebrated writer, with no other foundation than the fabulous tale of the grammarian Apion, who asserts in his book against the Jews that they preserved in Jerusalem an ass's head, which they adored.[87] We know that a sanitary motive was the cause of this animal being interdicted to the Israelites ;[88] and it has been also remarked that the ancient Britons abstained from it.[89]

This mammifer, everywhere very common, swarmed in the East, if we are to believe Xenophon, who saw a great number of them when marching with his troops to join young Cyrus.[90] Greece was abundantly stocked with them :[91] the inhabitants of islands of the Ægean sea had more than once to deplore the ravages which hunger caused these timid animals to commit, and whose fecundity they cursed.

Hegesander relates that, under the reign of Antigonus, an inhabitant of the island of Anaphe brought two hares into the neighbourhood. Their posterity became so numerous that the people were obliged to implore the gods to preserve the harvest, and to annihilate their formidable enemies. As the immortals turned a deaf ear to these complaints, recourse was had to Apollo alone, and the Pythonissa deigned to return this oracle : " Train hunting dogs, and they will exterminate the hares." [92] The advice was good, and deemed worthy of being adopted.

The Greeks esteemed highly the flesh of this quadruped, which was served roasted, but almost bleeding,[93] or made into delicious pies,[94] much in vogue in the time of Aristophanes.[95] Hippocrates had, however, forbidden the use of it. " The hare," said he, " thickens the blood, and causes cruel wakefulness;" [96] but epicurism will always think lightly of Hygeian precepts which do not accord with its own ideas. At all events, Galen was not of the same opinion as his colleague,[97] and Galen must be right.

The Emperor Alexander Severus eat a hare at each of his repasts.[98] Perhaps that prince shared the opinion of the Romans, who thought that a person who fed on hare for seven consectuive days became fresher, fatter, and more beautiful. A lady, named Gellia, had a large share of that unfortunate gift of nature which we call ugliness. She resolved to make a trial of this regimen, and submitted to it with a regularity really exemplary. She showed herself at the end of the week, and we are informed that no one thought her any the prettier for it.[99]

The epicures of Rome contented themselves with eating the shoulder of the hare, and left the remainder to less fastidious guests.[100]

THE RABBIT.

"The conies are but feeble folks, yet make they their houses in the rocks."[101] They taught mankind, it is said, the art of fortification, mining, and covered roads.[102] These skilful engineers come originally from warm climates ; from Africa, perhaps, whence they were brought to Spain.

They there became so numerous, and dug so well their holes beneath the houses of Tarragona, that that city was completely overthrown, and the greater part of the inhabitants buried beneath its ruins.[103]

Catullus calls Spain *Cuniculosa Celtiberia* (Celtiberian rabbit warren); and two medals, struck in the reign of Adrian, represent that peninsula under the form of a beautiful woman, clothed in a robe and mantle, with a rabbit at her feet. This animal was called in Hebrew, *Saphan,* of which the Phœnicians have made *Spania,* and the Latins *Hispania.*[104]

Strabo relates that the inhabitants of the Balearic Islands, despairing of being able to oppose the extraordinary propagation of rabbits, which nearly rendered their country uninhabitable, sent ambassadors to Rome to implore assistance against this new kind of enemy.[105] Augustus furnished them with troops, and the Roman arms were once more victorious.[106]

Aristotle says nothing of the rabbit, which, probably, was then little known in Greece. It afterwards became common enough, and that of Macedonia, in particular, found favour at tables renowned for delicacies.[107]

The Romans, those bold innovators in cookery, so desirous of strange and unheard of dishes, would only consent to eat rabbits on condition cf their being killed before they had left off sucking, or taken alive from the slaughtered mother, to be immediately transferred to the ardent stoves of their kitchens.[108] It was certainly reserved for that people to frighten the world by all kinds of culinary anomalies.

THE FOX.

A young fox, fattened on grapes, and roasted on the spit, is a tidbit for a king during the autumn.[109] Such was the idea of the Roman peasants; but we must be allowed, however, to differ from their opinion.

THE HEDGEHOG.

The Greeks willingly eat the hedgehog [110] in a *ragoût*—a dish the Romans never envied them.

THE SQUIRREL.

This charming little animal, which ought never to please but when alive, often appeared at Rome among the most elegant dishes of the feast.[111] At first it was only eaten by caprice: unfortunately for the little animal, it was found to be very nice.

THE CAMEL.

Aristotle gives the greatest praise to the flesh of this useful animal, and places it without hesitation above the most delicate viands.[112] The

Greeks, his countrymen, thought it worthy of being roasted for the table of sovereigns,[113] and the inhabitants of Persia and Egypt partook of the same enthusiasm. Rome thought the camel fit for the solitude of the Desert, but not for the ornament of banquets; and really, for this once, Rome appears to have been right.

"The flesh of the young dromedary is as good as that of veal, and the Arabs make of it their common food. They preserve it in vases, which they cover with fat. They make butter and cheese with the milk of the female."—DESMAREST.

The ancients, in their wars, made use of dromedaries. The soldiers when upon these animals formed a particular militia. In the Egyptian expedition Bonaparte renewed this ancient custom, and that cavalry caused a great deal of injury to the Bedouins and Arabs. Besides the rider, each dromedary carried provisions and munitions of war.

THE ELEPHANT.

Certain wandering tribes of Asia and Africa were thought formerly to be very fond of grilled elephant.[114] The Egyptians went so far in their pursuit of this delicacy, that the King Ptolemy Philadelphus was forced to forbid them, under pain of the most severe laws, to kill one of these animals, whose number diminished every day. The law was disregarded, and the elephant only possessed greater attractions for them.[115]

In our days, also, some semi-savage nations partake of the same taste. Le Vaillant, a celebrated traveller, and a most distinguished gastronomist, tells us that the first time he partook of an elephant's trunk, which was served him by the Hottentots, he resolved that it should not be the last; for nothing appeared to him of a more exquisite flavour.[116] But he reserves his greatest praises for the foot of the colossal quadruped. We will let him speak for himself:—

"They cut off the four feet of the animal, and made in the earth a hole about three feet square. This was filled with live charcoal, and, covering the whole with very dry wood, a large fire was kept up during part of the night. When they thought that the hole was hot enough, it was emptied: a Hottentot then placed within it the four feet of the animal, covered them with hot ashes, and then with charcoal and small wood ; and this fire was left burning until the morning. * * * My servants presented me at breakfast with an elephant's foot. It had considerably swelled in the cooking ; I could hardly recognise the shape, but it appeared so good, exhaled so inviting an odour, that I hastened to taste it. It was a dish for a king. Although I had often heard the bear's foot praised, I could not conceive how so heavy, so material an animal as the elephant, could furnish a dish so fine and delicate. * * * And I devoured, without bread, my elephant's foot, while my Hottentots, seated around me, regaled themselves with other parts, which they found equally delicious." [117]

The Romans never evinced fondness for the flesh of the elephant. This animal, with its gigantic proportions and rare intelligence, was found to be so amusing to the nation of kings, when dancing on the tight rope,[118] or in the terrible combats of the Circus,[119] that they hardly thought of roasting it, or making it into *fricassees*. We cannot, however, affirm that the gastronomic eccentricity of some Roman epicure did not dream of a monstrous feast, in which he may have offered to his guests an elephant *à la Troyenne* on a silver dish, made purposely for the occasion.

XX.

FEATHERED GAME.

Moses permitted his people to eat game, with the exception of birds of prey and some other species whose flesh appeared to him hard and unwholesome.[1]

The Egyptians piously offered to their priests the most delicate birds, which they willingly accepted, and eat, in order not to weaken their intelligence by the use of more simple and heavy food.[2]

Among the Greeks, at the commencement of the repast, little birds were served roasted, on which was poured a boiling sauce, composed of scraped cheese, oil, vinegar, and silphium.[3]

Feathered game appeared in Italy only at the second course. The Romans were very partial to it, and many epicureans, possessing strange tastes, found means to ruin themselves by eating pheasants and flamingoes.

The celebrated comedian, Æsopus, whom Cicero thought worthy of being his master in the art of declamation, had one day the fancy to regale himself with a dish of birds, the whole of which, when living, had both learned to sing and speak.[4] This gluttony of a new kind cost him very dear, and the supper of the barbarian was not any the better for it.

Some modern nations—the French among others—formerly eat the heron, crane, crow, stork, swan, cormorant, and bittern; the first three especially were highly esteemed, and Taillevant, cook of Charles VII., teaches us how to prepare these meagre, tough birds. Belon says that, in spite of its revolting taste when unaccustomed to it, the bittern is, however, among the delicious treats of the French.[5] This writer asserts also that a falcon, or a vulture, either roasted or boiled, is excellent eating; and that if one of these birds happened to kill itself in flying after the game, the falconer instantly cooked it. Liebaut calls the heron a royal viand!

These same men who eat vultures, herons, and cormorants, did not touch young game: they thought it indigestible; and, for instance, abstained from leverets and partridges.

The internal parts being the first to corrupt, the ancients carefully drew the game they wished to preserve. That done, they filled the inside with wheat or oats, and then placed it in the midst of a heap of flour or grain, with the feathers or hair on.

Thus protected from the contact of the air or insects, the game kept remarkably well.

THE PHEASANT.

The Argonauts discovered this magnificent bird on the shores of Phasis, a celebrated river of Colchis, and introduced it into Greece, where it was unknown.[6] This tradition, sung by the poets,[7] has only met with one contradictor, Isidorus,[8] who pretends that the pheasant is a native of an island of Greece, called Phasis.

All nations soon hastened to receive it with the favour its rich plumage and the exquisite delicacy of its flesh deserve. Carried in cages composed of precious wood, it adorned the triumphal march of Ptolemy Philadelphus, at his entry into Alexandria.[9] Ptolemy Evergetes, successor to that prince, caused pheasants to be sent from Media, which he destined for his aviary; and he never eat them, so much did he dread the idea of diminishing their number.[10] But, alas! custom and time, those jealous enemies of the greatest glories, eventually put an end to that. The unfortunate creature was stripped of its feathers and roasted; gluttony, an insatiable monster that never says "enough," rejoiced at being able to count it among the number of its conquests. The Greeks had coops for pheasants as we have for fowls, not to please the eye, but to ornament the table,[11] and a foolish prodigality caused a whole pheasant to be served to each guest in those luxurious repasts which the Athenians gave to display their pomp and ostentatious hospitality.[12]

Among the Romans, Pliny is the first (or we are mistaken) who mentions this bird, then very uncommon in Italy, since they went in quest of it to the banks of the Phasis.[13] Its rarity did not prevent Vitellius from having a *ragoût* of pheasants' brains,[14] mixed with other viands of an unheard-of delicacy, in the immense dish called by him " the Shield of Minerva."[15]

Pertinax willingly partook of pheasant, but on condition that they cost his miserly sensuality nothing. Heliogabalus would only eat them three times a week. Alexander Severus reserved them for solemn occasions.[16] They were sacrificed each morning to the statue of Caligula,[17] at the foot of which the vile troop of courtiers prostrated themselves at the very time even when Cæsar, in a fit of sanguinary monomania, wished that the Roman people had but one neck, that he might sever it at a blow.[18]

It is especially from the commencement of the 14th century that the pheasant, better appreciated in Europe, has resumed in banquets that remarkable place,[19] constantly assigned to it throughout this new era, in which our taste maintains it, and from which our posterity will never remove it, if they inherit that wonderful sentiment of the good and beautiful which so eminently distinguishes the epicures of the present day.

Let us add, for the comfort of weak stomachs, that the medical light of Pergamo—the illustrious Galen—recommends them the use of the flesh of pheasants;[20] that he prescribed it for himself, and found it a most delightful remedy.

"Mingrelia, or the antique Colchis, is the cradle of pheasants, that species of birds being stronger and finer there than anywhere else, but it is seen, however, all over Europe, in Africa, and Asia, even in the cold countries of the north. This beautiful bird forms an article of commerce with the Chinese, who sell them frozen in the market of Kiakta."—SONNINI.

THE PARTRIDGE.

The Greeks and Romans were acquainted with partridges, and eat them.[21] The red, at first very rare in Italy, were, however, advantageously replaced by the white, which true amateurs procured at a great expense from the Alps.[22]

The Athenians were fond of seeing them fight, and raised them for this cruel sport.[23]   Alexander Severus also sought in these sanguinary struggles relief from the cares of royalty.[24]

Aristippus, a more humane, perhaps a more luxurious, philosopher, gave as much as fourteen shillings for a fine fat partridge,[25] which, passing from the aviary to the kitchen, escaped the fatal vicissitudes of a desperate combat.

In Greece, people who knew how to enjoy life thought much of the leg of this warlike bird.[26]   It was fashionable not to touch any other part.   At Rome, when politeness was not of so much consequence, they sometimes ventured on the breast.   We, barbarians, eat the entire partridge.

THE QUAIL.

The dead may be raised by the means of a quail, said the ancients. Now for the proof: Hercules having been killed in Lybia, Iolaüs took one of these birds, which fortunately happened to be at hand, and placed it beneath his friend's nose.   The hero no sooner smelt it than his eyes opened to the light, and Acheron was forced to give up his prey.[27]

The learned Bochart denies this prodigy.[28] He affirms that Hercules was subject to epileptic attacks, and that, during a fit, they caused him to smell a quail, whose odour quickly cured him.[29]

The Phœnicians insisted that he was quite dead, and they all cried out, "A miracle!"[30] The reader must decide between them and Bochart.

In the Desert the Israelites fed on quails;[31] and this food, reserved for them by Divine goodness, caused no discomfort among the fugitive tribes.   The Greeks served them on their tables with partridges:[32] they raised them in aviaries, and eat them all the year round.[33] Aristotle speaks most highly of them, and does not attribute to them any dangerous property.[34] However, quails were banished from all Roman tables: they were no longer carefully fattened:[35] they were cursed, and accused of causing epilepsy in those who partook of their fatal and seductive flesh.[36] The authority of Galen confirmed this strange prejudice,[37] and these innocent birds, having lost all reputation in Italy, no doubt easily consoled themselves for the happy ostracism which delivered them from a too expensive glory.

At all events, it is probable that Rome had wickedly calumniated quails; two skilful men, devoted to the cause, undertook to defend them: they were called Hippolochus and Antiphanus.[38] Their eloquent pleadings caused a sensation; the epicureans were moved, and some of these birds were recalled, fattened, and roasted.

Quails, like cocks and partridges, seem born to fight to excess.[39] The Grecians encouraged their warlike ardour, and threw them into the arena, where they contemplated their furious attacks with as much pleasure as they experienced at the sight of gladiators murdering each other in order to amuse them.[40] Solon—the wise Solon—required that young men should be trained to courage at the school of these bold champions, and learn from them to despise danger, pain, and death.[41] We know that sensibility was little thought of in the plan of education formed by the great legislator. Long after him, however, the Areopagus gave a dreadful proof of this, by condemning to death a little boy who had amused himself by pulling out the eyes of all the quails unfortunate enough to fall into his hands. This precocious monster was too promising.[42]

THE THRUSH.

The immortal author of the Iliad did not disdain, it is said, to compose a poem in praise of thrushes. These verses were so beautiful that the Greeks learned them all by heart in their infancy.[43] The singular love of the ancients for this bird renders these poetical honours tolerably probable. More than once Comus has borrowed the lyre of Apollo.

In Greece, children were not allowed to eat thrushes, because it was feared that their delicious flesh might cause them to contract too early habits of gluttony and effeminacy. Young girls received them as presents from their bethrothed on the day of their marriage.[44] They were served at the most sumptuous feasts,[45] and Attica enriched with its gold the bird-catchers of that Daphne,[46] so celebrated for her luxury and scandalous voluptuousness.

Rome inherited this gastronomic rage. One of Varro's aunts reared thrushes in the country, and sold 60,000 of them every year, to the numerous epicures of the metropolis of the world. She derived an immense revenue from this speculation.[47] Magnificent aviaries were soon seen in all rich Roman villas; they were filled with thrushes; and the multitude of these birds became such that they furnished a plentiful manure for the land.[48] They were fed on crushed figs, mixed with wheaten flour; they had also millet, and great care was taken to preserve in the aviary a current of fresh and pure water to slake their thirst.[49] On days of triumph and rejoicing, a dozen of these tempting thrushes cost no less than twenty-seven shillings.[50]

On those solemn occasions more than one generous citizen, consulting his prodigality more than his purse, ruined himself[51] for love of his guests. More than one obsequious dependant spent his last sesterces in composing ingenious crowns of thrushes,[52] which his haughty patrons deigned to receive as a homage. It is true he was sometimes allowed to become a spectator of the repast which his gift was to embellish[53]—certainly a most flattering recompense for his gratitude and servility!

DESCRIPTION OF PLATE No. IX.

VARRO'S MAGNIFICENT AVIARY.—Adjoining his villa was a part of the house called the Ornithon, or the Aviary, of which some ruins are still remaining, between the two small rivers Vinius and Casinus, but can hardly be made out. More, perhaps, was in existence when the famous architect and antiquarian, Pierre Ligorio, drew the plan and profile more than 200 years ago. This drawing of Plate IX. is conformable with Varro's own description, who says that: "At the entrance there are two porticoes, or two large cages (in the Plate these are omitted for want of space); they are buildings with colonnades all round, on the top and sides there are nettings spread to prevent the escape of the birds. The entrance to the yards is between the two pavilions; two basins, long and wide, are alongside of the court-yard on the right and left of it; from them you pass to the grand double colonnade, the first circumference of which is of stone, and the second of pine; the distance from each other is five feet, and the whole of this middle space is filled with birds, which are prevented from escaping by small fillets all over the top and sides. There are, between the columns, like a small theatre, rails, like steps, put forward for the birds to perch upon. There are birds of various species, particularly singing birds, such as nightingales and blackbirds; a small canal supplies them with fresh water, and they are fed from under the netting. Facing the pedestals of the columns is a stone, raised one foot nine inches above the quay, and that is elevated two feet above the level of the water; its width is five feet, to enable the visitor to walk round. At the lower part of the quay, on the water-side, there are holes practised where the ducks can retire. In the centre of the large basin, about 200 feet in diameter, is a small island, bordered by a small colonnade, under which Varro treats his friends; in the middle, a round table, which a servant turns on a pivot, so that in succession the guests are supplied with dishes, plates, cups, and goblets. There is seen also an hemisphere, where the star Lucifer turns in the day, and Hesperus at night; both mark the hour, and are variable; on the same hemisphere the winds, to the number of eight, are marked with a hand that is always moving as the wind changes, the same as the clock of Cyprestus, at Athens."

The drawing of this Aviary is beautiful. It appears that Pierre Ligorio followed Varro's description; at all events, the drawing of this Plate perfectly agrees with it.

F. T. 2. Volant, del.

Grout & Saunders, sou

Heliogabalus eat only the brains of these birds.[54] This dish appeared to him most excellent, for it was very costly.

The extreme delicacy of this volatile, which poetical connoisseurs have celebrated in their verses,[55] recommends it to those with weak stomachs and to convalescents. Pompey being ill, his physician ordered him a thrush, but it was impossible to find one in Rome. Some one advised the celebrated general to apply to Lucullus, who fattened them throughout the year. "What," cried Pompey, ill-humouredly, "shall I have to thank Lucullus's pompous luxury for life!" He refused to eat the thrush, and he recovered.[56]

THE BLACKBIRD..

What has been already said of the thrush precludes the necessity of writing much on the blackbird, for both these kinds of birds were equally dear to the gastronomists of Greece and Italy.[57] They were fattened in the same manner,[58] served on the same tables. The blackbird, in fact, like the thrush, re-established the strength and health of the rich.[59] The poor were compelled to have recourse to less expensive remedies.

" The flesh of the blackbird, so delicate in the time of gathering grapes, acquires at that period a savour which makes it as precious as the quail, but becomes bitter when they feed on the juniper berries, the ivy, or other similar fruits. Some medicinal properties are attributed to it ; the oil in which the blackbirds have been cooked is recommended to persons afflicted with sciatica: and the soil of these birds, dissolved in vinegar, is, we are informed, a certain specific for removing the freckles of the face or spots on the skin."—VIEILLOT.

In 1468, Louis XI. ordered one of his authorised ruffians, named Perdriel, to seize all the tame blackbirds he could find in Paris. These poor birds were sent to Amboise, where a register was kept of what they said or sung. It appears that the king intended to punish those citizens of his capital who taught these innocent volatiles to repeat abuse of the sovereign, after which he would have wrung the necks of the too intelligent birds. Louis XI. could not carry out this singular idea, because he himself was shortly after the Duke of Burgundy's prisoner at Péronne. Blackbirds and citizens had a narrow escape.[60]

THE STARLING.

Drusus and Britannicus, sons of the Emperor Claudius, had a starling which spoke admirably the Greek and Latin. Alone he studied his lessons, and afterwards recited them to the astonished princes.[61] Science protected the learned bird from the fate reserved by the Greeks and Romans for the rest of its family, less distinguished by their erudition than by their culinary qualities. Starlings, roasted in the kitchens, honourably associated with partridges, blackbirds, and thrushes,[62] and the disciples of Galen recommended them to their patients, who willingly submitted to so nourishing and light a food.[63]

THE FLAMINGO.

A profound study of the art of good cheer caused the Romans to discover that the thick tongue of the phenicopter, or flamingo, presents towards its root a rather considerable adipose appendage. They tasted this lump of fat, and Rome was enriched with another dish.

It has been asserted that the glory of inventing this refinement in gluttony is due to Apicius. Italy possessed three gastrophiles of this name : the first flourished a short time before the dictatorship of Julius Cæsar; the second, Marcus Gabius, held a school of sensuality at Rome, under the reigns of Augustus and Tiberius; the third, Cælius, was contemporary with Trajan, and poisoned himself for fear of dying of hunger.

We possess, under the name of this last, a Latin work in ten books, from which we have borrowed largely, as the reader may have already remarked. It would be difficult to decide to which of the three Apicii it belongs. The author speaks of the flamingo, but does not mention its tongue : the treatise, then, is not the work of M. Gabius, who would doubtless have indicated the preparation of a dish of which Pliny assures us he was so fond.[64] As to Cælius, if he were the compiler of this

Pl. 10

Chas. K. Whittier, sculp.

EPICURUS.

APICIUS.

SEL BIOGRAPHY END OF ROMAN SUPPER.

Friant. del

curious volume, as it is thought, how comes it he has forgotten a dish so justly celebrated, in this magiric catalogue, in which no detail, however minute, seems to escape him? It would appear that this contested paternity rightfully belongs to the first Apicius, unless some of the learned contest it on the ground that the style of the work nowise agrees with the latinity of his century.[65]

May one of the learned societies of Europe some day take up this arduous question, and restore the ancient masterpiece to its admirable author. In the meantime the writer of the present work will continue to venerate the memory of Cælius Apicius, and offer him crowns of smallage, roses, and parsley, for his name embellishes the frontispiece of those pages which reveal to us the secrets of Roman cookery; and we repeat, with Sosie :—

> " Le véritable Amphitryon
> Est l'Amphitryon où l'on dine.[66]

Honour is due also to the other Apicius for his ingenious sauce of flamingo tongues. True, we have never tasted it, for this expensive fancy can only be satisfied in the marshes of the Nile.[67] It is still little known in Europe, but the most fastidious of the Romans regaled themselves with it.[68] Three Emperors, Caligula, Vitellius, and Heliogabalus—immortal triumvirate of incomparable polyphagists!—carried to indigestion their gastronomic delirium, their love for this famous *ragoût*.[69] These great authorities are conclusive.

The traveller, Dampier, wished to try the flesh of the flamingo, and he thought it very good, though lean, and very black.[70]

"The flesh of the phenicopterus is a dish more sought after in Egypt than in Europe; however, Catesby compares it for its delicacy to the partridge; Dampier says it has a fine flavour, although lean; Dutertre finds it excellent notwithstanding its marshy taste; the tongue is the most delicious part."—VIEILLOT.

FIG-PECKER, OR, BECAFICO.

The Duke of C * * * * had received from nature one of those culinary organizations which the vulgar assimilate with gluttony, and the man of art calls genius. Greece would have raised statues to him; the Roman emperor Vitellius would have shared the Empire with him. In

France he gained the esteem of all parties by inviting them to sumptuous banquets.

This rich patrician brought up with tender care a young *chef de
cuisine*, whom his *major-domo* had bequeathed to him on his death-
bed, as Mazarin did Colbert to Louis XIV. The disciple profited by
the learned lessons of the Duke ; already the young *chef's* head, eye,
and hand possessed that promptitude and certainty whose union is so
rarely combined: there remained for him only the instruction of experience.

One day, in the month of September, some guests of the highest
class, all professed judges in the order of epicureans, met together at
the residence of the noble Amphitryon, who often claimed the authority
of their enlightened judgment. The learned Areopagitæ had to pronounce on certain new dishes: it was necessary, by dint of seduction,
to captivate the favour and patronage of these judges by disarming
their severity.

Everything was served to the greatest nicety, everything was deemed
exquisite, and they only awaited the dessert—that little course which
causes the emotion of the great culinary drama to be forgotten—when
the young *chef* appeared, and placed in the centre of the table a silver
dish, containing twelve eggs. " Eggs! " exclaimed the Duke. The
astonished guests looked at each other in silence. The cook took one
of the eggs, placed it in a little china boat, slightly broke the shell, and
begged his master to taste the contents. The latter contined to remove
the white envelope, and at length discovered a savoury and perfumed
ball of fat. It was a fig-pecker of a golden colour—fat, delicate, exquisite—surrounded by a wonderful seasoning.[71]

The good old man cast on his pupil a look full of tenderness and
pride ; and, holding out his hand to him: " You are inspired by
Petronius," said he ; " to imitate in such a manner is to create. Courage !
I am much pleased with you."

This classic dish—a revival from the feasts of Trimalcio—enjoyed
only an ephemeral glory. Europe was on fire ; a warlike fever raged
everywhere ; and Paris soon forgot the eggs of Petronius.

The fig-pecker merits the attention of the most serious gastronomists.
The ancients reckoned it among the most refined of dishes.[72] The
Greeks made delicate pies of this bird, which exhaled an odour so
tempting, that criticism was disarmed beforehand.[73]

The Romans gave it their entire esteem,[74] and prepared it with truffles and mushrooms.[75] Among them, men who knew what good cheer means, thought there was nothing worth eating in birds but the leg and lower part of the body. Fig-peckers were the only exception to this rule : they were served and eaten entire.

"In the southerly parts of France, and in Italy, all the different species of linget, and almost all birds with a slender beak, are commonly called becafico, because in the autumn they attack and eat the figs, and thereby the flesh of these birds becomes then fat and exquisite ; but that really known as the becafico is remarkable for its delicacy ; therefore it has at all times been *recherché* as an excellent eating. It is like a small lump of light fat—savoury, melting, easy of digestion ; and, in truth, an extract of the juice from the delicious fruits it has fed upon."—VIEILLOT.

———

THE ORTOLAN.

Florence and Bologna sent to Rome cases of ortolans, the enormous price of which irritated instead of discouraging gluttony.[76] They arrived in the metropolis of the world, picked and separated one from the other by layers of flour to prevent decomposition.[77] Each of these little birds furnished only a mouthful ; but this incomparable mouthful eclipsed everything else, and produced a sort of epicurean extacy which may be called the *transcendantalism* of gastronomy.

Ortolans were submitted to the same treatment as fig-peckers in their preparation.

———

THE OSTRICH.

There were tribes formerly in Arabia who fed on ostriches, and who for this reason were called strutiophagists.[78] Marmot asserts that, in his time, they were eaten in Africa, although their flesh was glutinous, and had a bad smell. When the people of Numidia took any that were young, they reared and fatted them, and led them to feed by flocks in the Desert ; and as soon as they were fat they killed and salted them.[79]

The Arabs of the present day abstain from them ; but it is said they seek much the fat, which they use plentifully in cooking.

They were served at Rome on a few tables. This was nothing but a depravation of taste.

Heliogabalus, who understood good living better, contented himself with the brains of ostriches. Six hundred of these animals furnished enough for one meal.[80] The devastation was great, but the emperor had made a good supper.

The ostrich's eggs are very hard, very heavy, and very large; their weight often equals three pounds. The colour is of a dirty white, with light yellow veins; they are good to eat. In Africa they are sought after as a *friandise*, and cooked in various ways. The commonest and the best is, after breaking, to mix and cook them with a good deal of butter. They are large enough and sufficient for a man's meal.

When the Arabs have killed an ostrich they open its throat, and make a ligature under the opening; three or four men take the bird, and shake it, the same as rincing a pouch; after which, the ligature being undone, a considerable quantity of a greasy substance comes out, mixed with blood and fat as thick as coagulated oil. One ostrich produces as much as twenty pounds of it, and it is used for the preparation of dishes, for the cure of rheumatism, *humeurs froides*, and paralysis. The Romans used this grease for the same purposes, and believed it possessed the most precious qualities.

THE STORK.

In spite of the religious respect of the Romans for this bird, the emblem of peace[81] and domestic virtues, Sempronius Rufus, an ancient prætor, caused his cook to dress some young storks; and this brought into fashion[82] a dish which caprice alone could introduce at feasts.[83]

THE SEA-SWALLOW.

Among the ancients, the swallow—joyous herald of spring—possessed little attraction for those men whom their gluttony has rendered so justly celebrated. Alas! they knew not the "Salangan swallow," *hirundo esculenta;* they never tasted those birds' nests which Europe still envies the East.

The inhabitants of the Philippine Islands give the designation of salangan swallow to a little coast bird (the halcyon, or kingfisher), celebrated for the singular construction of its nest. These nests have been compared to those which the Greeks and Romans called halcyon's nests; but this comparison is false, since the marine productions to which they gave this name are not birds' nests but polypus's, or the cylindrical covering of the polypi—the *halcyonium*—a kind of medicament, of which there were several varieties.[103]

All travellers agree that the Chinese, and other eastern nations, have an extreme partiality for the salangan's nest, as a delicious seasoning for their viands, and that they value it excessively; but they differ strangely as to its nature, its form, and the places where it is found.

According to some, the material of these nests is a froth of the sea, or the spawn of fish, and strongly aromatic. Others say it has no taste. Some pretend that it is a juice gathered by the salangans from the tree called *salambouc;* some maintain that it is a viscous humour that they give out from the beak at a certain period of the year; and, lastly, many affirm that these birds compose it entirely from the remains of fish-zoophytes.

With respect to the form, some say that it is hemispherical; others that it resembles a shell valve.

As to the places where the salangans build their nests, some observers assure us that it is fixed on the rocks a little above the level of the sea; in the hollows of those same rocks; and, lastly, that they conceal them in holes which they burrow under ground. According to Kœmpfer, these nests, so far as they are known to us, are nothing more than a preparation concocted from the flesh of the polypi.

The celebrated traveller Poivre, while occupied one day in picking up shells and coral near Java, penetrated a rather deep cavern at a short distance from the sea shore, and found the sides of it covered with little nests, in the form of a deep shell, firmly fixed to the rock. These nests were taken on board, and several persons who had been in China immediately recognised them as being identical with those that the Chinese seek with such avidity. The birds which had built them were true swallows, of about the size of the humming bird. Poivre adds that, in the months of March and April, the sea from Java to Cochin

China is covered with spawn, which has the appearance of half-dissolved glue, and that he had learned from the Malays and the Cochin Chinese that the salangan builds its nest with this spawn. All agreed on this point. The bird picks it up as he skims the water, or from the rocks where the spawn coagulates. It is at the end of July and the commencement of August that the Cochin Chinese collect the nests, and, as the young birds are hatched in March and April, the species do not suffer by it.

By the subsequent examination of these nests it was found that they presented the form of the half of a hollow, lengthened ellipsoid. They are composed, externally, of very thin laminæ, nearly concentric, and laid one over the other. The interior presents several layers of irregular net-work, superposed one over another, and formed of a multitude of threads of the same matter as the external laminæ, and which cross and re-cross in every direction.

Their composition, which has a slight taste of salt, is of a yellowish white and demi-transparent; it softens in warm water without dissolving, and increases in volume. It is a substantial food, and would be excellent for persons suffering from exhaustion, whose debile stomachs ill perform their functions. Poivre declares that he never eat anything more fortifying than a pottage made with these nests and some good meat.

The salangan nests are of two sorts—the white and the black It appears that the white nests are those of the same year, and that the black ones belong to an epoch less recent. The birds are engaged about two months in preparing them, and the Chinese do not take them away until the young ones are feathered, and begin to be pretty strong on the wing.[104]

———

This nomenclature would be incomplete, did we not briefly mention some kinds of game which appeared with more or less favour on the tables of the ancients.

The *Wood-Hen*, dear to the Greeks,[84] was not common at Rome in the time of Varro. The curious reared them in aviaries with other rare birds.[85]

The *Bustard*, the *Water-Hen*, and the *Teal*, found many admirers.[86]

The Romans reared the last-named,[87] and judged it worthy of notice among the most delicate morsels of the feast.

The *Woodcock*, which is thought to be the *rustica perdix* of Martial,[88] and the *Snipe* do not appear to have obtained from the gastrophilists of antiquity that attention they deserved. This delicious game was ill-appreciated in Italy and at Athens. History, that "conscience of posterity," reproaches them with this oversight, and is astonished that the *Curlew* should have usurped, particularly in Greece,[89] a pre-eminence which it certainly does not deserve.

"The fat of the snipe is of a most delicate savour, which it acquires only after the first appearance of the frosty season. It is cooked like the woodcock, without being drawn."—VIEILLOT.

The *gourmets* have a way of knowing when the flesh of the woodcock is arrived at the degree of flavour required to be sought after : the bird is suspended by the beam-feather of the middle of its tail ; when the body gets loose and full, then is the time to eat it.

"The woodcock is cooked with the entrails in, which, being pounded with what they contain, form its own and best seasoning."—SONNINI.

The *Crow*, an object of superstitious worship among the Egyptians,[90] offered to the less scrupulous inhabitants of Alexandria a dish unequalled in delicacy ;[91] but which never seems to have tempted the nations of the west.

The *Turtle Dove*,[92] whose timid innocence caused it to be revered in Assyria,[93] had a less glorious destiny at Rome. It was roasted, and epicures greedily devoured the legs.[94]

The *Lark* joined to the delicate flavour of its flesh a more precious quality ; either roast or boiled, it infallibly cured persons attacked with the colic.[95] We cannot say whether it possesses this useful property at the present day.

"The common lark, which is called at Paris *mauviette*, is generally looked upon as a wholesome, delicate, and light game. It is dressed in various ways ; and the *gourmets* appreciate the value of the excellent lark pies which have established the reputation of the town of Pithiviers in France."—SONNINI.

The Romans went to almost fabulous expenses in order to procure game. What enormous sums, may we not imagine, were given for those dishes of flamingoes' tongues and ostriches' brains already mentioned ! What must have been the cost of the seven thousand birds which the brother of Vitellius served to the voracious emperor![96] And yet all these follies fall far short of those they committed through their love of fish.

The inventive genius of the Greeks discovered in ichthyophagy strange refinements, though always impressed with we know not what kind of propriety, which seems to palliate their excesses. The Romans at first imitated, and soon afterwards surpassed them. Their frightful gluttony was revived by crime, and exulted in barbarity. The sea eels (conger, or *muræna helena*) will not eat; let a slave be thrown to them, young and healthy, his flesh will be more tempting and alive, that his struggle against unspeakable tortures may the better irritate the devouring ardour of these beloved fish. And a few days afterwards, the grave patrician, or the noble knight, again offered them this human food; and no remorse, no doubt, no gloom, ever clouded his brow; no thrill of horror crossed his mind, while he feasted on those sea eels he had fattened so well.

More than two-thirds of the inhabitants of the most civilised countries were plunged in slavery, and employed solely to gratify the sensuality of the other third. That alone gives a terrifying idea of the contempt in which man was held by his fellow-man, of the power of egotism, and of the vast corruption resulting from it. And what cruelties were committed in the face of heaven, sanctioned by the law, and by the manners and customs of society! The masters had absolute power over their slaves, and could punish them with blows or death at their own will and pleasure.[97] If an unfortunate servant happened to taste a sauce, or the remains of a fish, this unpardonable crime was often punished by crucifixion.[98] The virtuous Cato sold his old slaves at whatever price they would fetch, rather than feed useless beings.[99] The senator, Q. Flaminius, put one of his domestics to death as a new spectacle for one of his friends, who had never enjoyed the pleasure of seeing a man killed.[100] If the father of a family was assassinated in his house, and the murderer was not discovered, all the slaves were subject to the capital punishment. One of the grandees of Rome, who possessed four hundred of them, having been killed by one of the number, they were all put to death.[101] At the funeral of rich persons, a certain number of slaves were often slain as victims agreeable to their manes.

And what is remarkable is, that these things, which we can hardly believe, were not viewed as excesses, not even as an abuse of power, but simply as the exercise of a natural right. Such scenes were witnessed daily, without exciting the least censure, or the slightest protestation, on the part of those numerous writers and sophists, who passed their whole lives in declaiming against the manners of the age. It is true that legislation had taken the lead by applying to slaves this dreadful aphorism: " They are still more null than vile ;"—*Non tam viles quàm nulli sunt.*[102]

Such were the conquerors of the world! Such were those Romans who invented dreadful crimes through love of good living!

XXI.

FISH.

PERHAPS it has not been sufficiently remarked that the science of ichthyophagy is generally developed in a direct ratio with the civilization of a people. Man began at first by satisfying the imperious necessities of his stomach; he then eat to live, and all was good to him. Experience by degrees gave rise to *eclectism*—choice. It was then discovered that a coarse and solid food might be replaced by a delicate and savoury alimentation; joyous appetite, and sensuality, its effeminate companion, took the place of hunger, and this happy couple gave birth to the more amiable of fairies, who, under the name of Gastronomy, was soon to govern the world and prescribe to it imperishable laws.

It is asserted that the art of preparing fish was one of the first boons of this powerful sovereign, and that, instructed by her, Thetis rendered ichthyophagist the god of light and the fine arts.[1]

The Jews, an agricultural people, living far from the borders of the sea, attached but very little importance to fishing and the researches necessarily attendant on it; so much so, that we hardly perceive any trace among them of this kind of food, which Moses did not entirely interdict, since that wise legislator was satisfied with prohibiting fishes without scales or fins.[2] What an immense wealth remained unexplored! Let us pity them for not having known how to profit by it, notwithstanding the good will of the Phœnicians, inhabitants of the coast, who brought them the produce of their maritime excursions.

Let us say it: the Hebrews were tolerably bad cooks. They possessed most admirable laws, a fertile country, courage and many virtues, but their sobriety never would allow them to understand the art of good living. In that, they are to be pitied.

We must agree that the Egyptians had better taste. Worshippers of certain fish, they used to embalm them[3] as a means of preservation; and what is still better, they eat others in spite of the example of their priests, who never touched them.[4] In fact, the preparation of those dishes required the trouble of a little study and culinary labour; therefore, to avoid it, they eat the fish raw when very hungry; the epicures dried them in the sun, and they were served salted on great solemnities.

But it was left to a woman to understand this wholesome and delicate food, and to raise it to the rank it ought always to have occupied.

Gatis—let her be named with admiration—Queen of Syria, and no doubt a beautiful woman, was so fond of fish that, in order to be continually supplied with the choicest quality, she ordered all caught in her kingdom to be brought to her, and that none should be eaten without the royal permission. This law, for it really was one, created great dissatisfaction; but she very sensibly allowed them to complain, and continued to treat herself and those of her privileged subjects whom she condescended sometimes to admit to her table, with the most exquisite dishes of fish, such as the tunny, conger eel; and carp.[5] It is much to be regretted that the chroniclers of that time have forgotten to transmit to us the name of the cook of this illustrious Queen, and the recipes of the sauces she preferred.

With great pleasure we turn to the Greeks, that charming people who had only to set their foot on the most barren soil to cover it with flowers, and who laid the foundation of ichthyophagy as well as all other sciences.

It appears, however, that, at first, they thought but little of fish as an aliment. None had ever been served to the heroes of Homer, and Ulysses, relating that his hungry companions had partaken of some fish, seems to excuse them, by saying: "Hunger pressed their digestive organs."[6] To be sure a celebrated philosopher,[7] and also an amiable epicurean,[8] attributed this grievous abstinence of those warriors to the fear of being enervated by dishes too delicious. And then, the terrible Achilles and the impetuous Ajax could not, perhaps, make up their minds to degustate under their tents a sole *au gratin*, or a fried herring, with the slow precaution more humble mortals willingly submit to.

But shortly after that, fresh and salt fish became one of the principal articles of diet with the Hellenes.

Aristophanes and the gastrophilist Athenæus, allude to it a

hundred times in their writings, and various personages are the subjects of biting sarcasms on account of their excessive partiality to the mullet, scar, and turbot. We may name, among others, Philoxenes of Cythera, who learning from his doctor that he was going to die of indigestion, for having eaten too much of a most exquisite fish: "Be it so," he calmly exclaimed; "but, before I go, allow me to finish the remainder." [9]

Everyone knows the witty jokes of Lucian, who informs us that he knew a philosopher who examined, with the most serious comicality, the nature of the soul of an oyster. [10]

Highly favoured by the neighbourhood of the sea, the Greek population applied themselves, with that peculiar taste which characterized them, to distinguish the best species; and skilful cooks knew how to give to fish the most refined flavour, thanks to the numerous combinations of ingredients which we too have learned from the ancient authors who have written on dietetics. They possessed various ways of preparing them with salt or oil, and aromatics. [11] Athenæus has transmitted to us some very important precepts upon their seasoning. Æschylus and Sophocles were not above lowering their tragic muse by sometimes introducing remarks on fish sauce.

The productions of the sea had for Athens such an irresistible interest, that a law of police forbad all fishmongers to sit down until they had parted with the whole of their stock; so that the uncomfortable position of standing made them more submissive, and induced them to dispose of the fish at a more reasonable price. [12] This regulation in the "Billingsgate" of Athens was very rigorously observed, and the purchasers were highly delighted with it.

They also required that the fish should always be out of the water; and this wise law, consequently, did not allow its being preserved, or the price to be increased. [13] And finally, as soon as any kind of fish was brought to market, they were required to call the customers together immediately, by a kind of market-bell, which was a sort of invitation to come and make their purchases. [14]

Some would-be philosophers, members of the opposition of that period, thought of raising their voices against the common taste. Symmachus, Polycrates, and Lamprias, tried to prove, in their writings, that those who eat fish were the most cruel and ferocious of men. These tender ichthyophilists were laughed at, and their works had no sale.

The Romans inherited the predilection of the Greeks, "For the dumb companions of the fair Amphitryte;" but, excited by the love of the marvellous, they stocked the sea with imaginary beings; and they saw whales of four acres, fishes of two hundred cubits, and even that eel, or that serpent, which veridical navigators have seen again in our days. It was then thirty feet in length,[15] but now it is much longer!

Pliny, who believed so many things, swore to these by the twelve great gods of Olympus. At all events, we are much indebted to that laborious naturalist for very precious information. He has made us acquainted with the scare, which the Roman epicures preferred to every other species. After the scare, the eel-pout or lotas'-liver enjoyed a great reputation. The red mullet, which is still much esteemed, was considered as one of the most delicate of dishes, and the Romans in fashionable circles employed it in a refinement of pleasure of a singular kind.

It is well known that this fish, when the scales are removed, still remains of a fine pink colour. The fops of Rome having remarked that, at the death, this colour passed through a succession of the most beautiful shades, the poor mullet was served alive, inclosed in a glass vessel; and the guests, attentive and greedy of emotions, enjoyed this cruel spectacle, which presented to them a gradation of colours, which insensibly disappeared.[16]

The greatest sensualists killed it in brine, and Apicius was the first who invented this kind of luxury. The brine most in use, in such cases, was made with the blood of mackerel, and that was one of the varieties of that famous garum so highly praised by the Latin authors, and which was to them, at that period, what the fish sauces of the English are now. We will give, in this work, the various preparations of this so celebrated condiment, and the reader will then be able to judge for himself.

Apicius, the man of culinary progress, proposed a prize to any one who could invent a new brine made with the liver of red mullets. History has not transmitted to us the name of the fortunate conqueror; but Juvenal informs us that Asinius Celer offered sixty pounds for one of these fishes which weighed six pounds.[17]

This was, after all, but a trifling folly, in the midst of so many extravagances which several writers have carefully registered. Lucullus, the most ostentatious of the patricians, had a mountain cut through in the neighbourhood of Naples, so as to open a canal and bring up the sea and its fishes to the centre of the gardens of his sumptuous villa.[18]

The love of fish became a real mania : turbots excited a *furore* of admiration—the *muræna Helena* was worshipped.   Hortensius, the orator, actually wept over the death of the one he had fed with his own hands ; the daughter of Drusus ornamented hers with golden rings ; each had a name, and would come with speed when it heard the voice of the master, whose happiness depended on his fish.[19]

Sometimes, in a moment of over tenderness for his dear *muræna Helena,* Vedius Pollio, a Roman knight of the highest distinction, and one of the intimate friends of the Emperor Augustus, could find nothing better to do than to feed them with the flesh of his slaves, who were thrown to them alive.[20]   It is true that these wretched creatures gene- rally deserved this terrible chastisement ; for instance, Seneca speaks of one who had the awkwardness to break a crystal vase[21] while waiting at supper on the irascible Pollio.   This unfortunate slave having managed to escape from the hands of those who were conducting him to this horrible death, he went and fell on his knees at the feet of Cæsar, whom he implored to inflict some less frightful torture. Augustus, moved to the very soul, granted him his liberty, had all of Vedius's vases broken, and ordered that the pieces should be used to fill up the reservoir in which the barbarous knight fed his *muræna Helena.*[22]

Having given this rapid sketch of the principal periods of ichthy- ophagy among the ancients, little remains to be said of later ages in which we find few traces of any particular or excessive predilection for this kind of alimentation.   If we are to believe Dio,[23] the first inhabi- tants of Great Britain never eat fish.   The English have not thought it expedient to imitate their ancestors in this respect.

Under the reign of Edward II., certain fish, especially the sturgeon, never appeared in England except on the table of the king: it was prohibited to all others.   In 1138, Stephen wanted to modify this interdiction ; but after his reign it was again in vigour, and considered as a royal prerogative.

In France, anybody could eat fish, of any and all kinds ; but every fishmonger was obliged to obtain permission from the king to sell it.[24]

The sumptuary laws of that kingdom inform us of nothing very interesting on this essential of gastrology.   We find, however, by the Edict of 1294, that Philip-le-Bel allowed, on fast-days, two herring- pottages, and only one sort of fish—a meagre dinner, if ever there was one, and which, thank heaven, has fallen into complete disuse.   Louis

XII. was very fond of good cheer, and, consequently, he appointed six fishmongers to supply his table with fresh-water fish;[25] Francis I. had twenty-two;[26] Henry the Great, twenty-four.[27]

Under the reign of Louis XIV. fish acquired a singular vogue in the city as well as at court, owing to the marvellous talent of that prince's cook, who discovered the art, supposed to be lost, of giving to the delicate flesh of the pike, the carp, and the trout, the shape and flavour of the most exquisite game.

At this period we have the celebrated Vatel, one of the most illustrious officers of the household that ever flourished in the palace of the Princes of Condé. This inimitable major-domo understood that a dinner without fish was a cheerless one. One day when his noble master entertained Louis XIV. at a royal banquet, at Chantilly, which the genius of Vatel rendered more brilliant, the fish from the coast failed; he sent everywhere, but none could be found. He was completely bewildered: he met his august master, whose kind words, full of benevolence, only served to increase his desperation; he left him, ran to his chamber, took his sword, and three times pierced his heart. Shortly after, fish arrived from all quarters. Vatel was called—no Vatel! He was sought for, and at last discovered—Vatel was no more!

It appears that, in former times, there was a remarkable consumption of fish in England on the 4th of July, the Festival of St. Ulric. The following verses, by Barnaby Gouge prove it :—

ST. HULDRYCHE.

" Wheresoever Huldryche hath his place, the people there brings in
   Both capes and pykes, and mullets fat, his favour here to win.
   Amid the church there sittieth one, and to the aultar nie,
   That selleth fish, and so good cheep, that every man may buie ;
   Nor any thing he loseth here, bestowing thus his paine,
   For when it hath beene offred once, 't is brought him all againe,
   That twise or thrise he selles the same, vngodlinesse such gaine
   Both still bring in, and plentiously the kitchen doth maintaine,
   Whence comes this same religion newe ? What kind of God is this,
   Same Huldryche here, that so desires and so delightes in fishe ?[28] "

An ordinance of King John informs us that, in the 14th century, people eat porpoises and even seals.[29] In the days of the troubadours, they fished for dolphins and whales in the Mediterranean, and the flesh of these sea monsters was considered excellent.[30]

STURGEON.

This enormous cartilaginous inhabitant of the ocean, the Mediterranean, the Red, Black, and Caspian Seas, received from the Greeks, after its death, honours in which none of the most delicate or renowned fish participated. It was announced to the guests by the sound of trumpets; and slaves, magnificently dressed, placed it on the table in the midst of garlands and flowers.[31]

Joy brightened every face; a more generous wine filled fresh goblets, and some flatterers—for the sturgeon possessed many—with eyes fixed on the noble accipenser, compared its flesh to the ambrosia of the immortals.[32]

The high price of the sturgeon contributed in no small degree to such brilliant praise. This king of banquets would have ruined a modest citizen of Athens, and hardly did the exiguity of its proportions permit its figuring among the expensive rarities of an Attic supper, when it had cost only a thousand drachms, or about £16 sterling.[33]

The Romans, imitators and emulators of the luxury of the Greeks, were almost equally fond of this fish; and, like them, reserved it for princely tables, or aristocratic opulence. It would seem, however, that the enthusiasm excited by the sturgeon somewhat cooled under the reign of Vespasian.[34] Perhaps at this period it became more common, or was sold at a more moderate price. Nothing more was requisite in Rome to deprive a dish of its most brilliant vogue and most powerful patronage.

However, the poet Martial, by nature no great flatterer, passes a pompous eulogium on the monstrous fish,[35] and judges it worthy of being placed on the luxurious tables of the Palatine Mount, that West-end of Rome, rendered illustrious by the presence of kings, nobles, and emperors.[36]

We have before observed that the sturgeon was formerly a royal dish in England.[37] A celebrated traveller assures us that, at the present day, the Chinese abstain from it, and that the sovereign of the Celestial Empire consigns it to his own kitchens, or dispenses it to a few of his greatest favourites.[38]

This gigantic accipenser, which often weighs two hundred pounds, is quite common in Siberia, where they even catch some of a much larger size, since some of the females have been found to contain two hundred pounds weight of eggs.[39] In 1750, one was caught in Italy which weighed 550 lbs. There are some in Norway, the head alone of which yields a tun of oil,[40] and whose immense proportions would formerly have astonished the most intrepid gastrophilists of Athens, Syracuse, and Rome.

An alimentary substance, called caviar, furnished almost exclusively by Russia to the rest of Europe, is prepared from the spawn of several kinds of sturgeons.

The spawn of the large sturgeon produces caviar of an inferior quality; that of the common sturgeon, and the sterlet, is prized as being more delicate, when it is carefully separated from the vessels and membranes with which it is intersected, well impregnated with brine, pressed, and slightly dried. White caviar, it is said, is the best of all. It is reserved for the court.[41]

There are two sorts of caviar: granulated caviar, and sack caviar.

The manufacture of the first named is performed by pressing the spawn on a sieve, and rubbing it in every direction to remove the pellicles which adhere to it, after which it is put into strong brine for one hour, then drained in a sieve, and, finally, pressed close into barrels, so as to entirely fill them before the head is fastened down.[42]

The manufacture of the other kind of caviar only differs in two particulars. The spawn is manipulated while in the brine, in order to soften it, and it is put, in small portions of about half-a-pound each, into linen bags, which are powerfully twisted to extract all the brine before it is pressed into the barrels.

The workmen employed in these operations make a third kind of caviar with the refuse. This sort, used only by the poorest classes, deserves no notice.

For some years past, they have introduced the method of salting the roes as they are taken from the fish, and packing them into barrels, where they remain seven or eight months; after which they are again salted, and then dried in the sun.

Caviar occupies a very distinguished place in Russian, Turkish, German, and Italian gastronomy. The Greeks, in particular, live upon it almost exclusively during the long Lent fasts prescribed by their Church.[43]

o

RED MULLET.

Philoxenes, of Cythera, supped one night with Dionysius, tyrant of Sicily. It happened that the prince was served with a magnificent mullet, whereas a very small one was presented to his guest. The philosopher took his fish in his hand, and, with a very serious air, held it to his ear. Dionysius asked him what he was doing. " I am busy with my Galathea," replied Philoxenes, " and I am questioning him on the subject of Nerea; but I can obtain no answer from him, because he was taken at too early an age. I am certain, however, that the other, evidently much older, which lies before you, is perfectly well acquainted with what I wish to know." The tyrant, who happened that evening to be in a good humour, laughed at the joke, and offered the larger mullet to the witty gastronomist.[44]

The unbridled and cruel luxury of ancient Rome required that this fish should be cooked by a slow fire, on the table and under a glass, that the guests might gloat on its sufferings before they satiated their appetites with its flesh.[45] It is true this barbarous gratification was very expensive, and it was necessary to be very rich to indulge in it—consequently it was decidedly very fashionable, quite natural, and in the very best taste.

Ordinary mullets weighed about 2 lbs. ;[46] these hardly deserved that their dying agonies should for an instant amuse the guests; they were worth only about £15 or £20 each. But sometimes fortune threw in their way much larger ones; and the opulent amateur esteemed himself only too fortunate when he could obtain a fish of three[47] or four pounds[48] for a much higher sum than he had paid for the slave, tutor of his children.

Crispinus was fond of mullets. He obtained one weighing four or six pounds, for which the fishmonger asked only £60.[49] This was giving it away; and certainly the man did not understand his trade. Crispinus, on becoming the possessor of this wonderful treasure, was astonished at his good fortune, and the whole of Rome long refused to believe it.

In the reign of Tiberius, three of these fish were sold for 30,000 sesterces,[50] or £209 9s. 8d.; and this emperor was one day generous enough to give up to P. Octavius, for the low price of 5,000 sesterces, a very fine mullet which had just been presented to him.[51]

And yet some persons of culinary authority paid but little attention to the flesh of this delicate fish; they sought only the liver and head; and if they paid for it so dearly, it was solely to find some few mouthfuls more in these two parts,[52] to which caprice, enthusiasm, that fever of admiration, and we know not what extraordinary gastronomic rage, gave an inestimable price, which at the present day excites only a smile of incredulity.

Pliny speaks of a mullet caught in the red sea, which weighed eighty pounds.[53] "At how much," adds this great naturalist, "would it have been valued had they caught it in the environs of Rome!" We may suppose, without the least exaggeration, that many a senator would have offered £1,500 to become its possessor.

It is thus that the mistress of the world foolishly dissipated in ephemeral whims the immense treasures poured into her lap by tributary kings—conquered and spoliated nations. Each day her patricians, knights, and nobles, tired of their importunate opulence, solicited new diversions, and invented new excesses. The mullet for a moment satisfied their prodigality, and amused their barbarity; but Heliogabalus appeared, and he imagined prodigies of gluttony which excited at once admiration and envy. The liver of this fish appeared to him too paltry; he took it into his head to be served with large dishes completely filled with the gills.[54] Now, we know that the mullet possesses only two. This dish, whose price would have enriched a hundred families, was worthy of the Sardanapalus of Rome, who, at the age of eighteen, had exhausted the treasures of the empire, and whom a violent death seized most *à propos*, at the moment when he had attained the extreme limits of crime and infamy.

The Romans served the mullet with a seasoning of pepper, rue, onions, dates, and mustard, to which they added the flesh of the sea hedge-hog reduced to a pulp, and oil.[55]

When the liver alone was to be eaten, it was cooked, and then seasoned with pepper, salt, or a little garum—some oil was added, and hare's or fowl's liver, and then oil was poured over the whole.[56]

The Greeks knew how to appreciate the mullet. They thought highly of those caught on their own shores[57], and placed them in the first rank of the most exquisite dishes of their delicate cookery.

" It is with the eggs of mullets, when salted, pressed, washed, and dried, that the preparation known as *botargo* or *botarcha* is made. It is very *recherché* in Italy, and other southern countries, as a seasoning." —Dr. Cloquet.

SEA-EEL.

The sumptuous abode of L. Crassus echoes with his sighs and groans. His children and slaves respect his profound sorrow, and leave him with intelligent affection to solitude—that friend of great grief; so grateful to the afflicted soul, because tears can flow unwitnessed. Alas! the favourite sea-eel of Crassus is dead, and it is uncertain whether Crassus can survive it !

This sensitive Roman caused this beloved fish to be buried with great magnificence : he raised a monument to its memory, and never ceased to mourn for it.[58]

This man, who displayed so little tenderness towards his servants, had an extraordinary weakness concerning his fine sea-eels. He passed his life beside the superb fish-pond, where he lovingly fattened them from his own hand. Ornamented with necklaces of the finest pearls, and earrings of precious stones,[59] all, at a signal, swam towards him; several fearlessly took the food he offered them ; and some, as familiar as their absent and regretted companion, allowed their master to caress them without seeking to bite or avoid him.[60]

This singular passion, which at the present day we can hardly believe, in spite of the respectable authority of the most serious writers, was very common at Rome, amongst those who were rich enough to rear such fish. C. Hirtius was the first to construct fish ponds on the sea shore, to which many visitors were attracted by their magnificence.[61] The family of Licinius took their surname of *Muræna* from these fish, in order thus to perpetuate the most silly affection, and the remembrance of their insanity.[62]

Sea-eels necessarily pleased men cloyed with pleasures, and who substituted a kind of cold and cruel curiosity for the terrible emotions which beings peculiarly organized hope to find in evil-doing:

gladiators murdering each other; lions or tigers lacerating the *bestiarii*;
all these agonies of the amphitheatre had long since lost the attraction
of novelty. It was a much more exciting spectacle to witness a swarm of
sea-eels tearing to pieces an awkward or rebellious slave; besides, it
greatly improved the fish. The atrocious Vedius Pollio, who understood these matters, never failed to have sea-eels served him after their
odious repast, that he might have the pleasure of eating some part of
the body of his victim.[63]

Thank Heaven! however, some amateurs of this dreaded fish were
not so barbarous; they fattened them very well without having recourse
to such criminal food. Veal was cut into thin slices, and steeped in the
blood of the animal for ten days, after which the fish greedily regaled
themselves with it.[64]

It was, doubtless, in this manner that the skilful speculator, Hirtius,
—the same already mentioned—nourished his sea-eels, which produced him an immense revenue. His fish ponds contained so great a
number that he was able to offer six thousand to Julius Cæsar on the
occasion of the public feast that general gave the day of his triumphal
return from the conquest of Gaul.[65]

The greater part of the Roman emperors were exceedingly fond of
sea-eels. The greedy Vitellius, growing tired of this dish, would at
last only eat the soft roes: and numerous vessels ploughed the seas in
order to obtain them for him.[66] This exquisite rarity again appeared
too common to the maniac child, who dismayed and astonished Rome for
the space of three years. Heliogabalus brought the soft roe of the sea
eel into disrepute by ordering that the peasants of the Mediterranean
should be gorged with it.[67] This folly amused him, and only cost several
millions. That was a trifle when compared with the blood which almost
always flowed to satisfy his whims.

The Greeks and Latins thought much of sea-eels caught in the
straits of Sicily.[68] They were sometimes served surrounded with craw-
fish;[69] but more frequently they were dressed with a seasoning much in
fashion, composed of pepper, alisander, savory, saffron, onion, and
stoned Damascus plums. These various substances were mixed together,
and to them were added wine, sweet sun-made wine, old wine reduced by
boiling, garum, vinegar, and oil.[70]

At Rome the fish market was abundantly supplied with sea-eels from
the Tiber. Connoisseurs thought nothing of them;[71] they were sold at a

low price, and their disgrace became complete directly they appeared on plebeian tables.

The Egyptians venerated this fish, and always esteemed it sacred.[72] Among the Sybarites, just appreciators of its culinary qualities, the fishers and sellers of sea-eels were exempt from all taxes.[73] They often procured some of such enormous size, that we should be tempted to accuse the old chroniclers of exaggeration, if we were not aware that this animal attains considerable dimensions. In the year 1786 a sea-eel was taken in the Elbe, weighing sixty pounds. This extraordinary fish measured seven feet two inches in length, and twenty-five inches in the girth.[74]

LAMPREY.

In spite of its soft and viscid flesh, this fish occupied in Rome a most honourable rank among the multitudinous dishes which intemperance was ever augmenting, and preference was given to that species caught by enterprising speculators in that strait which separates Sicily from Italy. These good people averred that lampreys which rise to the surface of the sea are immediately dried up by the sun, and cannot any more descend to the depths of the ocean.[75] This little story did no harm to their sale; on the contrary, they became on that account more curiously interesting.

It was also said, and the serious Gesner himself has repeated this fable:[76] That if the fish fastens its mouth to the side of a vessel it immediately stops, and that the combined power of the wind and the efforts of the rowers are unavailing.[77] The fact is that, by means of a kind of suction, it can fasten firmly on any bodies; and one weighing only three pounds has been seen to sustain in the air, with its mouth, a stone weighing twelve pounds.[78]

The lamprey has not always been the fashion, but it has had brilliant and glorious epochs In 1135 it caused so great a fit of indigestion to Henry I., King of England, that that prince died in consequence of it.[79] Since then, in the 16th century, it has been honoured with the reputation of having caused more than one death.[80] It was sold at a very high price, £3 at least, and at certain periods the Roman nobles even paid as much as £20 for one of these fish.[81] The ancient metropolis of the world had sometimes strange reminiscences of her former grandeur.

The Italian epicures of that remarkable era used to kill the lamprey in Candian wine. A nutmeg was placed in the mouth, and a clove in each of the openings of the gills. They rolled them round in a saucepan, and after adding crushed almonds, bread crumbs, Candian wine, and spices, the whole was cooked over a slow fire.[82]

SEA-WOLF.

Hicesius, one of the most estimable ichthyophagists of antiquity, does not hesitate to place the sea-wolf above all the fish which by their excellence were dear to Greece;[83] and the great Archestratus says, that the *lubridan* (a species of the sea-wolf) is a child of the gods.[84]

The Romans, touched no doubt by these magnificent praises, granted to the sea-wolf that favour which a high reputation commands. The immense sturgeon itself was eclipsed by it, and the sea-wolf had the glory of throwing this powerful and renowned rival into oblivion.[85]

Their love for its white and tender flesh knew no bounds,[86] and the fishermen of the Tiber were no longer equal to the task of supplying them for the impatient gluttony of the rich inhabitants of the Palatine Mount. Still this fish only fetched a high price when taken in a certain part of the river; from any other place it hardly commanded a few *as* (pence). Between the Sublicius and Senatorius bridges, a deep, black, and fetid water announced the presence of the continual flood of filth which the giant city poured into it night and day. It was in the midst of these impurities that shoals of sea-wolves were seen disporting; they fattened on that shocking slime, and thence passed to the delicate tables of Lucullus and Cæsar.[87]

The Greeks contented themselves with lubridans taken in clear water, and preferred the head to any other part.[88]

SCARUS, or, PARROT-FISH.

The scarus — its modern name is still problematic — furnished the Greeks with one of those exquisite dishes the remembrance of which never dies. The Romans were not yet acquainted with it, when Octavius, the commander of a fleet, brought on board the vessels a great quantity of this fish, which he ordered to be thrown into the sea along the coast of Campania, and which soon became the delight of the epicures of Rome.[89] History has shown too much disdain by neglecting to say more than a few passing words on the subject of this great service. May a tardy homage of gratitude be paid to the memory of the benefactor of his country.

The scarus was prepared without being embowelled, and epicures found it impossible to satiate themselves with the entrails,[90] which obtained for it a gastronomic vogue it long enjoyed without a rival.[91] It was asserted that the fish ruminates;[92] that it feeds only on herbage;[93] and that, far from being mute, like the other inhabitants of the water, it not only emits sounds, but is able to express by its cries the different sensations it experiences.[94] These anomalies, either real or supposed, had, perhaps, as great a share in rendering the scarus celebrated, as the delicacy of its flesh, and the exquisite flavour of its intestines. Merit the most real can so rarely keep the field unsupported by cajollery.

TURBOT.

Rome and Italy were indebted to the prætor, Sempronius, or to Rufus Rutilius,[95] for the turbot, which they taught their countrymen to appreciate. This fish quickly obtained the success which it merited, and was compared to the pheasant, as soles were likened to partridges, lampreys to quails, and sturgeons to peacocks. Some preferred turbot from the Adriatic Sea, others that of Ravenna;[96] but all united in declaring that there was not a more delicious food, and that a feast loses all its charm when this delicacy is wanting.

In the reign of Domitian a monstrous turbot was taken; such a one had never been seen in the imperial kitchens.[97] The emperor convoked the senate, and deferred to them to decide in what dish it should be cooked, in order that it might be served whole. The deliberation was long and stormy; all Rome was in a state of expectancy; and the august assembly strove to prove itself worthy of the high confidence reposed in it by Cæsar. At length the illustrious old men were tolerably unanimous in their idea that the best way would be to make a dish expressly for the fish—since there was none large enough ready-made—and also that a stove should be constructed vast enough to allow the dish to be placed commodiously upon it.[98]

The emperor, the city, and the court applauded the profound wisdom of this decision ; and " *le turbot fut mis à la sauce piquante.*" [99]

Aristotle does not mention this fish ; but his compatriots esteemed highly the turbots of Attica.[100]

———

TUNNY.

The Greeks greatly praised the tunny fish of Pachynum.[101] Persons who prided themselves on their knowledge in the art of good living, eat only the belly part,[102] and never touched the remainder.

The Synopians formerly gained immense sums by the tunny fishery along their shores,[103] the effigy of which, perhaps in gratitude, they stamped on their money. This fish came from Palus Meotides, and passed thence to Trebizond and Pharnacia, whence it followed the coast of Sinopus, and, at length, reached Byzantium, where they took nearly all those which escaped the fisheries of the two first-named stations.[104]

The Romans offered tunny fish in sacrifice to Neptune, in order that that god might deign to prevent the *xiphias* fish from tearing their nets, and forbid the too officious dolphins to assist in their escape.[105] They sold it at a very good price during the autumn and winter ; but it fetched less in summer because it was thought to be unwholesome during that season.[106] The jole and belly were thought the most delicate parts.[107] They were either fried or boiled, with pepper, alisander, cummin, onion, mint, sage, and dates, to which was added a mixture of honey, vinegar, oil, and mustard.[108]

Archestratus, who, on account of his gastronomic voyages, was looked upon as a high authority, asserts that Sicily and the neighbourhood of Constantinople furnished excellent tunny fish ; but that the best were those from Samos.[109] These latter were much renowned among the Greeks, who carefully prepared the entrails, and feasted on this dish. Athenæus relates, on this subject, a witticism of the poet Dorio, a keen and caustic spirit of the period of Aristotle and Philip of Macedon. Being at supper with that prince, a guest ridiculously praised a dish of tunny-fish intestines, just placed on the table. " They are certainly excellent," said Dorio, " when eaten as I eat them." " How, then, do you eat them ? " rejoined the gastronomic courtier. " With the firm determination," replied the poet, " of thinking of nothing better." [110]

This fish abounds in certain seas, and Pliny avers that it obstructed the navigation of the Indian Sea to such an extent, that the fleet of Alexander the Great was obliged to change its course, in order to avoid this impassable barrier.[111]

Tunny fish sometimes attain an immense size. Father Cetti tells us, that some were caught in Sardinia weighing no less than 1,000 lbs., and sometimes even 1,800 lbs.[112]

CONGER-EEL.

Near Sicyona, a city of the Peloponnesus,[113] they formerly caught conger-eels of such immense size, that it required a waggon drawn by oxen to carry a single one.[114] The body, the whole of the head, and even the intestines [115] were eaten. This dish, worthy of being offered by Neptune to his divine colleagues, was capable, like ambrosia, of bestowing immortality on those who had the good fortune of tasting it, and the dead would return to life, had it been possible to serve them with a piece of this exquisite fish.[116]

These childish exaggerations have not prevented Galen from treating the conger-eel with very little respect : he affirms, that nothing is more hard or indigestible.[117] And, indeed, epicureans of some repute allowed only the head to appear on their tables ;[118] and then only at rare intervals, and under the auspices of a relishing sauce which assured its reception.

The Romans had still less esteem for this too highly praised fish. However, sometimes a fried conger-eel occupied on the *sigma* an obscure place, in the midst of a seasoning flavoured highly with pepper, alisander, cummin, wild marjoram, dried onion, and hard yolks of eggs ; with which a skilful hand carefully mixed to the whole, vinegar, sweet wine, garum, and cooked wine.[119]

EEL.

In some parts of Egypt the eel was not eaten, because it was thought indigestible.[120]   In other places it received religious worship.[121]   They were ornamented, whether they liked it or not, with silver, gold, and precious stones, and priests daily offered them the entrails of animals and cheese.[122]

The Greeks thought highly of eels.   " Behold the Helen of feasts!" cried Eidicastes, at the moment when one was served ; " I will be her Paris ! "[123] and the glutton seized and devoured it immediately.

Bœotia—where this fish was immolated to the gods[124]—the straits of Sicily,[125] and the Copian lake, furnished eels remarkable for their delicacy and size ;[126] these were served fried and enveloped in beet leaves.[127] They enjoyed a high reputation among the Sybarites, a choice nation, who would have invented cookery if the art had not already existed, and among whom a repast was so serious a matter, that a whole year was not thought too long in order to meditate upon it and get it ready.[128]

But Hippocrates did not like the eel, and he forbade it to his patients, and to persons attacked with a pulmonary affection.[129]   So that this Queen of Luxury, as Archestrates calls it,[130] met with as many enemies as partisans.   Egypt adored it, Greece was enamoured of it, Rome despised it, and the plebeian alone reserved it to the humiliation in his brutal orgies.[131]

Apicius, however, has condescended to notice this fish.   Mix, says he, pepper, alisander, parsley seed, dill, and dates ; add to this honey, vinegar, garum, oil, mustard, and cooked wine ;[132] serve this sauce with the eel.

Nations have their ages of splendour—viands have their epochs of celebrity and glory.   This one seems to us fast falling into decay, in spite of some isolated efforts in order to make it reflourish.

When Rockingham was named member of parliament, he ordered thirteen barrels of eels to be brought to London, for the banquet he gave on that occasion.[133]   No one to our knowledge has since prepared so gigantic a *matelote*.

Travellers formerly saw in the Ganges beautiful eels 300 feet long[134] —a magnificent species never seen in Europe.

"The eel, so much despised by the Romans, is rather in favour in several countries; certain species are much esteemed, that named *Guiseau,* among others, deserves the preference it always obtains at Rouen."—Bosc.

PIKE.

The pike was very little esteemed by ancient gastronomists, who viewed it only as an ignoble inhabitant of muddy water, and the implacable enemy of frogs.[135] It was a received opinion that this despotic ruler of ponds lived for several centuries, and it may be correct.

Among the examples of longevity of this fish, the most remarkable is that of the pike of *kaisers'-lantern,* which was nineteen feet long, weighed 350 lbs., and had lived at least 235 years. It is reported that the Emperor Barbarossa himself threw it, on the 5th of October, 1262, into the pond where it was caught in 1497; and that this enormous pike wore a golden ring, which was made so that it would expand, and on which was engraved the date when the fish was spawned. Its skeleton was for a long time preserved at Mannheim.[136]

The multiplication of pikes would be immense if the spawn and pickrel, in the first year of their existence, were not the prey of several other fishes; for it has been calculated that in a female pike of middling size 181,000 eggs were found.

"In the north, and particularly in Siberia, the pike is preserved salted and smoked; the largest only are used, those weighing about two pounds. When they have been drawn, cleaned, and washed, they are cut in pieces, stratified with salt, in barrels. A brine is formed in which they are left for three days, then they are dried or smoked for one month. After this time they are put in another barrel, with fresh salt, wetted with vinegar."—Bosc.

CARP.

The carp occupied a very honourable rank with the Greeks and Latins, but only as a fish of the second order.[137] At Athens, they picked out the bones and stuffed it with silphium, cheese, salt, and marjoram.[138] The Romans boiled it and mixed it with sows' paps, fowls' flesh, fig-peckers, or thrushes; and when the whole was made into a kind of pulp, they added raw eggs and oil; then they sprinkled it over with pepper and alisander; after which they poured wine, garum, and cooked wine over it; and when the culinary combination was completed in the stewpan, by the assistance of a slow fire, it was then thickened with flour.[139]

In several countries it is known at what period the carp was naturalized. Peter Marshall brought it to England in 1514; Peter Oxe to Denmark in 1560. A few years after, it was introduced into Holland and Sweden. The fecundity of this fish is surprising; no less than 621,600 eggs were found in a carp weighing nine pounds; and it is very long-lived. Several have been seen in the moats of the castle of Ponchartrain, which were proved to be 150 years old. Carp are capable of acquiring considerable dimensions. The most gigantic on record was that caught at Bisshofs-hause, near Frankfort on the Oder; it weighed 70 lbs.[140]

EEL-POUT.

The liver of the eel-pout (also known by the names, *lota, lote,* and *lotus*) is particularly large, and so delicate that a certain Countess of Beuchlingen squandered a large portion of her income to gratify her taste for them.[141] That lady, worthy, by her refined and antique taste, of the proudest period of Roman extravagance, was, perhaps, not aware that the most fastidious epicureans of Italy, enthusiastic admirers of the liver of this fish,[142] had it served with a sauce composed of vinegar, grated cheese, and garlic; to which they added leeks and onions, chopped fine.[143]

TROUT.

Elian speaks of a fish found in the river Astræus, in Macedonia,[144] which Gesner believed to be identical with the trout. It does not appear, however, that the Greeks knew the real value and merit of this fish; but on the other hand, the Romans assigned to it the foremost rank, next to the sturgeon, red mullets, and the sea-eel, especially when they had been fattened in the thick waters of the Tiber, on the very spot where the labridans acquired their plumpness and value.[145]

The trout was dressed like the preceding fish.

GOLD FISH.

This fish, dear to the Greeks,[146] had the honour of giving its name to the celebrated icythyophagist, Sergius, who was passionately fond of it, and who took the name Orata (from *Aurata*—gold fish), to preserve in his family the remembrance of his gluttony or of his affection.[147] His compatriots, the Romans, highly valued the gold fish,[148] and sought with eagerness those which had fed on the shell fish of the lake of Lucrin[149]—that precious reservoir between Baiæ and Cumæ, which never deceived the hopes of the gastronomist, nor the greedy expectations of the fishermen.[150]

The gold fish was served with a gravy composed of pepper, alisander, carrots, wild marjoram, rue, mint, myrtle leaves, and yolk of eggs; mixed with honey, vinegar, oil, wine, and garum.[151] The slow cooking of these various ingredients gave them the required homogeneousness.

WHITING.

The flesh of this *gadus* is so light that, according to an old French proverb, the " *Merlans mangés ne pèsant non plus dans l'estomac que pendus à la ceinture.*[152] "Whitings weigh no more when eaten than when hung to the girdle." Nevertheless, the Greeks did not think much of it, and they said that the whiting was only good for those who could not obtain more delicate fish.[153]

The Romans, less severe or not quite so particular, cooked their whitings with a sauce composed as follows :—put with the fish, in a stewpan, some garum, chopped leeks, cummin, savory, and a sufficient quantity of cooked wine, and some wine slightly diluted ; cook it on a slow fire.[154]

COD FISH.

The cod fish supplied the ancients with the most exquisite dish next to the sturgeon.[155] The only fault found with it was, that it cost less than others. The Greek cooks sprinkled it with grated cheese, moistened with vinegar ; then they threw over it a pinch of salt and a few drops of oil.[156] Persons with delicate stomachs did not scruple to partake of this aliment, which Galen warranted as being excellent.[157]

The average size of this fish is about three feet in length ; but some are found of ten feet. The common weight is fifteen pounds, and some have been seen weighing 60lbs. Leuwenhoek has said that 9,344,000 eggs had been found in one fish. It is probable he made a mistake, as a cod fish of our days, weighing 50lbs., produced only 3,686,000 eggs— a number sufficiently prodigious, and which shows pretty well its great fecundity.[158]

It is supposed that the discovery of the great and small banks of cod fish is due to the Basque fishermen, who arrived there in pursuit of whales, one hundred years before Columbus' voyage. Others give that honour to James Cartier, a native of Falkland Islands.

" As early as the 14th century, the English and the inhabitants of Amsterdam busied themselves with cod fishing; and later, the Irish, Norwegians, French, and Spaniards competed with them more or less successfully. In 1533, Francis I. having sent J. Verrazzano, and afterwards, Jacques Cartier, to explore the neighbourhood of Newfoundland, the French fishermen followed them, and brought back also this fish from those distant countries in the beginning of the 16th century.

" Man annually seizes upon a prodigious quantity of cods, and were it not for the immense extent of the means of reproduction allowed to it by nature, the species for a long time past would have been annihilated.   It is even hardly conceived how it has been possible to preserve it; for it is well known, that as early as 1368, the inhabitants of Amsterdam had brought up fishermen on the coast of Sweden ; and, in the first quarter of 1792, according to a report presented to the minister, Roland, at the National Convention, that, from the ports of France only, 210 vessels, forming together 191,158 tons, went out for the cod fisheries; and that every year more than 10,000 vessels of all nations employed at this trade, throw in the commercial world more than 40,000,000 of salted and dried cod.   If we add to this enumeration the havoc made among the legions of these fishes by the great *squales*, sharks, and others, besides the destruction of a multitude of young ones by the other inhabitants of the seas and sea birds, together with the myriads of eggs destroyed by accident, it really is extraordinary to see this fish in so great a quantity now; but who can wonder, since each female can every year give birth to more than 9,000,000 of young ones."—Dr. Cloquet.

PERCH.

The Greeks were acquainted with the perch.[159]   Diocles used to give the flesh to the sick ;[160] Xenocrates extolled those from the Rhine ;[161] and Ausonius, the poet, has sung the praises of those fed in the Moselle.[162]

With the Romans, this fish obtained a renown almost equal to that bestowed on the trout; and all eyes bespoke its welcome at supper, when it appeared on the table, covered with a seasoning in which pepper, alisander, cummin, and onions were artistically combined with stoned Damascus plums—thanks to the clever use of wine, vinegar, sweet wine, oil, and cooked wine.   This ingenious amalgamation acquired over a slow fire the requisite consistence and cohesion.[163]

SCATE.

The ancients liked or disliked scate, according to the places where they eat it. So, now, this fish is rejected in Sardinia, and thought excellent in London and Paris.[164]

The Greek gastronomists of fashion sometimes partook of the back of the scate;[165] the remainder seemed unworthy of their attention, and a certain poet maintains that a piece of stuff, boiled, offers to the palate a flavour quite as agreeable.[166]

Italian gluttony always gave a cold reception to this dish, which they owed to the Greek cooks, and which their magiric writers have not sufficiently studied.

Aristotle knew of two species of scate;[167] Pliny speaks of them;[168] Lacépède enumerates thirty-nine species.[169]

That celebrated naturalist, Buffon's pupil and competitor, assures us that several eastern nations consider the smoke arising from the eggs of scates, thrown on burning coals, and inhaled by the mouth and nostrils, as an excellent remedy against intermittent fever.[170] It would cost but little to make the experiment.

SALMON.

It is reported that the salmon was thus named on account of its frequent leaping.[171] It has been sung by Ausonius.[172] Its absence left a chasm in the delights of Greece, and it was late before it became known in Rome. Pliny is the first of Latin authors who name it.[173] Ichthyophagy will cherish the memory of this laborious author. He speaks with praise of the salmon taken in the Garonne and Dordogne. He extols those of the Rhine, but he seems to give a decided preference to those magnificent fishes covered with a silvery mail, which disport in the limpid waters of that picturesque and beautiful Aquitaine.[174]*

Two centuries ago, there was such a great quantity of salmon taken in the rivers of Scotland, that, instead of being considered a delicate

* It is a question whether they could compete in quality with those caught in the Severn at the present day.

dish, it served commonly as food for servants, who it is said, stipulated sometimes, that they should not be obliged to eat that common, tasteless aliment more than five times per week.[175]

SEPIA, OR, CUTTLE-FISH.

Pliny has extolled the constancy of conjugal offection in the cuttle-fish, and the courage with which the male defends his companion in the moment of danger.[176] The poet Persius describes its flight, protected by the thick, black liquid with which it blinds its enemies. Apicius, struck more by its succulent qualities, opens this fish, empties it, and stuffs it with cooked brains, to which he adds raw eggs and pepper; he then boils it in a seasoning of pepper, alisander, parsley seed, and cooked wine, mixed with honey, wine, and garum.[177] Thus prepared, the cuttle-fish passed at Rome as an estimable dish, and which might be offered at an unpretending repast.

SWORDFISH.

The Greeks were fond of the swordfish, and often partook of it,[178] with a sauce of which oil was the basis, and with which were mixed yolks of eggs, leeks, garlic, and cheese.[179] The Romans thought very little of this fish, and prayed Neptune to send it far from their nets.

SHAD.

The shad was caught during the summer, and sold to the people,[180] who boiled it and dished it up with strong herbs and oil. This plebeian fish was excluded from all respectable banquets.

"Modern taste has allowed this estimable fish to re-appear on the

---

* We saw, in 1836, while at Colne Castle, about one ton weight taken out of the water in a few hours.

table, where it is always seen with pleasure. This fish is caught in most of the great rivers of Europe, Asia, and northern Africa."—Bosc.

———•———

RHOMBO, OR, RHOMBUS.

The rhombo claimed the attention of the discriminating ichthyophagists of Rome by the delicacy of its flesh, and few fish would have been preferred to it had it not been feared that it rendered digestion difficult.[181] Some intrepid stomachs, however, greeted this dish without much repugnance when presented to them fried and sprinkled with pepper, in the midst of a seasoning in which pepper, cummin, coriander, benzoin, wild marjoram, and rue, heightened by a little vinegar, were mixed with dates, honey, cooked wine, and oil. This boiling sauce was poured over the rhombo, but not before it had been enriched with garum,[182] which we had almost forgotten—that inevitable brine which the ancient magiric genius placed everywhere, and whose prodigious renown ought to have preserved it from oblivion.

———•———

MUGIL.

This fish, singular instrument of a punishment invented by Rome,[183] entered into the bill of fare of a fashionable supper, but one without that magnificence which a feast of parade exacts. It was prepared with pepper, alisander, cummin, onion, mint, rue, sage, and dates, mixed with honey, vinegar, mustard, and oil.[184]

The Greeks also esteemed mugils, and gave a preference to those sold by the fishermen of Scyathus.[185]

———•———

MACKEREL.

Commentators do not agree on the origin of this word. Scaliger, who perceived Greek in everything, says it is derived from *makarios*, "happy." But, then, in what does the felicity of this fish consist ? The old writer Belon, more wise in his conjecture, thinks this word comes from the Latin, *macularelli*, " little spots," because it is marked on the back with black stripes.[186]

Let the etymology be what it may, the epicurean cares very little about it. Mackerel was much liked in Greece, where it was believed to be a native of the Hellespont;[187] and throughout Italy, where it was supposed to come originally from Spain.[188]

It is .very probable that from mackerel was obtained one of the varieties of garum, known by the name of *garum sociorum*. Further on, we intend to devote a special chapter to the subject of this celebrated condiment.

" Neither the size nor the weapons of mackerel make them formidable; they have, however, a violent appetite, and on account, perhaps, of the confidence they feel in the number of each shoal, they are bold and voracious, frequently attack fishes larger and stronger than themselves, and even dart with blind audacity upon the fishermen who bathe where they happen to be. Thus Pontoppidan relates that a sailor, bathing in the port of Carcule, in Norway, missing one of his companions, saw him a few minutes afterwards dead, the body mangled and covered with a multitude of mackerel, tearing his remains to pieces."— DR. CLOQUET.

HADDOCK.

The haddock, like the sturgeon, was surrounded with the ridiculous honours of an almost divine pomp.[189] It was served interwoven with garlands, and trumpeters accompanied the slaves who, with uncovered heads and foreheads crowned with flowers, brought to the guests this dish, the merit of which was, perhaps, exaggerated by capricious fancies.[190]

TENCH.

Ausonius, who lived in the 4th century of the Christian era, is the first who has spoken of the tench, in his poem of the " *Mostella.*"[191] It was abandoned to the common people, who alone feasted on it.[192] This fish, long the victim of an unjust disdain, ultimately conquered from the great that esteem which they at first refused to it.

DRAGON WEAVER.

The dragon weaver traversed unseen the long and brilliant gastronomic period of the Romans. Greece rendered it more justice;[193] but its too modest qualities were not able to preserve it from forgetfulness and indifference.

———

LOLIGO.

At Rome the loligo, a species of cuttle-fish, was sometimes served with pepper and rue, mixed with garum, honey, sweet wine boiled, and a few drops of oil.[194]

———

SOLE.

This fish, which the Greeks caught on the coast,[195] was much sought after on account of the delicacy of its nourishing and light flesh.[196] The flounder, the brill, the diamond and Dutch plaice, which, together with the sole, were known under the general name of *passeres*, enjoyed an equal esteem, and had attributed to them the same qualities.

———

ANGEL-FISH.

In Holland there are angel fish of enormous size;[197] and Aldrovandus relates that some have been seen which weighed as much as 160 lbs.[198] In the time of this naturalist the common people did not eat them very willingly.

———

FILE-FISH.

The flesh of this species of the *bulistes* is only good when fried, according to Marcgrave. Columella thinks much of it,[199] and Pliny ranks it among the *saxatiles*, the most esteemed by connoisseurs.[200]

PILCHARD.

Among the Greeks this fish was considered only as fit for the people. Those from the environs of Phaleres were much esteemed, when left only an instant in boiling oil.[201] The Romans, who gave them the first rank among salt fish,[202] stuffed them, in order to render them better, in the following manner:—[203]

They bruised pennyroyal, cummin, pepper, mint, and pine nuts; these they mixed with honey, and with this paste they filled the anchovy, after having carefully boned them. They then wrapped them in paper,* and cooked them in a *bain-marie*, or saucepan, immersed in boiling water. They were served with oil, dregs of fish-brine, and cooked wine.[204]

LOACH.

The Greeks liked loaches,[205] but many abstained from eating them, lest the Syrian goddess, the protectress of these fishes, should gnaw their legs, cover their bodies with ulcers, and devour their liver.[206]

The inhabitants of Italy, free from this singular superstition, cleaned the loaches, left them some time in oil, then placed them in a saucepan with some more oil, garum, wine, and several bunches of rue and wild marjoram. Then these bunches were thrown away, and the fish was sprinkled with pepper at the moment of serving.[207]

GUDGEON.

The gudgeon—thought excellent by every one, but which no one mentions—appeared with honour in the most magnificent repasts at

---

* This paper did not resemble our own of the present day; it was a kind of papyrus, which perfectly resisted all moisture.

Athens.[208]   At Rome, it was served fried, at the beginning of supper;[209] and it disposed the guests to attack boldly the culinary *corps de réserve*, which took up the position as soon as the skirmish with the gudgeon was over.

" This fish is in abundance, principally in France and Germany; it is very good, and easily digested. They are served either fried or stewed; when done as last-mentioned, they must be drawn and wiped dry, put in a flat stewpan with butter, salt, pepper, good red wine, spring onions, mushrooms, shalots, thyme, bay leaves and basil—these last plants chopped very fine; stew the whole a quarter of an hour, and serve."—Bosc.

HERRING.

Herrings were unknown in Greece and Rome. Bosc says it is a manna that nature doubtless reserved for the northern nations, which they, however, have only turned to account in modern times.

The first herring fishery known in Europe was on the coast of Scotland; but that nation knew not how to profit by the treasure that the sea offered them. All the Scotch historians mention this fishery, the produce of which was bought by the Dutch. This transaction took place under the reign of King Alfred, about the year 836.

After some time the Scotch quarrelled with the Dutch, who undertook the herring fishery themselves. As they caught a great many more than they could consume, they salted them, and sold them in foreign countries. Such was the origin of that immense commerce, which had its rise, according to Eidous, about the year 1320, a short time after the Teutons had established themselves in the Baltic.

It is said that we owe the art of salting and barreling herrings to a Dutch fisherman, named William Beuckels, who died in 1449. The Dutch nation raised a mausoleum to his memory; and it is asserted that Charles V., who visited it in 1536, eat a herring upon it to render homage to the author of a precious discovery.

In the year 1610, Sir Walter Raleigh gave a statistical account of the commerce carried on by the Dutch in Russia, Germany, Flanders, and France, with the herrings caught on the coasts of England, Scotland,

and Ireland.   The sale of this fish amounted, in one year, to the sum of £2,650,000.

It has been erroneously thought that the herring was the *halec*, or, *alec*, of the Romans.   This name was given by them to a kind of brine; [210] it was not the name of any particular fish.

There are two prevalent methods of preserving herrings, and fishmongers sell them under the denominations of salted herrings and red herrings.

The process employed for the first-named is as follows:—

As soon as the herring is out of the sea, a sailor opens it, removes the gills and the entrails, washes the fish in salt water, and puts it into a brine thick enough for it to float.   After fifteen or eighteen hours, it is taken out of the brine and laid in a tub with a quantity of salt.   It remains in this tub until the port is reached.   There the herrings are placed in barrels, where they are artistically arranged one over another, with fresh salt between each layer.   Care is always taken to employ fresh brine.

Red herrings are prepared by leaving the fish at least twenty-four hours in the brine; and when they are taken out, little twigs are run through the gills, and then they are suspended in a kind of chimney, made on purpose, under which a small fire is made with wood, which produces a good deal of smoke.   The herrings remain in this state until they are sufficiently dry, that is to say, about twenty-four hours.

In Sweden and Norway they are somewhat differently prepared. The Icelanders and Greenlanders simply dry them in the air. [211]

ANCHOVY.

Sonnini thinks that garum was simply composed of anchovies cooked and crushed in their brine, to which was added a little vinegar, and chopped or pounded parsley.

The fishermen of the Mediterranean and the coasts of the ocean salt almost all the anchovies they take.   They cut off their heads, which are thought to be bitter, take out the entrails, wash them in soft or salt water, and stratify them in barrels with salt.   The fishermen of Provence think it is essential to the good preservation of anchovies that the salt be red; and, consequently, they colour it with ochreous earths. Moreover, these fishermen do not change the brine which is formed in the barrels: they simply fill them up when any is lost by evaporation or leakage.

The fishermen of the north only use bay salt, and they change the brine three times, whence it results that their anchovies keep much longer; but the greater acridness of those which have remained in the same brine is esteemed a good quality by most consumers, and therefore they are more sought after.

In sea ports, anchovies are eaten either fried or roasted. Salted anchovies are to be preferred when they are new, firm, white outside, vermilion coloured inside, and free from all putrid smell. After having taken out the backbone, and washed them well, cooks commonly make use of anchovies in salads, and to flavour sauces made with butter, cullis, &c. In this case they are employed raw.

They are not unfrequently fried, after having been deprived of the salt, and surrounded with an appropriate paste. Some persons toast slices of bread, cover them with strips of anchovies, and serve them with a sauce composed of oil, vinegar, whole pepper, parsley, scallions, and eschalots, all in abundant quantities, and chopped very small.[212]

SHELL FISH.

The Emperor Caligula had made immense preparations to invade Great Britain. He set off, and when he arrived in sight of that Albion he was going to attack, he commanded his troops to form in close array along the shore, the trumpets to sound the charge, and sat himself on the quarter-deck of his galley, from whence he might have directed the action. For a short time he contemplated his warlike cohorts, and having thus gratified his pride, he ordered his troops to pick up the shells which abounded on the strand, and returned to Rome, where he showed the "*spolia opima*" the ocean had delivered up to him. Caligula expected to receive the honours of a triumph; but the senate, having some sense of modesty left, would not award them, and the implacable Cæsar, from that moment, swore the ruin of the senators.[213]

The inhabitants of Greece and those of Italy thought a great deal of shell fish, which was always served at the beginning of the repast, just as they came from the sea : others cooked under the ashes, or fried. In most cases they were seasoned with cummin and pepper.[214]

The purveyors of fish in Rome gave the preference to those taken in the lake of Lucrinus.[215]   The Greeks esteemed those from the promontory of Polarea.[216]

The city of Baiæ, in Campania, celebrated for its charming position, and the unreserved lax manners of its inhabitants, was not less renowned for its culinary labours, and the nicety which presided over their joyful banquets.   Apicius has left us the recipe of a most exquisite stew, *emphractum,* which the epicureans of Rome often went to degust among their rivals, the Campanian gastronomists.

Cut up oysters, muscles, and sea-hedgehogs ; let the pieces be rather small ; put them into a stewpan with pine almonds, fried and chopped, some parsley, rue, pepper, coriander, and cummin ; add, with proper care and discretion, some cooked wine, garum, and oil ; cover, and boil the whole for a long time on a slow fire.[217]

We will point out the shell fish most in vogue in Italy, and for which the seasoning was generally composed of a mixture of pepper, parsley, dried mint, alisander, a great quantity of cummin, and a little of the decoction of spikenard.[218]

OYSTER.

The pontiffs of pagan Rome, men of exquisite delicacy and matured taste, caused oysters to be served at every repast.[219] This little piece of epicurism was very expensive, and it was necessary for these grave personages to carry the whole of the devotion which characterized them in their love of good cheer to the highest degree, to dare eat of a dish still uncommon a century before the Christian era.   At this epoch a *borriche* (a sort of basket) of oysters was worth one hundred sesterces. (£9).[220] It is unnecessary to remark that the poor never tasted them.

The Greeks and Romans, like ourselves, were remarkably fond of this delicious shell fish, and eat them (French fashion) at the beginning of a banquet.[221] For this reason Athenian epicures called oysters "the gastronomic prelude to the supper." [222] They were often served raw,[223] and were then dexterously opened by a slave on the table,[224] in presence of the guests, whose experienced eyes greedily sought the light purple net which, according to them, surrounds the fattest and best.[225]

The inhabitants of Italy preferred large oysters,[226] and exacted that this dainty manna of the sea[227] should be always fresh and abundant at their feasts.[228] This displayed wisdom on their part: this delightful fish excites the appetite and facilitates digestion.[229] To add to its delicate flavour, the "Roman club of epicureans," a useful association, which modern Europe envies antiquity, caused to be sent from Spain, at a vast expense, that precious garum,[230] the recipe of which seems to have been lost, and the condiment itself forgotten by the whole of the Peninsula.

The magiric genius of Rome did not hesitate to demonstrate that oysters do not form an exception to the law of perfectibility which governs all beings, and that it is possible to render their flesh more succulent and delicate by transporting them from their damp cradle into reservoirs exposed to the mild influence of the sun.[231] Sergius Orata, or, perhaps, Fulvius Hirpinus, was the first who received this happy inspiration. He caused to be constructed, near Pouzzole, a short time before the civil war of Pompey, a fishpond, where he stowed oysters, which he fattened with paste and cooked wine worked into the consistence of honey[232]—sapa et farre. This worthy Roman enriched himself by the sale of them,[233] and bequeathed a name to posterity —a two-fold happiness for the gastronomist Fulvius, whose good fortune the poet Homer did not partake.

Apicius esteemed highly oysters from the lake of Lucrinus, from Brindes, and Abydos, and studied deeply the succulent qualities of this shell fish. He knew how to preserve them fat, fresh, and alive, during long and fatiguing journeys; and, thanks to a delicate attention on the part of this immortal bon vivant, the great Trajan was enabled to regale himself with oysters sent from Rome while carrying on a distant war against the Parthians.[234] This present of the king of epicureans to the master of the world was worthy of both the giver and receiver, but it completed the ruin of the generous Apicius.

The Roman ladies shared their husbands' taste, and eagerly partook of oysters from the lake of Lucrinus, brought into fashion by Sergius Orata, and when their fatigued stomachs struggled painfully with gluttony, this delicacy soon obtained an easy triumph by disposing the appetite to fresh exertions. The means of defence, however, were not very formidable; sometimes a little warm and limpid water—oftener a dazzling plume from the bird of Juno—hastened the struggle, and, without effort, decided the victory.[235] This ingenious method was very much relished by polyphagists, and the Emperor Vitellius particularly honoured it.[236]

Cape Pelorus furnished the Greeks with highly prized oysters,[237] which were eaten alone, fried, stewed, or nicely dressed with marsh-mallows, dock-leaves, and with some kind of fish.[238]

The Romans at length became disgusted with those found on the coasts of Italy, or in the Dardanelles; an instinct of greediness caused them to prefer oysters from the Atlantic ocean, and especially from the shores of Armorica, now called Britany.[239] Bordeaux supplied imperial tables, and this high distinction is sufficient for its praise.[240]

It may not be useless to remark here, that no sooner had Ausonius praised this fish in his lines than it was forgotten, and did not re-appear till the 17th century on the tables of distinguished personages. May our descendants be more just than our forefathers.

At Rome oysters were served with a seasoning of pepper and ali-sander, mixed with the yolks of eggs, vinegar, garum, oil, wine, and a little honey.[241]

They were preserved in a vase smeared with pitch, washed with vinegar, and hermetically closed.[242]

"Oysters of a fine quality are generally of easy digestion, but not very nourishing, particularly when eaten raw. They are sought for to open the appetite, which is the case, owing to the nature of the water, agreeably salted, contained in them. Some mention is made of persons who can eat from fifteen to twenty dozen without being ill. It is not the same when cooked; then they become hard, more tough, and, consequently, indigestible. They are also eaten pickled with vinegar and sweet herbs In this state they are sent to countries distant from the sea, piled up one upon the other, without the shell, in small barrels."—DE BLAINVILLE.

SEA-HEDGEHOG.

Under this denomination were classed all animals, more or less orbicular, whose envelope bristles with calcareous points, on which account they were compared to hedgehogs.

The Greeks thought them delicious when caught at the full moon,[243] and prepared with vinegar, sweet cooked wine, parsley, and mint.[244] Oxymel often replaced vinegar.[245]

The Romans also esteemed highly this dish, which was recommended to sluggish appetites under the auspices of the faculty;[246] and Apicius furnished the following recipe for the preparation of it:—

" Procure a new saucepan," thus says the great master, " place in it a little oil, garum, sweet wine, and pepper. When the mixture begins to boil, stuff the sea hedgehogs, then submit them to the action of a slow fire ; add a large quantity of pepper, and serve." [247]

MUSSEL.

The two great nations of antiquity have granted uncommon praise to mussels, and partook of them at their most sumptuous feasts. At the wedding repast of the graceful Hebe, Jupiter wished the inhabitants of Olympus to exchange for this shell fish their celestial though monotonous ambrosia.[248] Epicharmus, who records the fact, does not inform us with what sauce the *chef de cuisine* of the gods dressed the flesh of those mussels. The reader must thus content himself with the seasoning invented by simple mortals, and which appeared good to them. It was composed of a suitable mixture of pepper, alisander, parsley, mint, with a quantity of cummin seed, a little honey, vinegar, and garum.[249] With this mixture they covered the boiled and widely opened mussels, and the guests found it impossible to satiate themselves with this dish, so much more digestible and nourishing than oysters.[250]

SCALLOP.

The effeminate inhabitants of Tarentum, the abode of luxury, delighted in good living, and boasted of possessing the finest scallops of
Campania, and of the whole empire.[251]   The infallible authority of this
voluptuous city in matters of taste gave a surprising vogue to this fish.
Rome, and all the population of Italy, believed it was forced to eat the
scallops of Tarentum prepared with oysters, and at other times with
mussels.

It now remains to be mentioned that some kinds of *testacea* appeared
worthy of the reputation they acquired among the ancients.

TORTOISE.

The Greeks and Latins speak with admiration of the enormous size
of certain tortoises in their time, the whole species of which were comprised under the generic word *testudo*.[252]   The Indian Sea produced
some so large, that the shell of one only amply served to roof a
comfortable and elegant cottage.[253]   The inhabitants of the shores of the
Red Sea never troubled themselves with building sloops; large shells of
tortoises spared them the trouble, by supplying them with charming
little barks, which lightly floated on the water.[254]   And, lastly, in the
Ganges, tortoise shells were found, capable of containing no less than 20
amphoræ, or about 560 pints.[255]

The inhabitants of the Peloponnesus did the tortoise the signal
honour of representing its image on their money.[256]   The blood cured
diseases of the eye,[257] and the flesh—in great request—was thought
excellent eating.   It was cut into pieces of a middling size, and placed
in a saucepan with pepper, rue, and scallions, crushed in the same
mortar; over this was poured honey, garum, raisin wine, common wine,
and a small quantity of good oil.   At the moment of ebullition, the
whole was thickened with flour.[258]

Sometimes the tortoise was boiled, and covered with a seasoning, for which the following is the recipe :—

Mix pepper, alisander, parsley, mint, and wild marjoram, with the yolks of eggs, honey, garum, wine, cooked wine, and oil; add mustard and vinegar.[259]

SEA-CRAWFISH.

Apicius sought relief from his culinary studies at Minturnus, in Campania, where that great master regaled himself with delicious sea-crawfish, in order to keep up his gustatory powers. Genius reposes amidst studious leisure. Being told that Africa produced some of these *testacea* of an immense size, immediately the worthy Roman tears himself away from the sweet solitude he had created; he freights a vessel, Æolus smiles on the undertaking, Neptune protects him, and he arrives in sight of the African shore. Scarcely was he disembarked when some fishermen brought him a few sea-crawfish; he examines, rejects them, and demands finer ones to be brought. He is informed that it will be impossible to procure any larger than those before him. At this Apicius smiles disdainfully, and commanding the presence of his pilot, orders him to steer back for Italy.[260] Decidedly magiric genius never revealed itself by a more sublime action.

However, Pliny somewhere mentions certain magnificent sea-crawfish, which he describes as being four cubits in length[261]—very large ones, certainly.

Roman tables often presented to the sight of guests boiled sea-crawfish, peppered and garnished with asparagus,[262] but they were generally covered with a gravy composed of honey, vinegar, wine, garum, oil, and cooked wine; to which were added scallions, chopped small, pepper, alisander, carrots, cummin, and dates. Mustard was then mixed with the whole.[263]

LOBSTER.

Antiquity rendered justice to the lobster, and the taste for it did not change, being founded on truly estimable and sterling qualities. It was opened lengthwise, and filled with a gravy, into the composition of which entered both pepper and coriander. It was then slowly cooked on the gridiron, and every now and then basted with the same kind of gravy, with which the flesh became impregnated.[264]

RIVER CRAYFISH.

The Greeks were remarkably fond of this fish,[265] especially when obtained from Alexandria.[266] They were not less esteemed in Rome, where they eat them boiled with cummin, and seasoned with pepper, alisander, parsley, dried mint, and a great quantity of cummin; the whole carefully and well ground, and mixed with honey, vinegar, and garum, to which was sometimes added some liquid perfume.[267]

" Crayfishes can be preserved several days, not too warm, in baskets with some fresh grass, such as the nettle, or in a bucket with three-eighths of an inch of water. If there were enough water in it to cover them, they would die in a few moments, because their great consumption of air does not allow them to live in water unless it is continually renewed."—Bosc.

CRAB.

Would you like to eat crab sausages? Boil some of these animals; reduce them to a pulp; mix with this some spikenard, garum, pepper, and eggs; give to this the ordinary shape of sausages, place them on the stove or gridiron, and you will, by these means, obtain a delicate and tempting dish.[268] Apicius assures us of the fact: Apicius was a connoisseur!

A crab may also be served whole, boiled, and accompanied by a seasoning of pepper, cummin, and rue, which the cook skilfully mixes with garum, honey, oil, and vinegar.[269]

Is it preferred stuffed? Then fill it with a skilful mixture of cummin, mint, rue, alisander, pine nuts, and pepper, the whole long soaked in garum, honey, vinegar, and wine.[270]

FROGS.

The ancients thought nothing of frogs, which they left at liberty to propagate. There was such a great number among the Abderites, that these good people gave up to them their native soil, and left the place in search of another spot.

At the present day, in some countries, frogs are sought for as a most agreeable and wholesome food; in other parts—England in particular—they are disdainfully shunned. But in France there is a great consumption of them, especially in the spring. About a century since, they were greatly in fashion at Paris; and it is stated that a countryman from the province of Auvergne, named Simon, made a considerable fortune by feeding and fattening them in one of the suburbs of that city, which were sent to him from Auvergne.

"In Germany, the various parts of the frog are eaten, the skin and intestine excepted; but in France they are satisfied with the hind legs, which, by the size of their muscles, are themselves equivalent to all the rest. They are dressed with wine as fish, with white or brown sauce; fried, or roasted; when tender, and properly done, it is a most delicate dish."—Bosc.

———•———

Before the conclusion of this article, we may as well mention a frightful fish which modern good taste has banished from our tables, but which the ancients allowed to appear at theirs. It is the *Polypus*, highly esteemed both in Greece and Italy, when caught at a certain period, and its numerous immoderate legs stretched far over the edges of the dish prepared to receive it.[271]

This monster was cut in pieces, and eaten with a sauce composed of pepper, garum, and benzoin.[272]

It will be easily understood that ancient nations must have early accustomed themselves to fishing, the origin of which, doubtless, goes back to the first ages of civilization. The holy writings often mention fishermen,[273] fish-hooks, and nets. Homer speaks of them,[274] and the poet, Hesiod, who flourished thirty years before Homer,[275] places on the shield of Hercules an attentive fisherman, ready to throw his net over some fish pursued by a dolphin.[276]

The Egyptians also practised this occupation; of which the following anecdote is a proof:—

Antony being in Egypt, the beauteous Cleopatra sought to amuse him by inventing for his entertainment each day new kinds of pleasure; but the Roman general, seized with a violent love of fishing, fled from the society of his numerous courtiers, and, alone on the borders of the sea, or an isolated lake, vainly waiting for the smallest gudgeon, he forgot long hours of vain expectancy and useless patience. The queen undertook his cure. She commanded a diver to plunge into the water, and there a hook a fish to the line of Antony. He, seeing it agitated, joyfully withdrew it from the water, and unhooked a *salted sardine.* Cleopatra then exclaimed: "Leave to Egyptians the task of fishing; Romans should take only kings, cities, and emperors."[277]

The inhabitants of Italy fished exactly in the same manner we do at this day;[278] but Roman luxury, always greedy of extravagant profusion, invented those celebrated fish ponds which cost immense sums, both to build and maintain;[279] and to which Lucullus, Hortensius, and Philippus, whom Cicero surnamed the "Tritons of fish pools,"[280] consecrated almost entirely their anxiety and fortunes.

This folly was carried to such a height that fish ponds were constructed on the roofs of houses.[281] More reasonable persons contented themselves with bringing river-water into their dining-rooms.[282] The fish swam under the table, and it was only necessary to stoop and pick them out the instant before eating them.[283]

These expensive habits could only suit the most opulent and least numerous class of Romans. The honest citizen modestly provided himself at the fish-market, and the part not eaten by him the first day was submitted to a very simple process, which assured its preservation. For this, it was only necessary to cover it with boiling vinegar as soon as it had been fried.[284]

Fish was also well preserved by surrounding it with snow, and placing it at the bottom of an ice-house.[285]

XXII.

THE COOK.

THE author of a rare and very curious work,[1] which no one at present has time to read, formed the charitable project of reconciling medicine and gastronomy. This was a noble enterprize, worthy of a true philanthropist, and which assuredly presented less difficulties than people may think. In effect, what was the moot question? To agree, *de forma*, without interfering with the substance; to examine whether culinary preparations poison, as has been said, the food which nature gives us, and unceasingly paralyze the salutary action of the dietetic, which the faculty prescribe.

For many centuries cooking has been exposed to these odious reproaches, the gravity of which we do not pretend to attenuate; and yet, ever pursuing its brilliant career amidst revolutions and ruins, the magiric art, endowed with eternal youth, embellishes each new era of civilization, receives its most constant homage, and survives it when it fades away. Let us speak plainly: mankind has thrown on cooks all the faults of which they ought to accuse their own intemperance. It was no doubt easier, than to avoid the fatal abuse of pleasure, and the evils it brings with it; but there was the crying injustice, which we do not hesitate to denounce; *there* lay the obstacle it was necessary to overcome, in order to bring about a peaceful understanding between the disciples of Galen and the followers of Apicius.

Gourmandise would never have rebelled against the kitchen if all polyphagists had obtained from the good Ceres the gift she granted to Pandarea—a celebrated eater, who could pass days and nights at table, without experiencing the slightest indigestion.[2]

"But," say you, "Seneca, the philosopher, perpetually combats, with the authority of his virtuous language, those dangerous men who are busied with a single stomach,[3] and who lay the foundation for a train of maladies."

The reply to this is, that Seneca, the pedant, should have thundered against the stomach, which alone is guilty (he has sometimes done so); that this atrabilarious preceptor of Nero, attacked with an incurable consumption, could only eat very little, which much enraged him; and that his imprecations on the subject of the excessive riches and prodigious luxury of the Romans of his age, neither hindered him from possessing, and unceasingly increasing, a more than royal fortune; nor from feeding—well or ill—several thousand slaves; nor from pompously displaying in his palace five hundred tables—only five hundred—of the most elaborate workmanship, of the rarest wood, all alike, and ornamented with precious incrustations.[4]

How often have people extolled the Lacedæmonians and their legislator, Lycurgus. Well, Lycurgus mercilessly commanded poor little children to fast when they looked fresh and fat.[5] Strange law-giver of a strange people, who never learned to eat, and yet who invented the celebrated " black sauce," the *jus nigrum*, for which the entrails of the hare served as the foundation. So true it is that cookery always preserves certain imprescriptible rights over the most fervent disciples of frugality.

Moralists do not cease to repeat that Rome would never have had sumptuary laws had it not been corrupted by cooks from Athens and Syracuse. This is an error. All the ordinances of the consuls proscribed profusion, excess—in a word, all the ruinous expenses of a passionate and ridiculous gastrophagy,[6] at the same time, respecting the magiric art itself; that is to say, that industrious chemistry which composes, decomposes, combines, and mixes—in a word, prepares different substances which gluttony, delicacy, the fashion, or luxury may confide to it for the space of a few minutes.

Why render the cook responsible for the extravagant tastes and follies of his age? Is it for him to reform mankind? Has he either the means or the right?

What is asked of him? and what can be asked? To understand exactly the properties of everything he employs, to perfect, and correct, if necessary, the savours on which he operates; to judge with a true taste, to degustate with a delicate palate, to join the skilful address of the hand, and the prompt and comprehensive glance, to the bold but profound conceptions of the brain; and above all—it cannot be too often repeated—to identify himself so well with the habits, the wants, even the caprices and gastronomic eccentricities, of those whose existence he embellishes, that he may be able, not to obey them, but to guess them, and even have a presentiment of them.[7]

Such is, to use an original expression of Rabelais, *"toute l'artillerie de gueule,"* which the cook can master. It is the sum total of what has been bequeathed to us by some great men, whose scattered instructions, lying here and there in books of morality and philosophy—there are numerous analogies between the act of eating and the art of living well—have been collected with scrupulous care, classed with all the attention we can command, and will serve, we hope, to beguile the studious leisure of the lovers of antiquity and the culinary science.

Mankind had long obeyed that imperious and periodical necessity which has been called hunger, when it announces its presence with its brutal exigencies, before any one thought to form a code of doctrine calculated to guide a sensation which, by its energy and duration, procures us the most thrilling and lasting pleasures.

The primitive nations no doubt gave themselves up to their native gluttony. They eat much, but they fed badly. They did not yet possess gastronomy; and, consequently, they had no cooks, in the serious and complete acceptation of the word.

The heroes of Homer prepared their repasts with their own hands, —and what repasts, gods of taste!—and prided themselves on their culinary talents. *Où la vanité va-t-elle se nicher?* Ulysses surpassed all others in the art of lighting the fire, and laying the cloth.[8] Patroclus drew the wine, and Achilles very carefully turned the spit.[9]

The conquerors of Troy shone more in the combat than under the tent which served them as kitchen.

At length the aurora of the magiric ages began to dawn: it is not a revolution, it is a creation which is preparing to appear. Man has only known hunger; he shall now become acquainted with the charms of an appetite. The King of Sidon learns how to eat, and it is Cadmus, the grandfather of Bacchus, the future founder of Thebes, who takes upon himself to instruct this august mouth.[10]

And since that time how many illustrious followers have descended into the arena, how many glorious names will not culinary annals have to register!

Somebody will, perhaps, one day publish a chronological history of celebrated cooks. In the meantime, it may not be amiss to recall to memory a few illustrious men, whose services and genius an ungrateful posterity has too soon forgotten.

Thimbron, among the Greeks, took the culinary art from its cradle: he watched devoutedly over its development, and only descended into the tomb after having won the heart of the whole of Greece,[11] for his favourite science. Timachidas of Rhodes, cook and poet of the highest renown, composed an epopee on the art which he professed, in the midst of emanations from the stoves and the spit'[12] His verses, glowing with the sacred fire which inspired him, lighted up the magiric vein of several of his disciples, among whom Numenius, Hegemon, and Metreas, are still cited.[13]

Artemidorus collected and commented on all the words in use in the kitchens of his time.[14] Greece owed to this patient terminologist the possession of a culinary language, subject to certain unchangeable rules.

Mithœcus gave the " Sicilian Cook "—a remarkable type of a multitude of tiresome and insipid imitations.[15]

At length Archestratus appeared. He was of Syracuse, and passed all his life in profoundly meditating on the functions, strength, anomalies, and resources of the stomach. He discovered the laws which govern that organ, and presented to the world his magnificent treatise on gastronomy [16]—an inestimable master-piece of laborious investigation of which time has deprived us, together with the works of his useful predecessors.

We must not omit the names of some celebrated theoricians, to whom the art owes its rapid progress :—Philoxenus of Leucadus, devoted himself to the difficult study of degustation, and practised several experiments, which were, however, ill-appreciated by his contemporaries. Thus, in the public baths, he accustomed his mouth and hands to the contact of boiling-water, in order to be able to seize and devour burning viands, the instant they were placed on the table. He recommended cooks to serve everything very hot, so that he alone exercised mastication and deglutition, while other guests less inured, were obliged to content themselves with looking at him.[17]

Pithyllus invented a sheath that covered the tongue, and protected it, without paralyzing its action, against a caloric dangerous to its delicate tissue.[18] This ingenious cuirass was not appreciated, and history, in its thoughtlessness, has not even transmitted to us a description of it.

It was then the good time of Athens: gluttons had made way for epicureans; hunger, to a less fierce and gross sensation, already subjected to examination and discussion. The magiric art possessed its rules, its various partisans, its professors, and disciples. Great masters studied deeply the appetite—indispensable basis, on which will always rest the culinary exegesis; and they finished by classing it definitively, according to the three degrees of intensity which observation discovers in it.

The bold appetite, said they, is that which is felt when fasting. It reflects but very little; is not squeamish about viands, and loses all reserve at the sight of a very indifferent *ragoût*.

The indolent appetite requires to be encouraged. It must be enticed, pressed, irritated. At first, nothing moves it—but after having tasted a succulent dish, it rouses, is astonished, its ardour becomes animated, and is capable of performing prodigies. It is this appetite which has consecrated the trivial but true proverb: "*L'appétit vient en mangeant.*"

The *eclectic appetite* owes nothing to nature; it is the child of art. Happy, thrice happy, the skilful cook to whom it says: "Thou art my father!" But how difficult is this creation—how rare! It is the work of genius —but listen. Some guests, chosen amidst veteran epicureans, seat themselves round a table covered with culinary offerings worthy only of the God of Feasts, and a small number of the faithful. Their *indolent appetite* examines, compares, judges, and, at length, abandons itself to the incomparable dainties from which it unceasingly seems to draw new ardour. But alas! pleasure, like pain, has its limits here below. Strength grows less, and becomes extinguished; the eye loses its greedy covetousness;[19] the palate languishes; the tongue becomes paralysed; the stomach sinks, and that which before pleased, now creates only fatigue and disgust. It is then that a *cusinier hors ligne*, tries a bold diversion, which must never be risked if the artist does not feel in himself that force of generous efforts which is no other than genius. By his orders, three or four dishes, prodigies of science and of luxury, appear on the altar, which the sacrificers no longer heed. At this sight, their looks brighten; desire revives; the smile reappears; the magiric *facies* shines forth with all its splendour; the chest dilates, and you no longer distinguish your former guests. A man has transformed them. Each one chooses, tries, tastes—is silent, and lost in wonder. The appetite is perhaps tired, but not satiated; and the skilful cook at length enjoys a deserved triumph.

In this solemn moment he received, among the ancients, a crown of flowers[20]—sweet and noble recompense of his arduous toil. Nay, a more substantial proof of gratitude often greeted his new dishes. In Greece, the inventor alone had a right to prepare them during a whole year, and drew from it all the honour and profit. It was necessary, in order that these culinary preparations should fall into the public domain, that some one of his colleagues should succeed in surpassing him.[21]

At this epoch, the best cooks came from Sicily. Trimalcio was one of the most celebrated. Athenæus tells us that, when he could not procure rare and highly esteemed fish, he understood so well how to imitate their form and flavour with common fish, that the most cunning epicures were always entrapped. This reminds us of a certain cook of Louis XIV., who, on Good Friday, served the king with a dinner, apparently composed of poultry and butcher's meat, which, in reality, offered nothing but vegetables, and prepared, too, *au maigre*.

The Romans, inheritors of the luxury of Asia and Greece, did not erect a temple to the greedy Addephagia, goddess of good cheer, who possessed altars in Sicily;[22] but they thought it impossible to repay too highly those who knew how to extend the limits of the pleasures of the table,[23] and a generous senator offered his *chef* at least four talents, or more than £800 a year.

This is yet but little compared with the magnificence of Antony. He gave a supper to Cleopatra; that princess praised the delicacy of the feast, and immediately her lover called for the cook, and presented him with a city, in recompense.

How times are changed! We, at the present day, treat all this as pompous and ridiculous prodigality. It is because our somewhat mean epoch judges the olden times by the narrow ideas of order, foresight, and economy. The ancients enriched their *Archimagiri*, wasted their revenue in feasts, and then killed themselves. We have adopted a very different style of living. But, at the same time, how far are our most sumptuous banquets behind the most modest collations of Greece and

Rome! Lucullus caused to be served to Cicero and Pompey a little *ambigu*, which cost £1,000. There were only three of them to partake of it!

The Emperor Claudius had generally six hundred guests at his table.[24]

Vitellius did not spend less than £3,200 for each of his repasts;[25] and the composition of his favourite dishes required that vessels should unceasingly ply between the Gulf of Venice and the Straits of Cadiz.[26]

It must be confessed that cooks of that gastronomic era had to fulfil an incessant and most laborious task. What was then more natural than to abandon to them some thousands of those sesterces, which the profusion of the master devoured by millions, in the form of pheni-copters' tongues, scarus or parrot-fishes' livers, and peacocks' brains?

We see that the Cæsars encouraged this frightful gastronomic mono-mania. Tiberius gave more than £3,000 to the author of a dialogue, in which the interlocutors were mushrooms, fig-peckers, oysters, and thrushes.[27]

Galba breakfasted before day-break, and the breakfast would have enriched a hundred families.[28] Ælius Verus invented the *pentaphar-macum*, a kind of *Macédoine*, composed of sows' flanks, pheasants, peacocks, ham, and wild boars' flesh.[29] Geta insisted upon having as many courses as there were letters in the alphabet, and each of these courses must contain all the viands whose name began by the same letter.[30]

These follies, which cooks were forced to obey, continued to astonish the world until the moment when Rome—with her gods, the monuments of her ancient glory, and of her recent turpitudes—crumbled beneath the invincible weight of that horde of barbarians, that mysterious and implacable scourge, which Divine vengeance reserved for the punishment of unheard-of crimes.

But, as we have before remarked, the magiric art always survives revolutions and ruin of empires. Modern Italy inherited the wrecks of Roman cookery, and, thanks to her, Europe is at the present day acquainted with the delights of good cheer, and the charm of joyous repasts.

Under the reign of Louis XII. there arose a company of sauce manufacturers, who obtained the exclusive privilege of making sauces. Their statutes (1394) inform us that the famous sauce *à la cameline*, sold by them, was to be composed "of good cinnamon, good ginger, good cloves, good grains of paradise, good bread, and good vinegar." The sauce, *Tence*, was to be made of "good sound almonds, good ginger, good wine, and good verjuice." We find in Taillevant, the celebrated cook of Charles V. and Charles VI., besides the *cameline*, *l'eau bénite* (holy water)—the sauce for pike, *le saupiquet*, *le mostechan*, *la gelatine*, *la sauce à l'alose*, *au moût*, that of milk-garlic, cold, red, and green sauces, *sauce Robert*, *Poitevine*, *à Madame rappée*, and *à la dodine*.

Platina, a Latin author of the 15th century, speaks of other sauces, in the composition of which sugar was frequently employed, according to the proverb of those times : "Sugar never spoiled sauce."

In the middle ages, poultry, butchers' meat, and roast game, were never eaten dry, as they are now, any more than fried fish. There were different sauces for all those dishes, and even for the different parts of each animal. The cooks of those days strove to acquire a reputation by inventing strange and grotesque sauces, which had no other merit than that of being surprising and difficult to make, as, for example : "eggs cooked on the spit," "butter fried or roasted." &c.[31]

We recognize in some of our most common *ragoûts*, those of which our ancestors were so fond in the middle ages, such as the *bœuf à la mode*, *à la persillade*, *au vinaigre et persil*, *le miroton de bœuf*, *veau percé de gros lard*, *fricassée de poulet*, *blanquette de veau rôti ;* but we have lost the *pot-pourri*, composed of beef, veal, mutton, bacon, and vegetables, and the *galimafrée*, a kind of *fricassée* of fowl, seasoned with wine, verjuice, and spices, and thickened with the famous sauce *cameline*.[32]

The cooks frequently placed on their masters' tables *ragoûts* and other dishes borrowed from foreign nations. They had a German *brouet*, a Flemish *chaudeau*, eggs *à la Florentine*, and partridges *à la Catalane*. They knew the *olla*—a mixture of all sorts of vegetables cooked with different kinds of meats, which we owe to the Spaniards, as well as the *ragoût* of fowl, called *à la Chipolata*, and the *keneffes*—a kind of forced-meat balls made of bread and meat, to which the Germans are very partial, and the *pilau*—a dish of mutton, fowl, and rice, borrowed from the Turks.[33]

The art of cooking with its innumerable paraphernalia of sauces with gravy, pepper, cinnamon, garlic, scallion, brains,[34] with its gravy soups,

Pl. II.

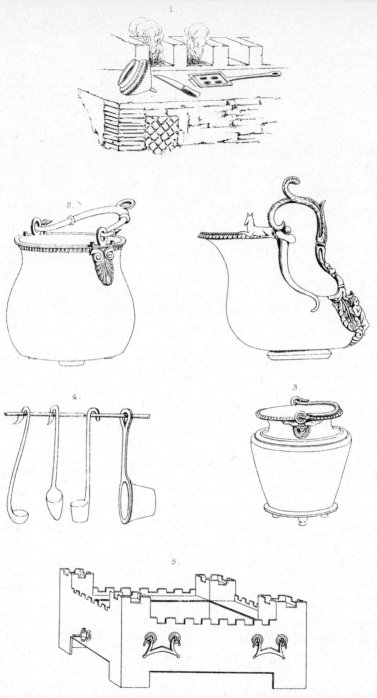

F. T. Z. Volant, del.

Chant & Saddler, scul.

milk pottage, and *ragoûts*, had a signal triumph at the wedding of Charles VI. of France. On that occasion a skilful cook covered the great black marble table of the royal palace [35] with a hundred dishes prepared in a hundred different ways.

The good physicians did not proscribe the art of cooking; several of their number even deigned to write treatises upon it. [36]

A certain monkish servant, moved by an indiscreet zeal, wished not only to mortify himself but all the Franciscans of the monastery. Consequently, he prepared the repasts in the worst manner he could. But the community held a chapter, and he was condemned to receive fifty lashes; many of the monks wanted to enforce a more rigorous discipline by giving a hundred. [37]

In the middle ages, the cook of a house of any note always seated himself in a high arm chair to give his orders; he held a long wooden spoon in his hand, with which he tasted, without quitting his place, the various dishes that were cooking on the stoves and in the saucepans, and which served him also as a weapon with which to chastise the idle and gluttonous. [38]

THE KITCHEN.

Let us enter together one of those vast kitchens, where two thousand years ago, the marvellous suppers of some rich senator were concocted. In every direction, slaves are coming loaded with meat, game, sea-fish, vegetables, fruit, and those expensive delicacies of which the dessert of the Romans was principally composed. The slaves have been over the principal markets of the city, especially those of the Trigemina gate,

DESCRIPTION OF PLATE No. XI.

No. 1. Remains of a kitchen-stove in the house of Pansa, at Pompeii, much like those of the present day; a knife, a strainer, and a kind of fryingpan with four cavities, probably intended to cook eggs.

No. 2. Stock-pot, in bronze, to hang over the fire, if we may judge from the eye at the top of the handle.

No. 3. A similar one of another shape, for boiling.

No. 4. Ladles of various forms, for making libation from larger vessels.

No. 5. A brazier; the thickness of the sides are hollow, and intended to contain water, and the four turrets, are provided with moveable lids, at the side is a cock to draw off the water. The centre of course was filled with lighted charcoal, and if a tripod, or trivet, were placed above it, many processes of cooking, such as boiling, stewing, or frying, might be performed.—"*Pompeii.*"—"*Lib. of Ent. Know.*"

of the Metasudante,[39] of the Suburd Way,[40] and the Sacred Way.[41] Each one lays his basket at the feet of the procurator or major-domo, who examines the contents, and registers them on his tablets ;[42] then he has placed in the pantry, contiguous to the dining room, those of the provisions which demand no preparation,[43] but whose graceful and symmetrical arrangement is confided to two Æolian servants designated under the name of *structores*.[44]

All these porters are under the immediate orders of a confidential servant—*obsonator*—charged with buying the provisions necessary for the household, and who is obliged to make himself acquainted with the taste of his master and also of each guest, that he may procure nothing which they dislike.[45]

The remaining comestibles are placed in an airy and spacious apartment adjoining the kitchen, and at the back of the house.[46] There, around a table loaded with numerous wooden figures, representing a variety of animals, some attentive young men are practising, under the direction of an experienced master, the difficult art of carving game and poultry ;[47] whilst a melodious symphony accustoms their skilful hands to hasten or retard their graceful movements according to the time of the music [48] In this learned rehearsal the eye and ear, alike charmed, pass alternately from the peaceful emotions of the pensive *adagio* to the lively cadences of the rapid *allegro*, and from the harmonious and calm *andante* to the captivating and joyous accents of a frenzied *prestissimo*.

In this spacious laboratory the most delicious emanations invite us. The chief of the cooks, the *Archimagirus*,[49] seated on a raised platform, embraces at a single glance the series of stock-pots and brick stoves,[50] very similar to those in use at the present day, at which the silent crowd of assistants,[51] ministers of his will, elaborate and watch the expensive dishes destined to form a splendid supper. As, at the moment of battle, the general, motionless on a height which commands a view of his army, hastens, orders, scolds his scattered battalions, absent and yet everywhere, animating with his own inspiration the warlike masses, and exciting them with the excitement of his own soul, he invokes victory, and victory replies, " Behold me !" The *Archimagirus* has also his days of triumph ; and in the evening, perhaps, the king of the feast will place on his head a crown of flowers, precious recompense of his talent and success.

At some distance from the culinary autocrat, on the opposite side, an

Pl. 12

NARGISS

F.T.Z Volant, del.   Chant & Saddler, sew.

immense iron grate,[52] carefully supplied with wood,[53] which an unhappy slave unceasingly blows with his breath into a flame,[54] throws around its lurid glare. The *Lares*, grotesque figures, roughly carved in stone, protect this spot. A cock is sacrificed to them in the month of December.[55]

Some learned men have supposed that the Greeks and Romans had no chimneys; it is, however, easy to prove the contrary. Philocleo, a character in the comedy of the "*Wasps*" of Aristophanes, hides himself in a chimney. A slave who hears him, cries out, "What a noise there is in the pipe of this chimney!" Philocleo, being discovered, exclaims, " I am the smoke, and I am trying to escape."[56]

Appian, speaking of the proscriptions of the triumvirs, relates that several citizens fled into the pipes of the chimneys.[57]

These two examples will preclude the necessity of more ample citations.

A vast cauldron of brass from Argos,[58] or Dodona,[59] placed on a tripod above the fireplace, furnishes the hot water required for the service of the kitchen. The frying-pan, beside it, serves in the cooking of certain delicate cakes or fish.[60]

The magiric laboratory, to which the reader is invited, is very nicely decorated with a profusion of utensils similar in every respect to our own in point of shape—such as gridirons, cullenders, dripping-pans, and tart dishes. These objects are of tolerably thick bronze, plated with fine silver.[61] Charming shells of the same metal serve to mould the pastry,[62] which is afterwards disposed with order on the shelves of a country oven,[63] or in the upper part of the authepsa,—a kind of saucepan of Corinthian brass, of considerable value, and made with such art that its contents cook instantly and almost without fire.[64] This simple and ingenious vessel possesses a double-bottom; the uppermost one holds

<hr>

DESCRIPTION OF PLATE No. XII.

From the ancients very little is left us of their kitchen utensils; however, the vessels and instruments which they used must have been in great variety; they had boilers called by the names of *caldarium*, *cacabus*, *cortina*, *adhenum*; chaldron, *lebes*; stewpan, *sartago*; saucepan, *pultarium*; the cullender, with small holes perforated, Pliny calls *colum*, and more modern writers *verna*; spoons, in Latin, *cochlear* or *cochleare*; forks and hooks, to draw the meat out of the stockpots, they named *creagra* and *fuscina*; the dishes were called *lances*, *disci*, *patina*, *patella*, or *catini*; and distinguished from plates by the size, and sometimes the shape.

No. 1. Stockpot, with a large ladle and cullender attached, with small holes; appeared on the column of Trajan, together with the stewpan of Silenus.

No. 2. Broken stewpan, in bronze.

No. 3. Smaller one. These three articles of kitchen utensils are from the cabinet of M. l'Abbé Charlet.—"*Antiquités de Montfaucon*."

the light delicacies destined for the dessert, and the fire is under-neath.[65]

The diploma, or double-vase, which has sometimes been confounded with the authepsa, does not in the least resemble the latter. It is thus they named the vessel called by us a " *bain-marie ;*"[66] the ancients made great use of this mild and gentle process of cooking, which is often men-tioned in the treatise of Apicius.[67]

These brass boilers, which boil on the hearth, supported by three feet, are precisely like those used by the French at the present day.[68] Boilers also of a rather different kind are sometimes used, in which the operation of ebullition takes place sooner than in the first mentioned; they are closed with a cover in the form of a dome, and a large hollow cylinder, fixed beneath, hastens and keeps up the action of the caloric.[69]

The saucepans, around which a host of cooks are busily engaged, are for the greater part made of brass or earthenware,[70] tolerably wide and deep, which they place on the stoves, and in which are concocted the delicate and scientific preparations. Some are of silver.[71] The caprices of luxury have led them to suppose that certain expensive viands acquire greater perfection when cooked in this precious metal.

A confidential slave, charged with the care of the plate, is cleaning and polishing near a dresser a large number of bronze chafing-dishes, which are to be used at table to prevent the plates from becoming cold. It is in speaking of this useful invention that Seneca, the philosopher, says, " Daintiness gave birth to this invention, in order that no viand should be chilled, and that everything should be hot enough to please the most pampered palate. The kitchen follows the supper."[72] Each of these elegant utensils is supported by three geese. It measures about seven inches from the extremity of one of the bird's heads to the op-posite edge of the circumference. This kind of tray is fifteen lines, or an inch and a-quarter deep, and the feet raise it about two inches above the plane. The three geese have their wings spread, and terminate by

DESCRIPTION OF PLATE No. XIII.

No. 1. This boiler is made of bronze; the lower part was filled with water, and made to boil by means of the cylinder, covered with a lid, in which lighted charcoal was introduced; the ashes escaped through holes perforated at the bottom, and the basin has a tap to let the water out.

No. 2. A flat saucepan, or *sauté* pan, with a fluted handle, and a ram's head at the end.

No. 3. A kettle similar to our teapots.

No. 4. A gridiron, and a dripping-pan.

No. 5. A trivet, a cleaver, and a butcher's knife.—ST. Non, " *Cabinet of Herculaneum.*"

Pl. 13.

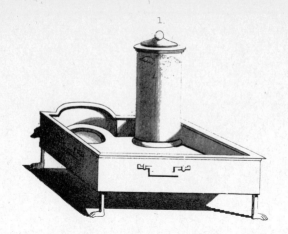

1.

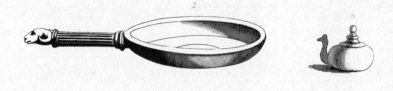

2.

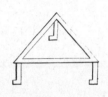

3.

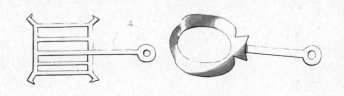

4.

5.

F. V. J. Solunt, del.

Chant & Saddler, scul.

Pl. 1.

2.

1.

T. H. Voland del.

Saddler & Chant

neats' feet.   The heads, raised on the breasts, form graceful handles.[73]
These chafing-dishes, arranged systematically on the sigma, produce a
delightful effect.

Dishes of massive silver occupy another compartment of the vast
cupboard.   An opulent family could not possibly do without this luxury.
Sylla had some which weighed 200 marks, and Rome would produce
more than five hundred of the same weight.[74]   It was in fact a perfect
furore, which afterwards greatly augmented.   In the time of the
Emperor Claudius, one of his slaves, named Drusillanus Rotundus,
possessed a silver dish weighing 1,000 marks, which was served in the
midst of eight smaller ones weighing 100 marks each.   These nine
dishes were arranged at table on a machine which supported and placed
them prominently in view.

The *patinæ,* such was the name of these magnificent pieces of plate,
served for *ragoûts* and fish; the *catinus,* an immense vase of earthenware among the poor,[75] and of silver with the rich, is more especially
reserved for liquid dishes, with much gravy, and what we call pottage.[76]

Those silver cups and saucers, of the same shape and size as those
we employ for tea, have a destination very strange to our ideas.   They
are used to drink hot water.   They are worked in relief, with a taste and
delicacy which we cannot too much admire.[77]

The Roman spoons, rather different from our own, end on one side
by a point, to pick shell fish from their shell, and at the other by the
bowl of a spoon, with which eggs were eaten.[78]

Doubtless, forks were unknown to the Greeks, since Athenæus relates,
" that Pithyllus "—surnamed the Dainty—" did not content himself with
covering his tongue with a species of net, to appreciate the taste of the
various dishes, but cleaned and rubbed it with a fish.   He also enveloped
his hands in a kind of glove, to eat everything burning hot;"[79] a useless
precaution if he had used a fork.

This indispensable addition to a modern table was, perhaps, not
common at Rome, but nevertheless, it was to be seen at the residence of
some wealthy families.   The slave before-mentioned holds several in his
hand.   These forks are remarkable for the beauty of their workmanship.

DESCRIPTION OF PLATE No. XIV.

No. 1.   Chafing-dish to keep everything hot.
No. 2.   Silver cup, beautifully chased, to drink hot water.

The stags' feet which terminate the handles, and the fillets with which they are ornamented, bear witness by their execution to the rare talent of the goldsmith. They are five inches and a half in length, and have only two prongs.[80]

Other servants dispose the earthenware pails, in which the wine is to be placed to cool,[81] and prepare the drinking cups and crystal flagons.[82] One of them replenishes with vinegar, salt, and pepper, little vases designated by the name of *acetabulum,* "vinegar cruet." [83] These are so many models of the most exquisite elegance, in bronze, silver, and, sometimes, gold. They are manufactured simply of earthenware, for the use of the middle classes of people.[84]

The knives, destined to serve at table, are of brilliant steel, and carefully sharpened; they bear each on the handle some whimsical ornament, and seem to have served as models for those which were so much in fashion towards the beginning of the 17th century, and which were called Chinese knives.[85]

The most precious plate is arranged before the arrival of the guests on the abacus, or sideboard, which decorates the dining room. This splendid piece of furniture, which will be noticed hereafter, was introduced into Rome 187 years B.C. It was also called the Delphic table.[86]

However, the *Archimagirus* has drawn up a list of the repast, which contains the bill of fare of the dishes, and which, both in Greece and Rome, was always presented to the guests.[87] He descends from his platform, and goes to cast an inspiring glance on the work of each subordinate. Nothing escapes his learned investigation, from the peacocks' eggs of the first service, to the soft cheese commonly eaten at the third.[88] Above all, he examines with minute attention the ovens, at which preside those second cooks of whose talents he is not certain, and who belong to that class of erratic artists who are to be met with every day at the forum,

---

DESCRIPTION OF PLATE No. XV.

No. 1. Roman silver spoon, found at Autun, in France. Martial says expressly that spoons were used by the ancients to eat eggs and shell fish.

No. 2. Brass knife, from Herculaneum. The shape of the handle is rather singular, being too small for the hand, but it was probably covered with horn, wood, or ivory. However, it may have been, the knife is thirteen inches in length, from the tip to the ring, which was used to hang it up. The handle is three inches long, and the blade in its largest width is one inch and a quarter. It was used no doubt for sacrifices.

No. 3. A simpulum, or a sort of spoon for salt or eggs.

No. 4. A simpulum, or cup with a long handle, commonly ending with a hook, which was used as a ladle to take wine or other liquids out of large vessels.

No. 5. Fork mentioned in the text, and given as antique in the "*Recueil d' Antiq.*," III., Pl. 84.

Pl. 15

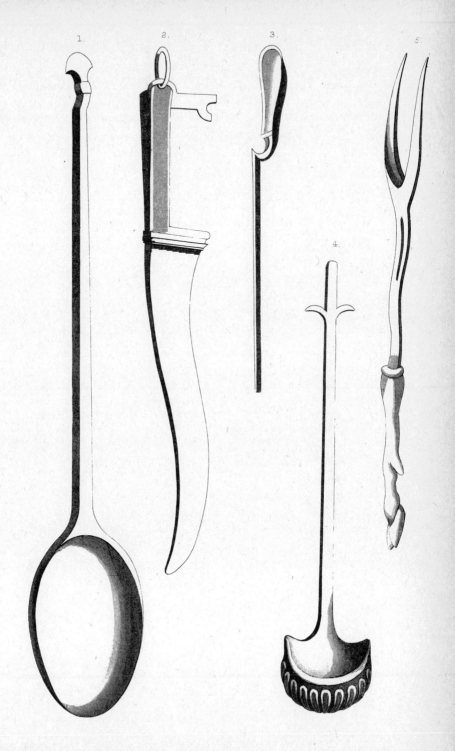

F. T. Z. Volant, del.

Saddler & Chant, scul.

Pl. 16.

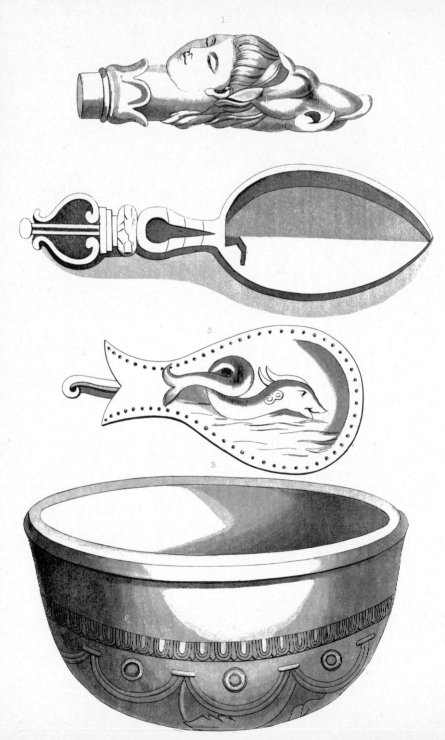

F.T.Z.Volant, del.

Chant & Saddler, scul.

where they wait till some one comes to request their services.[89]   His remarks, full of sense and precision, proclaim profound study and consummate experience.   "Never will this *depsiticius* bread,"[90] says he to one of them, " obtain the necessary lightness by baking; the flour should have been passed through a Spanish sieve of linen thread ;[91] Use the Gallic sieve of horsehair for the *artocreas*,*[92] and one of papyrus, or Egyptian rush,[93] for the coarser kinds of flour."   "The grasshoppers require great precaution," he exclaims, an instant after, approaching a young Sicilian ; "fry them so that they obtain only a light gold colour."[94]   Then, passing to a third stove, he shows to one of his favourite pupils how to season highly an excellent sauce of snails (this *hors-d'œuvre*, dear to the Romans), and by what marks to distinguish those fattened by art in particular inclosures, from those which feed in gardens and are only fit for the common people.[95]   He then stops before a stewpan, where a cook is browning large worms of a whitish hue, which breed in the hollows of trees, and are considered by the Romans[96] as a most delicious dish: " The flour with which these cossi were fed was heated," says he ; " they will present to the teeth only a soft and insipid substance."[97]

We will not accompany this great master any further: his instructions are already known to us.   An enthusiastic disciple of Apicius, he practises the lessons of that illustrious professor; and we should only hear from him precepts which we have already faithfully transmitted.

When the moment of supper is arrived, we shall find the *Archimagirus* presiding at that gastronomic order of battle on which depends the success of the day.   May Vesta and Comus be propitious to him.

In the 14th century, the refectories and kitchens of the numerous communities of Paris presented a curious scene.   Immense coppers contained the pottage and boiled meat, and monster gridirons, on four wheels, covered vast braziers.   All the utensils of these kitchens were of remarkable dimensions.

* Pie of meat and flour.

DESCRIPTION OF PLATE No. XVI.

No. 1.   Roman silver knife handle.
No. 2.   Roman silver spoons.
No. 3.   A very deep dish of metal, either for sauces or some kind of liquid.

XXIII

SEASONINGS.

THE animal and vegetable kingdoms furnish us with an abundant and wholesome food, whose flavour gastronomic caprice unceasingly modifies by the aid of various substances which we denominate seasonings. It is, above all, the perfect knowledge of these ingredients, the manner of employing them, and their skilful mixture, which constitute the art of the cook. Labour and custom, and a kind of routine which the palate acquires easily, will suffice for those who content themselves with this calling, and who, carefully preserving the timid traditions of the past, view progress as ruin and devastation, and the fruitful boldness of inspiration as ridiculous and fatal innovations.

Heresy, and even schism (pardon these expressions), should be allowed in cookery, as soon as they receive the sanction of the doctors *ès-banquets*—the sole judges competent in such matters. It is to the art professed by Apicius that the celebrated line of Voltaire appears more peculiarly to apply :—

"Tous les genres sont bons, excepté l'ennuyeux."

Innovate, then, studious disciples of the illustrious Roman : consult only the measures of your strength, the conscience of your genius, and the infallible good taste of some chosen guests. Create for your seasoning unheard-of combinations, the strangeness of which shall strike and astonish ; whose flavour shall subjugate and stifle criticism beneath the sweet efforts of a voluptuous mastication.

Learn how to make your areopagitæ eat : this innocent seduction will insure your triumph.

Treat not with too much disdain these Roman recipes ; for although the formidable list may excite a smile from the reader, and, perhaps, the scorn of the cook, a great and prolific idea slumbers beneath the cold ashes of the ovens of Apicius which a breath may rekindle; and, at the same time, resuscitate some of those culinary wonders of a bygone civilisation, and endow our modern age, so impatient of the future, so curious concerning the past.

Two Phœnicians—whose names are never mentioned by forgetful posterity—Selech and Misor, taught mankind the art of heightening the flavour of their food by mixing with it a certain quantity of salt. The science of seasoning has no other origin.[1]

———•———

SALT.

The law of Moses commanded the Jews to mix salt with everything offered in sacrifice.[2]   This prescription sufficiently testifies the use of this condiment at an epoch which the uncertainty of profane writers appears to invade on all sides, and which the great Hebrew legislator alone enlightens with a ray invariably steady and pure.

The Asphaltite lake produced abundance of salt.[3]   It was sent even to Rome, and was considered by Galen as the most desiccatory and digestive of any kind.[4]

The Greeks placed this substance in the list of things which ought to be consecrated to the gods; and it is in this sense that Homer gives it the epithet of divine.   Pagan superstition, of which some traces may still be remarked in the 19th century, threatened with some great misfortune any one who spilt salt; and it was deemed a signal impiety to forget placing salt-cellars on the table, or to dare go to sleep before removing them.   This strange superstition was common among the Greeks and Romans.[5]   Those nations never failed consecrating their repasts by filling salt-cellars, near to the vase in which they presented the gods with the first portion of meat and fruit.[6]

Certain nations, among others the Numidians, were not acquainted with salt;[7] and in the greater part of countries where it abounded, cupidity almost invariably subjected it to a heavy tax, which rendered its use less practicable.

The inhabitants of Troad provided themselves for a long time with salt from Tragase without cost.   King Lysimachus one day thought of exacting a duty for every measure carried away. But, wonderful to relate, hardly was the royal edict published, when the salt springs were found to be so nearly dried up, that they hardly furnished wherewith to season a small stew. Lysimachus comprehended the meaning of this prodigy, and abolished the tax. The salt re-appeared.[8]

At Rome, in the time of her Kings, every one was free to sell salt, and its price became excessively high. The republican government withdrew this right from private individuals, and from that time the common people easily procured all the salt they required, and which they willingly eat with bread.[9]

Ancus Martius was the first Roman who established salt works near Ostia towards the mouth of the Tiber.[10] Afterwards, others were formed, not only in Rome, but in the provinces. These were of two kinds, public and private. The first belonged to the republic, and formed part of the emperor's domain; malefactors were condemned to labour in the salt-works, and it was generally women on whom this punishment was inflicted.[11]

Ancus Martius was also the first who placed a duty on salt. It was abolished after the expulsion of the Kings, but was afterwards again established.

Down to the 14th century salt was a commodity of trade open to every one in France. Philip the Long and Philip of Valois were the first to impose a momentary tax on it; but after the fatal battle of Poictiers, in which John was taken prisoner, Charles, his son, in order to pay the ransom of that monarch, had recourse, among other extraordinary means, to the establishment of the salt tax. The idea was found to be good, and it has never since been given up.[12]

There are four sorts of salt which are employed to season dishes, obtained either from the evaporation of sea water, from certain lakes or salt marshes, and also from saliferous sources drawn out of the bosom of the earth in compact masses. Its particular savour is well known; it is soluble in water, and easily becomes damp. In the scientific language, this substance is called hydrochlorate of soda.

BRINE.

This was water in which bay salt had been dissolved. At Rome, it was served at table to be mixed with the meat precisely in the same manner as we serve salt in salt-cellars. The Romans plunged in this *muria* any fish or meat they might wish to preserve.[13]

Strong *muria dura* was water so completely saturated with bay salt, that no more could be dissolved in it.[14] Olives were washed in it.

The brine most sought after was that of Antibes, of Thurium, and of Dalmatia.[15] It was prepared with the blood and other juices which, after death, escaped from the tunny fish,[16] mixed with garum, which rendered it more fluid and less expensive.

At the end of the repast, enigmas were often proposed to the guests. Some delicious dish served as a reward to those who were fortunate enough to guess them; the others were compelled to pour *muria* into their drink, and swallow a cup-full without taking breath.[17]

DIGESTIVE SALTS.

The Romans were enormous eaters. Apicius, who was better aware of it than any one, imagined providing against those accidents to which his countrymen did not fear to expose themselves once every day, by offering to them a preparation which our habits of sobriety would, doubtless, render useless at the present day; but which the curious will not be sorry to discover in these sketches of antique gastrophagy. Take a pound of common salt, which torrefy and pulverize; mix it with three ounces of white pepper, two ounces of ginger, an ounce of lamoni, an ounce and a half of thyme, as much of celery seed, three ounces of wild marjoram, an ounce and a-half of rocket seed, three ounces of black pepper, an ounce and a-half of holy thistle, two ounces of hyssop, two ounces of spikenard, two ounces of parsley, and two ounces of anise-seed.[18]

Take a small quantity of these salts after a too plentiful dinner, and the stomach will immediately defy the most imminent indigestion.

GARUM.

When we have read all that has been written by the ancients on this famous preparation, we become convinced, in spite of the obscurities and continual contradictions of commentators, that if garum is no longer manufactured in the present day, it is not on account of the impossibility we find in discovering the recipe of the Greeks and Latins, but solely because this rather strange brine has not the same charm for us that it had for them. Let us, however, scan the authorities.

The Greeks called the shrimp *garos*, the Romans *garus* : it may hence be supposed that garum had originally for basis the flesh of shrimps, if Pliny had not taken the trouble to inform us of the fact.[19] It was afterwards composed of other fish, but it always retained the name which recalled its origin.[20] In like manner the signification of certain words is now applied to things quite different from the original type : chicory, or succory, is received under the mask of coffee : a certain pottage boldly usurps the honours due exclusively to turtle soup. Nothing more easy than to multiply these examples of catachreses : there are few figures which have become so common.

Well, then, they macerated the intestines of fish in water, saturated with salt, until putrefaction began to show itself; they then added parsley and vinegar.[21]

A thick garum was also frequently obtained, by allowing the entrails and other parts, generally thrown away, to liquefy in salt.[22]

In the time of Pliny, mackerel[23] was preferred, of which they employed either the gills and intestines, or only the blood, directly the fish left the water,[24] and while yet living. They thus obtained a precious liquid, and which the care necessary for its production rendered so dear, that eight pints of it cost no less than from fifteen to twenty pounds.[25]

This expensive garum was especially esteemed when it came from Spain : it was then called " garum of the allies"—*garum sociorum*— because it was received from a nation allied with the Romans ;[26] or, again, perhaps in allusion to the " band of gluttons," of Rome, a sort of fraternity of free-livers, who made great use of it.[27]

The blood and entrails of the tunny fish, mixed with salt in a vase, produced also a most elaborate garum. A hole was made in the vessel at the expiration of two months, and the rich seasoning flowed from it.[28]

This brine became exquisite, and obtained an exorbitant price when made from the liver of anchovies macerated in vinegar, pepper, salt, parsley, garlic, white wine, and sweet herbs.[29] But Apicius attained at the first step the apogee of refinement of the most sensual gluttony, by inventing garum made from the liver of red mullet.[30] What we have already said elsewhere with regard to this fish will enable the reader to appreciate the value of this new preparation.

Amateurs who were more economical contented themselves with very little saxatile fishes,[31] of which only the intestines were taken, or which were thrown whole into a vase with a great quantity of salt. These were exposed to the sun, and the mixture long and often stirred. When heat had caused fermentation, and the vessel contained only a kind of pulp, or paste, almost liquid, a kind of willow basket was introduced, into which the garum alone could penetrate. The thick part—the dregs which remained at the bottom of the vase—was termed *alec*.[32]

The following method was also frequently adopted:—

Mackerel, or small fish, were placed in a small vase with a large quantity of salt; this was well stirred, and the mixture was then left quiet all night. The next day it was transferred into an earthen pot, which remained uncovered in the sun. At the end of two or three months, it was hermetically closed, after having added a quantity of old wine equal to one-third of the mixture.[33]

When it was wished to obtain garum without waiting any length of time, they took brine, carefully filtered, and so saturated with salt that an egg would float on it; this was placed with the fish in a new sauce-pan; wild marjoram was added, and the whole boiled over a gentle fire, until the fish was entirely dissolved. Then wine, reduced to two-thirds by boiling, was added. It was left to get cold; the liquid was several times filtered, till it became quite clear, and was then finally placed in an uncovered vase.[34]

Although fish was generally used, the flesh of several animals was sometimes employed im the formation of garum.[35] It was, however, submitted to the same preparations as those already mentioned.

Such was this wonderful seasoning, forming the chief delight of the ancients, whose praises poets have sung, and the composition of which formerly exercised the singularly mad intelligence of Maître François Rabelais. The reader will doubtless remark, that the principal elements of garum are almost invariably the same: fish, salt, and a greater or less fermentation. But perhaps some one may exclaim: "This must be detestable!" No doubt, but then no one ever thought of regaling him-self with this liquid; it was never taken alone; it was but reserved as a seasoning for a host of dishes, in order to heighten their flavour.

It must also be observed, that a skilful cook always took care to

modify the garum before he sent it to table, by the help of various ingredients, such as pepper, vinegar, Falernian wine,[36] water, and oil,[37]
according to the use to which it was destined, or the degree of strength
it was expedient it should possess.   Hence that variety of seasonings
with garum,—sweet,[38] sharp, mixed with water, wine, vinegar, and many
other substances which changed or corrected the acid flavour of the
primitive condiment,[39] though without in the least depriving it of the
qualities which fermentation had communicated to it.

It results from the different citations of which this chapter is composed, that recipes for the making of garum are to be obtained more
easily than people seem to think at the present time.   Everyone may
not be of the same opinion with regard to the kind of fish generally
used by the ancients to obtain this liquid, although all difficulties would
be removed by admitting—which certainly is nothing but right—that
they chose at one time mackerel or tunny fish; at others, gudgeons and
small sardines; sometimes even the red mullet, in spite of its rarity and
price.   But it is evident that garum was prepared by either dissolving and
liquefying these fish in their brine, either whole, their intestines, or their
liver, and that, to effect this, it was only necessary to expose to the sun the
vessel containing them; or that they simply put small fish into a dish,
with vinegar and parsley, placed it on a charcoal fire, and stirred it for
some time, when it was wanted for immediate use.

It must have been remarked in reading this work, that Apicius very
frequently employs garum; he places it in every sauce, but never
makes use of this seasoning unmixed, never does he serve it by itself as
a special dish.   This celebrated gastronomist has bequeathed us the
recipe for a digestive garum.   It is as follows:—

Mix with some honey, half an ounce of pepper, three scruples of
eschalots, six scruples of cardamum, one scruple of spikenard, and
six scruples of mint; add vinegar to this mixture, and then pour in
some garum.[40]

The *Hypotrimma,* or stomachic condiment, of the same master, merits
also our attention:—Mix carefully some pepper, benzoin, mint, pine-nuts,
dried raisins, and dates, with fresh (not salt) cheese, vinegar, oil, honey,
and wine, reduced by boiling to one half; add garum to this mixture.[41]

The *Moretaria* appears to be a variety of the Hypotrimma; it is a
mixture of mint, rue, coriander, fennel, the whole fresh, with benzoin,
pepper, honey, and vinegar; to this, garum is added.[42]

Whatever may be the opinion the reader may form of this garum, of which mention has so frequently been made, and which has been alternately praised and despised by the moderns, it is certain that the most fastidious persons were madly fond of it, and that in the time of Pliny, it was so much esteemed, that its price equalled that of the most precious perfumes.

"At the present day this celebrated seasoning is forgotten in Italy, but in Turkey it is still in use. The inn keepers of Constantinople preserve in garum the cooked fish not consumed in the day."—Bosc.

HONEY.

What is sweeter than honey?[43] what is more pure,[44] or more nourishing?[45] It is the milk of the aged, it prolongs their existence,[46] and when they descend into the tomb, it still serves to embalm them.[47]

Pagan antiquity ascribed the honour of the discovery of this useful substance to the Athenian Aristæus, who taught mankind to feed on it. This valuable service procured him a patent of nobility. He was made a descendant of Bacchus or Apollo.[48]

It is not necessary to say that honey was known in the east long before the rise of Athens; it is already mentioned in the first book of the holy writings.[49]

It is said that Spain owed its knowledge of this delicious aliment to Gorgor, King of the Curetes, who was polite enough to take some on the occasion of a journey which he made into that country.[50] The Peninsula could afterwards furnish this delicacy for the tables of Rome and Italy.

The Greeks esteemed honey most highly;[51] they employed it in pastry, and in *ragoûts*;[52] their philosopher, Pythagoras, eat nothing else with his bread, and, as he lived to be ninety years old, he recommended his disciples to follow the same *régime*.[53] They profited by ths sage's counsel, and found themselves all the better for it.[54]

A benevolent goddess protected bees, hives, and the honeycomb. She was called Mellona, and a grateful piety offered her honey every new-year's day.[55]

Theophrastus distinguished three kinds of honey: that which the bees extract from flowers, that which comes from the air, and lastly, the honey from reeds.[56]   We clearly perceive that he means honey, manna, and sugar.

Virgil thought that a gentle dew falls on the flowers, and became immediately the prey of bees, which deposited it in their cells.[57]   Pliny has adopted the same graceful error,[58] and even Galen himself partakes of it.[59]

The ancients caused honey to be served at the beginning of a repast;[60] it was used in lieu of sugar in the preparation of preserves and some kinds of beverages, which will hereafter claim our attention. They preferred that of Attica,[61] and insisted on its being thick, clear, granulated, transparent, fresh, and aromatic, with a somewhat sharp flavour.[62]   The faculty attributed to it great virtues.[63]

Honey served as a basis to the wonderful seasoning of Apicius, which we present to the studious investigation of modern gastronomy :— Put fifteen pounds of honey into a brass vessel, containing two pints of wine.   Warm at a very gentle fire, stir, and when it rises, pour over more wine.   Let the mixture rise three times, then take it from the fire, and skim it the next day.   Then add four ounces of ground pepper, three scruples of gum, a drachm of spikenard, a drachm of saffron, five drachms of dried dates, after softening them in wine ; pour on the whole eighteen pints of light wine.[64]

The *Oxyporon* was another seasoning much in vogue two thousand years ago, and in which honey was the principal ingredient.   It was composed by mixing two ounces of cummin seed, one ounce of ginger, one ounce of green rue, and six scruples of nitre, with one ounce of pepper, and twelve scruples of fine dates ; nine ounces of honey were then poured over the whole.[65]

Sometimes they contented themselves with macerating cummin seed in vinegar, which they left to dry, and then pounded it ; that done, it was put into honey.[66]

" The honey most esteemed is the white, granulated, and of an aromatic flavour.   The honey from the French provinces of Narbonne, the Gatinais, or Britanny, is the most esteemed.   Honey is next of kin to sugar, having the same properties.   It is frequently used in domestic economy, and in medicine as a laxative.   It enters into a number of remedies, either as a corrective, or an excipient."—" *Dictio. Encycl.*"

SUGAR.

Theophrastus, the first among the ancients who speaks of sugar, classes it among the number of honeys.[67] Dioscorides also calls it "honey of reeds;" he adds that these reeds grow in India, or in Arabia Felix, and that the agreeable substance they contain has some analogy with salt.[68] Pliny also gives it the same name. It is, according to this naturalist, a kind of honey, with which certain reeds are filled, and used only in medicine.[69]

This was also the opinion of many ancient authors;[70] one of whom, Paul Eginetta, calls sugar—Indian salt.[71]

The sugar cane appears to be originally a native of the East Indies. From the most remote ages the Chinese have understood the art of cultivating it. The histories of the Egyptians, Phœnicians, and Jews, make no mention of it. The Greek physicians are the first who speak of it.

It was not till the year 1471 that a Venetian discovered the method of purifying brown sugar and making loaf sugar. He gained an immense fortune by this discovery.[72]

Sugar cane, well purified, and disburthened of all foreign matter, is white, solid, inodorous, soluble in water, of a soft and agreeable savour. Its specific gravity is 1.6065; it is used as a seasoning in a multitude of dishes, in preparing syrups, preserving of fruits, &c., &c.

CINNAMON.

In the time of Theophrastus, it was said that cinnamon grew in a dark and silent valley, guarded night and day by fearful serpents. Animated by the hope of gain, some individuals, careless of their existence, risked their lives by gathering some of this precious bark. When they had the good luck to avoid the vigilant reptiles, they consecrated to the sun part of their booty, which the radiant orb immediately consumed to prove his acceptance of the offering.[73]

Others, thinking this little tale on the subject of cinnamon rather too dramatic, pretended that the shrub furnishing it was found only on high mountains, to which man was forbidden all access. But fortunately certain birds—the phœnix, among others—great amateurs of aromatics, make their nests of its small branches; these nests are taken, and in this manner, whether the year be good or bad, a sufficient stock of cinnamon is obtained without much trouble.[74] Pliny recognises two kinds of it— one white, the other black, both of which were brought to Rome from Ethiopia, in the reign of Vespasian.[75]

Eighty years after (A.D. 164), Galen informs us that cinnamon was still very scarce in Italy; that the Emperors alone possessed any; and that they even preserved it among the curiosities they made it their pleasure to collect and keep in their palaces.[76]

The same writer regards this so precious and uncommon cinnamon as an excellent cordial and a good digestive.[77]

We may add that it was only well known in Europe after the frequent voyages of the Portuguese to India.[78]

However, in 1163, an abbot of St. Gilles, in Languedoc, having a favour to ask of Louis-le-Jeune, thought there was no better means of persuading him to grant it than to send him a small stock of cinnamon.[79]

Our forefathers (in the middle ages) had their tables furnished with cinnamon sauce; nutmeg, mustard, and garlic sauces; cold sauces; parsley and vinegar sauces, hot sauces, hell sauces, burgher sauces; cherry, plum, mulberry, grape, gorse, rose, and flower sauces. They were served with roast meat.

Cinnamon is daily employed in medicine, in diarrhœa, several fevers, &c., &c., and in pharmacy. That from China is much thicker than the others, its colour darker, and its odour more powerful; essential oil is drawn from it, and preserved in flagons, sealed with the arms of government, and sold at a very high price.

CLOVES.

Cloves were very little known to the ancients. Theophrastus, Dioscorides, and Galen do not speak of them.

Pliny says that some cloves were brought to Rome, very similar to grains of pepper but a little longer; that they were only to be found in India, in a wood consecrated to the gods; and that they served in the fabrication of perfumes.[80]

The conquest of India by the Portuguese rendered them common throughout Europe.

Cloves contain a considerable quantity of essential aromatic oil, thick, brown, and very heavy, to which it owes its aromatic properties and sharp burning savour. Cloves are employed as a seasoning or as medicine.

PEPPER.

The two great cities of antiquity knew how to appreciate pepper, and employed it largely in their culinary labours. They distinguished two kinds: one round, the other long and thin.[81]

Dioscorides and Pliny describe the shrub, on which are to be seen pods filled with seeds of pepper, resembling millet, according to the first of these writers, and like small beans, according to the other.[82]

Our readers no doubt remember the importance which Apicius ascribes to pepper, in the learned recipes of that skilful *Archimagirus*.

VERJUICE.

Verjuice, the use of which is very ancient, was used more in pharmaceutical preparations than in the seasoning of food.[83] Galen attributes to it refreshing qualities, and advises it in certain cases.[84]

Verjuice is a kind of grape, very acid, and which never gets perfectly ripe. The *suc* of verjuice is used in medicine and culinary preparation as an astringent. The juice is not proper to make wine, but a very agreeable syrup is obtained from it.

VINEGAR.

The greater part of ancient nations were acquainted with the use of vinegar. Reapers in the east soaked their bread in it, to freshen it.[85] The Greeks esteemed that of Cnide, of Sphette, of Cleone, and above all the vinegar of Egypt,[86] which was reputed to be the best among the Romans, who tempered its acrimony by mixing with it some sweet substance.[87]

These masters of the world did not fancy they possessed all the comforts of life when they wanted vinegar; therefore they always had a large provision of it in their cellars, as all their seasonings proved.[88]

This passion (for it certainly amounted to a passion) is easily explained by the admirable qualities they attributed to the pungent liquid. It was believed to be astringent, digestive, antibilious, refreshing, and an antiscorbutic.[89] Mixed with water, it was the drink of the soldiers,[90] who, thanks to this beverage, braved the intemperance of the seasons and the different climates of Europe, Africa, and Asia.

The Greeks and Romans esteemed highly their pickles: these consisted of flowers, herbs, roots, and vegetables, preserved in vinegar, and which kept a long time in cylindrical vases with wide mouths.[91] They were prepared with the greatest care; and these plants were often macerated in oil, brine, and vinegar, with which they were impregnated drop by drop.[92] Meat, also, cut in very small pieces, was treated in the same manner.

Vinegar of an exorbitant price was obtained from some precious wines, and that price was again increased by the proverbial cupidity of some butlers in great houses. We doubt much, however, whether any of those worthy personages ever made such a bill as a certain French seigneur dared to do under the reign of Louis XIII. It is said that the Duc de la Meilleraye, grand master of the artillery of France, presented to the minister a bill in which figured an article of 1,300,000 francs (£52,000), for vinegar to cool the cannons! The sum appeared rather large, but La Meilleraye was a near relation of Richelieu, and the article passed without the least contestation.[93]

TRUFFLE.

A truffled turkey was to be eaten at a dinner where Buffon was invited. A few minutes before setting down to table, an elderly lady inquired of the celebrated naturalist where the truffle grew. " At your feet, madame." The lady did not understand ; but it was thus explained to her : " *C'est au pied des charmes*" (yoke elm tree). The compliment appeared to her most flattering. Towards the end of the dinner, some one asked the same question of the illustrious writer, who, forgetting that the lady was beside him, innocently replied : " They grow *aux pieds des vieux charmes* " (old yoke elm trees). The lady overheard him, and no longer thought anything of his amiability.

Nevertheless Buffon was right. It was around the yoke elm trees of Lampsachus, Acarnidea, Alopecomesia, and Elis, that those famous truffles were discovered, whose reputation was spread in all parts and which Italy envied Greece.[94]

The truffle ! beloved treasure that the earth conceals within her bosom—as she does the precious metals, which she seems to have yielded grudgingly to the patient researches of the gastronomist; the magiric records do not tell us at what memorable epoch this exquisite tubercle astonished, for the first time, the palate of man ; but a doubtful tradition maintains that a vile animal (a pig), guided by his marvellous gluttony, found out the existence of this pearl of banquets.

Pliny was very much inclined to range the truffles amidst astonishing prodigies. He fancied that he saw it at its birth increase without roots, without the slightest fibre, without the least capillary vessel likely to transmit to it nutritious juices ;[95] therefore he believed that, sown by thunder-bolts in the autumnal storms,[96] this daughter of thunder grew like minerals by juxta-position, and relates on this subject the history of Lartius Licinius, governor of Spain, who, while biting a truffle with avidity, broke one of his teeth against a Roman denarius which chance alone had inclosed within it.[97]

The Greeks thought a great deal of a delicious species of truffles, smooth outside, red within, which were found just under the surface of the ground, and did not show the slightest appearance of vegetation.[98]

Another kind was also much sought after by amateurs, probably on account of their scarcity. They were originally from Africa, and called cyrenaïc, white outside, of an excellent perfume, and exquisite flavour.[99]

The Athenians, enlightened appreciators of all sorts of merits, accepted with gratitude a *ragoût* with truffles, invented by Cherips. That culinary genius did not long enjoy his glory; a premature death carried him off from his stoves, his honours, and his fortune; but the Greeks did not bury their gratitude in his tomb; his sons became citizens of Athens, and the name of their father, more fortunate than that of Christopher Columbus, clung for ever to his brilliant discovery.[100]

The doctors of other days did not exactly agree upon the quality either good or bad of truffles. Philoxenes, whose opinion met with many partisans, would have it that a great quantity should be eaten cooked under the ashes, and deliciously impregnated with a succulent sauce.[101] It was, however, recommended to choose them with the most particular attention, because some had the reputation of being as poisonous as mushrooms.[102]

The Romans were as fond of truffles as the Greeks, and that is not saying little.[103] Apicius gives a method of preparing them which is as follows:—

After they are boiled in water, put a little stick through them, and then place them for an instant before the fire; season them afterwards with oil, a little meat gravy, some skirrets, wine, pepper, and honey, in proper proportions. When the sauce is boiling, make a thickening, and serve.[104]

The illustrious epicurean prepared them also with pepper, benzoin, coriander and rue, to which he added a little honey, oil, and gravy.[105]

The estimable Platina insists that, in the first place, truffles should be washed in wine, and afterwards cooked under the ashes; and that they be served hot, and sprinkled over with salt and pepper.[106]

This is the composition of a syrup of truffles, taken from the old Arabian medicine. We believe it to be very little known, and should not be surprised if it were, some day, to obtain the renown it seems to deserve. It was composed of truffles, balm, and holy thistle, boiled in water with sugar; and to each pound of the decoction was added one scruple of water distilled from honey, and half an ounce of some spirit— say, for example, spirits of wine—to each pound of liquor. The whole was aromatised with musk and a little rose-water. Two ounces of this syrup were administered hot,[107] in cases of weakness.

Salmasius, who knew much of the Greek tongue, and very little of cookery, avers that the ancients knew two different kinds of truffles. One species was similar to ours, and the other a variety from Africa, already mentioned, white outside and the size of a quince.[108] Leo the African, says that the Arabs cook these truffles in milk, and that they think them exquisite. Thereupon Salmasius exclaims against the insipidity of this dish, or the ignorance of Leo the African; and immediately points out, with an air of triumph, the celebrated Avicenna, who informs us that, after the truffles were peeled and cut in small pieces, they were cooked in water and salt, and then dished up with oil, benzoin, and spices. Salmasius will have it that Avicenna's truffles had no other flavour than that given by the sauce, and he has no forgiveness for those poor Arabs who dared to dress them otherwise.

If this clever Hellenist had studied this savoury tubercle with as much care as he bestowed on the writers of the history of Augustus, he would have learned that the peculiar perfume which distinguishes it retains, in the midst of seasoning the most laboriously prepared, the same power it possesses when eaten by itself, and without any dressing.

Apicius had less of literature than Salmasius, but he was most assuredly gifted in a very superior degree with that *mens divinior* which makes great cooks and illustrious poets. This assimilation has nothing surprising in it, if we only remember that genius is nothing else than the faculty of producing; and who ever bequeathed to posterity productions more exquisite than those of Archestrates and Apicius?

Let us hear from this latter how to preserve truffles. You must be careful not to put them in contact with water; that is to say, that they ought to be kept very dry. They are placed separately in vessels, and covered with iron filings, or saw-dust. Close each vessel hermetically with plaster, and keep them in a dark and cool place.[109]

The truffle is a very remarkable vegetable, which, without stems, roots, or fibres, grows of itself, isolated in the bosom of the earth, absorbing the nutritive juice. Its form is round, more or less regular; its surface is smooth or tuberculous; the colour dark-brown outside, brown, grey, or white within. Its tissue is formed of articulated filaments, between which are spheric vesicles, and in the interior are placed reproductive bodies, small brown spheres, called *truffinelles*. Truffles vegetate to

s

the depth of five or six inches in the high sandy soils of the south-west of France, of Piedmont, &c., &c. Their mode of vegetation and reproduction is not known. Dogs are trained to find them, as well as pigs, and boars also, who are very fond of them. They are eaten cooked under the ashes, or in wine and water. They are preserved, when prepared in oil, which is soon impregnated with their odour.

Poultry is stuffed with them, also geese's livers, pies, and cooked pork, besides numerous *ragoûts*. They possess, it is said, exciting virtues.

MUSHROOMS.

Agrippina, desirous of securing the crown to her worthy son, Nero, went to a celebrated female poisoner, and procured a venomous preparation which defied the most powerful antidotes.[110] The Princess slipped this terrible poison in a very fine *morel* (a species of mushroom), which Claudius eat at his supper. The unfortunate Emperor died according to the desire of his amiable consort, who was, of course, inconsolable for a long time, and placed among the gods the husband she had murdered.[111] Nero ascended the throne, and every time that mushrooms were served at his table, true to the memory of his father-in-law, he facetiously called this preparation the " dish of the gods."[112]

To the poisonous effects of this vegetable have been attributed, also, the death of the Emperor Tiberius, that of Pope Clement VII., King Charles VI. of France, and many other important personages, who either knew very little of good cooks, or of *morels*. Notwithstanding these tragical events, mushrooms always retained a proud position, among the ancients, above the most inoffensive culinary plants; and their rather doubtful reputation has not prevented them from maintaining their ground down to our time, for we find that they now claim the same rank which they formerly occupied in the gastronomic *réunions* of Athens and Rome: a sad image of those fortunate criminals, whom society dreads, and yet often loads with its favours.

This "voluptuous poison," as Seneca, the philosopher,[113] calls it, which compels us to eat of it again, even when not hungry,[114] was much relished by the wealthy inhabitants of Rome and Italy. These free-livers, careless of the morrow, preferred the field mushroom,[115] which they devoured with delight, having previously covered it over with a pungent sauce, which they afterwards neutralized with various iced beverages.[116] It is true that this dish, worthy of the gods, often inflicted a severe penalty on those who yielded to its irresistible seduction ; but what mortal could think of the anguish of an uncertain poisoning, when he had the good luck to meet with some *boleti*, or mushrooms, of the rarest description, which the price of a beautiful toga would hardly have purchased,[117] and which promised some mouthfuls of ineffable, although ephemeral enjoyment? Besides, does not pleasure possess more piquant charms when danger is attached to it ? The greater part of mushrooms are very dangerous, say the ancients ;[118] but blind destiny, perhaps, reserves for us certain kinds which are not so. Re-assured by this judicious reflection, they gave orders to their cooks to stew some,[119] and season them with vinegar, oxymel, and honey.[129]

However, reasonable people—and there were still some to be found —abstained entirely from this vegetable, or procured it by the method which Nicander recommends ; that is to say, they frequently watered the trunk of a fig tree after manure had been placed around it. That philosopher assures us that by these means we may grow mushrooms perfectly wholesome.[120]

Those of our readers who are in possession of fig trees will be able to give their opinion on the merit of Nicander's method.

To obtain the seeds of most mushrooms, it only requires to expose them, when fresh, upon glass ; the superficies of the glass is soon covered with it. It is also obtained by shaking in the water the mushrooms which are sufficiently developed. This water, thus impregnated, is used to water the beds, which become thereby more productive.

The natural supply of mushrooms from the fields not being thought sufficient, the art of raising them on beds during the whole year was therefore indispensable, and required a mixture of *crottin de cheval*, rotten dung, and mould, which is deposited in layers of one foot and a-half in thickness and width Seeds of mushrooms are sown on these beds—that is to say, some of the mould of a former bog impregnated with it. It is then covered over with all the dung not consumed, and then copiously watered.

" At the end of a very few days, the beds begin to produce mushrooms, and keep on producing until the winter."—Bosc.

XXIV.

PASTRY.

THE art of the pastry-cook consists in preparing certain delicate and nice pastes in all sorts of shapes, in seasoning them with discretion, and in sufficient quantity, with meat, butter, sugar, preserves, &c.[1] It is a most important branch of the culinary science; unceasingly occupied with flattering the sight as much as the taste, it raises graceful monuments, delicious fortresses, seductive ramparts, which as soon as they are on all sides attacked, totter, crumble, and no longer present anything but glorious and ephemeral ruins, like every other work of man—all pass away whether they be temples, columns, pyramids, or pies.

This charming art was known to ancient nations as soon as their intellectual development had enabled them to understand a certain gastronomic truth, long since become a trivial axiom, and of which we dare scarcely remind the reader: "*On ne mange pour vivre que lorsqu'on ne sait pas vivre pour manger.*" (People only eat to live when they do not understand how to live to eat.)

The oriental nations were acquainted with the art of making pastry at a very early period. The Egyptians served many different sorts of cakes at their tables;[2] the Jews knew of at least three kinds—one sort kneaded with oil, another fried in oil, and the last was merely rubbed over with oil.[3]

The enlightened gluttony of the Greeks and Romans inspired them with a host of combinations more or less ingenious, and destined to revive a failing appetite, or one already greatly compromised by vigorous onslaughts.

Some of these pastries would appear very nice to us in the present

day; others we should think but little worthy of the epicures of Rome
and Athens. However, let us not be in too great a hurry to condemn
these great masters. Doubtless they had excellent reasons to like that
which modern taste may despise and dislike. In return, they might
have thought some of our most fashionable dishes detestable; perhaps
Apicius might have made a strange grimace at the sight of a dish of
sour-crout, an olla-podrida, or an immense plum-pudding.

Oublies, a light dainty for those who have weak stomachs, were
thin sheets of paste composed of flour and honey, which rolled into a
spiral form as soon as they approached the oven. They were eaten
soaked in cooked wine.[4] Persons of taste preferred *oublies* to fritters—
a bold mixture of flour kneaded with wine, seasoned with pepper, and
then worked up with milk, and, finally, with a little fat or oil.[5]

Some cooks employed the finest flour only, mixed with oil, and
served this paste after having cooked it in a dish.[6] Others worked
sesame flour a long time with honey and oil, and fried it.[7] These
various kinds of fritters were, doubtless, much sought after by the
populace, for Cicero speaks of them with profound disdain.[8]

The Jews, less dainty than the eloquent orator, offered some of this
paste in sacrifice. The recipe for its composition is given in Leviticus;
it was made of the finest flour, moistened with oil, and cooked in
the frying-pan.[9]

Women and children—those two fragile roots of society—were always
fond of sweet and delicate cakes. The pastry-cooks of Attica prepared
for them some very excellent kinds; sometimes it was merely a sweet
mixture of honey and milk;[10] others were made of honey, sesame flour,
and cheese or oil.[11] Delicious fruit was frequently covered with a light
and perfumed paste.[12] These Athenian dumplings met with a great
success.

Rome made the conquest of these precious recipes,[13] and vanquished
Greece, conquered by her, had still the glory of dictating laws to her
haughty enemy: she imposed her cookery.

Gingerbread was not unknown to the ancients. Rhodes owed its
reputation to it. It was sweetened with honey, and that island furnished
it to the whole of Europe. The Greeks called this delicacy *Melitates*,
and eat it with pleasure at the close of their repasts.[14]

Let us not forget, in this rapid survey of ancient sweets, that learned
and exquisite mixture now designated under the name of *Nougat*, which,

among the Greeks was composed of dried currants and almonds, and which has lost none of its attractions, nothing of its celebrity, after so many centuries.[15]

The *Mustaceum* did not deserve to occupy so high a standing ; and yet this rustic cake, composed of sweet wine and flour, a symbol of abundance and happiness, never failed to be presented to the guests at a wedding repast, and the newly-married pair sent a piece of it to each of their absent parents or friends, who, in return, addressed them congratulations, and wishes for their happiness.[16] The mustaceum was the wedding-cake of the Romans.

Modern civilization has also rejected with equal disdain the *Savillum* pie, always eaten with pleasure by the voluptuous inhabitants of Rome when they went to their villas in order to rest from their prodigious excesses, and from the fatigues of intemperance. This nourishing and agreeable dish required but little art in its composition. Half-a-pound of flour and two pounds and a-half of cheese were well mixed together ; three ounces of honey and one egg were then added. When the whole had been well beaten, it was placed in an earthen vessel rubbed over with oil, and which was covered with a tart dish cover. It was carefully watched to see that the process of cooking was going on ; afterwards it was taken from the dish, the pie was smeared with honey, and, for an instant, replaced under the tart-dish cover, after having dredged the top with pounded poppy seed It was always served in the dish in which it had been cooked, and was eaten with spoons.[17]

We have already mentioned the *Artocreas*, a kind of hashed meat mixed with bread, which Rome borrowed from Greece, together with its original name. This pie, welcomed by modern gastrophagy, has reached our days with merely some slight modifications, and deprived of its sonorous Hellenic appellation.[18] Formerly the Roman Emperors, for the greater part, ruled badly ; but, in return, they eat well. In that gastronomic era—gone, never to return—Cæsar's supper engaged the attention of the court, the city, nay, the whole empire. The conquered universe furnished the details for a banquet, and a royal hand sometimes deigned to write the ordinance. Now and then, even the monarch, wrapped in profound culinary meditations, long reflected, dictated to his *Archimagirus* a new dish, on which complaisant senators the next day bestowed enthusiastic praises and a sincere admiration. Thus the Emperor Verus, inventor of a pie, barely escaped an apotheosis of which his genius was deemed worthy. It is true that, without any exaggerated flattery, this pie was excellent, and that never was there imagined a more happy mixture, a more ingenious combination, of meats, or a more refined flavour. If any one be curious enough to wish to test this imperial dish, let him prepare a succulent amalgamation of sow's flank (*sumen*), pheasant, peacock, iced ham, and wild boar's flesh; let him inclose this mixture within the thick casing of a laboriously worked crust, and he may attack this kingly dish when a gentle and slow cooking causes it to emit burning yet sweet emanations.[19]

Here is a more modest recipe for a cake; but then it does not claim the paternity of an emperor. However, Cato brought it much into fashion, for the wise Cato often busied himself in the science of cookery, for which reason he is greatly worthy of esteem. Well, we recommend to the reader the *Libum* of that philosopher, who indicates the manner of preparing it :—

" Crush," he says, " two pounds of cheese; mix with it a pound of rye flour, or, in order to render it lighter, throw in merely half a pound of wheat flour and an egg. Stir, mix, and work this paste; form of it a cake which you will place on leaves, and cook in a tart dish on the hot hearth." This libum was much esteemed about twenty centuries ago; in honour of Cato may it again be brought to light, if not completely unworthy of our attention.[20] Could we not also rehabilitate the reputation of the most celebrated of ancient pies, the *Placenta*, which so delighted mankind, and by which the gods even allowed their fury to be appeased ?[21] Renowned writers have granted it the authority of their praise ;[22] and the illustrious geoponist, already cited, describes with lengthened complaisance the manner of preparing this important dish :—

" Place, on one side, two pounds of rye flour, which will serve to form the foundation, on which must be placed biscuits, formed of crisp paste; on the other, put four pounds of wheat, and two pounds of alica (grains of fine wheat, stripped of their husks and crushed; to which was added, in order to whiten them, a peculiar kind of chalk found between Naples and Pouzzoli[23]). This latter must be left to infuse in water, and, when well soaked, it must be thrown into a kneading trough, and well worked with the hand. You then mix with it the four pounds of wheat flour, in order to make the whole into biscuits, or dry marchpans. This paste must be worked in a basket, and, as it dries, each separate marchpan must be shaped. When they have acquired a convenient form, rub them on all sides with a piece of stuff soaked in oil, and the same must be done to the foundation of the placenta before placing the marchpans on it. During these preparations, make the hearth very hot, as well as the cover of the tart dish intended to cook it. Then spread the two pounds of rye flour you have in reserve over fourteen pounds of cheese of sheep's milk. Make of this a light paste for the foundation already mentioned. This cheese ought to be very fresh, and previously soaked in three waters. It is allowed to drain slowly between the hands, and when it has been left to dry, it is kneaded. Take a flour sieve, and pass the cheese through it before mixing it with the rye. Then add four pounds and a half of good honey; mix well; place the foundation, furnished with its band, on a board a foot square, covered with bay leaves rubbed with oil, and form the placenta. Begin by covering the whole of the base with a layer of marchpans, which you place one after the other, and cover slightly with cheese mixed with honey. ' Finally, you arrange the marchpans on the foundation, and prepare the hearth to a moderate degree of heat; place the placenta on it; cover it with the tart dish cover already heated, and spread live charcoal underneath and all around. The cooking must be done very slowly, and as soon as the pie is taken from the hearth, it must be rubbed with honey." [24]

The great desire we had to inform the reader of some of the methods of making ancient pastry will, perhaps, induce him to receive with indulgence the rather diffuse recipe of the worthy Cato. The following is much more concise; it relates to the relishing *Globi*, little globes, or balls, eaten at dessert:

Mix cheese and alica, and of this mixture make the globi, which cook one after the other, or two at a time, in boiling oil. Stir them constantly with a spoon; take them out; rub them over with honey, and serve, having previously dredged over them a little poppy-seed. [25]

Everyone will confess that all these cakes are inferior to the simple and elegant pastry with which the inhabitants of Picenum (marshes of Ancona) regaled themselves. They placed some alica to soak in water, and left it there for the space of nine days; the tenth day they kneaded it, and formed it into round, flat cakes, which they cooked in the oven in earthen baking-dishes easily broken. When these kind of biscuits were to be eaten, they were first softened in milk and honey. [26]

Apicius also made globi of great delicacy with the crumb of fine bread, shaped into balls, which were left to soak in milk, and which, on their being withdrawn from the boiling oil, he lightly covered with honey.[27]

We conclude with three recipes by this amateur cook, in the hope that they may appear worthy of his genius :—

" Mix pine nuts, pepper, honey, rue, and cooked wine ; cover with eggs well beaten ; submit this mixture to a slow fire, and serve, after having smeared it with honey."[28]

" Cook the finest flour in some milk, of which make a tolerably stiff paste ; spread it on a dish ; cut it in pieces, which, when you have fried in very fine oil, cover with pepper and honey."[29]

" Make a compact mixture of milk, honey, and eggs ; let it cook very slowly, and serve, after having sprinkled over it a little pepper."[30]

These details will, we hope, give a sufficient idea of ancient pastry. We must remember that these recipes form, as it were, the starting point. The oil fritter of the Hebrews and the meringues of our period are wide apart : more than thirty-three centuries separate the two ; two thousand years have elapsed since Cato wrote the recipe for his somewhat heavy tart. The author of the " Culinary Art," Apicius himself, is very old. The private life of the ancient people appears to be worthy of serious study ; but we too often only bestow on it our disdain. The author of this work has observed their customs in the kitchen and in the dining-room—the only places to which he had access—and he has taken the liberty of writing the result of his investigations. Sometimes he admires, but never does he despise, a civilisation different to our own, but which was not without its good side. He conjures the reader to believe him when he says, that whatever eccentricities the gastronomy of ancient nations may present to us, those people (he has, perhaps, acquired the right to venture such an assertion) doubtless eat in a very different manner from ourselves ; but they certainly knew how to eat.

The pastry just mentioned is certainly not altogether irreproachable— that is clear ; but many kinds reveal that exquisite sentiment of the good which is nothing else than taste—whether it relate to art, literature or cooking—and the entire development of which seems to have been the appurtenance of a small number of privileged centuries. Great epochs—such as those of Pericles, Augustus, Leo XII., Louis XIV., and Queen Anne—have seen roses and myrtles flourish by the side of the laurels with which the muses are crowned. Charles XII. was fond of tartlets; Frederic II. gave himself fits of indigestion by eating Savoy cakes; and the Maréchal de Saxe rested from the fatigues of glory before a plate of macaroons.

We have renounced the kind of pastry with which our ancestors used to regale themselves in the 14th century. Their stag pies[31] are no longer in vogue; neither have we any taste for their great pies which contained a lamb or a stuffed kid, surrounded with goslings by dozens and scores.[32]

Their tarts have fallen into the same oblivion. Who thinks now of their Janus, or double-faced, tarts, herb tarts, rose-leaf tarts, oat tarts, or chesnut tarts?[33]

The first statutes given to the pastry cooks by St Louis (May, 1270), sanctioned their custom of working on all festival days without exception. Now, the motive for such a toleration was probably this: the pagans had their festivals, which they passed in banqueting; the Romans called them *dies epulatæ*.[34] The early Christians, although they gave up the worship of false gods, preserved certain customs in which they had been brought up, among which was that of public and private banquets on festival days.[35] We still see some remains of these customs in the village rejoicings on the Continent, on the day of their patron saint. The Fathers of the Church and the Councils raised their voices against this abuse;[36] but they were obliged to tolerate it, and the pastry-cooks, who were very busy on those occasions, profited by the indulgence. It is as well to remark that they were, at one and the same time, publicans, roasters (that is they would roast anything for anybody), and cooks.

Under the ministry of the Chancelier de l'Hôpital, little pies, or patties, were hawked through all the streets of Paris, and there was an enormous consumption of them. The severe minister considered them a luxury, which it was incumbent upon him to suppress; so he prohibited, not their sale, but the crying of them, as a temptation to gluttony.

There is a kind of cake much in vogue in England, on Good Friday, designated hot-cross-bun, because it is always marked with a cross. The reader will, perhaps, take some interest in the observations of Bryant on the subject of this pastry:—

"The offerings," says he, "which people in ancient times used to present to the gods were generally purchased at the entrance of the temple; especially every species of consecrated bread. which was denominated accordingly. One species of sacred bread which used to be offered to the gods was of great antiquity, and called *Boun*." It was a kind of cake, with a representation of two horns. Julius Pollux mentions it after the same manner—a sort of cake with horns. Diogenes Laertius, speaking of the same offering being made by Empedocles, describes the chief ingredients of which it was composed:—" He offered one of the sacred *liba*, called a *bonse* (*bons*), which was made of fine flour and honey."[37] England seems, then, to have retained the name and the form of the ancient *bons*, though the people do not recognise in the bun anything sacred or holy.

Titus Livy said, in speaking of Rome, "The greatest things have small beginnings." This applies equally to pastry, which appears so unworthy of attention at the commencement of the middle ages that nothing seems to announce its high destiny. At first, in the southern provinces, people simply mixed flour, oil, and honey. The Roman school was still in force. The inhabitants of the north had a mind to innovate; they employed eggs, butter, and salt. Then came the idea of inclosing within this paste cooked meat, seasoned with bacon and spices; and, from progress to progress, they at last inclosed cream, fruit, and marmalades.[38]

We find pastry mentioned for the first time in a charter of Louis-le-Débonnaire (802). It is there said that a certain farm of the Abbey of St. Denis is to furnish, at certain festivals, sixteen measures of honey, eleven hundred oxen, and five hogsheads of flour to make pastry.[39]

A charter of the church of Paris, 1202, mentions simnels or wigs, under the name of "*panes leves qui dicuntur echaudati*." Joinville speaks, in "The life of St Louis," of cheese fritters cooked in the sun, which the Saracens presented to that king and his knights when they restored them to liberty. And, finally, so early as the 13th century, the *flans* of Chartres, the patties of Paris, and the tarts of Dourlans, were in great renown; and a charter of 1301 informs us that, at that epoch, several lords imposed on their vassals a tribute of *fugués*, or puff-pastry.[40]

The cook of Charles V. says, that the word *tourte* signified a household loaf of a round form; that this name was afterwards given to delicate pastry; and that, by corruption, it was called *tart* in certain provinces.[41]

Taillevant speaks of cream, almonds, and rose-water, as the accompaniments of *Darioles*, a kind of custard; and of *Talmouses*, a sort of cheese-cake, made of cheese, eggs, and butter, coloured with the yolks of eggs.[42]

Platina cites tarts made with radishes, quinces, gourds, elder-berry flowers, rice, oatmeal, millet, chesnuts, cherries, dates, May-herbs, roses, and, lastly, the white, or cream tart.[43]

XXV.

WATER.

THALES, who borrowed from Egypt the elements of philosophy, which he afterwards spread in Greece, taught that water is the vivifying principle of all things; that nature is thereby made fruitful; that without it the earth, arid and laid waste, would be a frightful desert, where every effort of man to support his existence must fail.[1]

These ideas, for a long time adopted by Pagan theology, peopled fountains, rivers, and seas, with divinities, and often confounded in the same worship those gods, sons of gratitude, with the limpid waters consecrated to them.

The Persians carried their veneration for this element so far, that they dared not wash their hands, and would have preferred being consumed to the very bone rather than dip themselves in a river.[2]

The Cappadocians were proud of treading in the same path.[3]

The Egyptians offered prayers and homage to water.[4] The Nile, in particular, received their adorations under the name of *Ypeus*, or *Siris*, and they offered to it—as a sacrifice—barley, wheat, sugar, and fruit.[5]

The Scythians honoured the Danube on account of its vast extent; the Thessalians prostrated themselves before the majestic shores of the Peneus; the ancient combat of Achelous with Hercules made it sacred to the Ætolians; by a special law, the Lacedæmonians were compelled to implore the Eurotas; and a religious precept forced the Athenians to incense in honour of the Ilissus.[6]

The Greeks and Romans did not fail to follow such good examples. The fountains and rivers had their altars. The Rhine was called a god; and when Æneas arrived in Italy, he prayed it might be favourable to him.[7]

However strange such superstition may appear, it is, nevertheless, conceivable that Paganism, struck with wonder at the flux and reflux of the sea, and at the phenomena presented by several celebrated springs, and seduced by the charming fictions of doubtful poesy, should have deified an element both beneficial and terrible, since it could not cry out with the prophet king: " The Lord on high is mightier than the noise of many waters, yea than the mighty waves of the sea." [8]

Thence came the innumerable number of tutelary gods to which the Ocean alone gave an asylum. By Thetis it became the father of the seventy-two Oceanides, and the fifty Nereides called it their grandfather. Hesiod numbered three thousand nymphs, and he probably forgot a few of them. We say nothing of the Naiades, the Napææ, the Limnades, and so many others whom fable was pleased to recognise, and whom it described as joyfully disporting in the water.

Greece exhausted the treasures of its poetical imagination to embellish her fountains, beloved retreats of the timid Naiades. Several were remarkable for the beauty of their architecture and the extreme delicacy of their execution.

Megara, in Achaia, possessed one celebrated for its magnificence. That of Pirene, at Corinth, was surrounded with white marble, in which were placed grottoes which unceasingly supplied a vast and superb basin. Another fountain of Corinth, named Lerna, offered to loungers an elegant portico, under which some very commodious seats allowed them to enjoy, during summer, the freshness which the water communicated to the atmosphere.

In the sacred wood of Æsculapius, at Epidaurus, a splendid fountain was seen whose marvellous beauty attracted all eyes.[9] Lastly, those of Messina, known under the names of Arsinoë and of Clepsydra, yielded nothing in richness of material and finish of details to the most renowned monuments of Greece.

The Athenians named four officers to keep watch and ward over the water.[10] The other Greek towns followed the example. These officers had to keep the fountains in order and clean the reservoirs,[11] so that the water might be preserved pure and limpid.

The Romans at first contented themselves with water from the Tiber. King Ancus Martius[12] was the first[13] to build aqueducts, destined to convey the water of the fountain of Piconia from Tibur to Rome, a distance of about thirty-three thousand paces. Some have honoured the censor, Appius Claudius, for this magnificent undertaking,[14] to whom is certainly due the celebrated Appian Way.[15] These gigantic works greatly multiplied in time. Under the reign of Nero, Rome had nine principal aqueducts[16] constructed, the pipes of which were of bricks, baked tiles, stone, lead, or wood.[17]

According to the calculation of Vigenerus,[18] 500,000 hogsheads of water were conveyed into Rome every twenty-four hours, by 10,350 small channels, the internal circumference of which was one inch. The water was received in large closed basins, above which were raised splendid monuments. These basins—or *châteaux d'eau—castella Aquarum*—supplied other subterraneous conduits connected with the various quarters of the town,[19] which conveyed water to small reservoirs—*fontes*—furnished with taps, for the exclusive use of certain streets.[20] The water which was not drinkable ran out by means of large pipes into extensive inclosures, where it served to water cattle. At these places the people washed their linen, and here, too, they had a ready resource in case of fire.[21]

Augustus created water commissaries, who took care that all water coming into Rome by the aqueducts was fairly distributed in every public place, and to those of the inhabitants who had obtained the privilege of having it enter their houses.[22]

But the "ingenious thirst"[23] of the conquerors of the world could not content itself with a delicious water which nature furnished free of expense. Was it not too much for human endurance, that not only the air and the sun could not be offered to the highest bidder,[24] but that the same spring was to quench the thirst of obscure plebeians on equal terms with the rich patrician ?

Intemperance and luxury very soon contrived to find excellent means of remedying a state of things so intolerable. The custom of preserving snow in cellars, to obtain cool beverages, is very old. Aristotle pointed out the method of boiling water, and putting the vessel afterwards in snow, in order to obtain ice. Rome had recourse to this expedient, which was afterwards replaced with advantage, under Nero, by constructing ice houses for the use of opulent epicureans.[25]

This even was not enough for voluptuous Romans, slaves to their strange caprices; their beverages did not appear to them as yet sufficiently cool,[26] and the summit of the Alps was put under contribution to furnish ice for the fashionable tables of the imperial city.[27]

The Romans were also frequently supplied with snow water,[28] clarified by being passed through the *colum nivarium*, or snow cullender,[29] a charming little utensil of silver, pierced with a great number of holes, through which the iced beverage passed into a recipient beneath. This drink was sometimes mortal, but always exquisite.[30] From this vessel, it was poured into an *ampula*, or a sort of crystal bottle of rotund form, which was often enormously dear on account of the elaborate chasing with which it was embellished.[31] This water bottle, with its long and narrow neck, was the principal ornament of the sideboards and tables, when it bore the name of some skilful artist from Campania or the Island of Samos.[32]*

Iced beverage lost all its charm at the end of the fine season, and hot water took its place during winter.[33] The same custom existed in Greece in the best classes of society.[34] At Rome, it was much more general, for there were a great number of taverns, where the middle classes and citizens of the lowest order gorged themselves copiously with pork and warm water. The Emperor Claudius caused them to be closed, and severely punished the proprietors of those houses who opposed his ordinance.[35]

At the commencement of the repast, a copper vessel was placed on the table purposely to boil water. It was much like a French *bouilloire* (which nearly resembles a tankard), and contained a cylinder of about four inches in diameter, covered with a moving lid, and pierced with holes for the ashes to pass through. They fell into the lower part of the cylinder. The space around was filled with water by means of a small funnel soldered to the boiler. The taps of these vases were always slightly above the bottom, so that the sediment of the water should not pass into the cups.[36]

Ancient medicine attributed to water a singular curative virtue, which it has also been supposed to possess in our days. This system, so much talked about now by some persons, is, therefore, not new. Hippocrates carefully distinguished the difference between good and bad water.[37] The best, according to him, ought to be clear, light, inodorous, without any flavour, and drawn from springs exposed to the east.[38] He interdicts all those which proceed from melted snow.[39]

Asclepiades made his patients drink plentifully of water, and frequently ordered them cold baths.[40]

* See Plate No. XXVII., No. 4., a plain bottle, with a long neck.

Pl. 17

F. T. Z. Volant. del.

Saddler & Chant, scul.

The physician, Musa, prescribed to Augustus the same regimen, and the Emperor found himself much benefited by it.[41]

Under the reign of Nero, Charmis acquired a great vogue by extolling cold baths,[42] even in the depth of winter. This dexterous native of Marseilles knew so well how to persuade people, that he could hardly attend to his immense connection; and as he sometimes required as much as £800 from his patients,[43] he soon became as celebrated for his riches as for his pretended medical genius. Who will say, after this, that the water-cure system is good for nothing?

"In Egypt, rich people have the water brought to them from the Nile in leather pouches. Large and porous earthen pots of an oval shape, kept up by supporters, are filled with it. The water at the end of a few hours has deposited the slime it contained. It is afterwards distributed in small vases of terra cotta, called *bardaks*, of the size of our water-jugs. These vases are taken in the most showy part of the habitation. In a short time the clay of the *bardaks* is impregnated; their surface is covered with water, which, after borrowing from the liquid within the caloric it requires for evaporation, reduces this to a temperature of six or seven degrees under that which it had before."— PARMENTIER.

More than five centuries ago the Sieur de Joinville described the same process. "The water of the Nile," he said, "is of such a nature, that when we hung it in white earthen pots, made in the country, to the rigging of our ships, the water became in the heat of the day as cold as spring-water."[44]

Sea-water is not potable, but it has long since been remarked that the vapours which rise from the sea are soft, and it was thence concluded that, by collecting and condensing them, it would be possible to obtain a potable liquid fit for domestic purposes. This phenomenon was known in the time of Pliny, who informs us that, "fleece spread about the ship, after having received the exhalations from the sea, becomes damp, and that fresh water may be extracted from it."[45]

About the middle of the last century means were found to remove

DESCRIPTION OF PLATE No. XVII.

No. 1. Pail, of bronze, with movable handle, covered with hieroglyphics, to carry water from the Nile for the Feast of Isis.

No. 2. Pail, with two handles, same metal, placed on a small tripod to stand upon, owing to the convexity of the bottom.—ST. NON, "*Herculaneum.*"

the saline substances from sea-water. Boyle, Leibnitz, the Count of Marsigli—all had made a great number of fruitless experiments. Mr. Poissonnier invented a very simple distillating machine, with which, and an absorbing powder, he succeeded in depriving sea-water of its insufferable bitterness, and rendering it perfectly salubrious. About 1784, a successful experiment was made at York with a machine which produced the same result.

Some travellers have related, that, at the Iron Island, the only soft water was that which was collected from a large tree, in the centre of the island, and which was incessantly covered with clouds. The water ran continually from the leaves, and fell into two large cisterns, constructed at the foot of the tree, which, according to Jackson, furnished enough for 8,000 souls, and 100,000 cattle. "Let us see," says Bory de Saint-Vincent, "what amount of credit is due to the mavellous tree of the Iron Island." Abreu Galindo, in his manuscript treatise on the Canary Islands, preserved in the archives of the country, says that he wished to see with his own eyes what the tree was. He embarked, arrived, took a guide to conduct him to a place called Tigulahe, which is separated from the sea by a valley, and there, at the extreme boundary, under a large cliff, was the holy tree, which in the country is called Garoë. Its trunk is twelve spans in circumference, four feet in diameter, and nearly forty feet in height. The branches are wide apart and tufted ; its fruit resembles an acorn, and the kernel is, in colour and taste, like the little aromatic almonds which pine nuts contain. It never loses its leaves, that is to say, the old ones do not fall until the young ones are formed. On the north side, are two large stone pillars, of twenty square feet, hollowed out to a depth of twenty spans. These pillars are so placed that the water falls into one, and is preserved in the other. Vapours and mists rise almost every day from the sea, particularly in the morning, and at no great distance in the offing ; these vapours are carried by the east wind against the cliffs, which block their passage, so that they cover the tree, become condensed on its smooth leaves, and run off drop by drop. The more the east wind reigns, the more abundant is the supply of water. It is distributed by a man who guards the tree. A whirlwind tore up the Garoë in 1625.[46]

XXVI.

BEVERAGES,

OF WHICH WATER IS THE FOUNDATION.

WATER is certainly the most ancient beverage, the most simple, natural, and the most common, which nature has given to mankind. But it is necessary to be really thirsty in order to drink water, and as soon as this craving is satisfied it becomes insipid and nauseous. What is then to be done? Cyrus would have said: "Drink no more;" so would a teetotaler of the present day. In the first ages of the world, the human race, bound by no oath of temperance, succeeded, by sheer application of their ingenuity, in finding something better, or perhaps worse, according to the ideas of certain moralists, whose wise teaching, however, commands respect. Certain it is that water, continuing to be regarded with peculiar favour, was called to play a principal part in various combinations by which it lost its insipidity and inoffensive properties, and acquired the wonderful power of provoking a sort of madness, known by the name of drunkenness.

Those beverages which man imbibes when he is no longer thirsty, which cloud his weak mind, and render him ill when in good health, are called fermented liquors.

Beer is one of the most ancient. If we are to believe Diodorus of Sicily, Bacchus himself invented it.[1] However, it is certain that the absolute injunction not to drink wine, caused the inhabitants of Egypt to have recourse to a factitious beverage obtained from barley,[2] often mentioned in history under the name of *zythum* and *curmi*,[3] and whose invention has been often attributed to Osiris—which means, that its precise origin is entirely unknown.

T 2

It was a kind of beer composed of barley, and capable of being preserved for a long time without decomposing;[4] for instead of hops, utterly unknown in that country, a bitter infusion of lupins was added.[5]

The Egyptians also used Assyrian corn in its composition, and probably other aromatic plants, in which each one followed his peculiar taste. The method of brewing varied much among them;[6] but the one here mentioned was that most generally in use to procure zythum in Lower Egypt, where it was converted, like our beer, into vinegar, which the Greek merchants of Alexandria exported to the European ports.[7]

The Egyptians long drank nothing but this fermented liquor, because the followers of Osiris believed that when Jupiter crushed the Titans with thunderbolts, their blood, mixing with the earth, produced the vine. They invented the zythum as a substitute for wine.[8]

It is not probable that the Greeks, whose wines were so renowned in antiquity, thought much of beer. Nevertheless, Aristotle[9] mentions drunkenness being caused by drinking a beverage drawn from barley. Æschylus[10] and Sophocles[11] mention a liquor procured from the same cereal.

The use of beer spread rapidly in Gaul, where wine was but little known before the time of Probus. The Emperor Julian, governor of this country, acquaints us of this fact in an epigram.[12]

The Spaniards, and the aborigines of Britany and Germany, also delightfully intoxicated themselves with an " infusion of barley," called by the first of these nations, *cœlia, ceria, cerevisia,*[13] and *curmi* by the two latter. These various denominations signify literally, *strong water,*[14] and this fermented drink was common to the nations just indicated.[15] All the people of Western Europe drank a strong liquor made with grain and water. The manner of preparing it was not the same in Spain, in Gaul, and elsewhere; but everywhere it possessed the same dangerous properties.

"Man," says Pliny, "is so skilful in flattering his vices, that he has even found means to render water poisonous and intoxicating."[16]

The Danes and Saxons gave themselves up to an enormous consumption of zythum and curmi, kinds of ale and beer, varying in no other respect than in the manner of preparing them.[17] The warlike piety of their ingenuous and coarse-minded heroes, desired no greater recompense, after a life of fatigue and rough combats, than to sing the praises of Odin amidst eternal banquets, where these exhilirating beverages might unceasingly maintain the joy and bravery of the warriors.[18]

The ancient Britons had many vines, but they esteemed them only as ornaments to their gardens; and they preferred, says Cæsar, the wine of grain to that of grapes.[19] It is historically demonstrated that the English, at a very early epoch, applied themselves to the making of beer.

It is mentioned in the laws of Ina, Chief, or King, of Wessex; and this liquor held a distinguished rank among those that appeared at a royal feast in the reign of Edward the Confessor.[20]

Under the Normans, ale acquired a reputation it has ever since maintained. Two gallons cost only one penny in the cities; in the country, four gallons might be obtained at the same price. Happy age! happy ale drinkers! At that period—the golden age for the apostles of the Britannic Bacchus—the brewers rendered no account of the preparation of this beloved beverage. The English nation did not yet purchase the right of intoxicating themselves: it was not till the year 1643 that this authorization was to be bought.[21]

The use of hops would appear to be of German invention. They were employed in the Low Countries at the beginning of the 14th century; but it was not till the 16th that they were appreciated in England.[22]

Can it be true that beer or ale possessed, in certain cases, strange curative properties? We find the following fact in a statistical account of Scotland.[23]

A poor coal miner of the county of Clackmannan, named William Hunter, had been long suffering with acute rheumatism, or obstinate gout, which deprived him of the use of his limbs. The eve of the first Monday of the year 1758, some of his neighbours came to pass the evening with him. Ale was drunk, and they got merry. The jolly fellow never failed to empty his glass at each round. Scotch ale is a seductive drink, and as perfidious as pleasure: it bewilders the senses, and finally masters the reason. William Hunter lost his, completely; but his legs were restored, and he was able to make marvellous use of them for more than twenty years. After that happy evening, never did his old enemy, the gout, dare approach him; and the worthy coal miner took care to keep it at a distance, by reiterating the remedy which had proved so beneficial. Nobody could blame him. Ale had become so dear to him! Gratitude and prudence combined to make it a duty to remain unalterably attached, and he was faithful to it till he breathed his last.

Antecedent to the use of hops beer was made in England as follows :

"*To make a Hogshead of Strong Ale.*—It was necessary, first of all, to make the *grout*, which was thus done :—Nine gallons of water was to be well boiled, and put into a brewing-vessel; when it was a little cool there was put therein three pecks of malt, which was left standing for an hour and a-half, and then it ought to be drawn off into a cooler. When it was near cold, it was put into a vessel provided for that purpose, perfectly clean, and having a cover to stop it down close. Being therein, it was closely covered down, that it might there stand to sharpen ; if the weather should be cold it might require about eighteen hours, but if it was hot not quite so long. When it was ripe enough, upon the sudden opening of the vessel, the strength of the fume arising from the liquour would near, if not entirely, extinguish a lighted candle, which ought to be provided short on purpose, and holden over for the proof thereof. When the brewer was satisfied that the grout was properly ripened, he poured it forth into the copper, and boiled it moderately upon a slow fire for about an hour, constantly stirring it all the while, and to know when it was boiled enough he provided a small ashen stick, which, being alighted at the fire, he thrust suddenly into the boiling liquor, drawing it forth as quick as possible, when, if the fire on the stick remained still unextinguished, it was well boiled, but not if it were otherwise. This being done, the liquor was put into a vessel of twenty gallons, or thereabouts, and yeast put to it, that it might work, which when it had sufficiently done, it was ready for the wort to be put to it. The wort might be brewed of what strength the brewer should please, so that it did not exceed sixty gallons to the above proportion of grout. The grout being now properly ripe, and having worked enough, a quantity of the wort, sufficient to fill up the twenty-gallon vessel into which the grout is put, must be poured upon it, and then the whole drawn off into the *yeeling fatt*, and there, being mixed with the remainder of the wort, is left to work together, which when it hath sufficiently done, it must be strained off into the hogshead, through a hair sieve made for that purpose, where it must also work like other beer or ale."[24]

In the ninth year of Edward II., things being very scarce, a gallon of ale was sold for twopence, of the better sort for threepence, and of the best for fourpence ; but the Londoners ordained that, in the City, a gallon of the bettermost sort of ale should be sold for three-halfpence, and of the small ale for one penny only.[25]

Holinshed says[26] that every kind of wine could be procured in England. " Nevertheless," he adds, "ale and beere beare the greatest brunt in drincking, which are of so many sortes and ages as it pleaseth the brewer to make them. The beere that is used at noblemen's tables is commonly of a yeare olde (or, peradventure, of twoo yeares' tunning, or more, but this is not general) ; it is also brued in Marche, and is therefore called Marche beere ; but for the household it is usually not under a monthe's age, eache one coveting to have the same stale as he might, so that was not soure, and the breade new as possible, so that be not hote."

Formerly, they drank beer in some parts of France—in others, wine. Perhaps it is the same now. This difference of taste gave rise to a rather jocose dispute between a grey friar and a white friar. One, who was a Fleming, was for beer ; the other, who was from Bordeaux, was for wine. The Fleming cited passages without number from antiquity in proof of the excellence of beer, known by the ancients under the name of *zithum*, or *curmi*. The one from Bordeaux was not so learned, but he was a native of Bordeaux, and with one word he terminated the dispute. "Brother," said he to his adversary, "I maintain that there is as much difference between wine and beer as there is between St. Francis and St. Dominick." The whole community were for the Bordeaux monk, and the Fleming was reduced to silence.[27]

Braket was formerly the cherished drink of the lower classes in England. Arnold describes the preparation of it, in his " Chronicles of London :"

" Take a pot of good ale and put thereto a porcyon of honey and pepper, in this manner:—When thou hast good ale, lete it stonde (stand) in a pott two dayes, and then drawe out a quart, or a pottell, of that ale, and putt to the honey, and set it over the fyre and let it sethe well, and take it of the fyre and scume it clene ; and then sat it over the fyre and scume it agayne, and then let it keele a whyle, and put thereto the pepper, and then set hym on the fyre and let him boyle well togyder, with esy fyre, but clere. Take four gallons of good ale, a pynte of fyn tryed hony, and about a saucerful of powder of peper."

Beer was not unknown in Italy, but the Romans never granted it their serious attention.[28] We will give a brief sketch of those beverages which, among them and the Greeks, replaced wine with greater or less advantage.

Convalescents, sober persons who resisted the sweet seductions of

Falernian and Chios wines, drank a kind of barley-water *ptisana*, a sorry liquid, of which the following is the recipe for the use of the abstemious of the present day: They placed barley in water, and left it there until it swelled; it was then dried in the sun, then beaten to deprive it of its husk, and ground. Then, when it had been boiled in water for a long time, it was again exposed to the sun. When they wished to drink barley-water, a small quantity of this flour was boiled, the water was strained off, and a few drops of vinegar were added.[29] The disciples of Comus have always shuddered at this beverage, when only mentioned.

The *oxycratus* was not much better. It was a mixture of water and vinegar, with which the lower orders contented themselves when they could obtain nothing more exhilarating to drink;[30] and with which the soldiers, especially in the camp, were compelled to quench their thirst.[31]

Some passages from Pliny, and also from other authors, prove that the ancients were acquainted with cider.[32] It is, however, asserted that the use of this beverage goes no farther back than three or four centuries, either in England or France;[33] but this cannot be a fact with regard to the last-named country, since the capitulars of Charlemagne place among the number of ordinary trades that of *sicerator*, or "cider maker." This "wine of apples,"[34] it is said, was very common among the Hebrews. That is possible, but it would, nevertheless, be difficult to prove it from the holy writings, since the word *schecar*, which has been translated by *sicera*, and which, again, has been rendered into cider, signifies all kinds of intoxicating beverage, whether made from grain, honey, or fruit.[35]

Gaul, covered with forests, and swarming with bees, possessed an immense quantity of wild honey, of which, by the aid of fermentation in water, the inhabitants composed a strong and intoxicating drink, called *hydromel*. This beverage, highly esteemed both in Rome and Greece, was prepared in the following manner: rain water was kept some time, and then boiled until reduced to one-third, to which honey was added.* This mixture was exposed to the sun for the space of forty days; it was then placed in a vessel, and by these means they obtained, in time, a vinous hydromel very similar to our Madeira wine.[36] To make *oxymel*, still more heady, ten pounds of honey were mixed with two pints and a half of old vinegar, and one pound of sea-salt; the whole boiled

---

* A pound of honey to three pounds of water.

only an instant in five pints of water. This liquor was left to get very old.[37]

Juice of quinces and honey, boiled in water, produced *hydromelon*, a delicious drink, which our century might envy the delicate drinkers of Athens and Rome,[38] especially when roses had been added to this nectar, which changed it into *hydrorosatum*.[39]

The *apomeli* was nothing more than water in which honeycomb had been boiled.[40] *Omphacomeli*, an ingenious mixture of honey and verjuice, quenched thirst during the summer, and produced that agreeable gaiety which is to drunkenness what doziness is to sleep.[41]

A mixture of honey and juice of myrtle seed, of course diluted with water, composed *myrtites*, the aromatic flavour of which flattered the palate, and rendered the breath more sweet.[42] Sometimes pomegranates were substituted for the myrtle, and it was then called *rhoites*, and possessed an agreeable and pungent flavour.[43]

Wine made of dates enjoyed a general esteem in the east. The Romans, who knew also how to appreciate it, prepared it by throwing into water some common, though very ripe, dates; and when they had well soaked, they were put under a press.[44] The same means were employed to procure fig wine; but often the sediment of grapes was used instead of water, to prevent its being too sweet.[45]

"Artificial wines" were also procured by the aid of several other kinds of fruits, such as sorbs, medlars, and mulberries.[46] Fermentation dispelled the sweet and insipid flavour which generally distinguishes these fruits; and, at the commencement of a repast, the guests swallowed with delight large cups of these beverages.[47]

It was also the custom to serve very cold water, in which certain plants had been infused, and which was freshened by being surrounded with snow after it had been boiled for some time. The invention of this iced water is attributed to the Emperor Nero, who made great use of it; and who appears to have bitterly regretted it when, dethroned and flying from his assassins, he was constrained through excessive thirst to drink muddy water from a ditch. The unfortunate Cæsar then, for the first time, thought of the strange vicissitudes of fortune, and casting a sorrowful glance at the disgusting fluid he held in his hand, "Alas!" he exclaimed, with a sigh, "is this the iced water that Nero drank?"[48]

TEA.

This plant is a native of China, and it is only in the Celestial Empire that tea is cultivated to any great extent. Why, then, is it neglected on all other points of the globe situated in the same latitude? Doubtless, because the soil of China is superior for its culture to that of any other country.

The shrub that produces tea is cultivated between the twenty-third and thirty-third degrees of latitude; it thrives on the mountainous parts, on the slope of the hills, and that which grows on high ground is far superior to that gathered in the valleys. It is the same with this plant as with the vine in France and in Europe; it grows on flat land, and succeeds wonderfully on plains exposed to the sun's rays.

The Chinese export teas of the first quality in much greater proportion than those of an inferior kind. In England there is a larger consumption than in any other country in the world.

In China, the tea that forms the habitual beverage of the people is a very inferior species of the *Boo* tea.

The provinces of Kiang-Nang, Kiang-Si, and Che-Kiang, furnish green tea to Russia, the United States, Calcutta, and various European countries; the province of Fo-Kien furnishes black tea to England, with the exception of a third of the *boo* tea, or *bohee*, which is exported from a district called Wo-Ping, lying to the north-west of the province of Canton.

It is in Fo-Kien that the cultivation of this precious shrub is held in the highest estimation. In this province it is deprived of a large number of its buds at the beginning of the spring. Of these are made the tea *Pé-ko*, the most renowned of all kinds. Congo tea serves to perfume part of these buds, and to impart to them a more agreeable flavour.

A first gathering of full-grown leaves takes place at the commencement of May, a second towards the middle of June, and a third and last at the end of the summer. This produces a tea inferior to the preceding kinds in point of quality and perfume.

The inhabitants of Fo-Kien cultivate tea in inclosures; and at the time of harvest sell the leaves to a class of persons who undertake their preparation, which consists in drying the leaves in houses, first by the simple contact with the air, afterwards in heated warehouses. When the preparation is terminated, the merchants come and make choice of the best qualities; then the desiccation of the tea is finished, and it is forwarded in packets, each bearing its proper designation.

As soon as the leaves have been gathered and selected, they are plunged in boiling water, where they remain about thirty seconds; they are then quickly withdrawn, strained, and thrown on iron plates, large and flat, placed above a furnace: the workmen's hands can hardly endure the heat of these plates. They continually stir the leaves till they are sufficiently heated, after which they take them off, and spread them on large tables covered with mats. Other workmen then busy themselves with rolling them with the palm of the hand, while others cool them as quickly as possible by agitating the air with large fans. This operation must be continued until the leaves have completely cooled under the hand of the person who rolls them, for it is by being quickly cooled that the leaves remain longer curled. Thanks to the operation of rolling them, which is repeated two or three times, the leaves are deprived of their humidity, and the unwholesome bitter juice they contain. For teas of the first quality, each leaf must be rolled separately; but for more common kinds, several may be rolled at once. Tea, thus prepared, is dried, and put into boxes or cases free from moisture. The Chinese then aromatise it with various odoriferous plants, such as the flowers of the *olea fragrans,* and those of the *camellia sesangua,* shrubs of the same family as tea; or those of the scented tea-roses and orange-flowers.

This tea is destined for mandarins of the higher class, for the *Calaos* or ministers, and even for the celestial sovereign of the *Centre of the Earth*—or, in more simple words, the Emperor.

There are, in reality, but two kinds of tea, black tea and green tea; each kind is again subdivided into many varieties. The best black tea is the scented *Liang-sing,* worth in China about 10*s.* the pound.

The first of all green teas, destined for the great, and bearing an exquisite perfume, is that called *Koo-lang-fyn-i.* M. de Rienzi assures us that he has seen it sold in Canton for 32s. a pound.

New tea is considered by the Chinese as a powerful narcotic, therefore it is never sold until a year after the gathering

The Europeans and Americans, who trade with tea in Canton, have recourse for their transactions with the Chinese to native tasters, or others, who know how to distinguish the different qualities at the sight of the colour produced by the infusion.

It is generally believed in Europe that tea exported thence has already served as a beverage to the Chinese. It is a mistake, propagated by persons who, having seen the tea put in water, have doubtless not well understood the reason of this operation. We must, however, admit that the merchants sometimes mix tea already used with tea of good quality; a fraud only to be discovered by the weakness of the infusion.

Tea seems likely to spread over the world. Our books, wines, brandy, cutlery, and jewellery, go round the globe, and are sought after by the civilized nations as well as the wild tribes. On the other hand, we receive our food, together with spices, from Malaisia; we sweeten them with sugar from the Antilles or Siam; we enjoy the flavour and perfume of coffee from Arabia and the Island of Bourbon; we intoxicate ourselves with tobacco from Manilla, Virginia, of Havannah, and Latakia; and we imbibe with luxurious pleasure the tea of those Chinese we are continually laughing at, but of whom we have borrowed so many useful things. We must, however, acknowledge that France is the country the least advanced in this respect, and the use of this beneficent drink is far from being as common as it ought to be. We do not fear to say that when once acquainted with the method of preparing it better than is generally done, this inferiority in the consumption will disappear. Some witty delineator of manners and customs has pourtrayed upon the joyous scene of a comic theatre of Paris, that famous tea party of *Mother Gibou* and *Madame Pochet*, one of those ridiculous Parisian and really home-scenes, much more common than is generally supposed, and although the picture is over-charged, it is nevertheless true.

It is not necessary here to give our private recipe to prepare an infusion in which that excellent lady, *Madame Pochet*, thought herself so perfect; suffice to say, that to make it agreeable to her guests she added salt, pepper, some cinnamon, the yolk of an egg, and a tiny drop of vinegar. We would beg the reader not to fail in attending these charming and daily meetings, at which each housewife presides, and we would say to strangers, let us seriously study an English tea.

" The use of tea in China dates from the greatest antiquity. The Japanese attribute to it a miraculous origin. They say that Darma, a very pious prince, and son of an Indian king, landed in China in the year 510 of the Christian era, and wishing to edify mankind by his example, imposed upon himself privations of all kinds. It happened, however, that after several years of great fatigue, in spite of his care he fell asleep; and believing he had violated his oath, and in order to fulfil it faithfully for the future, he cut off his eyelids and threw them on the ground. The next day, returning towards the same spot, he found them changed into a little shrub, hitherto unknown to the earth. He eat some of the leaves, which made him merry and restored his former strength. Having recommended the same food to his disciples, the reputation of tea soon spread, and has continued in use since that time."—DESFONTAINES. See, also, KŒMPFER, in his "*Aménités Exotiques.*"

We are ignorant of the period and motives which persuaded the Chinese to use tea in infusion. Perhaps it was to render water more agreeable, which is said to be brackish and of a bad taste in many parts of China. In 1641, Tulpius, a Dutch physician, was the first to mention this plant, in a dissertation he published. In 1657, Joncquet, a French physician, called it the divine plant, and compared it to ambrosia. In 1679, Cornelius Bentekoe, a Dutch physician, published a treatise, in which he declared himself a partisan of tea, and asserted that this beverage in no way could injure the stomach, even if drank to the extent of *two hundred cups* a day. Many of his countrymen went even beyond this: they made of it a universal panacea.

As at first the leaves of the tea plant were rare and but little known, many persons thought they had discovered in Europe what others fetched from such a distance. Thus Simon Pauli introduced the royal pimento (*myria gale* of LINN.), as the real tea of China. Others thought to have found the marvellous virtues of tea in plants growing in our own country, such as marjoram, veronica, myrtle, sage, agrimony, &c.; but it happily ended in granting the preference to the real tea of China and Japan.

COFFEE.

In the trade five principal kinds of coffee are enumerated—or rather, five sorts—according to the different countries from whence they come, although all derived from the same kind of coffee tree, *Coffea Arabica*. These five kinds are as follows :—

1st. Mocha coffee, thus called from the country whence this kind of coffee originates, a plant now so commonly spread over every American colony. The grain of this coffee is generally round and small. From Mocha coffee is derived the most sweet and agreeable beverage ; it is also the most esteemed, the dearest, and holds the first rank in the trade.

2nd. The Bourbon coffee, cultivated in the Island of Bourbon; for some time it occupied the second place in quality, but the *gourmets* prefer to it coffee from Martinique or Guadaloupe.

3rd. There are several kinds of Martinique or Guadaloupe, distinguished by the various preparations.

4th. The Cayenne coffee. This kind is less known on account of the small quantity cultivated there, and introduced in trade. This kind is superior to the Martinique coffee.

5th. The St. Domingo coffee, in which is comprised that from Porto Rico, and other leeward islands, is considered inferior to the four other kinds.

Let us mention a few of the methods by which coffee in infusion is obtained.

It is not exactly known who introduced the custom of taking coffee. Some attribute its use to the prior of a convent, who becoming acquainted with the properties of this plant by the effect it produced on the goats which fed upon it, tried its influence on his monks, in order to keep them awake during the performance of divine service. According to others, the discovery is due to a mufti, who, wishing to surpass in devotion the most religious dervishes, made use of coffee so as to banish sleep, and thus be enabled to pray longer without interruption. Whatever may be the origin of the use of coffee, it has become so general up to the present day that it may almost be classed among the articles of the greatest necessity. This extensive use has stimulated the industry of inventors to seek means of rendering it most pleasant to drink, as also its great consumption and high price have awaked both economy and fraud, in order to find a substitute for this agreeable beverage.

It would be useless here to describe the different methods of making coffee; it will be sufficient to mention that all those which tend to prepare it without boiling the water in which the pulverised coffee is placed, are almost equally good.

In order to supplant coffee, which in Europe was found very expensive, many different means have been tried. About fifty years since the Swiss porter of a nobleman in Paris thought of roasting acorns, which he mixed with roast coffee, ground; he sold it cheaper than any one; all bought it, and the Swiss made his fortune.

The trick, however, being discovered, all sought means of gratifying their taste without emptying their purses; barley and rye began to be mixed with coffee.

In the mountains of Virginia, in America, the inhabitants make a coffee simply of roasted rye; they by these means obtain a beverage in no way resembling coffee, but it goes by that name, and at least the imagination is satisfied.

In Belgium, in the province of Liege, coffee is mixed with wild chicory root. This method, generally known, is at the present time practised throughout the whole of Europe; and wild chicory root then opened for Liege a new branch of commerce. Lastly, in Flanders some of the inhabitants cultivate the lupin, which they complacently call coffee, and whose seed, roasted, they drink instead of real coffee.

"The infusion of coffee is thought to be beneficial to stout and phlegmatic persons, and for pains in the head; but it appears that its admixture with cream or milk prevents these good effects, on account of the relaxation it thus causes to the stomach. On the contrary, it gives strength when taken pure. It is doubtless for this reason that the inhabitants of the colonies take it three and four times a day—that is, at four o'clock in the morning, a very strong infusion, sometimes without sugar; at breakfast, with milk; after dinner, pure; and often in the afternoon, for the fourth time."—BEAUVAIS.

We are unacquainted with the period of the introduction of coffee into Europe. Rauwolf is the first who speaks of coffee, in 1583. Prospero Alpini then came, and described the coffee tree in Egypt by the name of *bon, bun,* or *boun:* his work appeared in 1591. In 1614, Bacon mentioned this oriental beverage, and Meissner published a treatise on it in 1621.

It was not, however, until towards the year 1645, that it began to be drunk in Italy. The first *cafés* were opened in London in 1652, and in Paris in 1669, a time at which a pound of coffee was worth forty crowns. It was principally Soliman Aga, the ambassador from Turkey, who caused coffee to become fashionable in Paris.

It penetrated into Sweden in the year 1674, where it was thought of use in scorbutic diseases. The first person who made trial of coffee with milk was Nieuhoff, the Dutch ambassador in China, in imitation of tea with milk.

"The physical effects of coffee are well known: it accelerates the circulation of the blood, but sometimes causes palpitation of the heart and giddiness; it has even been thought to occasion apoplexy and paralysis. Nevertheless, celebrated writers—such as Fontenelle and Voltaire—made constant use of it, almost to an abuse. They were told, *it is a slow poison;* it was indeed slow for these learned men, who died, the one at a hundred, the other eighty-four years of age. However, at the present time coffee is a beverage whose power over our intellectual or moral habits has, perhaps, never been calculated as it deserves, since it has become general, and almost suppressed the drunkenness which disgraced our ancestors at the end of their grand repasts."—VIREY.

The subject we have just slightly touched upon recalls to our recollection a whim of the charming Sévigné: "*Le café et Racine passeront,*" said this amiable lady, nearly two hundred years ago. The beautiful marchioness was mistaken: both coffee and Racine have remained, and do not appear likely soon to bid us adieu.

CHOCOLATE.

Every one is aware that chocolate is an aliment obtained from the cocoa-nut, roasted and reduced to paste, with sugar and aromatics.

But first, the choice of cocoa nuts is not indifferent.

Those from Soconusco, from Caracas, and Maracaibo, are the best and sweetest; it is, however, well to mix with them other kinds, to correct their insipidity by a certain sharpness far from being unpleasant; thus, to four parts of Caracas cocoa, earthed—that is, rendered mild by a sojourn of some weeks under the moist earth—a part of cocoa from the Antilles, or Maragnon and Para, is added; this kind contains more of sharp and bitter matter. These cocoas are slightly torrefied in an iron pan. The Spaniards burn their cocoa much less than the Italians. Being left to grow cold, this cocoa is slightly crushed, to separate the envelopes or shells, which are thrown away. However, in England, Switzerland, and Germany, these shells serve to make, with boiling water, a warm infusion, mixed with milk and drank in lieu of real chocolate. The envelopes of torrefied coffee are employed in a similar manner in the east for the "Sultana coffee." The mixtures of torrefied cocoa are reduced into a fat paste of a brown colour, either between stones, or by means of an iron roller upon a porphyry rock, warmed underneath by live coals; this paste, regularly ground, is at last incorporated with sugar, equal to its weight, then it is mixed together as perfectly as possible. In this *chocolat de santé* a small quantity of very fine cinnamon powder is admitted, which makes it more palatable, and neutralizes the action of the fat and heavy substance, or vegetable butter, contained in the cocoa.

"The term chocolate belongs, it is said, to the language of the Mexicans, and is derived from the two words *choco*, sound or noise, and *atle*, water, because it is beaten in boiling water to make it froth, according to the custom of this people. Before their conquest by the Spaniards, it formed the principal aliment of the Mexicans. They held the cocoa tree in such estimation, that its kernel served as current coin, and this custom even now remains."—HUMBOLDT.

The Mexican chocolate, besides the pimento, contained the *chile*, or Indian wheat-flour, with honey, or sweet juice of the agava. To this was added annotto, an astringent tinctorial juice, of a rosy hue, obtained from the seeds of the *Bixa Orleana*. The chieftains, or lords and warriors only, enjoyed the right of feeding on chocolate, as the most restoring aliment, and the most capable, in their opinion, of repairing worn-out strength and producing vigour. The addition of the perfume of vanilla, again, augments this quality, according to the testimony of physicians and travellers. Dias of Castilho relates that Montezuma drank vanilla chocolate, and the Maréchal de Bellisle says, in his "*Testament Politique*," that the regent, Louis Philippe d'Orléans regaled himself every morning with chocolate at his *petit lever*.

The ladies of Chiapa, in Mexico, are so fond of these perfumed chocolates that they even have them carried to eat in church. The Spanish Creole nuns have also brought to great perfection the art of preparing fine chocolate, perfumed with amber.

The use of chocolate was soon brought from Mexico, after its conquest by Fernando Cortes, into Spain, and this food has there become quite habitual. First, it easily deceives hunger by reason of its oily qualities and slow digestion; then it is softening and cooling, which renders it particularly desirable in warm climates, especially such as the Iberian peninsula. Thus the Spaniards but slightly roast their cocoanuts; they prefer preserving but a very slight bitterness, and mixing with it more aromatics. Besides, chocolate, so useful to dry and nervous temperaments, is an agreeable analeptic, recommended against hypochondria and melancholy, two affections so common to the Spaniards. The beggars, even, could not live without it, and they accost each other in the morning with inquiring if their lordships have taken their chocolate.

This aliment is favourable to idleness, augments the calm of the body and mind, and plunges one in a sweet quietude of *far niente* at a small expense.

From Spain the fashion of taking chocolate was introduced into Italy, especially by the Florentine, Antonio Carletti. The Italians extract from cocoa more exalted qualities by torrefication: they burn it till it becomes bitter. The grave question arose among them, whether chocolate taken in the morning by the monks broke the fast principally in Lent. The Cardinal Brancaccio, and other learned casuists, battled long in order to prove that chocolate, being evidently a beverage made of water, could not be in the least considered as an aliment, nor break the fast. We see, indeed, in the correspondence of the Princess des Ursins—all powerful at the court of Philip V. of Spain—and Madame de Maintenon, that the consciences of pious persons had been placed in full tranquillity by this decision, and that any one might fast during the whole Lent as perfectly by drinking chocolate as if he had only partaken of a glass of cold water.

" Chocolate became pretty common in France from the time of Anne of Austria, mother of Louis XIV.; however, it does not appear to have ever excited the same enthusiasm as coffee; it is not favourable to good cheer, nor is it exhilarating. To this may be traced, perhaps, the indifference of the English for this beverage."—VIREY.

In trade, as we have said, are distinguished a great variety of cocoas, and they are called by the name of the country whence they come. Thus we have the Caracas cocoa, the Surinam cocoa, &c. That which comes from the French possessions is called also " cocoa of the isles." The Caracas is the most esteemed of all : it is more oily than the other kinds, and has no sharpness of flavour. It is known by being larger, rough, of an ovoid, oblong shape, not flattened, covered with a greyish dust, and by the kernel being easily divided into several irregular fragments. " The name of *cacao*, of which in French has been made the word *cacaoyer*, is that given by the inhabitants of Guiana to this grain. As to the scientific name, *theobroma*, Linnæus formed it from two Greek words, signifying ' food of the gods.' "—DEMEZIL.

XXVII.

DRINKING CUPS.

IF men were wiser, the 19th century would probably not have seen a beneficent apostle preaching temperance everywhere, and making his name cherished and celebrated by a series of successes which could hardly have been expected; numerous societies of *Hydropotes*, or "teetotallers," would not alarm, in our days, those joyful disciples of Bacchus's temple, hydrophobes by profession, by taste, and interest, who sincerely bewail the desertion of newly made abstemious members; and no person would promise, by a solemn and formidable pledge, to forego the drinking of anything but water! The abuse must have been very great, since it was necessary to have recourse to such a remedy.

It is true that the evil had taken deep root, and that the most ancient people, the gods, and the heroes, have left us examples of this dangerous seduction. The Scythians, the Celts, Iberians, and Thracians,[1] were confirmed drunkards. The wise Nestor himself, who was so good a match for Agamemnon, often felt some difficulty in finding his tent.[2] Alexander the Great slept sometimes two days and two nights, after having paid too much devotion to the god of good cheer;[3] and Philip, his father, very frequently left the table with a very heavy head and staggering legs.[4]

It is reported that Dionysius the Younger, tyrant of Sicily, lost his sight through drinking too much, which will not be wondered at, if

DESCRIPTION OF PLATE No. XVIII.

No. 1. Drinking-cup, of terra cotta, in the form of a pig's head, found at Herculaneum.—HAMILTON, I., IIo.

No. 2. Also that of a dog's head.—CAYLUS, I., Plan 35.

Pl. 18.

F.T.Z.Volant, del.

Saddler & Chant, scul

Pl. 19.

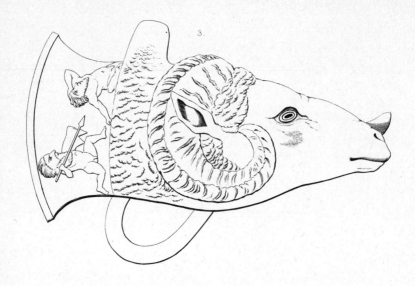

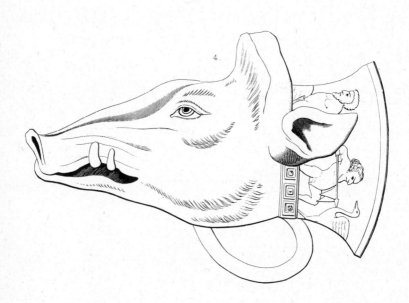

E. T. Z. Volant, del.

Chant & Saddler, sc.

what is supposed, be true, that this miserable man was drunk every day, without fail, for three months together![5] Shall we mention Tiberius— surnamed by the army, *Biberius* (Tippler)—who, after he became Emperor, passed the days and nights drinking with Flaccus and Piso, at the very time they were working at the reformation of the Romans?[6]

This pagan Solomon, having to choose from among several very distinguished candidates who offered themselves for the quæstorship, preferred the least known, because he had drunk a whole pitcher of wine, which the prince himself had condescended to fill.[7]

Intoxication, with the Greeks, was noted as belonging to low company, if we are to judge by certain personages whom Æschylus and Sophocles did not fear to bring on the stage, and who struck each other with vases—a thing which the modern theatre has judiciously banished.[8] Homer is more reserved ; for Achilles, after copious libations, only threw a neat's foot at Ulysses' head,[9] which probably was not of much consequence.

The fact is, that the ancients did not at all profess the same principles that we do respecting intemperance. Hippocrates himself, advised men to seek mirth now and then in wine ;[10] Seneca recommends us to drown cares and fatigue in it ;[11] and Musæus decorates with crowns of flowers the foreheads of the sages who, sitting by the side of Plato at all new banquets, should find in continual drunkenness the sweetest reward for their virtues.[12] A singular bliss, which only reason in delirium could have imagined.

We have spoken of the delicious beverage which was so costly a seduction to choice epicureans, who took merit to themselves for not resisting it ; for this reason, it was necessary to invent vessels worthy of containing it ; and art, encouraged by luxury, produced those magnificent vases of which ostentatious antiquity has only left us a faint idea.

The cups of the Homeric times were all of equal capacity ; one of them was offered to each guest, but several were offered to persons of high distinction.[13]

The Greeks thought much of their cups ; for them they were sacred relics from father to son, and were only used on certain solemnities. Thus Œdipus delivers the most frightful imprecation against his son Polynices, who had presented, at a common repast, the cup of his ancestors.[14] That of Nestor was so large that a young man could hardly carry it ; as to him, he lifted it up without the slightest difficulty.[15]

The Athenians drank from cups in the shape of horns.[16] Wax vases were sufficient for the Spaniards.[17] The Gaul who had thrown down an Urus (wild ox) took its horns, decorated them with silver and gold rings, and made his guests drink out of them.[18] Often the skull of an enemy, killed in single combat, was transformed into a cup of honour, and reminded a Gallic family of the memorable action of a valiant ancestor.[19]

The first cups of the Romans were made of horns, or of the earthenware of Samos.[20] Those conquerors of the world had not yet enervated their manly courage with the luxurious spoils of conquered nations. Afterwards, some very simple ones were made of beech-wood[21] or elder;[22] these possessed a marvellous property which they ought to have always preserved—the wine only escaped from them, and they retained the water which had been mixed with it.[23]

But Rome, already tired of its austere simplicity, and its disdain for the Greek cups of glass and crystal, soon began to desire something finer. Those magnificent chalices, master-pieces of patience and skill, in which gold and silver were amalgamated with a more brittle material,[24] were soon in much request, and appeared worthy of their renown.

But it is to be observed, that the crystal of which the most precious cups were made, had not the slightest similarity to that which we make use of now, and which the least shock will break; it was flexible and malleable;[25] it might be thrown on the pavement with impunity, and remained unhurt.[26]

Here is, on this subject, a curious anecdote, which has been left to us by Petronius:—

A certain skilful workman used to make crystal vases as strong as vases of gold and silver. He produced an incomparable masterpiece; it was a chalice of astonishing beauty, which he thought worthy of Cæsar only, and which he felt a pride in offering to him. Tiberius highly praised the skill and the rich present of the artist. This man, wishing to increase still more the admiration of the prince, and secure his favours to a greater degree, begged of him to give back the vase. He then threw it with all his might on the marble pavement of the

DESCRIPTION OF PLATE No. XIX.

Nos. 1. and 2. Drinking horns; these give us an idea how the ancient Greeks and Romans made use of the horns: taken from two paintings at Herculaneum.

No. 3. A horn, with a chimerical head, in Grecian terra cotta.—"*Herculan. Bronzi*," II., 2, 3.

Pl. 20

1.

2.

3.

F. T. Z. Volant, del.

Chant & Saddler, scul.

Pl. 20.

T. H. Volant, del.

Chant & Saddler, scul.

apartment : the hardest metal could never have resisted this terrible shock. Cæsar appeared moved, and was silent. The artist, with a triumphant smile, picked up the vase, which had only a slight dent, and which, by striking it with the hammer, was soon brought to its original state. This being done, no doubt remained on his mind that he had conquered the good graces of the Emperor, and the esteem of an astonished court. Tiberius asked him if he was the only one who knew how to work crystal in so remarkable a manner ? The workman immediately answered that no one possessed his secret. " Very well," said Cæsar, " let his head be struck off without loss of time; for if this strange invention were known, gold and silver would very soon have not the least value."[27] Thus did the Emperor Tiberius encourage artists and the arts.

There were, besides, cups made of the most pure crystal, " the brittleness of which seems to have added to their price,"[28] and which were paid for dearer than gold and precious stones;[29] but much less, however, than those famous Murrhine vases, which have so long exercised the useless sagacity of ancient commentators.

Among the rich spoils that Pompey, conqueror of Mithridates and master of a part of Asia, ostentatiously displayed in his triumph,[30] the Romans, for the first time, admired vases and cups, the material and workmanship of which surpassed all that the imagination could fancy the most graceful and delicate.[31] They were much in request; the price was exorbitant, and thenceforth they were indispensable. One of the ancient consuls thought himself too happy to give only a little more than £6,000 for one of those Murrhines. Such was the name given to this brittle and rare novelty. Petronius paid for a large basin £28,800;

DESCRIPTION OF PLATE No. XX.

This vase, made of one single piece of crystal, is in its original size; the delicacy of the work gives a great value to it. The body of the vase, and all other parts in relief, are of glass It was discovered in 1725, and is preserved in the cabinet of the Marquis of Trivulsi, at Milan. The fillet round the body, and those forming the ordinary motto of the feasts—" BIBE VIVAS MULTIS ANNIS "— are isolated from the body of the cup about one quarter of an inch, and are attached to it by threads or fillets of glass, very fine. They are not soldered to the cup, but the whole of the labour is worked on a turning lathe, being seen more or less angular as the instrument may have been led to penetrate in the most difficult parts. The inscription is green; the fillet is blue: these two colours are very bright. The cup is an opaque or changing colour, without being able to distinguish whether that hue was intended to be so, as it happens to glass which has remained a long while buried, exposed to the vapours of a dunghill, or a sewer, &c., &c. A second antique vase is known to exist, whose workmanship is similar.—" Histoire de l'Art," Liv. I., Chap. I., page 45.—Paris : Janson.

and Nero spent the like sum for a vase with two handles, which he forgot two days afterwards.[32]

The Murrhine cups appeared on the table with the wine of the "hundred leaves," and the Falernian was poured into them, so as to preserve all the generous delicacy of its odour.[33]

The Murrhines were much sought after, on account of their form and brilliant transparency : they were made of mother of pearl, according to Belon, but others say of agate. Their dimensions, however, would incline one to doubt it. Scaliger,[34] Cardan,[35] and Madame Dacier,[36] thought that the ancients gave unheard-of prices for simple porcelain vases, which were precious on account of their rarity. This opinion, which several modern *literati*[37] have adopted, rests plausibly enough, it appears, on one verse of Propertius, in which this poet speaks of "Murrhine cups, baked in the furnace of the Parthians."[38] It has been said that, perhaps the Parthians learnt from the Chinese how to make porcelain ; but this supposition, entirely void of proof, has been contradicted in a most peremptory manner by the author of a very curious book, who demonstrates irrefragably that the Murrhines were not of porcelain, but of stones of the species of onyx.[39] The following fact will leave but very little doubt on that subject :—

In 1791, the Constituent National Assembly, appointed a commission to make an inventory and valuation of all objects in the Garde-Meuble of the crown. They found, among other very beautiful sardonyx, two very antique vases : one made in the form of an ewer, ten inches in height and four inches in diameter, having its handle cut out of the same piece, and the second, hollowed out as a bowl, ten inches in diameter, which were recognised as real Murrhines—beautiful white and blue veins and other shades, circulated about the bowl without interfering with its semi-transparency ; the bottom was of the same colour as the ewer. The jewellers estimated these vases at £6,000 each, although there was nothing engraved in the hollow nor in relief, but merely on consideration of the beauty of the material, the fineness of the polish, and the difficulty that must have attended the hollowing out of the ewer.[40]

These valuations would appear exaggerated, if it were not known that the antique vase of the Duke of Brunswick, which formerly belonged to the Dukes of Mantua, in 1631, and made of sardonyx, in the cruet shape, was valued at 150,000 German crowns—or dollars of 4s. 3d. The relief

Pl. 27

MURRHIN CUP.

F. T. Z. Valant del.   Saddler & Chant, scul.

engraving represented the mysteries of Ceres and Bacchus; but it had no primitive handle, and the diameter was only two inches and a-half.[41]

By the side of these inestimable Murrhines were standing very graceful chalices of amber, the prodigious workmanship of which absolutely gave to them a most arbitrary value,[42] but which Roman prodigality never found too high.

Silver cups engraved were also nearly as much esteemed, when they came from the hands of some well-known workman—such as Myos, Mentor, or Myron.[43] They were even preferred to gold cups,[44] unless these latter were enriched with precious stones.[45]

All these vases presented still greater varieties in their forms than in the materials employed. There were very large ones, some narrow, some oblong; many ornamented with two handles, others had only one.[46] Some were much like a tympanon—or zoph, a musical instrument of the ancient Hebrews—a small boat or ewer.[47] In one word, the Greek or Roman artist never listened to anything but his own fancy, and was then far from supposing that he was preparing very long and wakeful hours of study to many antiquarians, zealous to explain seriously the strange wanderings of a fantastical imagination.

DESCRIPTION OF PLATE No. XXI.

MURRHINE VASE.—This vase is the most precious of all those which have come down to us. It is drawn here half the original size, and belongs to Prince de Biscari, in Sicily, which has been described by him in the dissertation entitled, "*De Vasi Murrini Ragionamenti.*" Three pieces of opal in the first place form the cup; the second, the stem; and the last, the base of the foot. If this vase is an antique, as it is said by the Prince de Biscari; if true that several pieces of opal have often been found as large and as fine (which appears doubtful, in the actual state of mineralogic knowledge), the question upon the Murrhine vases would be decided. They would have been of opal, and not porcelain; neither of sardonyx—*Pierre de lard*—as many have believed, nor of *cacholong* (a species of chalcedony, opaque, and of a yellowish white), as I have described it.

XXVIII.

WINE.

BACCHUS, son of Ammon, was born in Egypt, and was the first who taught his countrymen the art of cultivating the vine, and of making wine. He is the same as Osiris, the famous conqueror of India.[1] Should this assertion be contradicted, we shall only entreat any and every disputant to make his own choice of the god of vineyards, from among the five heroes bearing the name of Bacchus, as we are too impartial to prefer any one in particular.[2]

Œnopion, worthy son of one of these heroes, enriched the inhabitants, of Chios with the first rosy wine that ever yet obscured their reason.[3] Greece, Italy, and Sicily owed this wonderful liquor to the Egyptians. The Gauls received this sweet present from a Tuscan, who had been banished from Clusium, his country;[4] and the cultivation of the grape spread rapidly till the reign of the sanguinary Domitian, who completed the catalogue of his crimes by tearing up the vines.[5] The Emperor Probus restored them to the disconsolate Gauls.[6] That prince was certainly worthy of his name !

Modern science, agreeing with holy writ,[7] looks upon the east as the common cradle of the vine and the human race.

Palestine was renowned for its vines. Pliny speaks in praise of them.[8] The vineyards constituted a part of the riches of the country, and they were preserved with the greatest care ; so much so that Moses, with an especial view to vines, forbade the sowing of different seeds in the same field, on pain of confiscation :[9] and it was done to encourage their cultivation, that that wise legislator exempted every person who had planted one from military service, and from all public duties, until the first vintage.[10]

The growths of Lebanon,[11] of Helbon,[12] and of Sorec,[13] enjoyed an extraordinary reputation, and the delicious wine they produced was capable of inspiring the lyric David with that celebrated praise[14] by which intemperance has often dared to authorize reprehensible excesses.

However, the Hebrews, a sober people, like all eastern nations, rarely made use of pure wine; they generally mixed it with a quantity of water, and only drank a little at some ceremonial feasts, and at the end of their repasts.[15] They sometimes mixed with it perfumes and odoriferous drugs.[16]

Some nations seem to have had a great horror of wine. The Persians drank nothing but water;[17] and the inhabitants of Pontus, the Scythians, and the Cappadocians, partook of this strange taste.[18] The Arcadians, who lived on chesnuts and acorns, were not worthy of the favours of Bacchus; neither were the troglodytes, the ichthyophagists, and other swarms of hydropotes who were as yet too little civilized to ask of drunkenness its illusions and its enchantments.[19]

The Egyptians would have thought it a profanation of their temples to carry in a flagon of the rosy liquid; but Psammetichus came (670 B.C.), and that wise prince made them understand that a pot of beer is not worth a cup of good wine.[20]

The Romans asserted that their old king, Janus, planted the first vine in Italy,[21] and that, later, Numa taught them how to trim it.[22] That noble people knew how to appreciate such blessings, and in order to demonstrate that wisdom is always to be found in wine, they never failed to place on their altars the statue of Minerva beside that of Bacchus.[23]

The inflexible muse of history has preserved to us the name of the individual who doomed himself to a sorry sort of immortality by inventing the custom of mixing water with wine; it was Cranaüs, King of Athens, 1532 B.C.[24] The gods, doubtless to punish him, caused a great part of Greece to be inundated, and it was not long before he was dethroned.[25] Pliny accuses the obscure Staphil, son of Sithen,[26] of this depravation of taste, which gained upon imitators to such an extent that, in the time of Diodorus of Sicily (45 B.C.), the guests still mixed water with their wine at the end of the repast.[27] It is true that they were then all intoxicated.

Lycurgus was, no doubt, ignorant of this practice, when he had the barbarity to destroy the vines of the Lacedæmonians, under pretext of putting an end to the disorders caused by intemperance. It would have been preferable, says Plutarch, to have united the nymphs with Bacchus.[28] The ingenious philosopher insists on the mixture being made by a fourth, a fifth, or an octave, in the same manner as the chords in music, which charm our ears. The fifth was obtained by pouring three measures of water on two of wine; one part water and two parts wine made the octave; a quarter of wine and three quarters of water produced the fourth,[29] a most inharmonious chord, struck only by inexperienced and unskilful hands.

Hippocrates, great physician as he was, had already somewhere advised[30] this deplorable dereliction from all wise doctrines, so true is it, that science sometimes goes astray; but, happily for his glory, that learned man, further on,[31] recommends us to drink pure wine, and to drink enough for joy to dissipate our griefs, and rock us in the sweet errors of hope.

The god of grapes had everywhere fervent admirers, except, perhaps, among the Scythians. These schismatics refused to worship a divinity who caused the faithful to become intoxicated.[32] In other places they sacrificed to him a tiger, in order to show the power of his empire;[33] and zealous disciples, with their heads crowned with branches of the vine, holding in one hand a crater and in the other a torch, ran with dishevelled hair about the streets, shouting to the son of Jupiter, the terrible Evius,[34] in the silence of the night.[35]

The Romans addressed to him special prayers twice a year, on the occasion of the wine festivals,[36] which took place in the months of May and September. In the first, they tasted the wine;[37] and, during the second, they implored the god to grant Italy fine weather and abundant vintages.[38]

The god could not reasonably refuse this request, for the vine-dressers spared neither labour nor fatigue to procure an abundant harvest. They were constantly seen disincumbering the plant of a too luxurious foliage, thereby exposing the grapes to the sun's rays, which bring them to maturity, and breaking with indefatigable perseverance the least clods of earth which, accumulating around the tendrils, appeared to fatigue them by their weight.[39] And woe to the thief whom they detected by night stealing any of these carefully reared grapes; his crime was punished with death, unless the inexperience of youth pleaded in his favour. In that case a severe flagellation impressed on

Pl. 25.

F. T. Z. Volant, del.

Saddler & Chant, scul.

him permanently the remembrance of his fault and of the rights of property.[40]

The imperial jurisprudence afterwards softened the Draconian rigour of this law of the Decemviri.[41]

The ancients, like ourselves, were fond of seeing fresh grapes appear on their tables at all periods of the year. They preserved them by covering them with barley flour,[42] or by placing fine bunches in rain water, diminished to a third by boiling. The vase was hermetically sealed with pitch and plaster, and then placed in a spot where the sun's rays could not enter. This water was an excellent beverage for the sick.[43]

The method of making wine was precisely the same both in Greece and Italy.

The vine gatherers carefully rejected the green grapes,[44] and piled the others in deep baskets,[45] the contents of which were instantly emptied into large vats. There men, hardly clothed in the lightest garments, trampled them under their feet,[46] whilst joyous songs and sounds of flutes hastened their movements, and animated them to work faster.[47]

Wine obtained in this manner was much esteemed, and kept very well.[48] The wort which escaped from the vat as soon as they had thrown in the grapes, and which came from the pressure occasioned by their laying one on the other, enjoyed the preference. This first liquor was transformed into an exquisite wine.[49]

The grapes, crushed by the feet, were placed under the press,[50] and an opening made in the lower part of the vat allowed the wort to flow into earthen jars, whence it was subsequently poured into the barrels.[51]

The press was always raised at a little distance from the cellar and kitchen.[52] Its mechanism was very simple. The antiquities of Herculaneum will furnish us with an example. Two trees were firmly fixed in the ground, at a few feet distance one from the other, and a strong horizontal beam rested on their summit. Other pieces of wood, similar

DESCRIPTION OF PLATE No. XXII.

No. 1. Wine-press, explained in the text.

No. 2. A large vase, in which a man is sitting, supposed to be Diogenes. This amphora is broken, and the pieces are joined by ties of lead, cut dove-tailed. It is a bass-relief, from the Villa Albani, published by Winkelman

No. 3. Represents a beast of burthen, with a pack saddle, loaded with two amphoræ. This piece of terra cotta, drawn the size of the original, is taken from the collection of children's playthings of Prince de Biscari. The difficulty of carriage was so great in mountainous countries, that the inhabitants of the Alps substituted for vessels of terra cotta, casks, or wooden tubs, put together with wooden circles, similar to our own. (See Plate III., No. 4., Chariot with four wheels, loaded with a cask.)

to the top piece, were placed underneath. The grapes occupied the space between the vat and the lower plank. Between each of the cross planks wedges were introduced, and two persons kept striking them with hammers, one on each side; it is thus the pressure was effected.[53] Wine from the press, inferior to those just mentioned, served for the ordinary consumption of the family, and for the servants.[54] It was not racked, but simply taken from the barrel as it was wanted.[55]

The lees were taken from the press when it yielded no more liquor; a certain quantity of water was poured over them, and the whole subjected to a second pressure. The weak kind of wine obtained by this new operation must have somewhat resembled that acrid stuff called *piquette*, in France; it was the beverage of the people, and especially of the country people during the winter.[56]

A part of the wort—that which was required for immediate use—was put aside, and clarified with vinegar.[57] A portion of that obtained from the crushed grapes was put to boil on furnaces, supported on three legs, at a little distance from the press, in coppers, the contents of which were continually stirred.[58] This liquor, reduced by a third, was called *carenum*;[59] when the half only remained, it was called *defrutum*;[60] and, lastly, when the ebullition left only a third part remaining, this substance, very similar to honey, took the name of *sapa*.[61] It was mixed with flour, to fatten the snails reared by skilful speculators, who reserved them for the Roman sybarites.[62]

This wort, thus prepared by night, when the moon did not shine,[63] and carefully skimmed,[64] served to preserve wines, to give more body to those which were thought too weak, and became the base of several beverages sought in preference by Roman ladies, at that period of life when maturity of years made alliance with sensuality.[65]

Those who wished to preserve sweet wine during a whole year, filled with the second wort—that is to say, that which was produced by the pression of the feet—some amphoræ covered with pitch inside and out. They were then hermetically sealed, and buried in the sand, or plunged in cold water, where they remained at least two months.[66]

There still was left a large quantity of wort as it came from the grapes. This was taken into the cellar,[67] which was always situated a little below the level of the ground; or to the ground floor, where no kind of smell was allowed to penetrate, or any emanation capable of spoiling the bouquet of the wine it contained.[68]

Pl. 26.

F.T.Z. Volant, del.

Chant & Saddler, scul.

At Herculaneum a spacious cellar has been discovered, round which hogsheads were ranged, and built into the wall.[69] Another cellar, at Pompeii, remarkable for its small size, is divided into two compartments, both containing barrels, and divided one from the other by an horizontal wall.[70]

Large earthen vessels were found there, with and without handles, very carefully executed, and smeared with pitch.[71] We know that the cynic, Diogenes, dwelt in one of these vases; and that the king, Alexander, found him crouching in his strange kind of carapace.[72] The ancients had butts also, but they used them only in cold countries.[73]

The *Dolia*—for so they were named—were first subjected to a fumigation with aromatic plants; then watered with sea-water, and buried half way in the earth. They were separated each one from another, and strict attention was paid to see that the cellar contained neither leather, nor cheese, nor figs, nor old casks. Sometimes persons who inhabited the country paved the store-room, spread sand, and placed the dolia on it.[74]

At the end of nine days, when the fermentation had cleared the wine from those substances it rejects, they carefully covered the dolia, after having smeared all the upper part of the inside, as well as the covers themselves, with a mixture of defrutum, saffron, mastic, pitch, and pine nuts.[75] The butts of aqueous wine were exposed to the north; spirituous wines often braved the rain, the sun, and every change of temperature.[76]

They accelerated the fining of the wine by throwing in plaster, chalk, marble dust, salt, resin, dregs of new wine, sea-water, myrrh, and aromatic herbs.[77] The butts were uncovered once a month, or more frequently, in order to refresh the contents; and before the head was put on again, it was rubbed with pine nuts.[78] Wine was also clarified by drawing it off into another butt, and mixing yolks of eggs beaten with

DESCRIPTION OF PLATE No. XXIII.

COLUM NIVARIUM.—A strainer, used to separate the dregs from the wine. Two are preserved in the collection of Herculaneum; they are made of white metal, and worked with elegance. Each is composed of two plates, round and concave, of four inches in diameter, supplied with flat handles. The two dishes (as it were) and their handles adapt to each other so well, that when put together they appear as one; holes in great number are symmetrically perforated in the upper dish, which keeps the dregs, and lets the clear liquid pass through the lower one. The strainer here represented is taken from Montfaucon's " *Antiquities*," and was found at Rome, towards the end of the 17th century. It is of bronze, and ornamented. On the handles are reliefs in silver, referring to the worship of Bacchus.

salt,[79] or straining it through the *colum nivarium* (already described),[80] covered with a piece of linen.[81]

Fine wines were kept in the wood for two, three, or four years, according to their different properties; after which they were transferred to amphoræ, and that operation required the greatest care.[82]

The amphoræ were earthen pitchers with two handles,[83] reserved for choice wines.[84]   To prevent evaporation through their pores, they covered them with pitch, and stopped the neck with wood or cork, covered with a mastic composed of pitch, chalk, and oil, or any other fat substance.   The name of the wine was inscribed on the amphora; its age was indicated by the designation of the consuls who were in office when it was made.   When the amphora was of glass, it was ticketed with these details.[85]   For this kind of vessels they had store-rooms, which were commonly at the top of the house.[86]   By exposing them to the sun and to smoke the maturity of the wine was hastened.[87]   The discovery of this means of ripening, which the Roman œnophiles never failed to practice, was attributed to the Consul Opimius.[88]

Pliny assures us that the vineyards of the entire world produce 195 different kinds of wine; or double that number, if we reckon every variety.[89]   The whole universe, says he, furnishes only 80 of superior quality, and of this number, two-thirds belong to Italy.[90]   Modern agriculture must have singularly disturbed the calculations of the Roman naturalist.

Let that be as it may, the best Greek wines were those of Thasos,[91] Lesbos,[92] Chios,[93] * and Cos.[94]   Italy boasted of the Sentinum,[95] the

---

* We are not aware that any of our dramatic authors ever gave such proof of generosity after a triumph as did the poet, Ion.   Crowned at Athens, after the representation of a tragedy, he made a present to each Athenian of a vase filled with wine of Chios.— "*Athen.*," I., 5.

DESCRIPTION OF PLATE No. XXIV.

No. 1. Amphora, or Dolium. Upon one of the handles is engraved the *sigles* P. S. A. X.; the first two, probably, are the initials of the proprietor, and the last describes the capacity of the vase, being 250 quarts.—Montfaucon's "*Antiquities*," expl.

Nos. 2 and 3. Smaller Dolium, found at Herculaneum, buried at the bottom of a cellar. The mouths of these vases were fixed in a marble slab, and closed with a cover of the same material. There is in the Villa Albani, an amphora of terra cotta of this kind, which contained 18 Roman amphoræ, or 463 quarts, as marked by numerical letters, engraved upon the outside. In 1750, one of these amphoræ was found at Pouzzole, which was five feet six inches in height, and five feet in diameter, containing 1,728 quarts. Several amphoræ from Herculaneum and Pompeii have inscriptions written in colours, and which give the name of the Prætor Nonnius; the same as those found at Rome, which were inscribed with the name of the consul, to fix the year of the vintage.

Pl. 27

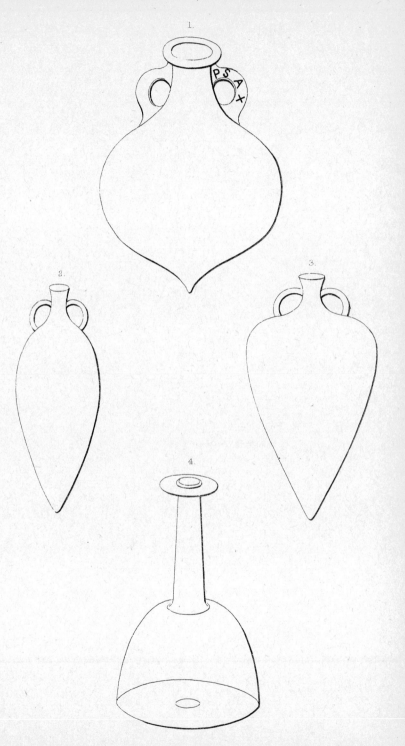

F.T.Z.Volant, del.   Chant & Saddler, cul.

Falernum,[96] the Albanum,[97] and the Mamertinum.[98] After these, a number of other excellent wines occupied a very distinguished place in a long nomenclature to be found in Pliny[99] and Athenæus.[100]

The ancients professed to have a very particular veneration for wines of a renowned growth, which had ripened slowly in amphoræ. Some gastronomic archæologists produced, on their tables certain wines which had so far dried up in leather bottles, that they were taken out in lumps;[101] others, placed in the chimney corner, became in time as hard as salt.[102] Petronius speaks of a wine of a hundred leaves.[103] Pliny says that guests were served with wine more than two hundred years old: it was as thick as honey.[104] This wine was thinned with warm water, and passed through the straining bag (*saccatio vinorum*).[105]

This predilection for good old wine was common to the Greeks;[106] the Romans—who liked it for the bitterness it had contracted by age;[107] and the Egyptians, who, notwithstanding their time-honoured love of beer, were not unjust towards the beverage with which their Osiris found it so delightful to intoxicate himself.[108]

Athenæus sets no bounds to his praise of old wine. He says it is excellent for the health ; it is the best thing to dissolve the food; it strengthens ; it assists the circulation of the blood, and assures a peaceful sleep.[109] Who, then, would be ungrateful enough to refuse to drink ?

The topers of antiquity did not disdain white wine, but they seem to have viewed it as of secondary importance. It digests easily, says the writer just cited, but it is weak, and has but little body.[110] Red wine, on the contrary, is full of strength and energy, and it is the first that the inhabitants of Chios learned to make,[111] when Œnopion, the son of Bacchus, had planted the vine in their country.[112]

However, there was no lack of amateurs of white wine, and, like ourselves, the ancients doubtless preferred it when they eat snails, oysters, or any of those shell fish with which the Lucrine lake abounded. They even took it into their heads (how ingenious is gluttony!) to change red wine sometimes into white. To do this it was only necessary to put three whites of egg, or some bean flour, into a flagon, and shake it a long time. The same result was obtained with ashes from the white vine.[113] Now, is Apicius jesting with us a little when he gives this recipe; or was it a legerdemain trick to amuse the guests at the end of a repast, when too frequent libations had rendered them incapable of distinguishing clearly one colour from another ?

v

The Greeks endeavoured to preclude the disastrous effects of intoxication by putting sea-water into the wine ; a mixture which they also thought had the effect of assisting digestion. One measure of water was enough for fifty measures of wine.[114] And, again, the merchants of that nation took so much interest in the health of foreign consumers that they never shipped the wines of the Archipelago for Rome or elsewhere without diluting them in this manner. Such, for example, was the course followed in concocting that celebrated wine of Chios, which Cato imitated so as to deceive the best judges.[115] That honest geoponic has transmitted us his secret. Fifty-six pints of old sea-water are thrown into a pipe of sweet wine made with grapes dried in the sun ; or two-thirds of a bushel of salt are put into a rush basket, and suspended in the middle of the pipe, where it is left to melt.[116]

This very simple process metamorphoses the most indifferent liquor into that delightful nectar which gave renown and fortune to the isle of Cos.

The saline wine of the Greeks (*vinum tethalassomenon*) was nothing else.[117] Their *thalassites* wine, so much in demand in Italy on account of its apparent age, owed its reputation to the fact of its having been plunged for some time in the sea.[118] This little trading knavery was a tolerably innocent means of increasing the profits of the speculator, who hastened the maturity of his wines without employing any of those deleterious ingredients which illicit traders have introduced at a later period. When the wine had remained a sufficient time in the sea to give it age, it was drawn off into goatskin bottles, well coated with pitch, and, in this manner it supported the longest sea voyages.[119]

The following are the made wines most in vogue in olden times.

The *Passum* was one of those most esteemed in Rome, particularly when it came from Crete.[120] It was made with grapes, spread in the sun until they were reduced in weight to one-half. The pips, thus dried, were then put into a butt containing some excellent wort. When they were well soaked, they were crushed with the feet, and then subjected to a slight pressure in the wine-press. Sometimes they simply plunged the fresh grapes into boiling oil, instead of exposing them to the sun, and the result was the same.[121]

The *Dulce* wine was obtained by drying the grapes in the sun for three days, and crushing them with the feet on the fourth, at the time of the greatest heat.[122] The Emperor Commodus thought this a most delectable drink.[123]

The *Mulsum,* or honeyed wine, was an exquisite mixture of old Falernian wine and new honey, from the Mount Hymettus.[124] The physician, Cœlius Aurelianus, recommends the holding of warm mulsum in the mouth as a palliative in cases of violent head-ache.[125]

The name of *Anisites* wine was given to that in which some grains of aniseed had been infused.[126]

The *Granatum* was prepared by throwing thirty broken pomegranates into a pipe of wine, and pouring over them ten pints and a-half of a different wine, hard and sour. This drink was fit for use at the end of thirty days.[127]

Apicius gives us the recipe for the *Rosatum :—*" Put," syas he, " some rose leaves into a clean linen cloth ; sew it up, and leave it seven days in the wine ; take out the roses, and put in fresh ones ; repeat the operation three times, and then strain the wine. Add some honey at the time of drinking. The roses must be fresh, and free from dew."[128]

The *Violatum* is made in the same manner, only violets are used instead of roses.[129]

Rosatum may also be obtained without roses, by putting a small basket filled with green lemon leaves into a barrel of new wine before the fermentation has taken place, and leaving them there for forty days. This wine is to be mixed with honey before it is drunk.[130]

Myrrh wine—*Myrrhinum,* among the ancients—was wine mixed with a little myrrh, to render it better and make it keep longer. They thought much of it.[131]

All these wines, like those previously mentioned, were strained through the *colum vinarium* before they were served to the guests. This strainer was composed of two round, deep dishes, of four inches in diameter. The upper part was pierced, and received the wine, which ran into the lower recipient, whence the cups were filled.[132]

In Rome the price of common wine—sometimes adulterated [133]—was 300 sesterces for 40 urns, or 15 sesterces for an amphora ; that is to say, about sixpence per gallon.[134] At Athens it was thought dear when it cost fourpence per gallon. This measure was commonly sold for not more than twopence.[135]

In the early days of the Roman republic women were forbidden to drink wine;[136] but that law fell into disuse, and noble matrons often carried intemperance as far as their toping husbands.

LIQUEUR WINE.

It must be owned that the Roman law was, for a long time, tyrannical in the extreme with regard to women. Totally interdict the use of wine! Kill the unfortunate creatures who were unable to resist the seductions of that dangerous liquor! For the Roman history furnishes us with more than one example of that atrocious chastisement inflicted on the guilty thirst of the fair sex. The barbarous Micennius immolated his wife on the butt, at which he caught her one day, quenching her thirst at the tap or the bunghole. The ferocious Romulus thought this act simple and natural: he did not even reprimand the cruel husband.[137]

Another unfortunate creature discovered the place where her husband kept the keys of the cellar. She took them, and had the imprudent curiosity to go and visit the mysterious and inauspicious treasure, to which she was forbidden all access. Her family perceived this innocent larceny, and refused her every kind of food, to punish her for an imaginary crime. She died in the tortures of hunger.[138]

Is it necessary to speak of C. Domitius, that uncourteous judge, who deprived a lady of her marriage portion because she had taken the liberty to drink a spoonful or two of wine unknown to her lord and master?[139] But, let us say it at once—Roman civilisation put an end to such strange manners; and so early as the age of Augustus, Livia, the consort of that emperor, affirmed, when eighty-two years old, that she was indebted to Bacchus for her long existence.[140] Let us remark, by the way, that the great prince, her husband, honoured the labours of the vine-dresser and the serious study of wines,[141] to which little attention had been paid down to his time. It began then to be understood that this grateful drink draws the ties of friendship closer,[142] and all honest people, all generous souls, were eager to taste it.

The good Trajan quaffed off numberless cups every day: of course he became the idol of the human species.[143] Agricola wished to drink before he died.[144] The imbecile Claudius often found some ray of wisdom at the bottom of an amphora.[145] Domitian merited the pardon of his crimes, thanks to the streams of wine which during the night ran from the fountains;[146] and Caligula would, perhaps, have obtained that popularity which always failed him, had he possessed sufficient sense to offer to the Roman people the delicious Falernian wine he allotted to his favourite horse.[147]

The ladies ventured, in the first place, to wet their lips with a few drops of those light wines which the sun seemed to ripen for them at Tibur, in the environs of Cumæ, and throughout Campania.[148] After a short time, they braved the Falernian itself—true, they generally mixed it with iced water or snow;[149] but the boldest are reported to have risked that dangerous liquor without taking such timid precautions. Falernian was a noble wine! They began to drink it as soon as it had reached its tenth year. Then it was possible to bear up against it. When it was twenty years old, it could only be mastered after it was diluted with water. If older, it was unconquerable; it attacked the nerves, and caused excruciating headache.[150] The ladies struggled a long time for the victory; but, alas! the Falernian always had the best of it. Tired out, at length, with so many useless efforts, the wisest of them left it to their husbands, and sought other beverages which possessed less dangerous charms. Greece and Italy invented new drinks for them, which had a well-merited vogue, notwithstanding the discredit into which they have fallen for many centuries past. Our modern beauties would smile with an air of incredulity if we were to extol asparagus wine, winter savory wine, wild marjoram wine, parsley seed wine, or those made from mint, rue, pennyroyal, and wild thyme; and yet these liquors were the delectable drinks of the most distinguished women of ancient Rome, of those women who could never find in the culinary productions of the entire universe anything sufficiently delicate or rare. Are we, then, to blame their taste, or question our own?

Leaving aside this knotty question, which we do not feel ourselves called upon to resolve, let us state that these different drinks were prepared in a very simple manner. Two handfuls of one of the above-named plants were put into a butt of wort; a pint of sapa and half a pint of sea-water were added.[151] This wine was drunk by the Greek and Roman ladies at breakfast,[152] and was an excellent substitute for the *silatum*, a drink prepared with ochre, and which we can hardly believe to have been introduced by sensuality alone.[153]

It frequently happened, after a banquet, that the wearied and palled stomach refused with loathing the least nourishment. An intelligent slave failed not, under such circumstances, to present his languishing mistress with a cup of wormwood wine, before she quitted her couch. Anon, the livid paleness of her complexion brightened into the rosy hue of health, the dimmed eye resumed its wonted lustre, and that very evening the brilliant matron could seat herself fearlessly at a fresh banquet. That precious wine, that fashionable tonic, which modern sobriety—be it said to our praise—has rendered almost useless, sold well in Rome under the reigns of the Emperors. It was composed by boiling a pound of wormwood in 240 pints of wort until it was diminished one-third. There was also a more simple method of making it, which was to throw a few handfuls of wormwood into a butt of wine.[154]

The live wood, or the leaves of the cedar, the cypress, the laurel, the juniper-tree, or the turpentine-tree, boiled a long time in wort, produced different bitter liqueurs, to which intemperance complacently attributed benign qualities and numerous medical virtues.[155] Equal praise may be accorded to hyssop wine, that famous mixture of three ounces of the plant in twelve pints of wort.[156] Its effects were surprising, and the most popular physicians would not have failed to prescribe it for their languishing patients, whose strength and gaiety it restored.

But, thank Heaven! our Roman beauties were not always obliged to have recourse to the gloomy experience of the disciples of Æsculapius; and when they were in good health, more exhilirating liqueurs lent their aid to toast their return to health and pleasure. They were then seen sipping myrtle wine, a mild beverage, the light vapours of which brought down calm and profound sleep. It was wisdom to drink it; for, alas! not all that would, can sleep! If the reader be troubled with wakefulness, he will hail with joy the recipe for this beneficent narcotic. Let him take young myrtle branches with the leaves, pound them, and boil one pound in eighteen pints of white wine, until it is reduced to two-thirds.[157] Let him drink this liqueur of the Roman ladies, and, without doubt, he will sleep as they did.

The *petites maîtresses*, those delicate women, whose life seemed to be a tissue of vapours mingled with tears—Rome abounded with them— would have fainted even at the smell of the wines made up in the manner indicated above. Their frail, nervous organization, required a different kind of drink, and one was invented for them,—the *Adynamon*. This adynamon, or wine without strength, was the most inoffensive of liqueurs. It was obtained by boiling ten pints of water in twenty pints of white wort.[158] A small cup of this salutary beverage restored a debile Cynthia, a sickly Julia, when, negligently seated at her toilet, a Bœotian slave brought a nosegay of lilies instead of a crown of roses. These charming creatures would soon have lost the use of their senses, if the adynamon had not been promptly applied to their lips. But hardly had they tasted the marvellous liqueur when animation resumed its calm and peaceful course; nay, after the lapse of a few seconds, they were enabled, without any inconvenience whatever, to witness the chastisement of the slave, whose naked shoulders and breasts were lacerated by their orders with a thong studded with sharp points.[159] Who, after that, would dare doubt the properties of the adynamon wine?

The *Œnanthinum* wine was destined for more vigorous constitutions, for natures of less exquisite delicacy. The Roman ladies, somewhat fond of rusticating, who passed a part of the year in their villas, prepared it by putting two pounds of wild vine flowers into a butt of wort. They were left there thirty days, and then the liquor was drawn off into other vessels.[160]

Such were the vinous drinks which fashion formerly brought into repute in the capital of the world. The women set no bounds to their taste for these concocted wines; but went on from one excess to another as long as the empire lasted. These strange habits, now buried under the Roman colossus, have been replaced by a new order of civilisation. Woman, that graceful being of whom antiquity was not worthy, now appears such as Christianity has made her, to reveal to us virtues which ancient Greece and Italy never knew. Daughter, wife, and mother, she consoles, encourages, and supports man amid the trials of life. Her sweet smile welcomes him at the cradle; her prayer accompanies him to the tomb. It was she who softened the ferocious instincts of the barbarous hordes that the forests of the north vomited over Europe; and still exercising her empire over modern society, she is hailed as a queen, whose virtues and chaste attractions render her the living embodiment of the flower and the angel, those sweet symbols of love and beauty, between which a modern poet has gracefully placed her throne.

———•———

The primitive inhabitants of Great Britain learned from the Romans to plant the vine, under the reign of the Emperor Probus. The conquerors taught them also the art of cutting it, and how to make wine. But, as Strutt observes, the vine could never be of any great utility in this country. It was more ornamental than useful, with the exception that it afforded the means of procuring a cool retreat and shade.[161] However, some provinces of England became celebrated for their wines. "The county of Gloucester is renowned for its vines," says William of Malmesbury; "and the wines it produces are scarcely inferior to those of France."[162]

Saint-Louis was the first who established statutes for the dealers in wine.[163] New ones were framed in 1585,[164] and the dealers were then divided into four classes, each of which was designated by a particular name, viz., the inn-keepers, the publicans, the tavern-keepers, and the wine-dealers by measure. The inn-keepers had accommodation for man and horse; the publicans served drink with table-cloth and plates—that is to say, they might serve food and drink at the same time; the tavern-keepers served drink alone; and the retail dealers could only sell it in considerable quantities at one time.[165] In 1680 these four classes were reduced to two—wine-merchants and retail wine-dealers.

Under the reign of Louis XIV., a great dispute arose concerning the relative merits of Burgundy and Champagne wines, and the preference due to the one or the other. This quarrel originated in a thesis, maintained at the commencement of the 17th century at the Medical School of Paris, in which it was asserted, that the wine of Beaune, in Burgundy, was not only the most agreeable but the most wholesome. This thesis excited no murmur at the time: from the 13th century the wine of Beaune had always enjoyed the highest reputation, and no one dreamed of disputing it. But forty years later they risked a proposition much more rash than the preceding one: it was maintained, in the same school, that the wines of Burgundy were not only preferable to those of Champagne, but that the latter attack the nerves, cause a fermentation of the humours, and infallibly bring on the gout in persons not naturally subject to it. They fortified this incredible opinion with the authority of the celebrated Fagon, chief physician of Louis XIV., who had just forbidden the king, as they said, the use of Champagne wine.

The Champagne people took fire—it was time—the dangerous heresy threatened to spread; so they attacked the Burgundians bravely. The latter defended themselves with equal courage. The battle waxed warm. Each party sought to crush their antagonists with heavy writings. The inhabitants of Burgundy pretended that the wine of Champagne owed its vogue entirely to the influence of Colbert and Louvois, the then ministers, one of whom was a native of Champagne, and the other in possession of immense vineyards. The Champagne growers proved that this assertion was false in every particular. Long before the time of these two statesmen, said they, the French got tipsy on Champagne wine ; ergo, they valued that exhilirating liquor. This argument was irrefragable. They might have added that, from the 16th century, the wine of Aï, a canton of Champagne, enjoyed such renown that the Emperor Charles V., Pope Leo X., Henry VIII. of England, and Francis I. of France, were anxious to possess this nectar, and tradition assures us that each of these great sovereigns purchased a close at Aï, in which a little house was built for a vine-dresser, who sent them every year a stock of wine, which enlivened their repasts.[166]

The epicureans took part in this great discussion, and that they might give their judgment after mature deliberation, founded on a perfect knowledge of facts, they have been tasting Champagne and Burgundy wines these two hundred years. May the vouchers in this suit never fail them !

Wine was long used for presents and fees—a custom established under Charlemagne. After a baptism, a marriage, or a burial, the priests received the *vicar's wine;* before marriage, *wedding wine* was offered to the intended bride ; after a law-suit, the counsellor was presented with *clerk's wine;* the *wine of citizenship* was given to the mayor of a town in which any person took up his abode. This present subsequently took the name of *pot-de-vin* (bribe), still in great favour. It has changed its character, certainly, but the variations have multiplied to infinity.[167]

In the middle ages sober people intoxicated themselves regularly once a month. Arnaud de Villeneuve examines seriously the advantages of this Hygienic custom.[168] There was a kind of glory attached to the swallowing of more wine than any other man without being *non compos mentis*. There was, however, a means of avoiding these bacchanalian encounters. It was, to choose a champion who, as in judicial combats, accepted the challenges for his candidate, to whom the victory or defeat was attributed, as if he himself had drank.[169]

In the middle ages, and in the 16th century, intoxication was severely punished in France.

By five ordinances, in the years 802, 803, 810, 812, and 813, Charlemagne declares habitual drinkers unworthy of being heard before courts of justice in their own cause, or as witness for another.[170]

Francis I. decreed, by an edict, in the month of August, 1536, that whosoever should be found intoxicated was to be imprisoned on bread and water for the first offence ; the second time, flogging in the prison was added ; the third time, he was publicly flogged ; and if the offender was incorrigible, his ears were cut off, he was deemed infamous, and banished the kingdom.[171]

Now every one is free to quench his thirst, and drink more if he chooses.

"*The Crafte to make Ypocras.*—Take a quarte of red wine, an ounce of synamon, ane halfe an once (ounce) of gynger, a quarter of an unnce (ounce) of greynes and long pepper, and halfe a pound of suger, and brose all this (not too small), and then put them in a bage of wullen clothe, made therefore (for that purpose), with the wire, and it hange over a vessel tyll the wine be run thorowe (through)."[172]—Quoted by STRUTT.

The English were extremely partial to a drink they called *Clarey*, or *Clarre*.   According to Arnold [173] it was compounded in the following manner :—

"For eighteen gallons of good wyne, take halfe a pounde of ginger, quarter of a pound of long peper, an ounce of safron, a quarter of an ounce of coliaundyr, two ounces of calomole dromatycus, and the third part as much honey that is clarifyed as of youre wyne, streyne them through a cloth, and do it into a clene vessell."

John, in the first year of his reign, made a law that a tun of Rochelle wine should not be sold for more than twenty shillings, a tun of wine from Anjou for twenty-three shillings, and a tun of French wine for twenty-five shillings, except some that might be of the very best sort, which was allowed to be raised to twenty-six shillings and fourpence, but not for more, in any case.   By retail, a gallon of Rochelle wine was to be sold for fourpence, and a gallon of white wine for sixpence, and no dearer.[174]

XXIX.

REPASTS.

MORTALS were formerly remarkably sober, and the gods themselves set them the example, by feeding exclusively on ambrosia and nectar.[1] The most illustrious warriors in the Homeric ages were generally contented with a piece of roast beef; for a festival, or a wedding dinner, the frugal fare was a piece of roast beef; and the king-of kings, the pompous Agamemnon, offered no greater rarity to the august chiefs of Greece, assembled round his hospitable table. It is true that the guest to be most honoured received for his own share an entire fillet of beef.[2]

The vigorous but uncultivated appetites of these heroes were hardly satisfied when everything disappeared, and none of them thought to prolong the pleasures of good cheer.[3] Happy times of ingenuous and ignorant frugality! what has become of you?

It must not, however, be imagined that they were entirely destitute of more refined aliments. Homer gives to the Hellespont the epithet of *fishy;* Ithaca, and several other islands of Greece, abounded in excellent game;[4] but the magiric genius was asleep—it awoke at a later period.

Beware, however, of a mistake: those men —with so little choice respecting their viands—all possessed stomachs of astounding capacity.[5] Theagenes, an athlete of Thasos, eat a whole bull;[6] Milo of Crotona did the same thing—at least once.[7] Titormus had an ox served for supper, and when he rose from table, they say not a morsel remained.[8] Astydamas of Miletus, invited to supper by the Persian, Ariobarzanes, devoured a feast prepared for nine persons.[9] Cambis, King of Lydia, had such an unfortunate appetite, that one night the glutton devoured his wife![10] Thys, King of the Paphlagonians, was afflicted with voracity nearly similar.[11]   The Persian Cantibaris, eat so much and so long that his jaws were at last tired, and then attentive servants used to press the food into his mouth.[12]

These are facts of which we do not exactly guarantee the truth, for history—it is no secret—has some little resemblance to the microscope : it frequently magnifies objects by presenting them to us through its deceitful prism.

We close this singularly incomplete list of the ancient polyphagists by adding that the Pharsalians[13] and the Thessalians [14] were redoubtable eaters, and that the Egyptians consumed a prodigious quantity of bread.[15]

In more modern times, some men have acquired, by the energy of their hunger, an illustration they would have vainly demanded from their genius or their virtues.   The Emperor Claudius sat down to table at all hours and in any place.   One day, when he was dispensing justice according to his own fashion in the market-place of Augustus, his olfactory nerves scented the delicious odour of a feast which exhaled from one of the neighbouring temples.   It was the priests of Mars, who were merry-making at the expense of the good souls in the surrounding locality.   The glutton emperor immediately left his judgment-seat, and, without any further ceremony, went and asked them for a knife and fork.[16]   Never, no, never, adds the biographer of this prince, did he leave a repast until he was distended with food and soaked with drink, and then only to sleep.   Yes, the ignoble Cæsar slept ; but still, the " peacock's feather," an unseemly invention of Roman turpitude, was called into requisition to prepare the monarch for new excesses.[17]

Galba could taste nothing if he was not served with inconceivable profusion.   His stomach imposed limits upon him, but his eyes knew none ; and when he had gloated to his heart's content upon the magnificent spectacle of innumerable viands for which the universe had been ransacked, he would have the imperial dessert taken slowly round the table, and then heaped up to a prodigious height before the astonished guests.[18]

Vitellius, the boldest liver, perhaps, of the whole imperial crew, and the most active polyphagist of past times, caused himself to be invited the same day to several senatorial families.   This deplorable honour often caused their ruin, for each repast cost not less than 400,000 sesterces (£3,200).   The intrepid Vitellius was equal to the whole, thanks to the peacock's feather, which, doubtless, was cursed more than once by the unfortunate victims of his dreadful gluttony.[19]

True, this poor prince was continually tormented with a hunger that no aliment seemed capable of satisfying. In the sacrifices, like the Harpies of whom Virgil speaks,[20] he took the half-roasted viands from the altars, and disputed the sacred cakes with the gods. As he passed through the streets he seized the smoking-hot food spread out before the shops and public-houses; he did not even disdain the disgusting scraps that a miserable plebeian had gnawed the evening before, and which a hunger-stricken slave would have hardly contested with him.[21]

Such were the masters of the world, the proud Cæsars! before whom haughty Rome bowed the head and trembled, and from whom it basely implored a smile, up to that day when some soldiers, tired of their shameful obedience, kicked the imperial corpse into the Tiber, after having mutilated it in presence of the populace, who crowded joyously around the Gemoniæ.[22]

These terrific examples of insatiable voracity have become rare and obscure. A few isolated facts may perhaps be met with at very distant periods, which remind us of the polyphagic celebrities of Greece and Italy. There are, however, two which would have merited the attention of Vitellius himself.

The ingenuous Fuller[23] speaks of a man, named Nicholas Wood, to whom the county of Kent proudly claims the honour of having given birth, who once eat a whole sheep at one meal. One day three dozen of pigeons were placed before him, of which he left only the bones. Another day, being at Lord Wootton's, and having a good appetite, he devoured eighty-four rabbits and eighteen yards of black-pudding for his breakfast. We leave to Fuller the responsibility of the figures. Any how, the brave Nicholas Wood must have been a vigorous trencher-man!

The second ancedote is from Berchoux:—

Marshal Villars had a house-porter who was an enormous eater. "Franz," said he, one day, "tell me, now, how many loins you could eat?" "Ah! my lord, as for loins, not many: five or six at most." "And how many legs of mutton?" "Ah! as for legs of mutton, not many: seven or eight perhaps." "And fatted pullets?" "Ah! as for pullets, my lord, not many: not more than a dozen." "And pigeons?" "Ah! as for pigeons, not many: perhaps forty—fifty at most, according to the appetite." "And larks?" "Ah! as for that, my lord—little larks—for ever, my lord, for ever!"[24]

A truce to gluttons. Let us speak of epicureans.

It is to them that gastronomic civilization owes the laws by which it is regulated; they were the legislators of the table: they introduced regularity and order at repasts. The breakfast, dinner, collation, and supper were created by those sages. Fashion has often modified the nomenclature, but assuredly it will never be able to supersede it.

The Greeks submitted to it for many years;[25] and then, that fickle people, whom everything wearied, declined the drudgery of masticating so frequently. The lower orders and the army eat twice a day;[26] the fashionable people contented themselves with one repast,[27] which some had served at mid-day,[28] but the greater part just before sunset.[29] The party of resistance had, as yet, yielded only on one point—the collation; and they continued bravely to breakfast, dine, and sup.[30] But the monophagists were not sparing in their jokes, and the new fashion triumphed at last over the prescription of ancient usages.[31] Pagan sobriety was doubtless far from suspecting that the Book of Ecclesiastes, in accordance with it on this subject, pronounces an anathema against the kingdom whose princes eat in the morning.[32]

The Greek manners were introduced in Rome, and persons of a certain rank, who did not make a profession of gluttony, gave themselves up to the pleasures of the table only once a day.[33]

The tyranny of fashion was not, however, such that all persons thought themselves bound to obey it under pain of being shamed and ridiculed. Many unscrupulously transgressed its laws, and more than one respectable Greek of good family, following the example of Ulysses, who prepared his breakfast at sun-rise,[34] had the *acratism* brought so soon as the crowing of the cock announced the return of day.[35] This frugal breakfast was composed of bread steeped in pure wine.[36] The adults restricted themselves to this slight repast, but the children received more substantial nourishment.[37]

The Romans, when they were not asleep, breakfasted at three or four o'clock in the morning.[38] A little bread and cheese,[39] or dry fruits,[40] enabled them to wait for the solemn hour of the banquets.

It would appear that the Jews dined at mid-day;[41] it was the hour at which St. Peter was hungry.[42] This repast took place also among the Greeks about the middle of the day,[43] if we are to believe Athenæus.

However, Cicero relates that the philosopher Plato appeared to be very much astonished, when travelling in Italy, to see the inhabitants eat twice every day.[44] It will only be necessary to repeat that the supper alone formed the rule, and that the breakfast and dinner were exceptions; they depended entirely upon the casualties of will.

About mid-day[45] the sober Romans had a slight collation.[46] Seneca, who never loses sight of himself in his fastidious treatises on wisdom, informs us that a little bread and a few figs were all that his virtue required.[47]

The senators, the knights, and the luxurious freed-men, spared no expense either for dinner or supper. The priests of Mars, of whom we have already spoken, set them an example too seductive for them not to follow it.[48] It is to be remarked, by the way, that those worthy ministers of the god of war took this repast in the most secret part of their temple, where they hardly allowed any one to come and interrupt them. This gastronomic quietude was also very much the taste of a celebrated modern sailor, the Bailiff de Suffrein. He was at dinner in Achem, India, when a deputation from the town was announced. Being a witty glutton, he conceived the happy thought of sending word to the importunate troop that an article of the Christian religion expressly prohibited every Christian from occupying himself with anything besides eating, that function being of the most serious importance. This reply singularly edified the deputation, who retired with respect, admiring the extreme devotion of the French general.[49]

The collation—*merenda*—was little in use. It took place about the end of the day, before supper, particularly in summer, among the workmen and farm labourers.[50]

We now come to the principal repast, to that which threw such brilliancy over the latter centuries of Rome, when a culinary monomania, a sort of gastronomic furor, seemed to have seized the sovereign people, who, no longer great by their conquests, betrayed a desire to become so by the number and audacity of their follies.

The Hebrews supped at the ninth hour, that is to say, about three o'clock in the afternoon.[51] Their custom of two repasts would be sufficiently proved by the fact that, on fast days, they took food only in the evening.[52] Hence, when they did not fast, they also eat at another hour. Their ordinary aliment was very simple; we shall have to speak of it hereafter.

In the primitive times, kings prepared their own suppers.[53]   Beef, mutton, goat's flesh—such were the viands which then satisfied the daintiest palates.[54]   Baskets, filled with pure wheaten bread, were carried round to the guests,[55] and heaps of salt, placed on the table, gave proof of the hospitality of those simple and unsophisticated ages.[56]

The fierce warriors of that warlike period never forgot to invoke the gods before they satisfied their appetites: libations of wine rendered them favourable.[57]   This pious duty once fulfilled, they gave themselves up without restraint, to the joys of good cheer; and the sounds of the lyre and the buffooneries of mountebanks enlivened the banquet,[58] which again received fresh animation from the copious healths, which persons the least versed in the forms of society never forgot.[59]

It often happened that each one paid his share, or brought provisions with him[60] to these joyous suppers, of which the last rays of the setting sun always gave the periodical signal.[61]   The uncertainty of these amicable meetings constituted their charm.   Pic-nics, as we see, may be traced rather far back.

It was then that pleasure presided at those repasts; dulness had its turn when luxury proscribed the supper in open air, and in common,[62] after the manner of the Jews, who assembled in gardens, or under trees,[63] and mingled the sweet harmony of music with the less delicate seductions of their banquets.[64]

The breakfast has always taken place after rising; dinner in the middle of the day; the collation in the course of the afternoon; and the supper in the evening.   In the 14th century, people dined at ten o'clock in the morning.[65]   One or two centuries later, they dined at eleven o'clock. In the 16th century, and at the commencement of the 17th, they dined at mid-day in the best houses.   Louis XIV., himself, always sat down to table at that hour.[66]   This order was not modified until the 18th century.

The Sicilian cooks taught unheard-of refinements, and were sought after with strange eagerness.[67]   The chine of beef and haunch of mutton of the Homeric epoch, gave way to sumptuous banquets, and a learned prodigality divided them into two or three acts, or courses,[68] the order and luxurious majesty of which have been adopted in modern times.

It appears that three or four o'clock in the afternoon—the ninth hour— was the time invariably fixed for the supper of the Romans.[69]   Like the

Greeks of yore, they contented themselves at first with simple aliments, and few in number; subsequently, three courses, sometimes seven,[70] or even many more, appeared to them to be hardly sufficient to satisfy the ardent voracity of their eyes, and glut stomachs which odious precautions assimilated to the buckets of Danaus's daughters.

These suppers, the details of which always appear to us as bearing the impress of exaggeration, notwithstanding the authority of the writers who furnish them, were insufficient for certain prodigies of extravagance and furious gluttony, who were served at midnight with a sort of "wake" (*comissatio*),[71] at which some of them gave proof of renewed greed and vigour.

Vitellius was renowned for this kind of nocturnal debauchery;[72] others shone in the second rank, but no one equalled that monarch-cook, who made the empire a market, and his shameful reign an unceasing banquet.

Sensual enjoyments, and every variety of barbarity that follows in their train, were carried to the highest pitch. There was something vast and monstrous, of which nothing can give us an idea, in the eclipse of mind, and the depravity of their hearts. All that force of intelligence and will which, under the influence of Christian spiritualism, has revealed itself in modern times by so many chivalric inspirations, so many moral institutions, so many scientific discoveries, so many industrial works, then ingulfed in the senses, was taxed solely for their gratification. The sensual organization of man had acquired a development apparently as vast as that of intelligence, because intelligence had become the handmaid of the senses: hence those colossal proportions in the tastes, the banquets, the pleasures of the ancients, when compared with ours, which make us regard them as an extinct race of giants, if we consider them in a sensual point of view; and as a race of pygmies, if we measure them by that power of ideas—that metaphysical and moral elevation—to which we have attained, and which would make a child of our days the catechist of all the philosophers of antiquity.[73]

Down to the time of the conquest of the north of Europe by the Romans, the food was very simple. Chopped herbs boiled in cauldrons, served in wooden bowls on the hide of an ox, spread on the ground, in the midst of the forest; balls composed of different kinds or flour, and some strips of meat grilled on the embers—such was the food of our forefathers.[74]

w

The table at which the Anglo-Saxons took their repasts, was covered with a very clean cloth. Each one received a horn cup, which contained some kind of pottage, or ale—the beverage for which they had a predilection.[75] The plates with which Strutt has enriched his work give a satisfactory idea of the culinary intelligence of the nation. They had spits, knives, plates, and dishes in abundance. England was marching with giant strides towards civilization.[76]

The Anglo-Saxons were particularly fond of boiled meat. They cut up the animal they intended to cook, put the pieces into a cauldron, supported by a tripod, and then lighted a fire on the ground. They stirred their *ragoût* incessantly with a long two-pronged fork, which also served them to take out the meat when it was done.[77]

All the deplorable excesses of the Romans ought not to divert us from the fact, that religion and sound policy seem to have consecrated repasts in common, as one of the means best calculated to unite men more closely in the bonds of concord and friendship.[78] The Scriptures furnish us with the first examples. Among the Israelites, the banquets which followed the sacrifices always took place in an assembly of relations, neighbours, or friends.[79] They eat together and in public on wedding days and solemn festivals.[80]

The first Christians promptly adopted this custom: their love feasts— their *agapæ*—were served in the church, after the Communion. The rich contributed to them abundantly; the poor according to their means; and the indigent who presented themselves with nothing in their hands, were received and treated as brethren.[81] Admirable association of penury and opulence, which will never be replaced by the crude Utopias of modern philanthropy!

As an act of justice to Pagan legislators, we are compelled to say that sometimes they had excellent views, which go far to extenuate many of their aberrations. The laws of Minos prescribed to the Cretans the annual levy of an impost, the half of which was to be consecrated to the nourishment of the people. No one could eat alone; a certain number of families met together to take their repasts in common.[82] At Lacedæmon, each one brought his share of the provisions necessary for the supper of the whole;[83] or he sent at the commencement of the month to the steward of the common halls, wine, cheese, figs, a measure of flour, and a small sum of money to defray other expenses.[84] Friendship, sobriety, and concord presided. without exception, at these meetings.

Solon decreed that the Athenians should assemble at the Prytanea to eat together—sometimes one, sometimes another—at the public expense. Each was invited in his turn, and was expected to be there on the day named.[85] The Prytanea of Athens, Megaræ, Olympia, and Cyzica, contained a great number of porticoes, under which were the tables at which the citizens sat.

The founder of Rome also had the wisdom to ordain that, in certain cases, the inhabitants of the same ward should take their repasts in common, as a sign of peace and good feeling; nay, more: he decreed these suppers to be a part of the religious worship, and they were called " sacred banquets."[86]

Man abuses every thing. The Romans, tired of eating merely to support life, and disdaining, little by little, that austere sobriety which rendered them the masters of the world, gave themselves up at last to unbridled luxury, which appears to have redoubled during the war of Italy, and the civil wars of Marius, 83 B.C. Cornelius Sylla assumed the government, and one of the terrible dictator's laws (*Lex Cornelia*) renewed the ancient sumptuary regulations, and fixed the prices of provisions.[87] Julius Cæsar also made great efforts to oppose the redoubtable invasions of Roman gastronomy. That prince stationed guards in the markets, with orders to seize whatever they found there in contravention of the laws. If, through want of vigilance or fidelity, they allowed anything to escape, it was sure to be confiscated by more active agents, on the very tables, and in presence of the assembled guests.[88] Resistance only increased the evil. Augustus thought to render the laws more efficacious by modifying them. He permitted twelve persons to meet in honour of the twelve great gods, and to spend eight shillings in ordinary repasts; twelve shillings in the banquets of the calends, the ides, and the nones; and even two pounds on wedding days and the day following.[89]

Tiberius granted still more. Under his reign, a worthy citizen might spend for supper the sum of four pounds, without having to fear that any one would find fault with it.[90]

Caligula, Claudius, and Nero—doubtless better judges of liberty than their predecessors—allowed every one the right to ruin himself as joyously as he pleased. These good princes, so far from repressing the luxury of the table, strove to fortify it with the authority of their examples.[91]

Vitellius was by nature a non-reformer. That voracious Cæsar operated on a large scale; he spent in four months, for his suppers, a little more than five millions sterling.[92] A trifle for a Roman emperor! Did not the riches and labour of Europe, Asia, and Africa, form his civil list? It is quite true that out of this modest revenue he had to find corn to stop the cravings of the proletarians, and provide the games of the Circus, in order to amuse them in their dangerous idleness. But Vitellius, who had no other passion than that of good cheer, was royally equal to the task. And these things cause no surprise when we remember that a Roman general, Lucullus, spent not less than £1,000 to offer a little collation to two of his friends, who refused him the time he required to treat them in a less unceremonious manner.

We find in the history of " *Jack of Newbury*,"[93] instructions relative to the manner in which an English tradesman was to feed the persons in his employment in the 16th century, which would certainly not be very pleasing now to that useful and laborious class :—

" You feed your folks with the best of beef and the finest of wheat, which is an oversight; neither do I hear of any knight in this country that doth it, and, to say the truth, how were they able to bear that part which they do, if they saved it not by some means? Come thither, and I warrant you that you shall see brown bread upon the board; if it be of wheat and rye mingled together, it is a great matter, and bread most highly commended, but most commonly they eat barley bread, or rye mingled with peasen or such-like coarse grain, which is doubtless of small price, and there is no other bread allowed except it be at their own board; and in like manner for their meat, it is well known that necks and points of beef is their ordinary fare; which, because it is commonly lean, they seeth therewith now and then a piece of bacon or pork, whereby they make their pottage fat, and therewith drive out the rest with more content : and this you must do. And besides that, the midriffs of oxen, and the cheeks, the sheep's heads, and the gathers, which you give away at your gate, might serve them well enough; this would be a great spareing to your meat, and by this means you would save much money in the year, whereby you might better maintain your French hood and silk gown."

The following is the style of living at the court of the Dauphin of France in the 14th century :—

As in all well-regulated houses, there were five repasts, viz.: the

morning (except on fast days), the breakfast; the repast of ten o'clock,
—(*dix heures*, or the *décimheure;* by abbreviation *décimer*, and by a
second abbreviation, *diner*)—the dinner; the second dinner, the supper
(*souper*), at which they eat no more soup than we do; and lastly, the
night repast, which they called a collation.

As an every-day fare, the Dauphin took for his dinner a rice
pottage, with leeks or cabbage, a piece of beef, another of salt pork, a
dish of six hens or twelve pullets, divided in two, a piece of roast pork,
cheese, and fruit; at supper, a piece of roast beef, a dish of brains, neat's
feet, with vinegar, cheese and fruit. Other days, other dishes, which
were also pre-arranged with respect to kind and quantity. The barons
of the court had always the half of the quantity of the Dauphin; the
knights, the quarter; the equerries and chaplains, the eighth. The distributions of wine and bread were made in the same proportions; such a
rank, such weight, such measure; so that the young and delicate baroness
had four pots of wine, while the chorister and the chaplain had but one.[94]

We are indebted to the learned Monteil for the following details
relative to the public repasts of Louis XIV. :—[95]

The usher of the court, at the hour named, goes and knocks with
his wand at the door of the hall of the body-guard, and says: "Gentlemen, to the king's table!" a guard is dispatched, who follow him to
the goblet, where one of the officers for the service of the table takes the
nave. The guard accompany him, marching by his side, sword in hand.

Having arrived at the dining-room, the officers spread the cloth,
try the napkins, the fork, the spoon, the knife, and the tooth-picks;
that is to say, they touch them with a morsel of bread, which they
afterwards eat.

The usher returns again to the hall of the body-guard, knocks at
the door with his wand, and cries: "Gentlemen, the king's meat!"
Four guards then follow him to the ambry, where the equerry of the
household and the chief steward, or major-domo, test the dishes, by
dipping a piece of bread, which they eat. After this, the king's meat
is carried, the guards marching with their drawn swords on either side;
the chief steward, preceded by the usher, walking in front. When he
arrives near the table, he approaches the nave, and makes his obeisance
to it; and if the announcer, or any other person desire also to do it, he
may. The gentlemen-in-waiting place the dishes successively, and the
table being covered with them, the king then enters.

It is to be remarked, that it is always a prince or a great personage who presents the wet napkin to him with which to wash his hands, whereas it is a simple valet who presents him with the dry napkin to wipe them.

The king takes his seat.

The equerry-carver carves the viands.

The king serves himself on a plate of gold.

When he asks for drink, the cup-bearer calls aloud : " Drink for the king !" At the same time he makes his obeisance to him, goes to the buffet, takes two crystal decanters, one of which is filled with wine, and the other with water, returns to the king, makes another obeisance, removes the cover of the glass, and presents it to the king, who pours out wine and water according to his own pleasure.

During the dinner or supper of the king, a group of lordly courtiers stand behind his chair, and endeavour—though frequently in vain—to divert him, and make him laugh ; and another group, composed of ladies of the court, stand behind the queen's chair, who, on their part, try to amuse her, and excite a smile.

Whether the king eat in public or private, the table is always served in the same manner :—

AT DINNER.

TWO LARGE TERRINES OF SOUP.
TWO MIDDLING-SIZED ONES.
TWO SMALL ONES AS SIDE DISHES.

FIRST COURSE.	SECOND COURSE.
TWO LARGE DISHES.	TWO LARGE DISHES OF ROAST.
TWO MIDDLING-SIZED ONES.	TWO MORE, AS SIDE DISHES.
SIX SMALL ONES, AS SIDE DISHES.	

AT SUPPER.

The same number of dishes, only there is but three-fourths of the quantity of soup.

The king eats only with the royal family and princes of the blood.

Sometimes, however, the Pope's nuncio has the honour of sitting at his table, but always at the distance of four places.[96]

The luxury of the table was carried so far under Edward III. of England, that that prince was constrained, in the 17th year of his reign, to impose sumptuary laws on his subjects, forbidding the common people the indulgence of costly food and fine wines.[97]

The necessity for this measure is demonstrated by the fact, of which we read in the chronicles of Stow,[98] that, " at the marriage of Lionel, Duke of Clarence, the third son of Edward III., with Violentis, the daughter of Galeasius II., Duke of Milan, there was a rich feast, in which above *thirty* courses were served at the table, and the fragments that remained were more than sufficient to have served a thousand people."

The same chronicler also informs us that King Richard II. held the Christmas feasts in the great hall of Westminster in 1399, " and such numbers came, that every day there were slain twenty-six or twenty-eight oxen and three hundred sheep, besides fowls without number."[99]

Richard Nevil, Earl of Warwick, kept so good a table, that his guests often eat six fat oxen for their breakfast.[100] " In number of dishes and change of meate," says Holinshed,[101] " the nobilitie of Englande do most exceede, sith there is no daye in maner that passeth over their heades, wherein they have not onely beefe, mutton, veale, lambe, kidde, pork, conie, capon, pigge, or so many of these as the season yieldeth, but also some portion of the redde or fallow deere, beside great varietie of fishe and wilde fowle, and thereto sundrie other delicates, wherein the sweet hand of the portingale is not wanting "

So early as the 16th century the inhabitants of the City of London were remarkable for the astonishing profusion of their repasts, if we are to believe the poet Massinger—

> " Men may talk of country Christmas, and court gluttony,
>   Their thirty pounds for buttered eggs, their pies of carps' tongues,
>   Their pheasants drenched with ambergrise ; the carcases
>   Of three fat wethers bruised for gravy, to
>   Make sauce for a single peacock :—yet their feasts
>   Were fasts, compared with the City's."[102]

The description of one dish will enable us to judge of the others—

> " Three sucking pigs, served up in a dish,
>   Took from the sow as soon as she had farrowed,
>   A fortnight fed with dates and muskadine,*
>   That stood my master in twenty marks a piece ;
>   Besides the puddings in their bellies, made
>   Of I know not what."[103]

* A sort of wine, much esteemed.

Hang thyself, voluptuous Apicius! thou hast never dreamed of such delicate fare!

In the comedy of the " *Parson's Wedding*,"[104] the captain orders for his supper " chines fry'd and the salmon calver'd, a carp and black sauce, red deer in the blood, and an assembly of woodcocks and jack-snipes, so fat you would think they had their winding-sheets on; and upon these, as their pages, let me have wait your Sussex wheatear, with a feather in his cap; over all which let our countryman, general chine of beef, command. I hate your French pottage, that looks as if the cook-maid had more hand in it than the cook."

The luxurious munificence of Norman kings is almost as remarkable as that of the emperors of degenerate Rome.

William the Conqueror had himself crowned three times in the same year, and the banquets he gave on those occasions were such that they impoverished the kingdom.[105]

At the dinner given on the marriage of Richard, Earl of Cornwall, and brother of Henry III., with the daughter of Raymond, Earl of Provence, more than *thirty thousand* dishes were served on the table of the bride and bridegroom.[106]

In the year 1252, "John Mansel, the king's counsellor, gave a stately dinner to the kings of England and Scotland and their queens; there was also present Edward, the king's son, the Bishop of London, and many earls, barons, knights, and citizens; in short, so large was his company, that his house at Totehill could not contain them; therefore he set up tents and pavilions for their reception; *seven hundred* messes of meat was not sufficient to serve them for the first course."[107]

The following details, which we borrow from Monteil's excellent work,[108] give us some idea of the style of living in the mansions of France during the 14th century:—

"Whenever there is a dinner of ceremony, the clerks of the church are requested to bring holy water. The repast is commenced and concluded with fruit. The bread eaten is in loaves of nine ounces only. Every bason of meat is surrounded with sage, lavender, or other aromatic herbs; and on Sunday, or any holiday, negus is given. The sideboard, or buffet, is always in the middle of the room, covered with jugs and large drinking cups of gold and silver.

" The cellars, store-rooms, kneading troughs, dairies, and fruit-stores, 'are filled and emptied unceasingly—take who will, when he will, and as much as he will. Provisions of every kind are heaped up with a profusion that announces magnificence allied with riches.

"The great number of nobles, knights, huntsmen, falconers, pages, kitchen servants, butlers, bakers, the numerous valets, workmen, gardeners, harbingers, door-keepers, porters, and guards are not equal to the task of consuming so much. From all sides come relations, allies, neighbours, friends, pilgrims, and travellers, all of whom remain or depart at will, being feasted as if it were the morrow of a wedding, or a patronal festivity.

"The kitchen chimney-places are not less than twelve feet in width. One man would not have strength sufficient to use the tongs or the shovels. The andirons do not weigh less than a hundred pounds, the trivets forty pounds; copper saucepans of thirty pounds are common, and so are spits of eleven and twelve pounds. One roast is composed of one, two, or three calves, two, three, or four sheep, besides game, venison, and poultry. The boiling of the saucepans, the exhalations from the grease, render the atmosphere so fat, so thick, that it is only necessary to breathe in it to feed. A person would not dare enter one of those kitchens on the eve of a feast day, for fear, as it were, of breaking his fast.

" In the 16th century persons washed their hands at the commencement of a repast, and a second time when it was concluded. When the master of the house was particular on the point of civility, he had a bason sent round at this second ablution, filled with perfumed water.[109]

"When the person seated in the chief place was a guest of distinction, politeness made it indispensable to present him with water to rinse his mouth.[110]

" One of the most difficult points of French civility in the 16th century was to drink to a person's health, or return the compliment in a proper manner.[111] A guest at one end of the table held up his glass, and called out: 'Mr. Such-a-one, to your health!' He replied: 'I love it from you!'[112] During the whole of the repast, healths were bandied to and fro, in every sense. At the end they touched glasses together at a central point, which created a very singular kind of clash, and, at the same time, the arms underneath formed a sort of fasces of sleeves and cuffs."[113]

XXX.

VARIETY OF REPASTS.

The fertile country inhabited by the Jewish people furnished them with a very great variety of excellent provisions. Those of which they made the greatest consumption, and which we find generally mentioned in the Scriptures, are bread, flour, barley, beans, lentils, wine, raisins, figs, honey, butter, oil, sheep, oxen, fatted calves, &c.[1]

The fat of animals offered in sacrifice was reserved for the Lord;[2] but, with this exception, the Hebrews could freely make use of it. They esteemed it much, and when they wished to speak of a rich banquet, they called it "a banquet of fat animals."[3] "He that loveth wine and oil,"* says Solomon, "shall not be rich."[4]

The extreme simplicity of the greater part of the Biblical repasts ought not to induce us to suppose that the Jews were entire strangers to the inspirations of good cheer. "Solomon's provisions for one day were thirty measures of fine flour, and three score measures of meal, ten fat oxen, and twenty oxen out of the pastures, and an hundred sheep, besides harts, and roebucks, and fallow-deer, and fatted fowl."[5]

That primitive nation also knew different kinds of banquets, which, conformably with their *naïve* manners, were associated with the celebration of a religious solemnity, a sad or a joyful event, a family festivity or mourning, a victory or a public calamity.[6]

The Greeks and Romans, skilful masters in the art of good living, were early on the alert to assure the collection of all things necessary for the support of life. "Take care," said Aurelian to Flavius, "take care, above all things, that the markets of Rome be well supplied: nothing

* *Fat meat*, according to the vulgate.

more gay or more peaceful than the people, when they are well fed."[7] This remark is much more profound than it at first appears.

At Athens, special officers visited the markets, and only permitted each citizen to purchase and keep in his own house the quantity of provisions necessary for one year.[8]

The ediles of Rome performed nearly similar functions.[9] The prefect of the town was invested with the power of making regulations for the markets,[10] and the prefect of provisions had the inspection of the sale of bread meat, wine, fish, and all other kinds of aliment required either for the table of the rich or poor plebeian.[11]

During a long time, in Greece and Italy, the only charm of repasts was, that they furnished an opportunity for the exercise of those duties of kind hospitality, which Apollodorus has described in the following ingenuous style: "As soon as a friend," says he, "steps on the threshold of his host, the porter receives him with a smiling face; the dog of the house comes immediately to caress him, amicably wagging his tail; then some one runs and presents him a seat without being told."[12] This last trait is charming.

But afterwards, they thought much more of honouring the god of good cheer than Jupiter Hospes, and joyous Comus became everywhere the fashionable divinity. One of the ancients describes him in the following manner: "He is seen at the door of an apartment communicating with the banqueting hall; his smiling face is fresh, plump, and ruddy; his head is crowned with roses, and he sleeps standing; his left hand rests on a thyrsus, but sleep makes him loose his hold; he staggers, and the torch will soon fall from his grasp."[13]

The Greeks were fervent in their worship of this god, at an epoch when Rome still prided herself on her transcendant sobriety. Conon gave a banquet to all the Athenians after the battle of Cnidos, about four centuries before the Christian era; and his celebrated contemporary, the handsome Alcibiades, conqueror in the Olympic games, magnificently regaled the numerous spectators who had just applauded his triumph.[14]

The pagan temples themselves often rung with the sound of the music, the chaunts, and the dances which always accompanied the religious banquets. These feasts in honour of the immortals must have been rather unedifying to the truly faithful, for gaiety generally degenerated into extreme licentiousness.[15]

The conquest of Asia was fatal to the Romans. Their savage rudeness yielded to the effeminate manners of the vanquished; and henceforth, the epicureans of Italy studied but one thing—gastronomic delectation; had but one worship—that of the goddess Victua,[16] protectress of food, and sovereign of the table.

Luxury made appalling progress. Nearly a century B.C., the Romans did not blush to give 50 denarii (£1 16s.) for a young fatted peacock; 3 denarii at least (more than 2s.) for a thrush; [17] and, a century later, 4,000 sesterces (£36) were given for a couple of fine young pigeons.[18]

Worse followed!

Seneca describes in few words the luxury of the table among the voluptuous Romans:—" Behold," says he, " Nomentanus and Apicius, those happy conquerors of all that is delectable on earth or in the sea. Behold them at table, stretched on their couches, and contemplating innumerable viands. Harmonious songs flatter their ears, a variety of pleasing objects occupy their eyes, and the most exquisite savours captivate their insatiable palates."[19]

The genius of gluttony multiplied the banquets by prescribing luxurious gastronomic assemblages, sometimes in honour of the gods, and often for the gratification of simple mortals themselves.

Each year, at the ides of November, a repast was offered to Jupiter in the Capitol (cœna Capitolina). The statue of the god was present at the banquet, reclining on a magnificent couch, with Juno and Minerva seated on either side. These divinities were splendidly served, and, as they touched nothing, in the middle of the night the seven epulary priests joyously eat the supper of the three immortals.[20]

The cereal banquet (cœna Cerealis) was equally splendid, and Ceres maintained the same frugality.[21]

A sterile reminiscence of the equality which reigned among men in the golden age, placed the slaves at table by the side of their masters, during the celebration of the Saturnalia (cœna Saturnalis).[22] This usage was common to the Greeks and Romans.[23]

The ninth day of the August calends, and the thirteenth day of the November calends, a gastronomic solemnity—a monstrous gala—brought together the Roman pontiffs to celebrate the day of their inauguration (cœna pontificalis). This banquet was worthy of the proverbial delicacy of those sacred stomachs.[24]

The augurs treated themselves magnificently in their turn (*cæna auguralis*), when they entered on their functions. The pagan priests of Rome vied one with another in a noble emulation of exquisite refinement and ruinous viands;[25] but it is said that the ministers of Mars, who had the reputation of being arch-epicureans (*cæna saliaris*), always won the palm in this struggle of magnificence and voluptuousness.[26]

The day the Emperor took the title of Augustus, he gave a supper (*cæna imperatoria*) to the senators and magistrates. The tributes of a year were sometimes hardly sufficient to indemnify the grand master of these imperial orgies.[27]

The triumphal banquets (*cæna triumphalis*) were less elegant, no doubt, but they cost the victor who invited the people immense sums.[28] The guests crowded into the vast inclosure of the temple of Jupiter Capitolinus,[29] or the temple of Hercules.[30]

They sat down to table to celebrate the anniversary of a birth-day (*cæna natalitia*),[31] the happy wedding-day (*cæna nuptialis*),[32] the arrival of a friend (*cæna adventitia*),[33] the sad day of his departure (*cæna viatica*).[34] The melancholy ceremony of interment was followed by a supper (*cæna funebris*), at which the guests were the relations and friends of the deceased.[35] They drank to his manes, and, by degrees, the wine not only stifled their laments but called forth joyous smiles. The Romans have bequeathed to certain modern nations more than the remembrance of their funeral repasts.

In the palmy days of Athens, the Greeks evinced more of the epicurean than the glutton—a fact which may be inferred from the description of the supper of Dinias.[36] The most magnificent of their repasts was, perhaps, that which Alexander the Great had served to ten thousand guests, who received, each one, a present of a golden patera.[37]

In Greece, as in Rome, the greater part of the events of life occasioned the joyous meeting of relations and friends. At the birth of a child,[38] a banquet was given in his honour; he was named on the tenth day, and the ceremony terminated with a banquet,[39] in which they offered the guests cooked Cherso cheese, cabbage boiled in oil, pigeons, thrushes, fish, and brimming cups of excellent wine.[40] The teething repast took place when the child had attained his seventh month, and the weaning supper when he began to eat.[41]

These family feasts, more or less sumptuous according to the fortune and rank of the individuals who gave them, were generally signalized by a custom which ridiculous and egotistical vanity could alone authorise and maintain. On the banquet day care was taken to throw the feathers of the poultry before the door of the house, in order to excite the fruitless greed of the poor wretches, who, as they passed,[42] prayed heartily that the infernal divinities might take the proud amphitryon, his guests, and even the meanest of his servants.

In France, about 1350, the setier (about twelve English bushels) of—[43]

	£	s.	d.
Wheat was worth	0	0	7
Rye	0	0	3
Oats	0	0	2½
Beans	0	0	5
Peas	0	0	6
A Hogshead of Wine	0	4	7
A Load of Hay	0	1	10
An Ox	0	6	10
A Horse	0	11	6
A Calf	0	1	2
A Sheep	0	0	4
A Fat Pig	0	2	0
A Gosling	0	0	1
A Hen	0	0	0¾
100 Eggs	0	0	1½
1℔ of Butter	0	0	3½
1℔ of Honey	0	0	10½
1℔ of Wax	0	1	10

Prices of a few articles in France during the 15th century :[44]

	£	s.	d.
1℔ of Bread	0	0	0¼
1 Pint of Wine	0	0	0¼
1 Pint of Mustard	0	0	0¾
1 Bushel of Salt	0	0	2½
1℔ of Pepper	0	0	2
1℔ of Cinnamon	0	1	2
1℔ of Bacon	0	0	0¾
A Pair of Pigeons	0	0	1¼

	£	s.	d.
A Pair of Partridges	0	0	2½
A Cart-load of Wood (*une voie*)	0	0	8
A Sack of Charcoal	0	0	1
1℔ of Candles	0	0	0½

In England, under the reign of Edward III., a royal proclamation fixed the price of the following articles :—[45]

	£	s.	d.
A Swan	0	0	4
A Porcelle	0	0	8
An Ewe	0	0	6
A Capon	0	0	6
A Hen	0	0	4
A Pullet	0	0	2½
A Poucyn	0	0	2
A Coney	0	0	4
A Teal	0	0	2
A River Mallard	0	0	5
A Snipe	0	0	1
A Woodcock	0	0	3
A Partridge	0	0	5
A Plover	0	0	3
A Pheasant	0	1	4
Twelve Eggs	0	0	1
Twelve Small Birds	0	0	1

The funeral repast of Sir John Redstone, Mayor of London, who died in 1531, occasioned the following expenses :—

	£	s.	d.
Shipe Brede	0	7	5
7℔s of Sugar for the same	0	4	1
Two unces of Saffrun	0	2	0
Two unces of Clovys and Mace	0	1	8
Seven unces of Pepper	0	0	10½
Sixty Eggs	0	0	7½
Seven dysshes of Butter, at 4¼d. the gallone	0	3	3¾
Manchet Brede	0	1	0

	£	s.	d.
400 of Peers	0	2	4
1℔ of Bysketts	0	0	8

TO THE PYKE-MONGER.

Sixteen Pikes, at 1s. 4d. a piece	1	1	4
Eight roundes of Sturgeon	1	2	0

TO THE PULTER.

Six roundes of Brawne	0	11	8
Ten Swannes, at 6s. a-piece	3	0	0
Two dozen of Quayles	0	10	0
Three dozen of Rabetts	0	6	6
Twenty-two Capons	0	12	10
Nine dozen of Pygeons, at 10d. per dozen .	0	7	6
Four Gese	0	2	8
300 Eggs	0	3	9

TO THE BOWCHER.

A Surloyne of Beffe	0	2	4
Half a Vele (Calf)	0	2	8
Four Marybones	0	0	8

TO THE MYLKE-WYFFE.

Two Gallones and Six Dishes of Butter . .	0	4	2
Eight Gallones of Creme	0	4	0
Twelve Gallones of Curdde	0	1	6

TO THE BREWER.

Three Barrelles of Ale	0	11	0
A Kylderkyn of Bere	0	1	0
For Double Bere to the Tabull	0	0	4
Yest	0	0	4

TO THE VYNTENER.

Thirty two Gallones of Redde and Clarett Wyne, at 10d. per gallon	1	6	8
Three Gallones of Mackeray	0	0	4
A Rundlett of Muskadine	0	6	0

THE GROCER.

	£	s.	d.
Six unces of Pepper	0	0	9
Four unces of Clovys and Mace	0	2	4
Two unces of Saffrone	0	1	10
18℔ of Pruenes	0	3	0
8℔ of Corans	0	1	8
6℔ of Dates	0	2	0
1℔ of Byskettes	0	0	10
12℔ of Sugar	0	7	0
Five unces of Cynimion	0	1	3
Four unces of Gynger	0	0	6

THE BAKER.

	£	s.	d.
Four busshelles of Chete, at 1s. 10d. the busshelle	0	7	4
For Hot Brede	0	4	0
For Fyne Flour	0	0	11
For Basterde Flour	0	1	10

THE CHAUNDELER.

	£	s.	d.
A Peck and a-half of Salt	0	0	6
For Candelles	0	0	4
For Vennyger	0	0	4
For Vergeys	0	0	6
For Pack-threade and Mustarde	0	0	2
For Cappys (Capers)	0	0	2
For Lop of Pottes	0	0	8
For Hyer of Pottes	0	0	4

THE COOKE.

	£	s.	d.
For hys labor and companye for eighteen messes of meat	0	15	0
For Yerbys	0	0	8
A Quarter of a Hundred of Fagottes . . .	0	1	2
For Coles	0	1	6
Paide the turners of broches and skulyons, four of them	0	1	4

The following is a correct copy of a monster bill of fare, from a paper found in the Tower of London :—*

300 Quarters of Wheat.	200 Pheasants.
300 Tuns of Ale.	500 Partridges.
104 Tuns of Wine.	5000 Woodcocks.
One Pipe of Spiced Wine.	400 Plovers.
10 Fat Oxen.	100 Curlews.
6 Wild Bulls.	100 Quails.
300 Pigs.	1000 Eggets.
1004 Wethers.	200 Rees.
300 Hogs.	4000 Bucks, Does, and Roebucks
3000 Calves.	155 Hot Venison Pasties.
300 Capons.	4000 Cold Venison Pasties.
100 Peacocks.	1000 Dishes of Jellies.
200 Cranes.	2000 Hot Custards.
200 Kids.	4000 Cold Custards.
2000 Chickens.	400 Tarts.
4000 Pigeons.	300 Pikes.
4000 Rabbits.	300 Breams.
4000 Ducks.	8 Seals, and
204 Bitterns.	4 Porpoises.
400 Hernsies.	

At the feast, the Earl of Warwick was steward; the Earl of Bedford, treasurer; the Lord Hastings, comptroller, with many noble officers; servitors, 1000 ; cooks, 62 ; kitcheners and scullions, 515.

In France (14th and 15th centuries) the repasts were commonly divided into five parts, called courses, or dishes.[47]

The first course was composed of cherries, tender fruits, citrons, and salads.[48]

Milk-porridge, puddings, and pottages followed; it was the second course.[49]

The third consisted of roast, with various sauces.[50]

The second roast, or fourth course,[51] presented the guests with venison and game.

The fifth course took the name of fruit-course. At this they served tarts made with all sorts of herbs, flowers, grains, vegetables, and fruit.[52]

* Dinner given by the Earl of Warwick, at the installation of an Archbishop of York, in the year 1470.

Pl. 28.

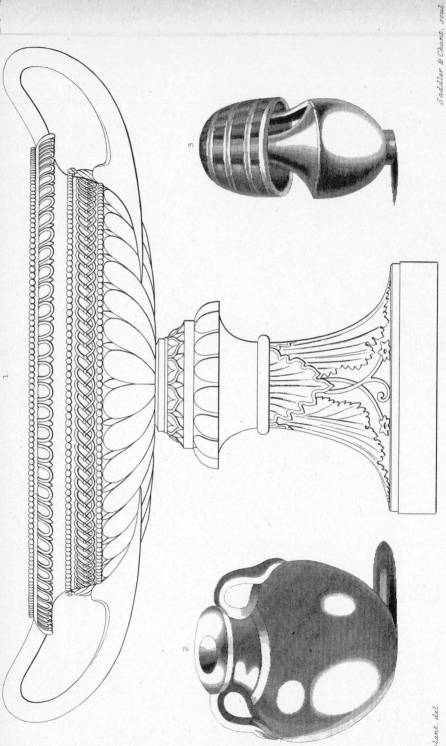

Saddler & Chant, sculp.

T. L. Volant, del.

XXXI.

THE DINING-ROOM.

THE *cœnaculum* (dining-room), properly so called, was the place in the upper part of the house where they eat.[1] It was reached by a staircase,[2] and thither persons repaired during the summer, particularly in the country. The Roman villas terminated by a platform, on which the Romans often collected at meal-time; the air was not so hot, and the panorama of the neighbouring country-seats was presented without obstruction, to the gaze of the guests.[3]

The dining-room was commonly decorated with fasces of arms and trophies,[4] which served as a momento of the warlike virtues of the ancestors of the master of the house. Enchanting frescoes stood out marvellously from the obscure shading of the wall, round which were twined fresh garlands of flowers; and a mosaic floor—master-piece of art and patience—harmonised with the fascinating landscape of the ceiling, the site of which varied with every course.[5]

The Emperor Nero, who carried this taste for the beautiful rather too far, devised a sort of vault, in the most elegant style, and entirely composed of movable leaves of ivory, which exhaled sweet

DESCRIPTION OF PLATE No. XXV.

No. 1. Large vase, or *cratère*: a vessel which was placed in the banqueting-room, and also on the empty space left on the tables. In it was put wine and water, which was taken out with a *simpulum*, a kind of small cup, fixed to a very long handle, bent at the extremity as a hook, to fill the cups of the guests. When the *cratères* were not fixed on tripods (*engytheca*, or *angotheca*), which supported them, they only differed from the cups by their size. Some were of such dimensions that Herodotus speaks of two *cratères*, one containing 300 amphoræ, and the other 600; these vases commonly exceeded ten-fold the size of the cups, to which they were very similar in shape and handles.

No. 2. A glass vase, with two handles, for iced water.

No. 3. Glass bottle. with its cup, placed on the table for each guest.

perfumes, and whence flowers fell on the guests. In another of his dining-rooms admiration was excited by a magnificent dome, the rotary movement of which imitated, day and night, the course of the celestial bodies.[6] These prodigies of ancient mechanism adorned the palace that the prodigal Cæsar called "the gilded house."[7] The colossal statue of that prince rose in the middle of the hall: it was 120 feet high![8]

Studious people, or those who wished to appear so, covered some part of the dining-room with books; for it was a custom introduced into Rome to have recitations or readings during the repast.[9] Atticus had always a reader;[10] and Juvenal promises the friend he invites to supper that he shall hear some fragments from Virgil and Homer.[11]

The Greeks yielded willingly to this intellectual pastime at the commencement of the banquet, whilst incense and other perfumes filled the room with a light vapour.[12]

Opposite the entrance-door stood a buffet, sometimes of iron, but more generally among the Greeks of sculptured wood, bronze, or silver, on which were represented the heads of oxen or satyrs.[13] This piece of furniture was placed under the protection of Mercury, and a curtain commonly veiled the front of it. It served for the display of precious plate—vases of silver, silver-gilt, and gold, enriched with magnificent precious stones.[14]

The buffet of the Romans,—a sort of sideboard, of rare workmanship,—was appropriated to the same use.[15] Sometimes a single foot supported a white marble table, surrounded with a border of *vert-antique,* and plates and dishes were arranged on two elegant shelves placed above.[16] Again, the artist frequently conceived the idea of giving a whimsical form to the buffet, which enhanced its price—it was a ship laden with the vases necessary for the banquet; four enormous amphoræ occupied the deck, on the two sides of the mast; towards the prow was a candelabrum, and at the stern was displayed a large-bellied cantharus, or vase, with mobile handles;[17] the main-topmast

DESCRIPTION OF PLATE No. XXVI.

No. 1.   A glass vase, with two handles.
No. 2.   A glass vase, with three handles.
No. 3.   Etruscan vase, with three handles, terra cotta.
No. 4.   A large silver vase, to hold wine and water; when placed on the table, the liquor was taken out with a simpulum, to fill the drinking cups.
No. 5.   A large-bellied cantharus—"*Herculaneum.*"

Pl. 30.

F. T. Z. Volant, del.

Saddler & Chant, scul.

Pl. 21.

1.

2.

3.

F. T. Z. Volant, del.

Chant & Saddler, scul.

was replaced by a large urn, and two cups of Bacchus were gracefully balanced at either extremity of the yard,[18] along which were suspended craters, or vases, used in drinking wine.[19]

The buffet of the Greeks and Romans survived the ruins of those two celebrated nations; we find it again in the middle ages, and even in more modern times. Then also, rich people loved to display their plate on a very apparent piece of furniture, which, being dressed, took the name of "dresser." Monstrelet, describing the magnificence of the Duke of Burgundy during his sojourn in Paris, relates: " that in the room of his mansion in which he eat was a square dresser (dressoir) with shelves, which dresser was covered and loaded with very rich gold and silver plate." [20]

Sovereigns who affected great munificence had buffets of metal; there were three—one for silver, one for silver-gilt, and one for gold. At the banquet which the King of France, Charles V., gave to the Emperor Charles IV., his uncle, each of the three buffets was of the same metal as the plate it supported.[21]

After the birth of a child, ladies, when they received visits, had a dresser placed in their room. Those of countesses and great ladies had three shelves; those of the wives of the younger sons of baronets had two; women well-connected but not titled could have no shelf. Those who enjoyed the honours of the court placed by the side of the buffet a little table, covered with a white cloth, destined for the hippocrass and spiced wine they offered their visitors,[22] and which they drank in hanaps, or a kind of chalice of earthenware, gold, or silver. Those of crystal were much esteemed. Charles the Bald gave to the Abbey of St· Denis a hanap, said to have belonged to Solomon. "It was of pure gold, fine emeralds, fine garnets, and the work so marvellous that in all the kingdoms of the world never was there anything so perfect." [23]

The great lords also indulged in metal dressers,[24] to which the 16th century gave the name of " buffets " Under Henry II. of France the court called them crédence, from an Italian word bearing the same meaning,[25] and which they have retained.

The Hebrews probably knew nothing of chimneys. When King Jehoiakim burned the book which Jeremiah had written, " he sat in the winter-house in the ninth month: and there was a fire on the hearth burning before him." [26]

When, among the Greeks or Romans, they wanted to warm the

dining-room, they also had recourse to braziers or bronze furnaces of the dimension of a middling-sized table, resting on lion's claws. Foliage in copper, bronze, and silver, was artistically incrusted round the edge. The bottom was a very thick iron grating. Above and beneath, brick-work prevented the coal from touching the upper part, or escaping through the interstices.[27]

They also made use of two kinds of stoves to warm the dining-room—the one was concealed under ground in the massive wall, and little pipes extended from its orifice to the apartment; the other, portative and light, disappeared whenever it was judged expedient.[28]

Among the pagans, the dining-room was lighted by torches made of a resinous wood,[29] or tallow candles.[30] The rich had lamps, candelabra,[31] or magnificent lustres suspended from the ceiling.[32] They even knew the luxury of wax candles.[33]

In the middle ages, the sovereigns and the great lords had, in the middle of their dining-rooms, fountains playing, which poured fourth wine, hippocrass, and other liquors. Some gave rose-water and divers odoriferous liquids to perfume the banqueting-hall.

Rubruquis found in Tartary a Parisian goldsmith, Guillaume Boucher, who had settled under the sway of the Khan, and had made him one of those fountains.

DESCRIPTION OF PLATE No. XXVI A.

THE DUKE OF BRUNSWICK'S VASE.—This is one of the finest monuments we have yet seen, which has reference to the mysteries and sacrifices of Ceres and Bacchus. It is a precious vase, made of one single piece of onyx, from the cabinet of the Duke of Brunswick, and of the size represented in the engraving. It was published, and learnedly explained, in 1682, by Jean Henry Eggeling, and printed in the same year. This vase is of a singular form; has one handle, and on the other side a spout, which begins at the bottom, and finishes by a bend towards the top, to pour out the liquor. Eggeling believes that this vase is of the number of those the ancients called *guttus*, because the liquor came out drop by drop: he comes to that conclusion from a passage of Varro—"*Quo vinum dabant, ut minutatim funderent, a guttis guttum appellarunt.*" The vase is divided in three parts by two bands of gold, by which it is girdled: that of the middle, which forms the largest space, contains also a larger number of figures. The third diminishes towards the foot, and has figures also, all of which represent the mysteries and sacrifices of Ceres and Bacchus.

The reader will probably feel interested how this vase came into the possession of the Duke of Brunswick. It was in the cabinet of the Duke of Mantua. When that city was taken and sacked, in 1629, a soldier, who had possession of the vase, offered it to Francis Albert, Duke of Lower Saxony, his commander, who gave him a hundred ducats as a reward. This prince left it by will to the Princess Christina Marguerite of Mecklenburg, his wife, who left it in the same way to her sister, the Princess Sophia, Duchess of Brunswick. She also gave it by will to her son, Ferdinand Albert, Duke of Brunswick. The lapidaries thought so much of it, that they offered, in turn, from sixty to ninety thousand imperials. In the inventory of the Princess Sophia it was valued at one hundred and fifty thousand imperials.*

*Imperial, a gold coin, current in Russia. The imperial of ten roubles (1755) was worth nearly £2 2s. 0d.

Pl. 26 b.

DUKE OF BRUNSWICK'S VASE.

The municipal bodies adopted them. At the entrance of Charles VII. into Paris, one of this kind was seen in the Rue St. Denis:—" One of the tubes spouted milk, another vermilion-coloured wine, another white wine, and another pure water; and persons stood all round with silver cups to give drink to the passers-by."

In the 17th century playing fountains were still used at repasts.[54]

THE TABLE.

It is pretended, says Athenæus, that in the Homeric times each guest had a table to himself,[1] on which he was served with " a saddle-back of beef, or a whole sheep or goat." It was the custom among the heroes, all men of high lineage, and tolerably aristrocatic in their tastes. The burghers of those warlike times and the villeins of the epoch eat their dinner, without form or ceremony, on a heap of grass, which also served them as a seat or couch.[2]

Wooden tables—at first very clumsy ones, no doubt—only came into use when the development of human industry had enabled men to understand that they might be preferable to a truss of hay.[3] A passage in Homer would seem to show that they were very much like ours.[4] Perhaps the circular form was generally preferred.[5]

Luxury soon called for the most precious materials, and the Greeks had, at a very early period, tables of bronze,[6] and even of fine silver.[7] The isle of Rhenea produced magnificent ones,[8] and an expensive fashion caused those luxurious pieces of furniture to be prized when they pre sented delicate incrustations of silver, bronze, or ivory, and rested on lions' claws or leopards' feet.[9]

Cneus Manlius introduced these rarities into Rome after the conquest of Asia.[10] He was also the originator of tables veneered with plates of gold,[11] which ere long adorned the dining-rooms of princes and senators, and the excessive price of which was only surpassed by that of tables made of precious woods from distant countries.[12] The maple, the whitten, and a species of African lemon-tree occupied the first rank,[13] and the prodigious skill of the workmen gave them a value superior to gold and silver.[14]

The most beautiful of these tables were spotted or veined to imitate the tiger's or panther's skin; but they acquired an exorbitant claim upon the admiration of connoisseurs when they bore the marvellous design of a peacock's tail. This fantastic play of nature commanded a boundless price.[15]

An artist of unrivalled talent, Carvilius Pollio, was the first, according to Pliny,[16] who enriched these magnificent woods with buhl-work of ivory and shell in the acme of perfection.[17] Under the reign of Nero, the Romans dyed this shell, and thought to increase its primitive value by giving it the tints and accidental shades of the cedar, the maple, and the lemon tree.[18]

These splendid pieces of furniture were at first square;[19] then round;[20] then in the form of a half-circle or half-moon, and this horse-shoe-shaped table they called a *sigma*, from the name of that Greek letter, which resembled our C.[21] The guests whom any person wished to honour most were placed at the extremities of this hemicycle,[22] overlaid with magnificent covers, which replaced the skins of beasts, formerly used for their adornment; and, in addition, they were spread with tissues of fine linen and rich stuffs elaborately worked.[23]

The tables were changed at each course.[24] The Greeks cleaned them with sponge;[25] the Latins used a sort of thick, plushed, linen cloth.[26]

The opulent citizens possessed a great number of tables; some were of ivory,[27] others of maple wood, cedar of Mount Atlas,[28] or lemon.[29]* Cicero had one of this latter kind of wood which cost him 200,000 sesterces—about £1,480.[30] They rested on one, two, or three feet,[31] and were called monopedes, bipedes, and tripedes.

The Romans often changed tables only twice during the repast. Fish and flesh appeared on the first, and the fruit was served on the second.[32] The same custom was common to the Greeks and the oriental nations. The Hebrews had also two tables in their solemn feasts and sacrificial banquets; on one was served the flesh of the victim, and on the other they placed the cup of benediction, which passed round from one to another, and was called " the cup of praise.[33]

The luxury of Rome seemed to revive after she had become extinct.

---

* This lemon-tree wood was a species more precious and more beautiful than that which we now possess.

Saint Rémi, Bishop of Rheims, left to his heirs a silver table, embellished with figures.[34]   Charlemagne had three made of the same metal—the first represented the ancient capital of the world; the second, Constantinople; the third, every known region of the earth.[35]   Aymar, Viscount of Limoges, found on his estate a treasure, which consisted of a table, round which were seated an emperor, his wife, and several children—all as large as life, and of massive gold.   Richard Cœur-de-Lion pretended that the treasure belonged to him as Lord of Limousin, and went to lay siege to the castle of Chalons, to which Aymar had retired, where the king received a wound, of which he died the 6th of April, 1199.[36]

Silver tables still existed in the 17th century.   Madame de Sévigné (1689), speaking of persons who, following the example of Louis XIV., sent their plate to the mint, says : " Madame de Chaulnes has sent her table, two *guéridons*, and her beautiful toilet of silver gilt."

At some distance from the sigma, on a slightly raised platform, were three kinds of elegant *crédences* for the cups, wines, and vases.[37]   The major-domo himself generally attended to this part of the service.

A very curious old book, cited by Strutt, " *The Booke of Ker-vynge*,"[38] contains the following instructions as to the manner of laying the cloth for the King of England :—

" Serve your Soverayne with wafers and ypocras.   Also loke your composte be fayre and clene, and your ale fyve dayes olde before men drynke it, and be curtays of answere to eche persone ; and whan ye laye the clothe, wype the borde clene with a cloute (*cloth*); then lay a couch (*cloth*), take your feluwe, that one ende, and holde you the other ende, then drawe the clothe straught, the bought on the utter edge, take the utter parte and hange it even, then take the thyrde clothe, and laye it bought on the inner edge, and laye estat with the upper parte halfe a fote brode, then cover thy cupborde and thyne ewery with the towel of dyaper ; than take thy towell about thy necke, and laye that on syde of the towel upon thy lefte arme, and thereon laye your soveraynes napkyn, and on thyn arme seven loves of brede, with thre or foure trenchour loves, with the ende of the towel, in the lefte hande as the maner is ; then take thy salte seller in thy lefte hande, and take the ende of the

DESCRIPTION OF PLATE No. XXVII.

No. 1.   Etruscan flat vase, of terra cotta, with a cover, to hold a particular drink (warm, perhaps).
No 2.   A marble vase, ornamented, for water.
No. 3.   A metal vase, to fill the cups of the guests.
No. 4.   A Greek Etruscan drinking vase, of terra cotta, in form of a seated Bacchanal.—" *Hercul.*"

Pl. 30.

towell in your ryght hand, to bear in spones and knyves; than set your salte on the ryght syde, where your soverayne shall sytte, and on the lefte syde the salte set your trenchoures; than laye your knyves, and set your brede one lofe by another; your spones, and your napkyns, fayre folder besyde your brede, than over your brede, and trenchours, spones, and knyves, and at every ende of the table set a salte seller, with two trenchour loves, and yf ye wyll wrappe youre soverayne's brede stately, ye must square and proporcyon your brede, and see that no lofe be more than another; and than shall ye make your wrapper manerly; than take a towell of reynes, of two yerdes and an halfe, and take the towell by the endes double, and laye it on the table; than take the ende of the bought a handfull in your hande, and wrape it harde, and laye the ende so wrapped betwene two towells, upon that ende so wrapped laye your brede, bottom to bottom, syx or seven loves; than set your brede manerly in fourm, and whan your soverayne's table is thus arrayed, cover all other bordes with salt, trenchours, and cuppes; and se thyn every be arrayed with basyns and ewers, and water, hote and colde; and se ye have napkins, cuppes and spones; and se your pottes for wyne and ale be made clene, and to the surnape make curtesy, with a clothe, under a fayre double napry; than take the towelle's ende next you, and the utter ende of the clothe, on the utter syde of the table, and holde these three endes at ones, and folde them at ones, that a plyte passe not a fote brode; than laye it as it should lye: and after mete wasshe with that, that is at the ryghte ende of the table, ye must guyde it out, and the marshall must convey it; and loke on eche clothe, the ryghte syde be outwarde, and draw it streygthe; than must ye reyse the upper parte of the towell, and laye it without ony grouyng, and at every ende of the towell, ye must convey halfe a yarde that the sewer may make reverently and let it be. And whan your soverayne hath washen, drawe the surnape even; than bere the surnape to the myddes of the borde, and take it up before your soverayne, and bere it into the ewery agayne; and whan your soverayne is set, loke your towell be aboute your necke; then make your soverayne curtesy; than uncover your brede, and set it by the salt, and laye your napkyn, knyfe, and spone, afore hym; than knele on your knee till the purpayne passe eyght loves; and loke ye set at your endes of the table foure loves at a messe; and se that every persone have napkyn and spone, and wayte well to the server, how many dysshes be covered, that so many cuppes cover ye; than serve ye forth the table manerly, that every man may speke your curtesy."

THE TABLE SEATS.

The Jews originally sat down to their meals; but when they became subject to Persia they laid on couches at their repasts, like their conquerors, and other oriental nations, from whom the Greeks and Romans borrowed their custom.[39]   The most distinguished place was at the head of the table, at the extremity of the room, near the wall.   Saul sat in this place of honour.[40]   Under the reign of Solomon, the Hebrews still used seats.[41]   The Egyptians were early acquainted with the effeminate sumptuousness of table couches.   They often placed on them the venerated images of Jupiter, Juno, and their king himself.[42]

Before they had adopted this refinement of oriental luxury, the Greeks sat at their repasts on chairs, more or less costly, but all very elegant, similar to those which adorn our drawing-rooms, and which have been modelled from theirs.[43]

Homer's heroes sat down to table,[44] and Alexander the Great appears to have preserved the custom.   That prince giving a repast to ten thousand persons, caused all to be seated in silver arm-chairs, covered with purple.[45]   However, Hegesander assures us that, among the Macedonians, he who had succeeded in killing a wild boar, reclined at full length, whilst the other guests remained seated.[46]

Italy always imitated Greece, and, like her, had table couches, which at first, were only used by men: a feeling of propriety interdicted their use by women.[47]   But the relaxation of morals, seconded by fashion, soon banished this seeming reserve, and the two sexes could only eat in a reclining posture.[48]

A round, low table, made of common wood, and resting on three legs, was placed in the dining-room of persons in humble life; the rich had it made of lemon or maple wood, and supported by a single ivory foot.[49]   Three couches at most were arranged round this table (*triclinium*);[50] sometimes two, which Plautus names *biclinium*;[51] and these they covered with purple or other magnificent stuffs.[52]   Before they placed themselves, the guests performed their ablutions and threw off their togas, to substitute the "dinner robe."[53]   They then took off their sandals,[54] and lay down, three or four on each couch.[55] The rules of good society did not allow that number to be exceeded.

The upper part of the body was supported by the left elbow; the lower part was extended. The head was slightly raised, and downy little cushions supported the back.[56] When several persons occupied the same couch, the first placed himself at the head, in such a manner that his feet nearly reached the shoulders of the second guest, whose head was before the middle of the body of the preceding one, from whom he was separated by a cushion; and his feet descended to the back of the third guest, who followed the same order with respect to the fourth.[57]

When a couch contained three persons, the one in the middle occupied the place of honour; when there were four, that distinction belonged to the second. The place at the head of the couch was only offered to the most worthy, when not more than two persons were on the couch.[58]

Among the Persians, the middle place was reserved for the king. Cyrus placed on his left the guest to whom he wished to do the most honour, the next on his right, the third on the left, the fourth on the right, and so on, down to the last.[59] In Greece, the most distinguished personage occupied the head of the table.[60]

The voluptuous Heliogabalus only made use of couches stuffed with hares' down or partridges' feathers.[61] The Emperor Œlius Verus introduced a more exquisite novelty: he had his filled with lily and rose leaves.[62] The first of these princes—a cruel monarch, or capricious child, according to his strange whims—amused himself, sometimes, by placing on a couch, round the sigma, at one time eight bald men; at another, eight gouty men; one day, eight grey-headed old men; another day, eight very fat men, who were so crowded together that it was almost impossible for them to raise their hands to the mouth. And the brainless dolt shook with laughter at their efforts and their contortions.[63] One of his favourite diversions consisted in filling a leathern table-couch with air, instead of wool; and while the guests were engaged in drinking, a tap, concealed under the carpet, was opened, unknown to them; the couch sank, and the drinkers rolled pell-mell under the sigma, to the great delight of the beardless emperor, who enjoyed greatly his *espiéglerie.*[64]

The Celts seated themselves at their repasts on hay, before very low tables;[65] the Belgians reclined on a kind of couch;[66] the Gauls on

the skins of dogs or wolves.[67]   These different authorities are easily reconciled ; for they relate to different cantons of Gaul.

The use of couches was not unknown in the middle ages; we find
the proof of it in the *fabliaux* of the 13th century.   We have also the
description of a magnificent repast given by a bishop to two great officers
of Charlemagne, at which the prelate was seated, or lying, on feather
cushions.[68]   But this fashion was unsuccessful, and people preferred
wooden seats and stools, covered with carpet.   When they gave a great
feast, they seated the guests on benches—*bancs*—whence comes the
word " banquet."[69]   Henry III. of France introduced arm-chairs for
himself, and folding stools for his suite.[70]   Sometimes people eat on
the floor.   St. Arnold, Bishop of Soissons, took his repast in that
manner on the day of the dedication of a church, after having had
carpets spread on the ground.[71]   In winter the banqueting place was
spread with straw or hay, and in summer with grass and leaves.   Publicans and tavern-keepers decorated their rooms in like manner.[72]

The gallantry of the middle ages had led to the adoption of a rather
singular custom, which consisted in placing the guests two and two,
man and woman, and serving for each couple one common dish, which
they called " eating in the same porringer."   Neither had they more
than one cup.   In families the same goblet served for all.   Saint Ber-
landa was disinherited by her father, who was exasperated because,
under pretext that he was leprous, she had washed his goblet before
making use of it for herself.[73]

A passage in Martial would seem to imply that the guests, among
the Romans, laid the cloth themselves ;[74] that is to say, they spread on the
sigma the stuff, more or less precious, with which it was to be adorned.

A somewhat whimsical custom was established in the middle ages of
chivalry.   When it was intended to affront any one, a herald, or king-at-
arms, was sent to cut the cloth before him, and turn his bread upside
down.   That was called " cutting away the cloth," and was practised in
reference to cowards and faithless vassals.   It is thought that Bertrand
Duguesclin was the originator of this custom.[75]

Mention is made of table-cloths in the life of St. Eloi.   They were
in use on common tables; but the costly ones were not covered.   These
cloths were plushed and shaggy, as we find by the description of
Nigellus, the author of a poem on Louis-le-Débonnaire.   They were
of vast dimensions.   In the inventory of certain effects in the monastery

of Fontenelle, in the 9th century, we read of four table-cloths, each of which measured twelve yards and a-half by two and a-half; another, twelve and a-half by three and three-quarters; and thirteen, three yards and three-quarters wide.

In the 12th and 13th centuries table-cloths were called, in France, *doubliers*, doubtless because they were folded in two. This practice was eventually given up; and instead of a doubled cloth, the first was covered by a smaller one, and removed at the last course. Henry III. required this dessert cloth to be artistically plaited, so as to present pleasing designs.[76]

Napkins were much used in Greece and Italy. In the time of Augustus, and many years after, each guest brought his own, as we bring our pocket-handkerchiefs. Catullus complains of a certain Asinius, who had stolen his. Martial brings a similar accusation against a parasite named Hermogenes.[77]

Napkins were sometimes made of asbestos, and they were thrown into a brazier to clean them.[78] But these rarities were seldom possessed by any but princes, for asbestos was as expensive as jewels.[79]

The constitution of St. Ansegisius for the monastery of Fontenelle mentions plush napkins to wipe the hands, but they were only used before and after the repast. The town of Rheims was renowned in the middle ages for the manufacture of table linen. When Charles VII. made his entrance there they presented him with napkins, " very rich and curious by reason of the beautiful flowered work."

XXXIII.

THE SERVANTS.

ALL the opulent families had a great number of servants, or slaves, whose low extraction,[1] the chances of war,[2] or the parental will,[3] subjected to the caprices of the rich as a mere thing possessed, a right, a property (*res*).

They were known, like the slaves of the Jews[4] in former times, by their ears, which were pierced with an awl;[5] an ineffaceable stigma, which always reminded the freed-man of his former humiliation. The slave was also often marked with a hot iron on the back, the hands, the cheeks, or the forehead; and the characters thus imprinted served the master as an evidence against his fugitive servant in whatsoever place he might find him.[6] It is, perhaps, to similar marks that the prophet Zechariah makes allusion, when he says: "What are these wounds in thine hands?"[7] Plautus, whose comic vein respects neither the power of the Gods nor the sanctity of misfortune, calls these unfortunate creatures "lettered slaves" (*servos literatos*).[8]

A house of any note could not do without a crowd of servants, to whom the steward (*dispensator*) apportioned the labour, the food, and the chastisements.[9]

In a lodge near the vestibule was the porter (*ostiarius*),[10] whose watchful eye observed every one who went in or out by day or night. They made sure of his vigilance by chaining him to his place.[11]

The hall (*atrium*) was guarded by an intelligent and confidential servant, whose functions raised him above the other slaves.[12] The *atriensis*—such was his designation—had the care of the arms, trophies, precious furniture, and books, which adorned this apartment. He had also to take extreme care of the paintings and wax figures there pre- served from motives of vanity or by a sentiment of respect; and it was he who carried those images of venerated ancestors before the funeral procession of the head of the family when, in his turn, death had num- bered him with his progenitors.[13]

The *obsonator* bought in the markets the meat, fruit, and delicacies necessary for the repasts.[14]

The *vocatores* carried the invitations, received the guests, and placed them at table according to their rank.[15] These functions required a peculiar kind of urbanity and long experience on the part of the indi- vidual who fulfilled them.

The arrangement, the keeping in order, and adornment of the table- couches belonged exclusively to the *cubicularii* (valets).[16] These servants are mentioned in Suetonius and other ancient authors. The Cæsars had a great number of *cubicularii* who obeyed one particular chief.[17]

The *dapiferi* brought the dishes into the dining-room,[18] and the nomenclators (*nomenculatores*) immediately informed the guests of the names and qualities of the things with which they were going to be served.[19]

The *structor* arranged the dishes symmetrically.[20] The *scissor* (carver) cut up the meats to the sound of musical instruments, of which he followed the measure. Finally, young slaves (*procillatores*),[21] served the guests attentively, and poured out their drink. Those chosen for this employment were fine, beardless, adolescent youths, with a fresh complexion, whose long silky hair fell in curls over the shoulders. A wide riband which went twice round the waist confined their fine, white tunic—a light, graceful vestment, which descended in front to the knees, and behind hardly covered the hamstring.[22]

While the guests, softly reclining on their table-couches, were en- joying the agreeable surprise reserved for them by an amiable amphi- tryon, slaves (*sandaligeruli*) attended to their sandals, and fastened them on at the moment of departure.[23] Others, (*flabellarii*) armed with fans of peacocks' feathers,[24] drove away the flies, and cooled the banqueting-hall.[25]

The banquet terminated, servants with torches and lanterns (*adver- sitores*) conducted their masters home, and pointed out to them the

Y

stones that might be lying in their path, and which repeated libations might have prevented their visual organs from discovering.[26]

We must not omit, in this nomenclature of the principal servants of a good house, the taster (*prægustator*), who tasted or tried the viands before the guests touched them ; [27] nor the chief steward (*triclinarches*), and director of the repast, who had to occupy himself with an infinity of details in the kitchen, the cellar, the pantry, the buffet, and the dining-room.[28]

A living synthesis of these multiplied services, he performed them all himself. The least negligence, the slightest absence of mind on his part, would have ruined the reputation, utterly marred the sumptuous hospitality, of his master.

Never did the general of an army tremble under the weight of a responsibility so redoubtable.

Procillatores, or cup-bearer, an officer whose duty was to fill and present the cup to the king and princes. This charge was known in Egypt, and the ancients transformed Ganymede into a cup-bearer to the gods.

Charlemagne had master cup-bearers. These officers signed royal charters, and kept rank amongst the great officers of state. The head one took the title of *Echanson* to the king, of master, premier, or great *échanson*. In the 15th century the *échansons* exercised their functions only on the coronations, marriages, and entries of kings and queens. Louis XVIII. re-established the office of *premier échanson*. It was abolished in 1830.

There was, moreover, a class of miserable, obscure, despised slaves, whose useful labours rendered them necessary, and who were treated much the same as beasts of burden. This order of subaltern servants were composed of :—

The *lecticarii*. They carried the elegant palanquin in which the haughty matron or the noble senator were conveyed to the banqueting-hall.[29]

The stokers (*focarii*), who cut the wood, lighted, and attended to the fires.[30]

The sweepers (*scoparii*), whose indefatigable activity kept the apartments and furniture clean.[31]

TRICLINIUM.

1.

PROCILLATORES.

T. L. Yolart. del.   Saddler & Chant, scul.

The washers (*peniculi*). With a sponge and a cloth they cleaned the precious tables which adorned the *cœnaculum*, or dining-room. Sometimes, also, they had to lay the covers.[32]

This rapid sketch will enable the reader to form a sufficiently correct idea of the comfort and luxury which prevailed among the Romans, and of which the Greeks set them the example. It is hardly necessary to remark that the cup-bearers, stewards, carvers, and other household officers, whose names belong to modern Europe, perform functions analogous to those which similar servants performed formerly in Italy. But these last were debased by the stigma of slavery, and degraded by long habit, whilst the others were citizens.

XXXIV.

THE GUESTS.

THE Jews and the Egyptians washed the feet of the persons whom they received into their houses, and offered them larger portions as a mark of greater honour.[1] These homely and hospitable usages have disappeared with the simplicity of the primitive ages.

The Greeks required their guests to arrive neither too soon nor too late. It was a rule of politeness from which nothing could exempt them,[2] and which we ourselves observe at this day.

In the Homeric ages each one received his share of meat and wine,[3] and the man who at that epoch piqued himself on his knowledge of the science of life, never failed to offer his neighbour a part of his dinner. So Ulysses gives Demodochus one-half of the "chine of beef" with which he is served.[4] It is true that the King of Ithaca was regarded as a perfect model of complaisance and delicacy.

Another custom (adopted it is said only in the modern taverns and dining-rooms) was that of warming the remains of a preceding banquet for other guests.[5] It must have constituted very poor fare, for the Greeks were remarkable for a formidable appetite, and their repasts were prolonged indefinitely. The banquet of Menelaus, noticed by Athenæus, is a proof of it. They eat at first without speaking, and after prodigies of mastication they began to discourse. Then, having washed their hands, face, and beard, a fresh attack was commenced, more formidable than the first; and when the ardour and energy of the assailants seemed to be exhausted, they hardly took time to breathe ere they fell on the viands with renewed avidity. Nothing resisted them; the dishes were cleared; only a few bones remained to certify their achievement.[6] A saddening, unsatisfactory trophy for future guests.

Archestrates, whose gastronomic axioms we cannot respect too much, was averse to large dinner parties. Three or four persons—five at most —chosen with care, assembled with taste, appeared to him sufficient[7] for those solemnities in which silence was to be maintained so long, under pain, said Montmaur, of no longer knowing what one eats.

The Lacedæmonians admitted as many as fifteen guests, but they elected a king of the banquet, and that ephemeral autocrat decided without appeal all questions which might have compromised the tranquillity of the banquet.[8]

Greater numbers met together in Athens. Plato gave a supper to twenty-eight of his friends.[9] Hundreds of citizens often met together at the public repasts; but then a magistrate was deputed to see that modesty, moderation, and temperance were observed.[10]

The Romans understood that it is at table that one lives; so they gave those whom they invited the name of *conviva* (*cum vivere*, living conjointly), a charming type of that easy, gentle cordiality which arises, is fortified, and displayed between those who partake of the same dishes, drain in friendship cups of the same wine, and separate with the hope of soon seeing a return of the same pleasures.

People were very polite in Rome, as in Greece, when they met in the dining-room. Never did they fail to make a low bow.[11] This act of Roman courtesy recalls a very pretty expression of Fontenelle's, which we cannot refrain from citing. This grand nephew of the great Corneille passed, on his way to the table, before Madame Helvétius, whom he had not perceived. Fontenelle was then ninety years of age. "See," said she, "what esteem I must have for your gallantry: you pass before me without looking at me." "Be not surprised, Madam," replied the old gallant; "if I had looked at you I should never have passed."

In the year of Rome 570 (182 B.C.), the tribune of the people, C. Orchius, was the prime mover of the first sumptuary law, which enacted that the number of guests were not to exceed that of the Muses, nor be less than that of the Graces.[12] Subsequently seven were thought to be sufficient, and some insisted that when there were more the banquet ought rather to be called a rout.[13]

In the year of Rome 548, the Consul C. Fannius carried a law (*Lex Fannia*) which prohibited the assembling of more than three persons of the same family on ordinary days, or more than five at the nones, or on festival days.[14] This rigorous measure was pressingly solicited by the rational portion of every order of citizens, who could not witness without a shudder the whole of Italy plunge into the most brutifying excesses, after obscene orgies which we dare not describe.[15]

But who could dissipate that fearful bewilderment with which nations seem to be seized when they are about to fall? Rome blushed for her ancient virtues, and veiled them with dissolution and crimes. She had exhausted all the prodigies that the genius of debauchery could invent —she created monsters!

Ruinous banquets soon revived, and the number of guests had no other rule than the unbridled desire of ostentation and expense.

Let us not forget those miserable parasites who managed to get to the corner of a table in Greece and Italy, and to whom meagre portions were conceded as a reward for cringing servility, such as the vilest slave would have been ashamed to exhibit. There were three kinds of parasites. Some, under the name of buffoons, amused the company with their grotesque attitudes and ridiculous sayings.[16] Others allowed their ears to be boxed, and suffered a thousand different torments, provided a piece of meat or a bone were afterwards thrown to them. These patient sufferers[17] diverted the Greeks and Romans very much. The adulatory parasites were the most skilful of these hungry parias. They were well treated and almost respected. They were persons who possessed a kind of merit which was always equally appreciated, and to which we still render justice—they flattered whosoever gave them a supper.[18]

An energetic, familiar expression in French often replaces the word *parasite*, transmitted to us by the Greeks and Romans: that expression, which conveys the same idea, is *pique-assiette*, an image necessarily associated with disdain and insult.

The Count de Gerval had invited to his table several persons of high distinction, among whom was remarked one of those intruders who find means to get themselves received, notwithstanding the profound contempt they inspire. The dessert was just served, and a magnificent pear attracted the attention of the parasite, who endeavoured to bear it off on the point of his knife, but, in so doing, he broke a valuable plate. "The deuce take it, sir," said the master of the house; "*piquez l'assiette* as long as you like, but don't break it!"

The guests always washed their hands, and frequently their feet, before they placed themselves on the triclinium.*[19] They received that

---

* See Plate XXVIII., p. 378, for the triclinium.

custom from the orientals, and we find numerous examples of it in the Old and New Testaments.[20] Perfumes were then poured on their heads,[21] as among the Jews,[22] and wreaths of flowers were offered them.[23]

It was at this solemn moment that the guests turned their attention to the election of the king of the banquet, whose grave functions consisted in regulating the number of cups that each one was expected to empty during the repast.[24]

Among the Anglo-Saxons, he who wished to drink asked the nearest person to pledge him. The latter replied affirmatively, and immediately armed himself with his knife or his sword to protect the other while he emptied his cup. The death of Edward the Martyr, it is said, gave rise to this custom. Elfrida, his mother-in-law, caused him to be basely assassinated from behind whilst he was drinking.[25]

"The following," says Strutt, "according to ancient historians, is the manner in which Rowena, daughter or niece of Hengist, drank to the health of Vortigern, King of the Britons. She entered the banqueting-hall where the prince was with his guests, and, making a low curtsey, she said : 'To your health, my lord and king.' Then, having put the cup to her lips, she presented it on her knees to Vortigern, who took it and emptied it, after having replied : 'I drink to your health.'"[26]

We find in the works of Pasquier an affecting anecdote of the unfortunate Queen of Scotland, Mary Stuart : "On the eve of her death," says he, "towards the end of the supper, she drank to all her attendants, commanding them to pledge her ; the which obeying, and mingling their tears with their wine, they drank to their mistress."

Divers spectacles, of which we shall have occasion to speak hereafter, occupied the leisure of the guests during the interval necessary to remove the remains of one course and serve the next. These representations and amusements, of which they never tired in the middle ages, received from our ancestors, in France, the name of *entre-mets;* a designation much more true and just than the modern acceptation imposed on the word—anything served between the roast and the dessert.

The *entre-mets* were interludes, pantomimes, concerts, and even melodramas performed between each course. So that a piece which in our days attracts crowds to one or other of the theatres, would have been then a little *entre-met,* or a cold side-dish (*hors-d'œuvre*).

In 1237, at the marriage of Robert, son of Saint-Louis, with Machault, Countess of Artois, very singular spectacles were given between

each course of the banquet. A horseman crossed the hall by making
his horse walk on a thick cord, extended above the heads of the guests.
At the four corners of the table were musicians. seated on oxen; and
monkeys, mounted on goats, seemed to play the harp.[27]

A droll custom prevailed at the court of the Frank kings. St. Germier
having come to solicit some favour from the King of the Franks, Clovis,
that haughty Sicamber received the bishop with kindness, and had an
excellent dinner served for him. The holy bishop took leave of the
king after the banquet, and the king, who sometimes piqued himself
upon his politeness, pulled out a hair, according to the custom of the
time, and offered it to his guest. Each of the courtiers hastened, in his
turn, to imitate the benevolent monarch, and the virtuous prelate returned to his diocese enchanted with the reception he had met with at
the court.[28]

Among other amusements prepared for Queen Elizabeth, during
her sojourn at the celebrated castle of Kenilworth, "There was," says
Laneham, "an Italian juggler who performed feats of strength and leaps,
and cut such capers with so much suppleness and ease, that I began to
ask myself whether it were a man or a sprite. Indeed I know not what
to say of that comical fellow," adds the artless chronicler; "I suppose
his back must resemble that of a lamprey—it had no bone." [29]

In England, during the middle ages, the courts of princes and the
castles of the great were crowded with visitors, who were always received
with sumptuous hospitality. The pomp displayed by the lords was
truly extraordinary, and it is difficult to understand how their fortunes
could suffice for it. They had their privy-counsellors, treasurers, secre-
taries, chaplains, heralds, pursuivants-at-arms, pages, guards, trumpeters
—in a word, all the officers, all the servants, with which royalty itself is
surrounded. And besides this numerous domestic establishment, there
were troops of minstrels, clowns, jugglers, strolling players, rope-dancers,
&c., lodged there at the great banqueting times. Each of the apartments open to the guests presented spectacles in harmony with the gross
taste of the epoch. It was a marvellous confusion, a prodigious chaos,
in which the ear was struck at once with the sound of dishes, of cups
clashing one against another, of harmonious music, with the bustle of
the dance, the notes of the song, pasquinades, somersaults, and everywhere the most boisterous laughter. The face of decency alone was
slightly veiled.[30]

Sometimes the term *entre-mets* was also applied to decorations, which were paraded through the banqueting hall, and which represented cities, castles, and gardens, with fountains, whence flowed all kinds of liquors. At the dinner which Charles V. of France gave to the Emperor Charles IV. there was a grand spectacle, or *entre-met*. A vessel appeared with its masts, sails, and rigging; it advanced into the middle of the hall, by means of a machine concealed from the view of all. A moment after there appeared the city of Jerusalem; its towers covered with Saracens. The vessel approached it, and the city was taken by the Christian knights who manned the vessel.[31]

Among the Egyptians a funereal idea was made the means of rousing the erewhile buoyant spirits of the guests at the end of a repast. A servant entered carrying a skeleton, or the representation of a mummy, which he took slowly round the dining-room. He then approached the guests, and said: "Eat, drink, amuse yourselves to-day; to-morrow you die"[32]

Greece, and Rome in particular, adopted this lugubrious emblem of the rapid flight of time and pleasure. This sepulchral image hurried them on in the enjoyment of the present: it never revealed to paganism a "hope full of immortality."[33]

XXXV.

A ROMAN SUPPER.

Two lustres had passed since the world obeyed Domitius Nero, son of Agrippina. The Romans, a herd of vile slaves, docile adulators of the infamous Cæsar, had already celebrated nine anniversaries of his happy accession to the empire, and the Flamen of Jupiter solemnly thanked the gods at each of these epochs for all the benefits that the well-beloved monarch had unceasingly lavished on the earth.

Few princes, it is true, ever equalled Nero. He and his mother had poisoned Junius Silanus, the pro-consul of Asia; subsequently the young emperor made away with Agrippina, and the senate applauded that horrible crime, which was only the prelude to outrageous enterprises which astonish the historian who narrates them.

The Flamen was, indeed, bound to offer up solemn thanksgivings to Jupiter for having hitherto restrained the crowned monster from the commission of evil which afterwards marked his flagitious career.

It was the 64th year of the Christian era. The emperor had passed some time at Naples, whence it was thought he would go into Greece; but suddenly changing his project, he returned to the capital of the world, to prepare, it was said, a spectacle of unheard-of splendour, and such as Nero alone could conceive.

One of his ancient freed-men, Caius Domitius Seba, resolved to celebrate the return to Rome, and the tenth anniversary of the reign of his master, who was now become his patron and friend. That man possessed immense riches, a formidable credit at court, and an insolence which had struck so much terror into the souls of the proudest families of the empire, that they had long since humbled themselves before him.

Saddler & Chant; sculpt

IN THE YEAR 64.

So that it was no sooner whispered among the Roman aristocracy that the magnificent Seba intended to give a banquet, than one and all became anxious to be numbered with the guests of Cæsar's favourite.

However, days past, the time for the nocturnal festival approached, and the Invitor had not made his appearance.

Among the Hebrews, nothing was more simple and unsophisticated than an invitation to dinner;[1] but, with the Romans, etiquette required that the amphitryon should send one of his servants to each person who was to participate in his pompous hospitality. This servant, who was generally a freed-man, went from house to house, and indicated, with exquisite politeness, the day and precise hour of the banquet.[2]

Seba's Invitor was at last announced to the two consuls of the year, Lecanius Bassus and Licinius Crassus, who accepted with tender gratitude the distinguished honour which the enfranchised slave deigned to confer upon them.

After them the same favour was received with the same gratitude by the Agrippas, the Ancuses, the Cossuses, the Drususes, and all those who were the most noble, powerful, and proud in Rome.

The next day, about two o'clock in the afternoon (the repast was to begin at six o'clock), an unusual movement reigned in the Palatine baths, and those of Daphnis, near the Sacred Way. The *mediastini* kept up a steady fire under the coppers; the *capsarii* folded with care the clothes of the bathers; the *unguentarii* sold their oils and unguents; and the *fricatores*, armed with the *strigil*—a sort of wooden, iron, or horn spoon—rubbed and scraped the skin before the *tractatores* came gently to manipulate the joints, and skilfully shampoo the body, which gained by this operation more elasticity and suppleness.[3]

The upper classes of the Romans never sat down to table until they had undergone all these preliminaries of minute cleanliness.[4]

The future guests return home, after the bath, to employ the skill of the barbers (*tonsores*), who are in waiting to give more grace to the hair, and remove, with the aid of tweezers and pumice, the first silvery indications of the lapse of years, which, though incessantly effaced, still re-appeared.[5]

A more serious occupation succeeded. Epicureans should never neglect their teeth—particularly at the approach of a banquet. Nor did the ingenious gastronomy of the first century of our era neglect to invent tooth-powder, which cleaned the enamel without injuring it, and fortified the gums—those fortresses of mastication. Some persons made use of substances which no one would adopt in the present day, because our delicacy revolts against them.[6] But preparations less offensive were employed, and men of good taste, as well as fashionable ladies, extolled ox-gall, goats' milk, the ash of stags' horns, of pigs' hoofs, and of egg-shells.[7]

Thus were the teeth equipped, as the comic Plautus has it;[8] or, rather, thus were they prepared to undergo the labour required of them.

Those who had had the misfortune to lose some of those powerful gastrophagic auxiliaries substituted false ones of ivory, which art found means to render absolutely similar to their neighbours. The eye was deceived: what more could be required?[9]

But the clepsydræ[10] and the celebrated clock of the field of Mars[11] announce that it is time to put on the white, light robe, a little longer than the pallium of the Geeeks, and to which the Latins have given the names of *vestis cœnatoria, vestis triclinaria, vestis convivalis.*[12] This last part of their toilet finished, the guests set out for the magnificent abode of their host, preceded by a few slaves, and followed by their shadows—those hungry hangers-on of whom mention has already been made, and who strive to obtain, on the road, a smile or a word by dint of cringing obsequiousness.

Arrived at the *atrium*, the crowd of Roman nobles are conducted into the interior of the house by the parasites of Seba. The proud freed-man disturbed himself for nobody; but, like the opulent Greeks, whom he aped, he left to these ignoble familiars the care of replacing him in the honours of his palace.[13]

They enter an immense hall, decorated with unheard-of luxury, lighted by lustres,[14] and round which are several ranks of seats, not unlike the folding-stools and arm-chairs we meet with in the present day in the most elegant *boudoirs.*[15] The guests seat themselves, and anon Egyptian slaves approach with perfumed snow-water, which flows from golden vases of the most graceful forms, and cools the hands of senators and Roman knights,[16] whilst other servants disincumber them of their patrician shoes, the end of which represents a crescent.[17] The feet then received a similar ablution, and fresh slaves, skilful orthopœdists, accomplish in a twinkling the delicate toilet of these extremities,[18] and imprison them again in elegant and commodious sandals, fastened by ribands which cross on the top.[19]

Here and there a few persons are remarked who still wear their togas, having doubtless forgotten to substitute the banqueting dress. So soon as the major-domo perceives them he makes a sign to some youths clothed in white tunics, who hasten to present to each of these guests a *synthesis*, or short woollen vestment of different colours,[20] which envelopes the whole body, but leaves the shoulders and breast uncovered if the wearer desire it.[21]

These indispensable preliminaries being terminated, the seats disappeared, and the guests stood waiting for the freed-man, Seba, who speedily entered accompanied by the two consuls, for whom places of honour had been reserved on couches beside their pompous amphitryon. The latter deigned to address a few words of welcome to his noble company, and each one stretched himself on his couch of gold and purple. The fourth couch was given up to the parasites and shadows.[22]

Meanwhile, slaves were burning precious perfumes in golden vases (*acerræ*), and young children were pouring on the hair of the guests odoriferous essences, which filled the banqueting hall with balmy fragrance. Rome had borrowed this custom from the east.[23]

The golden panelling of the hall shone with dazzling brightness as it reflected a torrent of light from the crystal candelabra,[24] and the melodious sounds of the hydraulic organ[25] announced the commencement of the banquet.[26]

At this signal, servants, richly dressed, place within the circle formed by the couches lemon-wood tables of inestimable price,[27] which they immediately cover with a rich tissue of gold and silk. That done, sylph-like hands spread them over with a profusion of the rarest flowers and rose leaves.[28]

Musicians (*symphoniaci*) then occupy a kind of orchestra or platform, raised at one of the extremities of the hall,[29] among whom the flute and harp players are to be particularly remarked.[30] The former constitute, among the Romans, a special body dubbed with the name of *College*, and they have the exclusive right to attend banquets and enliven the pomp of ceremonies.[31]

These musicians execute a slow, dulcet melody while the slaves are placing on the tables the statues of some of the principal gods,[32] together with that of the divine Nero, whom a pusillanimous flattery ranks already with the immortals. At this moment they also arrange here and there the salt-cellars,[33] while the more meditative of the guests invoke Jupiter, before they give themselves up to the pleasures of the feast.[34] Hardly is this short prayer finished when joyous cup-bearers distribute charming little crystal cups,[35] which Æthiopian slaves[36] fill to the brim with a generous, honeyed wine, drawn, in the first instance, from those large pitchers which the Greeks have named *amphoræ*.

Some drops of the exhilirating liquid are offered to the *Lares* (household gods), by sprinkling it in their honour on the floor and the table.[37] This pious libation precedes the entrance of the first course (*antecœna*),[38] composed of the lightest and least succulent kinds of viands, by means of which a generous host stimulates the appetites of his guests, as a preparative for brilliant exploits.[39]

Lettuces, olives, pomegranates, Damascus plums,[40] tastefully arranged on silver dishes,[41] serve to encircle dormice, prepared with honey and poppy juice,[42] forcemeat balls of crab, lobster, or cray-fish, prepared with pepper, cummin, and benzoin root.[43] A little further, champignon and egg sausages, prepared with garum,[44] are placed by the side of pheasant sausages, a delicious mixture of the fat of that bird, chopped very small, and mixed with pepper, gravy, and sweet sun-made wine, to which a small quantity of hydrogarum is added.[45] Tempting as these delicate viands may be, the practised epicureans seem to have a decided preference for peacocks' eggs, which they open with spoons. These eggs, a master-piece of the culinary artist, who presides over Seba's stoves, are composed of a fine perfumed paste, and contain, each one, a fat, roasted, ortolan surrounded with yolk of egg, and seasoned with pepper.[46]

We will not go through the list of all the dishes which composed the *antecœna*. The nomenclature was offered, according to custom, to the guests of the rich freed-man, but the reader would doubtless think it a little tiresome. We must, however, inform him, that the true gastronomists—and there were many at that banquet—did no more than give note of preparation to their appetite, by plying it with pickled radishes,[47] some few grasshoppers of a particular species, fried with garum,[48] grey peas, and olives fresh from their brine.[49]

DESCRIPTION OF PLATE No. XXX.

No. 1. A Greek Etruscan vase, or amphora, of terra cotta, for wine and water, commonly placed on the dinner table.—HAMILTON.

No. 2. A Greek terra cotta vase, for a particular wine.—CAYLUS.

No. 3. Etruscan terra cotta vase, to hold wine on the table.—CAYLUS.

No. 4. A glass amphora, or vase, of large dimensions, for Falernian wine. All found at Herculaneum.—SAINT-NON.

Pl. 26.

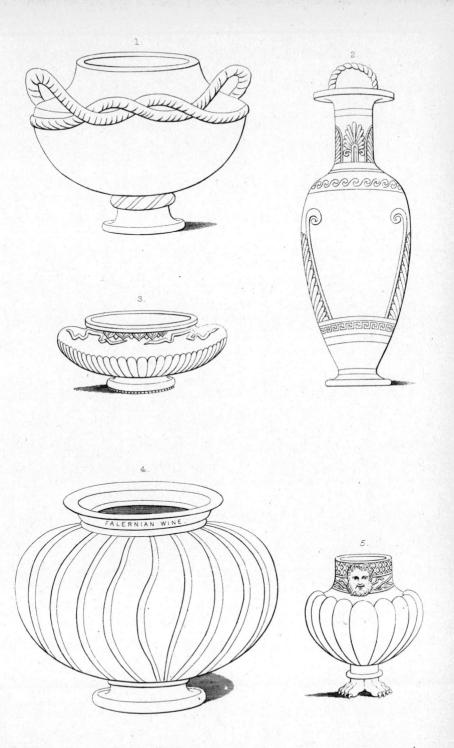

1.

2.

3.

4.

FALERNIAN WINE.

5.

F.T.Z. Volant, del.

Saddler & Chant, scul,

Pl. 34.

F. T. N. Volant, del.

Saddler & Chant, sculp.

The first course was removed to the sound of music.[50] Now came chased silver cups, much larger than those of crystal [51]—no doubt because thirst is excited by drinking. Amphoræ of a secular wine were ranged by the major-domo on the mosaic flooring of the hall, at some distance from the triclinium, and they proceeded, by the invitation of the consuls, to the choice of the *symposiarch* (or master of the banquet), upon whom devolved the duty of regulating how often any person was to drink, and of preventing the guests, in the best manner he could, from yielding too easily to bacchic provocations, which commonly led to unseemly gaiety and the loss of reason.[52]

This sort of magiric magistracy was obtained by lot, or the unanimous call for a personage worthy of such a distinction.[53] That memorable evening every voice named the senator Drusillus, one of the most determined drinkers of the Roman aristocracy. Drusillus smiled, snapped his fingers,[54] and, by the order of his master, thus intimated, a slave, who was standing behind him, filled a golden crater* with wine, and presented it to the symposiarch.

Thereupon, the latter, slightly raising his head from the downy cushions on which it rested, and supporting it from the left elbow,[55] makes a graceful bow to the amphitryon, the consuls, and the rest of the assembly. Then, with a stentorian voice : " Slaves," he cried, " bring wreaths of flowers.[56] Fugitive images of the spring and of pleasure, they shall bind our brows.[57] At the same time let garlands adorn our craters, in which the cherished liquor of the son of Semele sparkles ;[58] and let us bestow no thought, during the fleet joys of the banquet, on the uncertain and fatal hour when Atropos shall pronounce our doom."

This speech, slightly impregnated with the epicurean philosophy so much in fashion during the reign of Nero, had at least the merit of a praiseworthy conciseness. Nor did it fail to attract applause from the auditors, whose brows and cups were speedily adorned with wreaths of roses, which young boys, clothed in white tunics, arranged with marvellous art.

The slight rustling of the flowers was soon drowned by the shrill noise of the trumpets which announced the second course. A flattering buzz welcomed this profusion of viands, which encumbered the tables, and well-nigh crushed them with their weight. There were the peacock,[58] the duck, whose breast and head are so much coveted ;[59]

* Cup, or *crater*, used by the Greeks and Romans at their repasts, made either of gold, silver, or earthenware (terra cotta).—HAMILTON, "*Herculaneum*.".

capons' livers,[60] peppered becaficoes,[61] grouse, the turtle-dove, the phenicopter,[62] and an infinite number of rare birds, the costly tribute that Europe, Asia, and Africa, exchanged against the gold of the prodigal Seba. Other gold and silver dishes contained those inestimable fishes which Roman luxury brought so much into fashion; the scarus, or parrot fish, sturgeons, turbots, mullets, and those numerous inhabitants of every sea with which the tanks were stocked, to supply the kitchen of the freed-slave.

Moreover, there were wild boars *à la Troyenne*,[63] ranged in the centre of the table, in silver basins of a prodigious value; stuffed pigs, quarters of stag and roebuck, loins of beef, kidneys surrounded with African figs,[64] sows' paps prepared with milk,[65] sows' flank,[66] and some pieces of Gallic bacon,[67] which certain gluttons loved to associate with a piece of succulent venison.

While the carvers were cutting up the meats with incredible address, to the sound of a light but animated music, Numidian slaves filled the cups from small leathern bottles with old Greek wine,[68] a servant carried bread round the tables in a silver basket,[69] and others ventilated the apartment,[70] or offered the guests warm and iced water.[71]

In every direction trays circulated, covered with divers kinds of meats,[72] which they took care to humect with peppered garum,[73] that strange condiment, which the freed-slave procured from Spain at a price equal to its weight in gold.

Suddenly the symposiarch commands silence: the musicians obey —the slaves are motionless.

" Let us drain our cups," said he, " in honour of Cæsar. Let us celebrate the tenth anniversary of his glorious reign, and his happy return to the metropolis of the world. Let us drink, senators and knights, as many craters as there are letters in the cherished name of the emperor."[74]

Sense and reason must have succumbed, had the patrician assembly toasted Caius Lucius Domitius Nero: it would have been constructive treason not to empty twenty-three cups; but they limited themselves to four, which represented the last of these names.

Joy unrestrained floated with the fumy wine, furnished from large

DESCRIPTION OF PLATE No. XXXI.

No. 1. Curious silver dish, with Etruscan letters engraved around the head of Medusa. Petronius speaks of two silver dishes, upon which were engraved the name of Trimalcion, and the weight of each dish.—ATHEN.; STUART.

Nos. 2 and 3. Silver dishes.—GORRIE, " *Etruscan Mus.*"

Pl. 35.

F. T. Z. Volant, del.

Chant & Saddler, scul.

glass amphoræ, on which were these words: "Falernian wine of a hundred leaves, made under the consulship of Opimius." [75]* The consuls and the Roman nobles almost forgot, in the voluptuousness of the splendid repast, that the executioner of Britannicus and Burrhus, the crowned tiger, was doubtless thinking at that very moment of taking some of the heads then present. A funereal spectacle soon aroused their dormant fears.

An officer of the palace presented himself at the door of the banqueting hall. He advanced slowly, followed by two slaves, who laid on the table an object covered with a winding-sheet. "Pressing occupations," said the imperial messenger, "prevent Cæsar from sharing with you the hospitality of Seba; but he thinks of you, and sends you a testimony of his remembrance."

"Long live Cæsar!" cry the consuls, the freed-slave, and some few trembling voices. The officer retires. The veil which shrouds Nero's present from every eye is removed, and all perceive a silver skeleton, of terrifying truthfulness, and which, by its admirable mechanism, proclaims artist to be one of those Greeks who have come to Rome to seek fortune and celebrity.[76]

This episode engrossed the thoughts of the greater part of the guests, and the old senator, Lucius Vafra, could not help saying, with a sigh, to his neighbour, Virginius Rufus, one of the consuls of the preceding year: "Fear the Greeks: fear this disastrous present!" [77]

But the hot wine which was being served,[78] and the healths which succeeded without interruption, drove the sinistrous presage from their minds; and, moreover, the present of the emperor was nowise contrary to the manners of the epoch, and the thought of death would only have enlivened the repast, if it had been presented by any other than Nero.

At first healths were drunk in the Greek fashion,—that is, beginning by the most distinguished personages, he who drank bowed and said: "I wish you every kind of prosperity;" or simply: "I salute you." In pronouncing these words, he who drank the health took only a part of the wine contained in the cup, and sent the remainder to the guest he had just designated.[79]

Many craters were then emptied in honour of the mistress of the house (dominæ); neither were the illustrious dead nor absent friends forgotten. The formula was nearly the same for all: "To your healths,'

* See Plate XXX., No. 4.

Z

said the symposiarch, "to our own, to that also of the friend whom we cherish."[80]

Sometimes Drusillus, still fascinated with that dulcet poetry of the Greeks with which, when young, he had stored his mind, would take up the harmonious cadences of Horace, and thus personate, as it were, those divine chanters of Attica who have immortalised themselves by celebrating love, wine, and pleasure.

One of his extempore strains, while sipping the sparkling liquor from his cup, was:—

> This dream of bliss maintain, prolong these happy hours,
> O, all-enchanting wines! perfumed with flowers
>   Which Cos and Cyprus rear;
> Let nothing ever change this soul-felt, rich delight;
> For I would say, when parting for the realms of night,
>   I never knew a tear.

This sensual philosophy found numberless echoes in that vainglorious Rome, who exhausted her disdain, outrage, and punishments on the (so called) new fantastic folly that the Nazarenes were endeavouring to introduce. A few years more, and their doctrine will subjugate the universe!

Time passed rapidly, and the meats, divided into equal portions, were served to the guests, who frequently did not touch them, but gave their share to their servants, or sent it home.[81]

So soon as the major-domo perceived that appetite began to flag, he ordered the whole to be cleared, and the dessert, spread on ivory tables,[82] to be substituted for the more substantial comestibles, with which the guests were satiated.

Exquisite drinks, artificial wines, delicate and light aliments,[83] still came to titillate the palate and the burthened stomach—pears, apples, walnuts, dried-figs, grapes;[84] a thousand different kinds of raw, cooked, and preserved fruits; tarts, cakes, and those incredible delicacies which the Latins designated by the collective generic term *bellaria*, wooed the epicurean—if we may be allowed the expression—with their mild, material, dangerous, and irresistible eloquence.

Some one proposed to replace the half-faded flowers by Egyptian wreaths, and every brow was soon bound with garlands of roses and myrtle, interspersed with little birds, which, by their fluttering and chirping, soon restored the drowsy company to that animation which seemed to wane.[85]

Then began the amusements of the evening.

A troop of strolling players were admired for their agility and suppleness. Some rolled round a cord like a wheel which turns on its axle; they hung by the neck, by one foot, and varied these perilous exercises in a thousand different ways. Others slid down a cord, lying on the stomach, with their arms and legs extended. Some revolved as they ran along a descending cord. Some, in a word, performed feats of strength and address on the horizontal rope which were truly incomprehensible, and at an elevation from the flooring which would have rendered a fall fatal.[86]

To these acrobats succeeded prestigiators, who appeared to receive a peculiar degree of attention. One placed under cups a certain number of shells, dry peas, or little balls, and he caused them to disappear and reappear at will.[87] The spectators strained their eyes without being able to comprehend anything. Another of these mountebanks wrote or read very distinctly while whirling rapidly round.[88] Some vomited flames from the mouth, or walked, head downwards, on their hands, and beat with their feet the movements of the most agile dancers.[89] Then a woman appeared, holding in her hand twelve bronze hoops, with several little rings of the same metal, which rolled round them. She danced gracefully, throwing and successively catching the twelve hoops, without ever allowing any of the rings to fall.[90] After that, another juggler rushed, with his breast uncovered, into the midst of a forest of naked swords. Every one thought him to be covered with wounds, but he re-appeared, with a smile on his countenance, whole and sound.[91]

These feats were followed by an interlude, in which the parts were amusingly sustained by marionettes. The Greeks knew this childish pastime,[92] and Rome did not disdain it.[93] These little bronze and ivory figures[94] played some comic scenes tolerably well, and obtained the applauses of grave senators, who more than once forgot their senility as they contemplated the grotesque pantomime.

The only thing now wanting to render Seba's supper a worthy specimen of nocturnal Roman feasts was, to produce before the guests one of those spectacles which outrage morals and humanity. Nero's freed-man had been too well tutored to refuse them this diversion. Young Syrians,[95] or bewitching Spanish girls,[96] went through lascivious dances,[97] which raised no blush on the brow of rigid magistrates, who forgot, in the abode of the vile slave, the respect due to their age and dignity.

After the voluptuous scenes of the lewd Celtiberians, blood was required: for they seem to have been formed by nature to take a strange delight in sudden contrasts. Ten couples of gladiators, armed with swords and bucklers, occupied a space assigned to them, and ten horrible duels recreated the attentive assembly. For a long time nothing was heard but the clash of arms; but the thirst for conquest animated those ferocious combatants, and they rushed with loud cries on one another. Blood flowed on all sides; the couches were dyed with it, and the white robes of the guests were soon spotted. Some of the combatants fell, and the rattles announced approaching death; others preserved, in their last struggle, a funereal silence, or endeavoured to fix their teeth in the flesh of their enemies standing erect beside them.[98] The spectators, stupified with wine and good cheer, contemplated this carnage with cold impassibility; they only roused from their torpor when one of those men, happening to trip against a table, struck his head on the ivory, and his antagonist, prompt as lightning, plunged his sword into the throat of his foe, whence torrents of black, reeking blood inundated the polished ivory, and flowed in long streams among the fruits, cups, and flowers.

The deed was applauded; servants washed the tables and the floor with perfumed water, and these stirring scenes were soon forgotten. A last cup was drunk to the good genius,[99] whose protection they invoked before returning home.

Meantime a stifling atmosphere pervades every part of the hall, and a hollow noise, rumbling in the distance, excites at intervals in the minds of the guests a sort of undefinable apprehension—the ordinary presage of an unknown but imminent catastrophe. The consuls raise themselves on their couches and listen; their host endeavours to calm their fears; but at this moment a slave, panting for breath, rushes towards Seba, and pronounces a few inarticulate words. "Fire!" cries the anguished freed man. "Where is the fire?" inquire all the terrified guests, who have heard but this one sinistrous word. "Everywhere!" replies the slave; "it has burst forth simultaneously in every part of the city!" No one waits to hear more. Consuls, senators, knights, mu sicians, and servants, jostle one another; and, abandoning those who fall, arrive pell-mell at the atrium. The porter still chained, trembles at his post; the flames already envelop the sumptuous edifice—the entire street is one vast brazier! Rome burns, and will soon be a heap of ruins and ashes! Flight is impossible—the flames intercept every issue! * * * Nero has taken his measures well.

We will not attempt to depict the mute but terrible despair of those proud patricians, at bay in the midst of an ocean of fire, in which they are fated ere long to perish. The wreaths of flowers which bind their brows are already parched by the scorching breath of those roaring flames, which engulf and consume everything as they sweep along. A thick smoke begrimes the lustrous robes, whose graceful folds erewhile displayed the exquisite urbanity of Seba's guests, and which now exhibit only a sad emblem of festive joys. The dread of death, and I know not what strange anguish at this all-important moment, blanch those human faces, to which the choicest wines of Greece and Italy had just given a hue of purple. These men feel—instinct tells them—that life is theirs no longer, and they have not the courage to die!

The opulent freed-man calls to his slaves, and promises them their liberty if they consent to risk their lives in an attempt to save his. But the vile herd is already dispersed; the porter alone remains—for no one has thought to liberate him—and he, in his impotent fury, replies by insulting clamours to the cowardly supplications of his quondam master.

This horrible scene soon changed by the very action of that torrent of fire which was pursuing its devastating course; and the next day, when Aurora appeared, a heap of ruins was all that remained of the odious Seba's magnificent palace.

The two consuls and some of the senators were fortunate enough to escape the common danger. Less besotted, perhaps, by the wine and good cheer, and finding in despair that incredible energy which some-times operates the same prodigies as courage, they rushed through the flames, and gained the country, or those obscure portions of the city which the son of Agrippina had apparently forgotten.

Thus it was that Lucius Domitius Nero celebrated the tenth anniversary of his glorious reign. While the fire was rolling on with its resistless flood of flame from temples to palaces, and from the Circus to the Pantheon, the young, poetic Cæsar, his brow bound with laurel, and holding in his hands a golden lyre, viewed from the top of a tower—where he was surrounded by a troop of histrions and buffoons—the conflagration he had just kindled.

And while the imperial Apollo sang some melancholy verses on the fatal destiny of the antique city of Troy, his ignoble courtiers cried with enthusiasm : "May the Gods preserve Nero, their august son, and the delight of the human race!"

Such was the last gorgeous feast at which the magiric genius presided in that Rome which Romulus had founded, and which engulfed the treasures and wonders of the world. Destroyed by the imperial incendiary, it arose from its ashes with increased beauty and voluptuousness ; and the wild joy of its new banquets caused the thoughtless queen of nations quickly to forget the disasters of the past, and the sinistrous presages of the future.

Pl. 32.

HELIOGABALUS.

NERO.

F. T. Z. Volant, del.   Saddler & Chant, scul.

BIOGRAPHICAL NOTES.

NERO.

Lucius Domitius Nero's father was Caius Domitius Ænobarbus ; Agrippina was his mother. He took the reins of the empire at the age of eighteen (A.D. 54), and governed at first with clemency and equity. The Roman people, transported with love for their young prince, indulged the fond hope of long and unalloyed felicity ; but they were soon aroused from this delusion to a sense of the dire reality. Nero had forgotten himself in the path of virtue ; he rallied by trying his hand at crime, and found at last his true vocation. Others have recounted his detestable infamies : we will merely remind our readers that he poisoned Britannicus,—that he caused his mother to be slain,— that he killed his wife Octavia by kicking her,—and that Seneca, his preceptor, only escaped his cruelty by having his veins opened. In the year 64 he took it into his head to set fire to the city of Rome, and then accused the Christians of that prodigious atrocity. Language cannot describe the unbridled luxury of this ignominious emperor. His gilded house, his ivory ceilings, his murrhine vases, the nets of gold and scarlet with which he fished, the incalculable profusion of his repasts—everything connected with Nero betrayed a species of pompous monomania, leading to excesses so immeasurable and abominable that in these days they excite doubt or incredulity.

The entire world detested the monster. Galba and the Roman army revolted against him, and the pusillanimous Cæsar fled bare-footed, and wrapped in a sordid robe. But, alarmed at the idea of the tortures he would have to undergo if he fell alive into the hands of the cohorts and the people, and finding no executioner more infamous than himself, he plunged a sword timidly into his breast, while a freed-man, Epaphroditus, guided his trembling hand. This happy event happened in the year 68. Nero had reigned thirteen years !

This prince sat down to table at mid-day, and did not quit it till midnight (Sueton. in Neron. 27),—he had reservoirs stocked with the most rare and exquisite fish,—and he gave to his boon companions suppers which vied in delicacy with their astonishing magnificence. Let this, then, plead our excuse for having classed the cruel but epicurean Cæsar among the high culinary notabilities whose names, glory, or excesses we record in this work.

HELIOGABALUS.

Heliogabalus (Marcus Aurelius Antoninus Verus), son of Antoninus Cara-
calla and Semiamira, immortalised himself by his follies, and merited the name of
the *Sardanapalus of Rome*.   His grandmother, Mœsa, had a fancy to have
him invested with the functions of Priest of the Sun, and the following
year (218) the army elected him to succeed Macrinus.   He was then only
fourteen years old.   It would be impossible to give a complete catalogue of
the crimes which stained this precocious monster.   His luxury knew no
bounds, and his insatiable gluttony led him to send into distant provinces for
rare birds, unknown in Italy.   The golden lamps of his palace were supplied
with a precious balm, and scented waters of exquisite delicacy were daily renewed in the vast piscina of this beardless Cæsar.   His beds were adorned
with coverlets of a cloth of gold, and in his kitchens none but skilfully chased
silver utensils were employed.   It is said that Heliogabalus invented after-
dinner lotteries : his guests took the tickets at random, and fate gave to one
some vase of inestimable value, to another a simple toothpick ; a fortunate ad-
venturer would receive for his allotment ten elephants, richly caparisoned, and
his less lucky neighbour had to content himself with ten flies, and loud bursts
of laughter from the imperial stripling.

Thank Heaven ! this frightful phenomenon of turpitude and folly never
attained manhood.   The soldiers of his guard massacred him after a reign of
something less than four years, and threw to the populace the dead body of
a young man of eighteen, who, in the course of his brief existence, had exhausted the treasures of the empire, and enlarged the sphere of every crime.

The gastronomic art is, however, indebted to the odious Heliogabalus for
some useful discoveries, and for that reason alone is he here mentioned.

EPICURUS.

Epicurus—born 337 years B. C., in the market-town of Gargettus, near
Athens—taught in his gardens a system of philosophy, which, though indulgent
towards the requirements of the senses, possessed the merit of a sovereign
disdain for every kind of superstition.   Epicurus had a great number of disciples among the ancient pagans, and the sensual philosophy of modern times
hails him as a patron. At this very day the dainty livers rally under the joyous
banner of the moralist of Gargettus, and his cherished shade inspires the guests
and presides over the soothing intoxication of banquets

MODERN BANQUETS.*

WE have endeavoured to describe in the preceding pages some of those antique entertainments, which seem to be the *summum bonum* of the gigantic power of those shameless dominators of the Roman empire, whose reigns might be counted as so many banquets, and for whom the entire world was transformed into one vast market.

We are reduced to despair when we attempt to depict such sensualism, and we also despair of inspiring belief. When one goes back into those old pagan times,—when one shuts out the world as it is, to evoke the manners and customs of days gone by, and breathe in their atmosphere,—the mind experiences a sort of stupefaction, so much is it immersed in the senses, so thick is the moral darkness, so low has man fallen !

And, as if it had been decreed that everything should concur to consummate the annihilation of the human species, on the one hand, almost the whole family of man was, for the first time since their dispersion, collected into one body under the Roman domination, which spread its corruption throughout the several members ; while, on the other hand, the hordes of barbarians who pressed round—like ferocious beasts waiting till the arena opened—were about to over-run the earth, in the absence of any civilising element that could interpose to stay the destruction, by snatching the conquered from the hands of victory, and the conquerors themselves from their own ferocity.

It belongs not to us to portray this fearful cataclysm, this sudden transition from the development of all the arts which perpetuate the enjoyments of life to the profound ignorance, the savage rudeness, which the northern conquerors imposed on enslaved Europe.

The fifth was the last century of Rome. It was then that barbarism became everywhere victorious. The Vandals were masters of Africa, the Lombards of Italy, the Visigoths of Spain, the Franks of Gaul. Literature followed the destiny of the empire, and seemed to perish at the same time. It is, however, impossible for nations not to receive, as an inheritance from people civilised before themselves, a great part of their intellectual cultivation. Happily modern Europe was swayed by this law : the barbarians reduced Rome by the force of arms, —Rome triumphed in the long run over the barbarians by the genius of civilisation and her arts.

---

* The following descriptions of various banquets and bills of fare are here introduced, in the anticipation that in after years they may prove interesting, and induce, for the future, culinary artists to enlarge and preserve those magiric archives.

It is known that even after the introduction of vulgar idioms, the learned of the middle ages continued the use of Latin, and that in the 15th century that beautiful language, purified from barbarian corruptions, became once more classic, particularly in Italy.

At that epoch, an obscure inhabitant of Mentz, John Guttenberg, immortalised himself by the discovery of printing, just as the love of antiquity was causing the old literary masterpieces to be sought out, and creating a demand for copies of the manuscripts.

Then, as if they had risen from their tombs after a thousand years of forgetfulness, all the writers of antiquity re-appeared, to charm, instruct, and renovate the world.

It was the era of regeneration, when you, O, beloved masters! Pliny, Apicius, Petronius, Athenæus,—and you, ingenuous and faithful chroniclers of the gastronomic follies of the people-king,—were resuscitated in all your glory! Others instructed the universe in philosophy, eloquence, and history,—you taught man how the ancients dined; and, thanks to your lessons, our fathers began to comprehend that, since the table is the great scene of life where bonds of friendship are formed and cemented, banqueting is indispensable to the prosperity of nations.

No one will accuse us, we hope, of endeavouring to establish a paradox for which we could hardly find an excuse, in our love of the culinary art, as long experience, and public facts within the memory of all, victoriously confirm our assertion.

Let us interrogate the 19th century. Hardly had the lamentable wars which divided the nations of Europe ceased,—hardly had the vibration of the last cannonshot died away,—when the people of every clime—too long disunited—sealed by fraternal banquets their tardy but frank reconciliation. The destructive genius of war is succeeded by those grand struggles of commerce and industry, which, aided by the arts and sciences of civilisation, dispense to all the blessing of reproductive wealth.

And then dinner is the *sine quâ non*,—to that goal all our efforts tend. The Englishman dines in Paris, the Frenchman dines in London; the time-honoured national dishes become cosmopolite, like those who dwell on the banks of the Thames or the Seine; on both sides the people are proud to communicate the arcana of those delicate preparations, which have only to cross the frontier to obtain, under a favourable sky, a more ample illustration and a new right of citizenship. Appetite, the roasting-jack,—in a word, gastronomy, serves perhaps to unite men much more firmly than motives of interest; and more than one thought useful to the human species has often originated in the midst of the creative excitement of a banquet, where, to say the least, we meet with that hearty goodwill and friendly aid which might be wanting elsewhere.

Shall we mention that prodigious enterprise with which a noble prince—the enlightened protector of industry and the arts, and so worthy of our love and respect—has deigned to couple a name dear to public gratitude?

The royal plan was nothing less than this: to erect an immense, costly, and sumptuous palace, in which each nation should deposit the material proofs of its intelligence. Neither Rome nor Greece ever conceived such a thought! Louis XIV., with all his magnificence, and the magic pomp of his reign, imagined nothing equal to it!

This great and complex idea struck many persons no doubt with surprise; but England—we must do her the justice which facts prove to be her due—is always ready to undertake impossibilities, and generally performs them.

However, it was necessary to bring together a certain number of influential, scientific, patriotic, and wealthy men, and obtain their co-operation to realise that modern arch of crystal, into which the industry of the world would be summoned to send its most marvellous productions. Banquets were proposed, and banquets took place, in honour of a prince who was about to connect all parts of the globe in the bands of commercial fraternity. The Lord Mayor of the city of London—that celebrated factory of the world's trade!—invited all the mayors of the three kingdoms to come and place themselves by the side of the august spouse of their sovereign, at a feast worthy of such guests by its delicate profusion and splendid magnificence. There his Royal Highness Prince Albert received the enthusiastic assurance of the realisation of a colossal project, a philanthropic thought,—the union of nations, by rousing the noble pride of their nationality!

In their turn, the mayors of Great Britain and Ireland were desirous of offering to the Lord Mayor of the city of London a banquet, at which his Royal Highness would be present; and this feast, a grandiose and sympathetic demonstration on the part of the votaries of the memorable London Exhibition, took place the 25th October, 1850, in the gothic Guildhall of York, where remembrance of the past was blended with hopes for the future.

It was resolved to intrust us with the direction of the gastronomic department, and, let us add, the artistic arrangement of that banquet, which, by reason of its unprecedented richness and truly magic aspect, no pen can describe, owing partly to the magnificence of the maces, swords, banners, &c., of each county being for the first time displayed under the same roof. The engraving which we present to our readers* will perhaps convey an idea of a portion of the splendour of the entertainment.

The guests at the royal table consisted of the following distinguished personages:

The Lord Mayor of York being in the chair, there were seated on his right his Royal Highness Prince Albert, his Grace the Archbishop of York, Earl Fitzwilliam, Lord John Russell, Earl Minto, Lord Overstone, Lord Beaumont, and the Right Honourable Sir Charles Wood. On his Lordship's left were the Lord Mayor of London, the Marquis of Clanricarde, the Earl of Carlisle, the Earl of Abercorn, Lord Feversham, the Earl Granville, the High Sheriff of Yorkshire, the Right Honourable Sir G. Grey, Bart., and Sir J. V. Johnstone, Bart.

As this table formed a prominent feature in the entertainment, the following distinct bill of fare was provided:—

---

* For the general illustration of the banquet, see the "*Illustrated London News*," of November 2nd, 1850.

BILL OF FARE FOR THE ROYAL TABLE.

FIRST COURSE.

Venaison. Rissolettes à la Pompadour.

Trois Potages.	*Trois Poissons.*
Potage à la Victoria.	Turbot à la Mazarine.
Id. à la Prince of Wales.	Rougets à l'Italienne Blanche.
Id. Tortue Transparente.	John Dory à la Marinière.

Trois Relevés.

L'Extravagance Culinaire à l'Alderman.*
Chapons à la Nelson.
Quartier d'Agneau de Maison à la Sévigné.

Quatre Flancs.

Timballe de Riz à la Royale.
Jambon à la York.
Vol au vent à la Talleyrand.
Cannetons Canaris, Macédoine de Légumes.

Six Entrées.

Sauté de Faisans au fumet de Gibier.	Côtelettes de Mouton à la Réforme.
Blancs de Volaille à la York Minster.	Riz de Veau à la Palestine.
Turbans de Quenelles de Lapereaux aux Truffes.	Filets de Canneton à la Séville.

Rissolettes à la Pompadour. Venaison.

SECOND COURSE.

Trois Rôtis.

Paon à l'ancienne Rome garni d'Ortolans.
Bécasses aux Feuilles de Céleri. Guillenôts des Ardennes.

Dix Entremets.

Crême de la Grande Bretagne à la Victoria.	Crême de la Grande Bretagne à l'Albert.
Galantine d'Oisons à la Volière.	Salade de Grouse à la Soyer.
Gelée de Fraises Françaises à la Fontainebleau.	Chartreuse de Fruits aux Pêches.
Miroton de Homard.	Gâteaux crêmants à la Duke of York.
Tartelettes prâlinées aux cerises de Montmorency.	Rocailles aux Huîtres gratinées à l'Ostend.

Légumes à la Française. Petits Pois Verts.

Trois Relevés.

Hure de Sanglier à l'Allemande en Surprise.
Jambon Croquant aux Abricots.
Paniér de Fruit glacé à la Lady Mayoress.

Dessert Floréal à la Watteau.

Raisins de Fontainebleau.	Raisins Muscats.
Fraises des bois Françaises.	Melons.
Pêches de Montreuil.	Bananas.
Ananas.	Compote de Chaumontelle.

Légumes à la Française. Grosses Asperges à l'Américaine.

* See page 406.

YORK BANQUET IN

Pl. 33

Chant & Saddler, sculp.

T IN THE YEAR 1850.

GENERAL BILL OF FARE FOR 248 GUESTS.

FIRST COURSE.

Trente-deux Potages.

Quatre Potages à la Victoria.
Quatre Id. à la Prince of Wales.

Huit Potages à la Tortue Transparente.
Seize Id. à la Moderne.

Trente-deux Poissons.

Huit Turbots à la Mazarin.
Huit Truites Saumonées à la Marinière.

Huit Filets de Merlans à la Crême.
Huit Crimp Cod aux Huîtres.

Trente-deux Relevés.

Six .Chapons à la Nelson.
Six Saddleback de Mouton Gallois.
Quatre Aloyaux de Bœuf au Raifort.
Six Haunches de Venaison.

Six Quartiers d'Agneau de Maison à la
Sévigné.
Quatre Dindonneaux en Diadême.

Trente-deux Flancs.

Huit Jambons à la York.
Huit Poulardes à la Russe.

Huit Timballes de Riz à la Royale.
Huit Pâtés chauds à la Westphalienne.

Quarante-huit Entrées.

Huit Sautés de Faisans au fumet de Gibier aux Truffes.
Huit de Côtelettes de Mouton à la Vicomtesse.
Huit de Blancs de Volaille à la York Minster.
Huit de Riz de Veau à la Palestine.
Huit de Rissolettes de Volaille à la Pompadour.
Huit de Salmi de Gibier à la Chasseur.

SECOND COURSE.

Quarante Rôtis.

Huit de Perdreaux aux feuilles de Céleri.
Huit de Faisans bardés au Cresson.
Six de Cannetons au jus d'Oranges.

Six de Grouses à l'Ecossaise.
Six de Levreaux au jus de Groseilles.
Six de Bécasses et Bécassines au jus.

Cent Entremets.

Dix Chartreuses de Pêches.
Dix Gelées de fraises Françaises à la
Fontainebleau.
Dix Salades de Grouses à la Soyer.
Dix Galantines Aspiquées à la Volière.
Dix Crêmes transparentes au Kirchenwaser.

Dix Crevettes au Vin de Champagne.
Dix Gâteaux crêmants à la Duke of York.
Dix Petites Macédoines de fruit cristallisé.
Dix Mirotons de Homard aux Olives.
Dix Tartelettes prâlinées aux Ceris es de
Montmorency.

Vingt Relevés.

Dix paniers de Fruits Glacés à la Lady Mayoress.
Dix Jambons en Surprise à l'Ananas.

Side Table—Vegetables.

Céleri à la Crême.
Choux Fleurs au beurre.
Haricots Verts.
Choux de Bruxelles.

Céleri à la Crême.
Choux Fleurs au beurre.
Sea Kale.
Choux de Bruxelles.

Grand Dessert Floréal à la Watteau.

L'Extravagance Culinaire d l'Alderman, or the One Hundred Guinea Dish.—
The opportunity of producing some gastronomic phenomenon for the royal table on
such an occasion as the York Banquet was irresistible ; accordingly, the following
choice morsels were carefully selected from all the birds mentioned in the general
bill of fare, to form a dish of delicacies worthy of his Royal Highness and the
noble guests around him.

The extravagance of this dish, valued at one hundred guineas, is accounted for,
by supposing, that if an epicure were to order a similar one for a small party, he
would be obliged to provide the undermentioned articles, viz. :

	At the cost of £ s. d.
5 Turtle heads, part of fins, and green fat	34 0 0
24 Capons, the two small *noix* (nuts) from each side of the middle of the back only used, being the most delicate part of every bird	8 8 0
18 Turkeys, the same	8 12 0
18 Fatted pullets, the same	5 17 0
16 Fowls, the same	2 8 0
10 Grouse	2 5 0
20 Pheasants, *noix* only	3 0 0
45 Partridges, the same	3 7 0
6 Plovers, whole	0 9 0
100 Snipes, *noix* only	5 0 0
3 Dozen Quails, whole	3 0 0
40 Woodcocks, *noix* only	8 0 0
3 Dozen Pigeons, the same	0 14 0
6 Dozen Larks, stuffed	0 15 0
Ortolans from Belgium	5 0 0
The *garniture*, consisting of cockscombs, truffles, mushrooms, crawfish, olives, American asparagus, *croustades* (paste crust), sweetbreads, *quenelles de volaille* (strips or slices of fowl), green mangoes, and a new sauce	14 10 0
	£105 5 0

In order to present to the reader the striking contrast of extravagance in
ancient and modern cookery, we here give an engraving of the celebrated Roman
dish (Wild Boar à la Troyenne) described in page 185. It appears to have been
one of those extraordinary efforts of genius which the artist could only produce under
the sanction of a lavish patron. It was a veritable *tour-de-force*, and, no doubt
deserved the commendation it received, not only because it was of colossal size, and
the good taste displayed, but also on account of the various culinary delicacies of which
it was composed. We have no account of the cost of such a dish, but, judging
from the excessive prices given in ancient times for all *recherché* articles at the
tables of the great, it must have been enormous.

We will now resume our description of the York Banquet. In front of the

Alfred Adam del.

WILD BOAR A LA TROYENNE.

EXTRAVAGANCE CULINAIRE A L' ALDERMAN

Pl. 35

LORD MAYOR OF LONDON'S CUP.

HIS ROYAL HIGHNESS PRINCE ALBERT'S CUP.

LORD MAYOR OF YORK'S CUP.

principal table, on a raised platform, covered with purple cloth, was a collection of maces, swords, &c., estimated by competent judges to be worth £12,000.

The most conspicuous ornament was placed immediately behind the great circular table ; it was designed by the author, and is represented in the accompanying engraving. It consisted of a large emblematic vase, twenty feet in height, painted and modelled by Mr. Alfred Adams. Around the base are Europe, Asia, Africa, and America, presenting specimens of industry to Britannia. From the centre of the base springs a palm tree, surrounded by the arms of the cities of London and York ; medallion portraits of her Majesty and Prince Albert, encircled by the shields of the principal cities and towns of the United Kingdom, form the body of the vase ; two figures of Ireland and Scotland the handles ; the Prince of Wales's emblem the neck, and the royal arms the apex. Appended were graceful wreaths of flowers, in which the symbols of the Houses of York and Lancaster (red and white roses) predominated ; and when a brilliant flood of gaslight, aided by powerful reflectors, was thrown upon this splendid decoration, the effect was truly magnificent.

Having illustrated this volume with a murrhine vase, belonging to the House of Brunswick, and a curiously worked crystal cup, as gems of ancient production, we give here, as modern works of art, an engraving representing three superb drinking cups,—one for his Royal Highness Prince Albert, and one each for the Lord Mayors of London and York : the first is in ruby glass, a portion of the stem and base internally checquered with silver, and on the sides bearing white sunken medallions of her Majesty and the Prince Consort, and the royal arms of England. The other two cups were of the same size and shape, but, instead of being ruby and silver, the colours were emerald and silver ; and on the sides were the private arms of each of the Lord Mayors, together with the usual heraldic emblazonments of the cities of London and York respectively. They were presented by the author of this work in the name of the Patent Silvered-Glass Company.

This banquet was of so interesting a nature, that we could not omit giving some particulars of it in this work ; at all events, the pomp and splendour of modern times, as far as banqueting is concerned, must prove that—from the Greeks and Romans, down to the middle ages—we have not been exceeded, except, perhaps, in waste and extravagance.

The national entertainments given within the last fifty years, to commemorate striking events, are too fresh in our memory to pass them in silence.

Many persons can still remember the coronation of the Emperor Napoleon in 1805. On that occasion a grand banquet was given to all the dignitaries of the Empire and their ladies, nothing being omitted that was calculated to solemnise with sumptuosity such an event.

In 1810 the city of Paris offered to Napoleon and Maria-Louisa (Archduchess of Austria) a banquet as extraordinary as it was costly. A semicircular gallery of the Corinthian order was erected on the whole square of the Hôtel-de-Ville, where above a thousand guests joined the festival.

In 1815 a magnificent entertainment was given to the allied sovereigns by the city of London, where richness of decoration, massive gold and silver plate, and profusion of culinary rarities struck the beholder with wonder.

At the Coronation Banquet of George IV., in 1820, the old customs and privileges were ransacked to give *éclat* to that solemnity, one of the grandest, and perhaps, the most sumptuous that ever could be imagined in ancient or modern times.

In France, in the year 1824, the coronation of Charles X. was celebrated at Rheims with royal magnificence ; the banquet excited the admiration of all present. At that solemnity the Duke of Northumberland was appointed Ambassador Extraordinary from England, and few, if any, ever equalled the liberality of his Grace, or the display he made of his wealth, to represent and honour his sovereign and country at the court of Charles X. The fêtes and banquets given by his Grace —and at which the author was present—were of the most costly if not extravagant description, for we are told that the expenses of that munificent nobleman were not less than £200,000.

The grand banquets and receptions of King Louis Philippe during eighteen years exhibited too much liberality and splendour to be forgotten ; and at the marriage of his eldest son, the unfortunate Duke of Orleans, Versailles presented a scene of banqueting and rejoicing unparalleled since the time of Louis XIV.

On her Majesty's visit to the city of London a banquet was given in the Guildhall, the grandeur of which was scarcely ever exceeded, showing the loyalty, devotedness, and noble hospitality of the wealthiest commercial citizens in the world.

In 1838, at the coronation of Queen Victoria, Buckingham Palace witnessed a most elegant, chaste, and splendid banquet. The Ambassadors Extraordinary, sent from all the foreign courts, were not more conspicuous for the brilliancy of their costumes than the native nobility who graced the festive-board of the youthful Queen of Great Britain.

On this occasion a very elaborate and graceful fountain of massive gold of about three feet in height and two feet in diameter, was prominent on the royal table. It spouted four different sorts of delicious wine into as many shells, from which it dripped into four reservoirs, and was served to the guests by means of a golden ladle. This fountain can be seen, with the regalia, in the Tower of London.

On that joyful day the members of the Reform Club intrusted to our care, at Gwyrdir House, a sumptuous entertainment for fifteen hundred persons, on a scale of liberality deserving of the highest praise.

The marriage of Her Majesty with H. R. H. Prince Albert formed one of those memorable epochs to be preserved in the annals of banqueting.

The opening of the Royal Exchange, in 1846, was also one of those extraordinary days on record, where the Queen of a great nation gave proof of her sympathy in the prosperity of her merchant-princes, by presiding over a splendid entertainment to commemorate the re-establishment of that commercial edifice.

On the 3rd of July in the same year, his Highness Ibrahim Pacha, son of Mehemet Ali, Viceroy of Egypt, was entertained by the members of the Reform Club to a magnificent and most sumptuous banquet provided for two hundred guests. The author, having full scope to do honour to the invitation, provided the following liberal selection of gastronomic dishes, many of which were innovated for the occasion :—

BILL OF FARE.

Seize Potages.

Quatre à la Victoria.

Quatre à la Comte de Paris.

Quatre à la Louis Philippe.

Quatre à la Colbert, aux Légumes Printaniers.

Seize Potages.

Quatre de Turbots, Sauce à la Mazarin.

Quatre de Buissons de Filets de Merlans à l'Egyptienne.

Quatre de Saumons de Severn à la Crême.

Quatre de Truites Saumonées en Matelotte Marinière.

Seize Relevés.

Quatre de Chapons à la Nelson.

Quatre de Saddleback of Southdown Mouton, rôti à la Soyer.

Baron of Beef à l'Anglaise.

Quatre de Poulardes en Diadême.

Quatre de Saddleback d'Agneau, rôti à la Sévigné

Entrée Pagodatique de riz à la Luxor.

Cinquante-quatre Entrées.

Six de Poussins Printaniers à l'Ambassadrice.

Six de Côtelettes de Mouton à la Reform.

Quatre de Riz de Veau piqués en Macédoine de Légumes.

Quatre de Petits Vol-au-vents aux Laitances de Maquereaux.

Quatre de Timballes de Riz aux Queues d'Agneau.

Quatre de Jambonneaux Braisés au Vin de Madère.

Quatre de Volailles Farcies à la Russe aux Légumes Verts.

Quatre de Pâtés Chauds de Cailles à la Banquière.

Quatre de Rissolettes à la Pompadour.

Quatre de Grenadins de Bœuf à la Beyrout.

Six de Côtelettes d'Agneau à la Vicomtesse, et

Quatre de Turbans Epigramme de Levreau au Fumet.

Seize Rôts.

Quatre de Turkey Poult, Piqués et Bardés.

Quatre de Cannetons au Jus de Bigarades.

Quatre de Levreaux au Jus de Groseilles, et

Quatre de Gros Chapons au Cresson.

Cinquante-quatre Entremets.

Six de Gelées Macédoine de Fruits au Dantzic.

Quatre Turbans de Meringues Demi-Glacées.

Quatre de Charlotte Prussienne.

Six de Croquantes d'Amandes aux Cerises.

Quatre de Galantines à la Volière.

Quatre de Mirotons de Homard à l'Indienne.

Quatre de Salades de Volaille à la Soyer.

Quatre de Haricots Verts au Beurre Noisette.

Six de Tartelettes Prâlinées aux Abricots.

Quatre de Pain de Pêches au Noyeau.

Quatre de Petits Pois à l'Anglo-Française, et

Quatre de Gelées Cristallisées à l'Ananas.

Relevés de Rôts.

Crême d'Egypte à l'Ibrahim Pacha.

Gâteau Britannique à l'Amiral.

Quatre de Jambons Glacés en Surprise.

Quatre de Côtelettes en Surprise à la Reform.

Quatre de Manivaux de Champignons au Curaçao en Surprise.

Deux de Meringues Chinoises-Pagoda aux Fraises.

A A

We hardly need mention the annual entertainment which takes place on the 9th of November, when the city of London makes a king of a citizen.

In the course of the year 1844, King Louis Philippe paid a visit to her Majesty Queen Victoria at Windsor Castle, and during the time a series of banquets were given in honour of the King's visit by her Majesty. The gold plate—worth, it is said, a million sterling—was used on that occasion. We shall not attempt to describe the extraordinary beauty of that service: the value in itself must leave the impression that nothing like it is in existence.

In the year 1848 the return of Lord Hardinge, Governor-General of India, from his glorious campaigns in the East, was solemnised by a sumptuous banquet offered to his lordship by the members of the Carlton Club.

In the year 1850 the annual meeting of the Royal Agricultural Society was held in the fine old city of Exeter, where the Society was welcomed with the most enthusiastic rejoicings, and we had the honour of being selected by the committee to provide a dinner for one thousand and fifty members. As this rustic banquet was admitted to be one of no ordinary kind we give here the general bill of fare, and a short narrative of the first attempt to roast a whole ox by gas.

GRAND AGRICULTURAL PAVILION DINNER.

Baron of Beef à la Magna Charta.

33 Dishes of Ribs of Beef.
35 Dishes of Roast Lamb.
99 Dishes of Galantine of Veal.
29 Dishes of Ham.
66 Dishes of Pressed Beef.
2 Rounds of Beef à la Garrick.
264 Dishes of Chicken.
33 French raised Pies à la Soyer.
198 Spring Mayonnaise Salad.
264 Cherry, Gooseberry, Raspberry, and Currant Tarts.
33 Exeter Puddings.
198 Dishes of Hot Potatoes.

Grand Agricultural Trophy.

Homer tells us that a royal culinary artist placed before Ajax and his voracious companions in arms a whole bullock roasted. Since those heroic ages many no doubt have shared the same fate; and we know that in this country, on the occasion of a rich heir coming of age, a roasted ox is often given to the tenants as a substantial fare, with a well-nursed butt of ale, twenty-one years old. Many can remember that in the winter of 1812 a bullock was roasted on the frozen Thames, which certainly was something to wonder at. Another monster effort was attempted at Hammersmith some years ago, but the animal, clumsily suspended from the summit of an apparatus formed of three beams, was burnt, emitted a rank smell, and did not roast. All those who have had to attend such an operation agree that it is rather an awkward affair, and not performed without great difficulties, on account of the immense fire, which requires constant attention to keep up and regulate the necessary heat,—and, after all, it is seldom entirely successful.

For the present festival, the author, who knew well the power and efficacy of gas, wished to honour the guests with a dish of *his own*, never yet attempted, and which he has entitled the "*Baron and Saddleback of Beef à la Magna Charta.*" He therefore proposed to roast a baron and saddleback of beef, weighing five hundred and thirty-five pounds, in the open air. The magistrates very willingly put the castle yard at his disposal, and it was anticipated that a large Pandemonium fire would have been seen; but, to the surprise of every one, a few bricks, without mortar, and a few sheets of iron, forming a temporary covering to a space six feet six inches in length, and three feet three inches in width, were the only appearance of an apparatus, with two hundred and sixteen very small jets of gas coming through pipes half-an-inch in diameter. It was hardly credited that such a monster joint could be properly done by such means; however, incredulity soon vanished on seeing it frizzling and steaming away; and after eight hours' roasting it was thoroughly dressed, at a cost of less than five shillings for gas.

After having allowed it to cool it was removed, and carried by eight men through the principal streets of the ancient and loyal city of Exeter, accompanied by a band of music, playing "The Roast Beef of Old England," and followed by thousands of the incredulous of the previous day. On its arrival at the pavilion it was deposited under the grand triumphal arch, designed and erected by the author; it was 17 feet high, and 10 feet wide, and composed of all the produce of agriculture and the farm.

The following list will give some idea of its magnitude: it consisted of—

One swan, two turkeys, four geese, four ducks, eight fowls, eight pigeons, four rabbits, one fine barn-door cock, six ox heads, four calves' heads, two rams' heads, two stags' heads, two whole lambs—all natural, and in their plumage or skin— ornamented with vegetables, fruit, and flowers, viz., cabbages, turnips, potatoes, carrots, leeks, celery, rhubarb, onions, French beans, peas, asparagus, sea-kale stalks; sheaves of wheat, oats, barley; pine apples, citrons, cherries, grapes, melons, peaches, apricots, greengages, apples, gooseberries, strawberries, currants, and the choicest kinds of flowers—all being the production of the county— and surmounted by various implements of agriculture. There was also an elegant jug, ornamented with flowers, filled with clotted cream. On the top of the huge piece of beef, was placed a black pig's head, weighing eighty pounds when killed.

It was in the recollection of many persons, that thirty-five years ago a baron of beef, weighing only two hundred and forty-two pounds was roasted in Exeter, under the superintendence of twelve blacksmiths, at their forge fire, for a banquet given at the time peace was proclaimed.

The Parisians have not forgotten the great fête of the distribution of eagles by his Majesty the Emperor of the French, on that day when he relinquished the functions of President of the Republic for a more august title. That military solemnity was followed by a splendid banquet, at which there were several thousands of guests. It would be superfluous to add, that the arrangements for that gigantic repast evinced the intelligent taste and incredible resources of imagination of our continental neighbours.

An entire volume would not suffice, if we attempted to recount all the pompous feasts which followed in succession during the last century, "the age of powder and suppers." But we cannot pass in silence the memorable punch given in 1746 by Sir Edward Russell, Commander-in-Chief of the British forces, which can only be assimilated in point of extravagance to the great banquet of the Earl of Warwick, the description of which was extracted from the " Gastronomic Regenerator," and reproduced in this work, page 362.

The bowl was the marble basin of a delightful garden, forming the central point of four vast avenues, bordered with orange and lemon trees. A magnificent collation was served on four immense tables, which occupied the whole length of the several avenues. The basin had been filled with four large barrels of brandy, eight barrels of filtered water, twenty-five thousand citrons, eighty pints of lemon juice, thirteen hundred weight of sugar, five pounds of nutmeg, three hundred biscuits, and a pipe of Malaga wine. An awning over the basin protected it from rain, which might have disturbed the chemical combination of the delicious beverage; and, in a charming little rose-wood boat, a cabin boy, belonging to the fleet, rowed about on the surface of the punch, ready to serve the joyous company, which numbered more than six thousand persons.*

We cannot terminate this rapid sketch, without mentioning that, after several years of research in compiling this work, we completed our task on the day following that on which her Most Gracious Majesty the Queen of England offered the largest royal banquet since her accession to the throne, to an assembly of kings, queens, and princes, and the flower of the British aristocracy, consisting of a hundred and twenty guests, on the occasion of the baptism of his Royal Highness Prince Leopold George Duncan Albert. This regal entertainment took place on the 28th of June, and never, perhaps, did the august sovereign display so much magnificence and majesty. We shall not publish the details of this imposing banquet; and, moreover, we should inform our readers of nothing new, were we to tell them of the artistical selection, execution, and perfection of the bill of fare,—of the richness of the ornaments and service,—of the royal and feminine gracefulness of the mother, wife, and queen. " May Heaven grant," say we, in the words of the immortal Bossuet, " that the children of this illustrious princess, like a crown of olive saplings, may cling round her, and grow in virtue, strength, and renown; may the Ruler of empires throw a halo round the destiny of the august mother, and show to all that His mighty hand upholds thrones and protects kings!"

---

* While thus hastily enumerating some modern banquets, we cannot refrain mentioning that illusive feast of the most effeminate of Assyrian kings, the plan of which seems to have been imparted by the magiric genius himself to our celebrated tragedian Charles Kean. Every night, Sardanapalus, the sensual king of the too joyous Ninevites, rising from his tomb, with his twenty-six centuries of renown, seats himself at table, in order to unveil to us long buried splendours, and confirm our belief in those sumptuous orgies of which history preserves to us but uncertain details.

The admirable works of Botta, Flandin, Layard, and Bonomi, have allowed the ingenious major domo who presides at these Assyrian feasts of the 19th century, to invest them with that *couleur locale* which would formerly have been sought in vain; and, should the shade of the voluptuous prince wander amidst the guests seated at his table, it may still recognise the cup from which he imbibed intoxication and forgetfulness of his tragic destiny. Altogether, this scenic representation appears to us the realisation of an extraordinary dream, and we have been tempted to place this fictitious repast of Sardanapalus amongst the modern banquets here called to remembrance.

TABLE OF REFERENCES

TO

Ancient and Modern Writers.

I.

AGRICULTURE.

1. Plutarch. De Isid. et Osirid.; Ovid. Fabul. lib. v. 6, 7; Aurel. Vict. De Orig. Gent. Roman.
2. Genes. cap. ii. 15.
3. Ibid. cap. iii. 23.
4. Cuvier, Discours sur les Révolutions du Globe, 6e. édit. p. 171.
5. Judic. cap. vi. 11,14.
6. Ruth, cap. ii. 3, 5.
7. I. Samuel, cap. xi. 5.
8. I. Reg. cap. xix. 19.
9. Guénée, Lettres de Quelques Juifs, tom. iii. p. 23, edit. in 12mo.
10. Levitic. cap. xxv. 23.
11. Diodor. Sicul. lib. ii. § 3.
12. Aristot. De Republ. lib. ii. cap. 7.
13. Levitic. xxv. 3, 6.
14. Mishna, passim.
15. Exod. iii. 8.
16. Joseph. De Bello Judaic. lib. iii. cap. 8.
17. Juvenal. Sat. xv. 10.
18. Genes. cap. xii. 10.
19. Ibid. cap. xlii. 1, 2, 3.
20. Varro. De Re Rustic.; Plin. xviii. 7; Plutarch. In Cæsar.
21. Plutarch. De Isid.; Tibull. lib. i. eleg. vii. 29.
22. Fabretti. Inscript. p. 574.
23. Homer. Il. x. 351; Odyss. viii. 124.
24. Polydor. Virgil.
25. Plin. xviii. 4.
26. Aul. Gell. i. 23.
27. Plin. iv. 3; Flor. i. 2.
28. Flor. viii. 3.
29. Columell. ii. 5.
30. Ibid. ii. 2.
31. Varro. i. 29.
32. Encyclopédie Méthodique; Antiquités Planches.
33. Cato. De Re Rustica, x. xi.
34. Strutt, Manners and Customs, &c., vol. i. p. 32, fig. vii.
35. Plin. xvii. 5, 8.
36. Varro. i. 13, 38; Columell. ii. 5, 6, 9.
37. Geoponic. xii. 4; Virgil. Georg. i. 81 Plin. xvii. 9.
38. Cato. cap. xxx.; Plin. xviii. 53; Varro. ii. 2.
39. Column. Trajan. tab. 83.
40. Passerii Lucern. Fictil. tab. 9.
41. Gessner. ii. tab. 32, no. 75.
42. Mongez. Encyclop. Méthod. Antiquit. Planches.
43. De Re Rustica, i. 50.
44. Virgil. Georg. lib. iv.
45. Plin. viii. 30.
46. Columell. ii. 21.
47. Isaias, xxviii. 27.
48. Herculan. v. 95.
49. Geoponic. ii. 27, 31; Plin. xviii. 30; Varro. i. 57; Columell. i. 6.
50. Dioscorid.; Diodor. Sicul.; Dio. Nicæus.
51. Id.
52. Strab.; Plin.; Strutt, Manners, &c., of the Ancient Britons, vol. i. p. 7.
53. Strutt, Ibid. p. 43.
54. Id. Ibid. pp. 43, 44.
55. Fontan. tom. ii. liv. iii. titre 33, p. 1190.

II.

CEREALS.

1. Tit. Liv. Decad. i. lib. 1.
2. Plin. xviii. 8.
3. Cato. R. R. cap. 86.
4. Virgil. Georgic. i. 210.
5. II. Samuel, cap. xvii. 28.
6. Sueton. In August. xiv.
7. Exod. cap. ix. 31.
8. Virgil. Georgic. i. 216.
9. Xenophon. De Expedit. Cyri, lib. vii. ; Plin. xviii. 7.
10. Geoponic. ii. 38.
11. Plin. xviii. 40.
12. Id. xviii. 16.
13. Dioscorid. ii. 16.
14. Virgil. Georgic. i. 153.
15. Plin. xviii. 17.
16. Id. xviii. 7, 10.
17. Dioscorid. ii. 117.
18. Galen. De Facultat. Aliment. i. 17.
19. Herodot. ii. 36.
20. Dioscorid. lib. ii. cap. 3 ; lib. iii.
21. Plin. xxii. 25.
22. Id. ii. 7.
23. Petron. cap. i.
24. Plaut. Pœn. act. i. sc. 2, 112.
25. Leg. xii. Tabul. pars ii. L. ix.
26. Ulp. 50 Dig. t. v. l. 2 ; Arc. ad. Charis. D. 50, t. iv. l. 18, § 5 ; Wolfius, t. v. Oper. Demosth. f. 358.
27. Samuel Petit. Comment. lib. v. tit. 5.
28. Plin. lib. xviii.
29. Dio. lib. xi. 3 ; Isidor. lib. ult. cap. 14.
30. Panem et Circenses.
31. Demosth. In Phorm.
32. Plutarch. In Cat. Maj. ; Cic. in Verrem.
33. Sueton. In Jul. Cæsar. cap. 41.
34. Dio Cassius, lib. xliii.
35. Id. lib. lv.
36. Sueton. In Neron. cap. 10 ; Tacit. lib. xv.
37. Spartian. In Sever. ; Liv. lib. ii.
38. Socrat. ii. 10, 13 ; Sozomen. iii. 6.
39. Cic. Pro Leg. Manil.
40. Liv. lib. xxxiii. ; Cic. Ad Attic. ep. ix. et seqq. ; Varro. R. R. ; Plin. xviii. 7.
41. Stow's Chronicles, p. 167.
42. Fabian. vol. ii. p. 30.

III.

GRINDING OF CORN.

1. Apud Athenæum.
2. Ovid. Fast. iv. 399.

3. Tibull. ii. eleg. 3.
4. Pausan. In Arcad.
5. Virgil. Georg. iv. 81.
6. De Mensura Cibi.
7. Lucret. v. 14.
8. Plin. vii. 51.
9. Encyclop. Méthod. Antiquit. Planches.
10. Varro. apud Nonnium.
11. Plin. xviii. 3.
12. Polyb. i. 22.
13. Deuteronom. xxiv. 6.
14. Exod. xi. 5.
15. Numer. xi. 8.
16. Pausanias, v. μυλη, Histor. Laconicor.
17. Homer. Odyss.
18. Id. Ibid. vii. 105.
19. Plin. xviii. 11.
20. Gell. xxxi. 3 ; Terent. Andr. act i. sc. 2.
21. Gell. xiii. 22.
22. Virg. Georg. i., et ibi Servius, v. 267, 274.
23. Ovid. In Fastis ; Rosin. Antiquit. Roman. iv. 10.
24. Paschal. Coron. p. 260.
25. Rosin. loc. cit.
26. Apul. Milesiar. lib. ix.
27. Terent. Andria. act. i. sc. 2.
28. Meursius, Criticar. Exercitat. part i. cap. 9.
29. Id. Ibid.
30. Gell. iii. 3.
31. Vitruv. x. 10.
32. Plin. xviii. 10.
33. Vid. Turneb. Salmas, et Perrault, section Vitruve.
34. Goetzius, De Pistrinis Veterum.
35. Strabo, Geograph.
36. De Canone Frumentar, Urb. Rom. L. iv. Cassiodor. Variar. iii.
37. 5th century.
38. Decernimus de Aquæductu, L. x.
39. Anno 536.
40. Procop. De Bello Gothico. i. 15.
41. Vitruv. x. 5 ; Schneider ; Palladius, R. R. i. 42.
42. Plin. xxxvi. 30.
43. Odyss. xx. 105, 119 ; Cato. R. R. cap. 56.
44. Leges Ethelberti.
45. Strutt, Manners, &c., vol. ii., p. 13.
46. Apud Strutt, ibid.
47. Ibid. p. 14.
48. Heringius.
49. Monast. Anglic. t. i. p. 816 ; t. ii. p. 459 ; t. iii. p. 107.

IV.

MANIPULATION OF FLOUR.

1. Montaigne, Essais.
2. Genes. xviii. 6.
3. Exod. xii. 39.
4. Reg. xix. 6.
5. Levitic. vii. 9.
6. Calmet. Bible, tom. vi. p. 257, fol.
7. Waserus, De Antiq. Mensuris, ii. 5.
8. Genes. iii. 19; Exod. ii. 20; xviii. 12; et passim.
9. Calmet. loc. cit.
10. Fleury, Mœurs des Israélites, chap. 12.
11. Ruth, ii. 14.
12. Calmet. loc. cit.
13. Plin. xviii. 11.
14. Exod. xii. 15, 17 to 20, 34, 39.
15. Levitic. vii. 9.
16. Genes. xv. 17.
17. Levitic. ii. 4; vii. 9; xi. 35; xxvi. 26; Calmet. Bible, tom. vi.
18. Genes. xl. 1, et seqq.
19. Cassiodor. Variar. vi.; Olai Magni Hist. xiii. 13; Panis a Pane.
20. Cic. Pro Cluentio; Isïdor. xx. 2.
21. Paître—Manger.
22. Nonnius Marcellus, De Prop. Sermon.
23. Athen. iii. 13.
24. Id. Ibid.
25. Id. Ibid.
26. Id. Ibid.
27. Aristoph. Ran. v. 856.
28. Galen. De Aliment. Facultat. lib. i.
29. Athen. iii. 29.
30. Cæl. Rhodig. xxvi.
31. Athen. loc. cit.
32. Id. Ibid.
33. Id. Ibid.
34. Id. Ibid.
35. Id. Ibid.
36. Id. iii. 13.
37. Plin. xviii. 7.
38. Athen. loc. cit.
39. Plaut. Pœn. et Mostellar; Plin. xviii. 8.
40. Tit. Liv. Dec. i. lib. v. cap. 48—Florus.
41. Galen. De Aliment. Facultat. i. 18.
42. Festus; Lactant. Divinar. Institut. cap. 20; Ovid. Fast. ii. 525.
43. Plin. xviii. 11.
44. Pomp. Sabin. In Moret. Virgil.
45. Maximar. C. De Excusat. Muner. L. xii.
46. Vitruv. Architect. vi. 9.
47. Plin. xviii. 10.
48. Plin. xviii. 11.
49. Aurel. Vict.; si quis De Pistorib. L. ii.; si cui, Ibid. L. iv.
50. Optio, Ibid. L. iv.
51. Nulli Pistori, Ibid. L. xxi.
52. Ne Quis, Ibid. L. xv.
53. Quicumque, Ibid. L. xxii.
54. Gell. xv. 19.
55. Brod. Miscellan. v. 21; Plin. xix. 1; Columell. v. 10; Petron. 35.
56. Juvenal. Sat. x. 82.
57. Ammian. Marcellin. xxvi.; Sueton. In Claud. cap. 18.
58. Plin. xviii. 7, 9, 10, 11.
59. Id. xix. 4.
60. Id. Ibid.
61. Gronovius.
62. Richard. Gorræi. Annal. Principio.
63. Plin. xviii. 11.
64. A.D. 75.
65. Ovid. Fast. vi., 260, et seqq.
66. Pitt. Ercolan. tom. ii. p. 141.
67. Gronovius.
68. Cels. ii. 18; Galen. De Facultat. Aliment. i.
69. Id. iv. 6.
70. Ammian. Marcellin. xvii. 17; Senec. Epist. 83.
71. Athen. iii. 28.
72. Encyclop. Méthodiq. Antiquités.
73. Plaut. Aulul. act ii. sc. 9, ver. 4; Plin. xviii. 11.
74. Encyclop. Méthod. Antiq.
75. Ibid.
76. Ibid.
77. Strutt, loc. cit.
78. Delamarre, Traité de la Police.
79. Réglement du 20 Mars, 1635.
80. Monteil. Hist. des Français, tom. ii., pp. 47, 48.

V.

FRUMENTA.

1. Servius.
2. Theophrast. ex versione Gazæ.
3. Hippocrat. De Victûs Ration.; Galen. De Aliment. Facult. lib. i.
4. Plin. xviii. 7; xx. 25; Bruyerin. v. 7; et seqq.
5. Deuteron. viii. 8.
6. II. Samuel, xvii. 28.
7. Paralipomen. ii. 9.
8. Sueton. In August. cap. 14.
9. Theophrast.; Menand.; Plin. xviii. 7.

10. Galen. De Aliment. Facultat. lib. i.
11. Id. Ibid.
12. Athen. iii. 36.
13. Bruyerin. v. 6.
14. Hippocrat. De Victus Ratione.
15. Id. Ibid.
16. Plin. xviii. 17 ; Villichius, cap. xii.
17. Colman, Lexicon ; Meursius.
18. Cato. R. R. cap. lxxxvi.
19. Galen. De Aliment. Facultat. i. 17 ; Bruyerin. v. 21.
20. Varro. De Ling. Lat. ; Columell. ii.
21. Virgil. Georg. lib. iv.
22. Plin. xviii. 7.
23. Id. Ibid.
24. Dioscorid. ii. 120.
25. Plin. xviii. 24.
26. Plin. Jun. Epist. ad Septic. Clar.
27. Cato. R.R.
28. Columell. xii. 55 ; Cato. cap. 86.
29. Plin. xviii. 7 ; Bruyerin. v. 23 ; Galen. De Aliment. Facultat. lib. i.
30. J. A. St. John, The Hindoos, vol. i. p. 357.
31. Martial.
32. Athen. vii.
33. Plat. in Gorg.
34. Athen. i. 13.
35. Andrieux, " Les rois malaisément souffrent qu'on leur résiste."
36. Athen. 13.

VI.

GRAINS : SEEDS.

1. Plin. xx. 22.
2. Nonnius, De Re Cibariâ, i. 14.
3. Plin. xix. 8, 22.
4. Matth. xiii. 31 ; xvii. 20 ; Marc. iv. 31 ; Luc. xiii. 19 ; xvii. 6.
5. Boerhaave, Hist. Plant.
6. See Les Bigarrures du Seigneur des Accords. Paris, 1662, p. 62.
7. Plin. xx. 20.
8. Varro. R. R.
9. Plin. xviii. 7, 14.
10. Id. Ibid.
11. Athen. i. 15.
12. Ibid. ii. 14.
13. Plin. xviii. 14.
14. Bruyerin, vii.
15. Plin. xix. 1.
16. Galen. De Aliment. Facult. i. ; Bruyerin. vii. 12.

17. Plin. loc. cit.
18. Bruyerin, vii. 13.
19. Simeo. Sethi, De Aliment. Facult.

VII.

VEGETABLES.

1. Nonnius, De Re Cibar. i. 5.
2. Plin. xviii. 10.
3. Genes. ix. 3.
4. Ibid. xxv. 34.
5. Samuel, xvii. 28.
6. Daniel, i. 12, 16.
7. Athen. i. 45.
8. Iliad.
9. Athen. ii. 8.
10. Varro. De Re Rust. i. 23, 32 ; Isidor. Orig. xvii. 4.
11. Cato. 35, 36 ; Virgil. Georg. i. ii. ; Varro. De Re Rust. i. 23, 32. ; Ovid. Fast. v.; Gell. iv. 11.
12. Virgil. Georg. translat. by Delille.
13. Sigonius, De Nominib. Roman.
14. Cic. lib. vii. Epist. 26 ad Fab. Gall.
15. 97 years B. C.
16. Dio. Epitom. Tiber.
17. Apicius, De Obsoniis. i. 23.
18. Caroli Magni Capitul.

VIII.

DRIED VEGETABLES.

1. Ovid. Fast. iii. ; Festus, De Verb. Signif. ; Nonnius, i. 5.
2. Festus, loc. cit.
3. Nonnius, loc. cit.
4. Id. loc. cit.
5. Theophrast. De Caus. Plant. ; Clem. Alex. Strom. ; Cic. De Divinat. i. ; Plin. xviii. 7, 12. ; Simeo. Sethi, De Aliment. Facult. p. 134.
6. Hippocrat. iii. aphor. 20.
7. Plin. xviii. 12.
8. Pollux et Eustath.
9. Isidor. Orig. vii. ; Nonnius, i. 5.
10. II. Reg. xvii. 28.
11. Ezech. iv. 9.
12. Athen. iii. 1.
13. Id. Ibid.
14. Id. Ibid.
15. Dioscorid. ii. 99 ; Athen. loc. cit. ; Plin. xxi. 15 ; Theophrast. v.
16. Plin. xvi. 30 ; xxiv. 2.

17. Pinkerton's Ancient Scot. Poems, vol. ii. p. 431.
18. Anecdotes of Some Distinguished Persons, vol. iii. p. 317.
19. Boemus Aubanus. Mores, Leges, &c., Omnium Gentium, Genev. 1620, p. 266.
20. Brand's Popular Antiquities, vol. i. p. 24.
21. Athen.
22. Virgil. Georg. i. 227.
23. Athen. ii. 15.
24. Galen. De Aliment. Facult. ii.
25. Id. Ibid. v.; Nonnius, i. 5.; Platina, De Tuend. Valetud.
26. Columell. ii. 10.
27. Mélanges Tirés d'une Grande Bibliothèque.
28. II. Reg. xvii. 28.
29. Martial. i. 42.
30. Lambinus; Erasm. In Adagiis.
31. Columell. ii. 10.; Plin. xviii. 12.
32. Martial. loc cit.
33. Horat. Sat. i. 3.
34. Athen. iv.; Nonnius, De Re Cibar.; Bruyerin. vii. 3.; Florentin. ap. Constant. Cæsar. xi.
35. Athen. vi. 4.
36. Id.; Nonnius; Bruyerin. loc. cit.
37. Genes. xxv. 34.
38. II. Reg. xvii. 28.
39. Ibid. xxiii. 11.
40. Ezech. iv. 9.
41. Cic. Tuscul. iv.; Virgil. Georg. i. ii.; Isidor. Orig. xvii.
42. Appian. De Bello Parthico; Plutarch. In Vitâ Crassi.
43. Virgil. Georg. i. 228.
44. Plin. xv. 12.

IX.

KITCHEN GARDEN.

1. Delille, Préface du Poème des Jardins.
2. Num. xxiv. 6.
3. Virgil. Georg. iv.
4. Esth. vii. 7, 8.
5. Ex Trog. Pompeio. Justin. xxxvi.
6. Q. Curt. v. 1.
7. Odyss. vii.
8. Dio. xlvii.; Sueton. Cæs. 83.
9. Cato. Varro. Columell. passim.
10. Cal. Siculus. Eclog. ii.
11. Frontin. Cœl. Sympos. Œnigm. 72; Pallad. ix. 11.
12. Scriptores Rei Rustic. passim.
13. Ibid.
14. Hippocrat. Aphorism.
15. Plin.
16. Cato. De Re Rustic. 156, 157.
17. Athen. ix. 2.
18. Cato. loc. cit.
19. Ch. St. Laurent, Diction. Encycloped.
20. Apicius, De Obsoniis, iii. 9.
21. Id. Ibid.
22. Id. Ibid.
23. Id. Ibid.
24. Olivier de Serres.
25. Columell. x. 251 et 254.
26. Plin. xix. 8.
27. Athen. i. 6.
28. Id. ix. 2.
29. Id. Ibid.
30. Martial. xiii. 13.
31. Apicius, iii. 2.
32. Id. Ibid.
33. Id. iii. 11.
34. Dioscorid.
35. Stephan. Thesaur. Ling. Latin.; Ch. St. Laurent, Dict. Encyclop.
36. Beckmann, Hist. of Invent.
37. Hispanicum Olus.
38. Athen. ii. 18.
39. Id. Ibid.
40. Horat. Epod. ii. 58.
41. Martial. iii. 89.
42. Cic. vii. Familiar. 26.
43. Plin. xx. 21.
44. Apicius, iii. 8.
45. Id. Ibid.
46. La Fontaine, Fables.
47. Athen. ii. 21.
48. Id. Ibid.
49. Id. Ibid.
50. Plin. xix. 4.
51. Id. xix. 8.
52. Sueton. Oct. Cæs. 87.
53. Apicius, iii. 3.
54. Plin. loc. cit.
55. Dictionnaire des Sciences Naturelles.
56. Plin. xix. 5.
57. Id. Ibid.
58. Id. Ibid.
59. Athen. ii. 18.
60. Id. Ibid.
61. Propert. iv. 2, 43.
62. Juvenal. Sat. xiv. 47.
63. Athen. ii. 18.

64. Athen. ii. 18.
65. Id. Ibid.
66. Id. ix. 3.
67. Id. Ibid.
68. Apicius, iii. 4.
69. Id. Ibid.
70. Id. Ibid.
71. Id. Ibid.
72. Athen. i. 6.
73. Scriptores Rei Rustic.
74. Apicius, iii. 13.
75. Plin. xix. 5.
76. Id. xxi. 15.
77. Apicius, iii. 21.
78. Id. Ibid.
79. Id. Ibid.
80. Festus.
81. Dr. Charbonnier.
82. Plin. xx. 20.
83. Id. Ibid.
84. Id. xix. 12.
85. Apicius, iii. 11.'
86. Plin. xix. 8.
87. Athen.
88. Apicius, iii. 9.
89. Ruell. i. 20.
90. Athen. ii. 13; Pollux, vi. 9.
91. Id. Ibid.
92. Dioscorid. iii. 14.
93. Plin. xxi. 16.
94. Id. Ibid.
95. Hermolao Barbaro.
96. Ruell. i.
97. 2nd cent. A.C.
98. Galen. De Aliment. Facult.
99. Columell. x. 236.
100. Geoponic. xii. 39.
101. Ibid.
102. Apicius, iii. 19.
103. Ch. St. Laurent, Dict. Encycl.
104. Apicius, loc. cit.
105. Id. Ibid.
106. Tertullian, De Animâ, cap. 32.
107. Id. Adv. Marc. iv. 40.
108. Plin. xx. 2.
109. Num. xi. 5.
110. Apicius, iii. 4.
111. Id. Ibid.
112. Ch. St. Laurent. Dict. Encyc.
113. Apicius, iii. 5.
114. Num. xi. 5.
115. Athen.
116. Geoponic. xii. 7, 4.
117. Plin.
118. Apicius, iii. 6.

119. Apicius, i. 31.
120. Id. Ibid.
121. Id. iii. 6.
122. Id. Ibid.
123. Id. Ibid.
124. Exod. xii. 8; Num. ix. 11.
125. Athen. ii. 18.
126. Id. Ibid.
127. Martial. xiii. 14.
128. Bibl. Sacra. loc. cit.
129. Athen. i. 12.
130. Theophrast. Hist. Plant. vi. 7.
131. Galen. De Aliment. Facult.
132. Sueton. In August.
133. Ch. St. Laurent. Dict. Encycl.
134. Apicius, iii. 15.
135. Id. Ibid.
136. Platina; Taillevant.
137. Plin. xx. 8.
138. Virgil. Georg. i. 120.
139. Columell. x. 3.
140. Pallad. i. 30; Apul. De Herb. 47.
141. Apicius, iii. 18.
142. Geoponic. xii. 31.
143. Num. xi. 5.
144. Socrat. In Zenophont. Symposio.
145. Plin. xix. 6.
146. Horat. lib. i. Epod. xii. 21.
147. Apicius, iii. 15.
148. Alexand. v. 10.
149. Num. xi. 5.
150. Geoponic. xii. 29.
151. Ibid.
152. Athen. ix. 3.
153. Apicius, iii. 10.
154. Id. Ibid.
155. J. A. St. John, The Hindoos, vol. i. p. 357.
156. Suidas. Tiber. iii.
157. Geoponic. xii. 20.
158. Ibid.
159. Ibid.
160. Apicius, iii. 7.
161. Pasquier, Recherches sur la France.
162. Babylonic Talmud.
163. Athen. i. 6.
164. Plin. xix. 5.
165. Id. Ibid.
166. Id. Ibid.
167. Varro. R. R.; Columell. xi.; Plin. xviii.
168. Geoponic. xii. 21; Varro. i. 11.
169. Sueton. In Vespas. iv.
170. Apicius, iii. 13.
171. Id. i. 24.
172. Athen. ii. 16.

173. Plin. xix. 5.
174. Athen. loc. cit.
175. Theophrast. Hist. Plant. vii. 4.
176. Id. Ibid.
177. Id. Ibid.
178. Geoponic. xii. 22.
179. Ibid.
180. Ibid.
181. Ibid.
182. Ibid.
183. Apicius, iii. 14.
184. Plin. xx. 6.
185. Suidas.
186. Plaut. Pœn. v. 5, 34.
187. Suidas.
188. Virgil. Eclog. ii. 9.
189. Dict. des Sciences Naturel.
190. Athen.
191. Geoponic. xii. 30.
192. Ibid.
193. Plin. xix. 16.
194. Banier, Mytholog. tom. vii. p. 198.
195. Plutarch. Sympos. v. 3.
196. Anacreon, passim.
197. Horat. Od. i. 36.
198. Paschal. Coron. p. 436.
199. Homer. Iliad. ii.
200. Plin. xx. 1.
201. Apicius, iii. 2.
202. Id. iii. 15.
203. Plutarch. Sympos. v.
204. Columell. xi. 3.
205. Apicius, iii. 12.
206. Cic. In 5 Tuscul. cap. 34.
207. Id. De Finib. ii. 92.
208. Plutarch. De Virtute et Vitio, sub fin.
209. Dr. Charbonnier.
210. Geoponic. xii. 27.
211. Ibid.
212. Ibid.
213. Plin. xix. 8.
214. Apicius, iii. 16.
215. Id. Ibid.

X.

PLANTS USED IN SEASONING.

1. Plin. xix. 8.
2. Id. Ibid.
3. Nonnius, De Re Cibariâ.
4. Dalechamp, Ad Plin. xx. 25.
5. Petron. cap. i.
6. Plin. loc. cit.
7. Dioscorid. ii. 120.
8. Plin. xx. 20.

9. Geoponic. xii. 26.
10. Ibid.
11. Ovid. Remed. Amor. 402; Juvenal.
   Sat. ix. 134; Columell. x. 171.
12. Isidor. xvii. 11.
13. Geoponic. xii. 34.
14. Virgil. Eclog. ii. 48.
15. Columell. xi. 3.
16. Dioscorid. i. 52.
17. Id. v. 41.
18. Apicius, vi. 9; vii. 6.
19. Plin. xx. 17.
20. Id. Ibid.
21. Psalm l. 9.
22. Columell. vii. 5.
23. Plin. xxv. 11.
24. Columell. xx. 35.
25. Plin. xx. 17.
26. Dioscorid. v. 38.
27. Cato. R. R. 127.
28. Columell. x. 233.
29. Id. xii. 35.
30. Plin. xx. 22.
31. Id. xxi. 22.
32. Id. Ibid.
33. Const. Cæs. vi. 14.
34. Plin. xx. 14.
35. Geoponic. xii. 33.
36. Athen.
37. Macer. i. 12.
38. Athen.
39. Geoponic. xii. 25.
40. Turneb. Advers. viii. 5.
41. Ovid. Metam.
42. Plin. xx. 14.
43. Geoponic. xii. 24.
44. Ovid. Art. Amat. ii. 418.
45. Apicius, i. 29; iv. 2.
46. Plin. xix. 8.
47. Martial. iii. 77, 5.
48. Apicius, i. 30.
49. Id. x. 2, 7.
50. Plin. xii. 7.
51. Apicius.
52. Lamprid. Elogab. 21.
53. Plin. xxvii. 7.
54. Strabo. Geograph. vii.
55. Apicius, i. 3.
56. Martial. viii. 68.

XI.

FRUITS.

1. Genes. ii. 16.
2. Deuteron. xx. 19.

3. Levitic. xix. 23, 24.
4. Deuteron. xx. 6.
5. Ovid. Metam. xiv. 623.
6. Propert. iv. 2, 10.
7. Ovid. Fast. i. 415.
8. Virgil. Georg. i. 18.
9. Natalis Comes. vii. 15.
10. Id. ii. 1.
11. Id. i. 10.
12. Tibull. ii. 3, 67.
13. Athen. ix.
14. Sueton. In August. 76.
15. Vid. Stuckium, Nonnium, Bruyerinum, &c.
16. Seneca, Epist. 122.
17. Id. De Irâ, i. 16.
18. Id. Controv. v. 5.
19. Apicius, i. 20.

XII.

STONE FRUIT.

1. Constant. Cæs. ix. 1.
2. Id. Ibid.
3. Æsch. Agam.
4. Statius. Theb. ii.
5. Euripid. Heracl. act ii.
6. Apollon. Rhod. iv.
7. Id. ii. et ibi Scholiast.
8. Id. Ibid.
9. Diodor. Sicul. vi.
10. Genes. i. 11, 12.
11. Genes. xxviii. 18.
12. Diodor. v.; Justin. xiii.
13. Exod. xxv. 6.
14. Ibid. xxix. 7.
15. Ibid. xxiii. 40.
16. Exod. Levitic. Numer. Deuteronom. passim.
17. Mishna.
18. Plin. xv. 4.
19. Athen. ii. 25.
20. Id. Ibid.
21. Id. iv. 4.
22. Plin. xxiii. 3.
23. Ruellius.
24. Athen. ii. 8.
25. Theophrast. Hist. Plantar. passim.
26. Plin. xv. 1.
27. Id. i. 2.
28. Id. viii., xii., xv., xvi.
29. Cato. i. 1, 3, 31, 67, 68, 144.

30. Varro. R. R. i. 2.
31. Columell. i. 6, v. 8 ; xii. 50.
32. Plin. xv. 3.; Mathiol. In Dioscorid. i.
33. Plin. loc cit.
34. Martial, xii.
35. Tit. Liv.
36. Spartian. xxii.
37. Horat. Od. 6. lib. ii.
38. Plin. xiii. 2.
39. Sueton. In Cæs. 53
40. Salmas. De Homonym. Hyles Iatricæ. cap. 103.
41. Plin. xxii. 24.
42. See p. 269.
43. Apicius, i. 5.
44. Vid. Pontan.
45. Natal. Com. vii. 15.
46. Bibl. Sacr. passim.
47. Levitic. x. 9 ; Deuteron. xiv. 26.
48. Guénée, Lettres de Quelques Juifs, tom. iii. p. 270, edit. 8vo.
49. Joseph. De Bell. Judaic. ii. 2.
50. Theophrast. ii. 8.
51. Plin. xiii. 14.
52. Plutarch. ; Athen.
53. Hieronym. Ad Eustochium, epist. 19.
54. Plin. xv. 25 ; Ammian. Marcell. xx. 13.
55. Plin. xv. 25.
56. Virgil. Georg.
57. Athen. ii. 11.
58. Theophrast. iii. 13 ; ix. i.
59. Plin. xv. 25.
60. Id. Ibid.
61. Columell. v. 10 ; xi. 2.
62. Galen. De Aliment. Facultat. ii. ; Dioscorid. i. 131.
63. Plin. xv.
64. Theophrast. iii. 5.
65. Plin. xv. 14.
66. Columell. x. 17.
67. Plin. xiii. 9 ; xv. 13.
68. Galen. ii.
69. Dioscorid. i. 131.
70. Apicius, i. 26.
71. Theophrast. i. 11 ; iv. 3 ; ix. 1.
72. Athen. ii. 10.
73. Theophrast. et Athen. loc. cit. ; Geoponic. x. 40.
74. Virgil. Eclog. ii.
75. Plin. xiii. 10 ; xv. 12.
76. Dictionnaire des Origines.
77. Mémoires de Dangeau.
78. Gaillard, Hist. de François I.
79. Théâtre d'Agriculture.

XIII.

PIP FRUIT.

1. Theophrast. ii. 4.
2. Athen. iii.
3. Cato. De Re Rusticâ.
4. Plin. xv. 11.
5. Galen. De Aliment. Facult.
6. Columell. v. 10.
7. Pallad. xi. 20.
8. Forum Cupedinarium.
9. Dioscorid. v. 20.
10. Ulpian. ix. Sess. de Trit. Vin. Ol.
11. Athen. iii. 6.
12. Id. Ibid.
13. Apicius, i. 19.
14. II. Reg. v. 23, 24 ; 1 Paralip. xiv. 14, 15.
15. Theophrast. ii. 23, et passim.
16. Plin. xv. 15.
17. Galen. De Simpl. Medicam. v. ; De Aliment. Facult. ii.
18. Grandes Chroniques Françaises; Vita B. Francisc.
19. Cant. ii. 3, 5 ; vii. 8 ; viii. 5 ; Joel, i. 12.
20. Cant. ii. 3.
21. Bruyerin. xi. 16.
22. Athen. i. 21.
23. Strab. xv.
24. Turneb. De Vino. p. 22.
25. Virgil. Georg. ii. 126, et seqq.
26. Athen. iii. 4.
27. Theophrast. i. 22 ; iv. 4 ; viii. 8.
28. Athen. loc. cit.
29. Dioscorid. i. 136.
30. Athen. loc. cit.
31. Lib. i. cap. 21. Lond. 1705, 8vo.
32. Plin. xii. 3 ; xxiii. 6 ; xxv. 28.
33. Pallad. xii. 7.
34. Athen. iii. 4.
35. Apicius, i. 21.
36. Plin. xxiii. 6 ; Athen. iii. 4 ; Galen. Simplic. Medic. vii.
37. Année Littéraire, 1755.
38. Nouveau Dict. Class. d'Hist. Nat. Paris, 1844.
39. Année Littér. 1755.
40. Brand's Popular Antiquities, vol. i. p. 9.
41. Dictionnaire d'Histoire Naturelle.
42. Genes. iii. 7.
43. Num. xx. 5.
44. Ibid. 24, 28.
45. II. Reg. iv. 25.
46. IV. Reg. xviii. 31.

47. Guénée, Lettr. de Quelq. Juifs, tom. iii. pp. 271, 272.
48. Pausan. In Atticis.
49. Athen. iii.
50. Id. iii. 2.
51. *Sukon*, fig, and *phainô*, I detect.
52. Plutarch. De Curiosit.
53. Athen. xiv.
54. Plin. xv. 18.
55. Cato. R. R. 94, 99, 133.
56. Varro. R. R.
57. Plin. loc. cit.
58. Athen. iii. 14.
59. Bruyerin. xi. 37.
60. I. Reg. xxv. 18, 27.
61. Clem. Alex. In Pædag.
62. Plin. xii. 1 ; Plutarch. In Camill. 390 B C.
63. Athen. iii.
64. Galen. De Cibis Boni et Mali Succi.
65. Hippocrat. De Diœt. ii.
66. Plin. xxiv. 14 ; Dioscorid. iv. 33.
67. *Uva crispa*, and *ribes*.
68. Mathiol. In Dioscorid. i. 105.
69. Virgil. Eclog. iii. 92.
70. Ovid. Metam. xiii. 816.
71. Id. Ibid. i. 104.
72. Plin. xvi. 25.
73. Athen. ii. 12.
74. Apicius, i. 22.
75. Psalm lxxxiv. 6 ; I. Chron. xiv. 14, 15.

XIV.

SHELL FRUIT.

1. Macrob.2 ; Saturnal. 14; Columel. v.10.
2. Athen. i. 49.
3. Genes. xliii. 11.
4. Athen. iii.
5. Id. Ibid.
6. Apicius, iv. 2.
7. Plin. xxiii. 4.
8. Id. xvi. 25.
9. Dutour ; Amandier.
10. Theophrast. Hist. Plant.
11. Exod. xxv. 33 ; xxxvii. 19.
12. Cant. vi. 10.
13. Plin. xv. 22.
14. Varro. L. L. iv. ; Dioscorid. i. 141.
15. Theophrast. i. 3, et passim.
16. Catul. In Epithal. Tulliæ et Malli.
17. Servius, In Virgil. Eclog. viii.
18. Plin. xv. 22.
19. Pers. Sat. i ; Hesych. Lexic. voc. Nux.

58. Cod. Theod. L. x. De Suariis et Pe-
    cuariis.
59. Ibid.
60. Cod. Valent. De Suariis.
61. Ibid.
62. Ibid.
63. Ibid.
64. Onuphr. Panvin. Descript. Urb. Rom.
65. Sext. Rufin. Descript. Urb. Rom.
66. Geoponic. iii.
67. Apicius, i. 10.
68. Id. i. 8.
69. Delamarre. liv. v. titre 23, chap. 6.
70. Monteil. Histoire des Français, tom. ii.
    p. 46.
71. Arrêt du Parlement, 18 Mai, 1366.
72. Delamarre.
73. Règlement du 20 Mars, 1635.

XVI.

ANIMALS.

1. Athen. iii. 7.
2. Id. ix. 5 ; Bulenger. ii. 24.
3. Herodot. ii. 47.
4. Plutarch. De Isid. et Osirid ; Ælian. De
    Animal. x. 16.
5. Levitic. xi. 7, 8.
6. I. Macchab. i. 65, 66 ; II. Macchab. vi.
    18, et seqq.
7. In Barakama. vi. 7. § 7 ; Maimonides,
    In Niskemamon. cap. v.
8. Kibuschim. 49.
9. Hoorabeck. De Conviv. Judæis, vii. 1.
10. Herodian. v.
11. Ælian. xvi. 37.
12. Koran, chap. vi.
13. Varro. R. R. ii. 4 ; Clem. Alexandr.
    Stromat. ii.
14. Scholiast. Aristophan. In Acharn.
15. Macrob. Saturn. i. 6 ; Aul. Gell. iv. 6.
16. Varro. loc. cit.
17. Fest. De Verb. Signific.
18. Varro. loc. cit.
19. Id. Ibid.
20. Johan. Pierius, Hieroglyph ix.
21. Plutarch. Sympos. v. 10 ; Cic. De Natur.
    Deor. ii.
22. Galen. De Aliment. Facult. iii.
23. Id. De Cib. Boni et Mali Succi.
24. Id. Method. Medendi. vii.
25. Athen. passim.
26. Id. iii. 7, 9 ; ix. 6, et passim.
27. Id. iv. 1.

28. Athen. ix. 4, 5.
29. Bulenger. ii. 24.
30. Petron. Satyr.
31. Macrob. Sat. iii. 13.
32. Athen. ix. 7.
33. Varro. R. R. ii. 41.
34. Plin. viii. 51.
35. Petron. Satyr.
36. Lamprid. In Alexand. Sever.
37. Macrob. Saturn. iii. 13.
38. Plin. xi. 37.
39. Nonnius, ii. 3.
40. Strabo. vi. 3, 7 ; Martial. Lemmate de
    Pernâ.
41. Nonnius ; Stuckius.
42. Cato. R. R. cap. ultimo.
43. Strabo, iv.
44. Plutarch. Sympos. v. 10 ; Varro. R. R.
    ii. 4.
45. Bruyerin. xiii. 1.
46. Athen. ix. 1 ; Petron. Satyr.
47. Juvenal. Sat. xi.
48. Spartian. In Adrian.
49. Plin. viii. 57.
50. Dio. ex Xiphil. In Vespasian. cap. x.
51. Id. In Claud. v.
52. Apicius, i. 9.
53. Plutarch. Apophteg.
54. Apicius, viii. 7.
55. Id. Ibid.
56. Id. Ibid.
57. Cato. R. R. 163.
58. Apicius, vii. 3.
59. Id. vii. 9.
60. Athen. iii. 21.
61. Id. ii. 4.
62. Id. Ibid.
63. Id. vii. 2.
64. Id. Ibid.
65. Id. vii. 3.
66. Id. Ibid. ; Plin. viii. 51.
67. Apicius, vii. 9.
68. Id. ii. 1.
69. Id. ii. 4.
70. Id. ii. 1.
71. Id. ii. 2.
72. Fontan. Ordonnances.
73. Delamarre, Traité de la Police.
73 A. Trésor de la Santé, liv. iii.
73 B. Champier, xiii. 2.
74. Clem. Alexandr. Stromat. v.
75. Banier, Mythologie, tom. i. p. 354.
76. Ælian. Hist. xii. 34.
77. Euripid. Alcest. act v.
78. Pollux, ix.

20. Galen. Simpl. Medicam.
21. Mathiol. In Dioscorid. i. 141.
22. Avicen. v. 4.
23. Athen. ii. 7.
24. Id. Ibid.
25. Plin. xxiii. 8 ; Q. Seren. Sammonic.
26. Theophrast. i. 5 ; Athen. ii. 7.
27. Cato. R. R. 8 ; Macrob. Saturnal. iii. 18.
28. Nucula. Festus.
29. Nonnius. i. 37.
30. Galen. De Aliment. Facult. ii. ; Dioscorid. i. 42.
31. Hospinian. De Orig. Festor. Christian. fol. 113. B.
32. Plin. xiii. 5.
33. Theophrast. iv. 5.
34. Plin. xv. 22.
35. Galen. De Alim. Facult. ii.
36. Avicen. lib. ii.
37. Athen. ii. 13.
38. Virgil. Eclog. ii. 52.
39. Id. Eclog. i. 82.
40. Nicand. Interp. Turneb.
41. Sipont.
42. Natalis Comes. iii. 16.
43. Martial. i. 44.
44. Columell. xii. 41.
45. Plin. xiii. 19.
46. Columell. loc. cit.
47. Apicius, i. 18.
48. Athen. xiv.
49. Pausan. et Diodor. passim.

XV.

ANIMAL FOOD.

1. Genes. i. 29 ; iii. 17, 18, 19.
2. Ibid. iii. 21.
3. Ibid. iii. 19.
4. Ibid. iv. 4.
5. Ibid. xviii. 8.
6. Xenoph. De Cyri Expedit. ; Varro. R. R. ii. 1 ; Bruyerin. ii. 1 ; iv. 1.
7. Hieronym. Adv. Jovin. Arnob. Cont. Gent. ii.
8. Plutarch. De Esu Carn. ; Porphyr. De Non Necand. &c.
9. Bossuet, Discours sur l'Hist. Universel.
10. Genes. ix. 3.
11. Herodot. Hist. i. ; Virgil. Georg. i. ; Ovid. Metam. i. et xv.
12. Bruyerin. ii. 1 ; Plin. xvi. 5.
13. Ovid. Metam. i. 3.

14. Porphyr. De Non Necandis ad Epuland. Animantib. i.
15. Plin. vii. 5 ; Porphyr. i. ii. ; Polyd. Virgil. De Rer. Inventor. iii. 2.
16. 756 years after the Deluge.
17. 943 years after the Deluge ; Athen. ix. Var. R. R. ii. 4 ; Ovid. Metam. xv ;
18. Ibid. loc. cit.
19. Plin. vii. 56.
20. La Fontaine, Les Animaux Malades de la Peste.
21. Plin. loc. cit. ; Nonnius ii. 1 ; Ælian. Var. Hist. i. 3 ; Paus. i.
22. 895 B.C.
23. Porphyr. loc cit.
24. Homer. passim.
25. Plutarch. De Esu Carnium.
26. Genes. ix. 3.
27. Levitic. xxii. 24.
28. Deuteron. xxv. 4.
29. Exod. xxiii. 5.
30. Deuteron. xx. 10.
31. Exod. xxiii. 12.
32. Genes. passim.
33. Xenoph.
34. Homer.
35. Leg. xii. Tabul. L. 72 ; Ulric. Zasii Catalog. Leg. Antiq.
36. Ibid. lxxi.
37. Columell. i. 3.
38. Cic. In Brut.
39. Hyginius in Frontin. De Controvers. Agror. cap. De Loc. Publicis.
40. Leg. i. De Abigeis. iii. Oves ss. De Abigeis.
41. *Scrofa*, a sow.
42. Varro. ii. 1.
43. Geoponic. passim ; Cato. Varro. Plin. Columell. Pallad. passim.
44. Varro.
45. Aul. Gell. xiii. 21.
46. Ovid. Fast. iii. 523.
47. S. Augustin. De Civitat. Dei. vi. 9.
48. Geoponic. xvii.
49. Paralipom. xxiii. 15 ; xxxiii. 14 ; II. Esdras, iii. 1, 28 ; xii. 38 ; Sophon. i. 10.
50. Tit. Liv. xxix. 37.
51. Rosin. Antiquit. Rom. p. 39.
52. Id. Ibid. p. 38.
53. Ulpian. De Officio Præfect. Urbis.
54. Homer.
55. Turneb. Advers.
56. Gruter. p. 647, n. 6.
57. Encyclop. Méthod. Antiquit. ; Gruter. loc. cit. ; Montfaucon, Antiq. Expliq.

79. Banier, tom. i. p. 448; Ælian. Hist. viii. 3.
80. Cic. De Natur. Deor. ii.
81. Aristophan.
82. Plutarch. Solon.
83. Homer. passim.
84. Genes. xii. 16; xx. 14; xxi. 27; xxiv. 35; xxxii. 5, et passim.
85. Ibid. xviii. 7, 8.
86. Ibid. ix. 3.
87. Ibid.
88. Deuteron. xiv. 4.
89. Galen. De Ration. Vict. ii.
90. Poseidip. apud Athen. x. 2.
91. Theodor. Ibid.
92. Marm. Sandwic. p. 35.
93. II. Reg. vi. 19; Homer. et Athen. passim.
94. Nonnius.
95. Homer. Iliad.
96. Athen. iii. 7.
7. Id. Ibid.
98. Id. iv. 7.
99. Id. vi. 9.
100. Encyclop. Méthod. Antiquités.
101. Horat. ii. Sat. 5; I. Epist. 15.
102. Apicius, viii. 5.
103. Id. Ibid.
104. Apicius, viii. 5.
105. Id. Ibid.
106. Pers. Sat. ii. 43; Apul. Metam. ii.; Fulgent. De Vocib. Antiq.
107. Valer. Maxim. viii. 1.
108. Sonnini; Desmarest: Bœuf.
109. Taillevant.
110. Senec. Natur. Quæst. iv. 6.
111. Banier, tom. i. p. 354.
112. Natal. Com. Mytholog.
113. Exod. xix. 38 to 42.
114. Banier, tom. i. p. 447.
115. Exod. xii. xxiii.
116. Genes. xxiii. 19.
117. IV. Reg. iii. 4.
118. Amos, vi. 4, 7.
119. Athen. i. 16.
120. Id. iv.
121. Id. vii. 24.
122. Id. passim.
123. Cels.
124. Apicius, viii. 6.
125. Id. Ibid.
126. Id. Ibid.
127. Id. Ibid.
128. Id. Ibid.
129. Beckwith's edition of Blount's Jocular Tenures, p. 281.

130. Genes. xxvii. 9, 17.
131. Exod. xii. 5.
132. Judic. xv. 1.
133. Luc. xv. 29.
134. Herodot.
135. Ibid.
136. Athen. iii. 1; iv. 7.
137. Id. ix. 3.
138. Athen. i. 6; Clem. Alexandr. Pædagog. ii. 1.
139. Athen. ix. 13.
140. Juvenal. Sat. xi.
141. Varro. R. R. ii. 3.
142. Apicius, viii. 6.
143. Id. Ibid.
144. Id. Ibid.
145. Id. Ibid.
146. Id. Ibid.
147. Levitic. xi. 26.
148. IV. Reg. vi. 25.
149. Galen.
150. Plin. viii. 43.
151. Galen. De Aliment. Facultat. iii.
152. Id. De Ration. Vict. cap. 7.
153. Id. De Alim. Facult. iii.
154. Id. Ibid.
155. Hippocrat. De Diœt. ii.
156. Fest. Pomp.
157. Athen. viii.
158. Plutarch. De Fortunâ Romanorum.

XVII.

POULTRY.

1. Aristot. De Longit. et Brevit. Vitæ, cap. 4.
2. Galen. De Aliment Facult. iii. 18.
3. Macrob.; Dio.
4. Genes. i.
5. Lucian. xvi. De Syriæ Deâ.
6. Oppian. Cilix. Cyneget. ii. 189.
7. Aristophan. In Avibus.
8. Ælian. Var. Hist. ii. 28.
9. Plin. x. 21; Columell. viii. 2.
10. Plin. loc. cit.
11. Erasm. Chiliad. i. cent. 1; Columell. viii. c. 2.
12. Plin. x. 50.
13. L. Fannia. Sumptuar. In Catalog. Leg. Antiq. Ulrici. p. 143.
14. Macrob. Saturnal. iii. 17.
15. Aul. Gell. ii. 24; Plin. x. 50.
16. Martial. xiii. 63, 64.

17. Apicius, vi. 9.
18. Rosin. Antiquit. Roman. p. 207.
19. Galen, De Aliment. Facult. iii. ; Nonnius. ii. 22.
20. Athen. ii. 12 ; iv. 1 ; ix. 4.
21. Plin. x. 50.
22. Varro. R. R. iii. 9.
23. Columell. viii. 7 ; Plin. x. 51.
24. Plin. Ibid.
25. L. Fannia. loc. cit.
26. Nonnius. ii. 22.
27. Apicius, vi. 9.
28. Cic. De Divinat.
29. Val. Maxim. i. 4.
30. Aristot. ; Vopiscus.
31. Athen. iv. 7, et passim.
32. Apicius, iv. 1.
33. Id. vi. 9.
34. Id. Ibid.
35. Id. Ibid.
36. Id. Ibid.
37. Aristophan. In Avib.
38. Id. Acharn. iv. 1, 14.
39. Athen. ii. 12 ; iv. 1, et passim.
40. De Comp. Medic. Secund. loc. v. 4.
41. Plutarch. In Caton.
42. Athen. ix.
43. De Aliment. Facult. xiii.
44. Avicen. Canon Medicinæ.
45. Macrob. Saturnal. iii. 13.
46. Martial. xiii. 52.
47. Apicius, iv. 2.
48. Id. iv. 5.
49. Ælian. v. xii. ; Gessner. iii. ; Aldrovand. xix.
50. Aristot. Hist. Animal. i. 1.
51. In Aristotel. loc. cit.
52. Homer. Odyss.
53. Athen. ii. 12 ; iv. 1, et passim.
54. Diod. Sicul. ii. 3.
55. Athen. ix. 7.
56. Aristoph. In Avib. ; Porphyr. De Abstin. iv.
57. Cæsar. De Bello Gall. v.
58. Brand's Popular Antiquities.
59. Plin. x. 22.
60. Polyb. ii. ; Plut. In Camillo.
61. Pierii Hieroglyph.
62. Columell. viii. 13.
63. Alex. ab Alex. Genial. Dier. iii. 12.
64. Plut. De Roman. Fortunâ.
65. Nonnius. ii. 3.
66. Plin.
67. Lamprid. In Sever.
68. Pallad. i. 30 ; Athen. ix. 7 ; Plin. x. 22.

69. Plin. Ibid.
70. Id. ix. 20.
71. Id. Horat. Sat.
72. Plin. viii. 51.
73. Martial, xiii. 58.
74. Plin. x. 22 ; Galen. De Aliment. Facult. iii. 20 ; Æginet. ii. 82.
75. Athen. ix. 7.
76. Pallad. i. 30.
77. Apicius, vi. 8.
78. Id. vi. 5.
79. Id. vi. 9.
80. Brand's Popular Antiquities.
81. Strab. vii.
82. Homer. Odyss.
83. Hesychius.
84. Selden, De Diis Syris. ii. 3 ; Tibull. i. 8, 18.
85. Bibl. Sacr. passim.
86. Cantic. passim.
87. Levitic. i. 14, 17.
88. S. Chrysost. Homil. de Patientiâ Job.
89. Homer.
90. Athen. ii. 12 ; iv. 1, 5 ; ix. 11, et pass.
91. Id. Ibid.
92. Quintilius, In Geoponic. ap. Gessner de Avibus, iii.
93. Plin. x. 37.
94. Id. Ibid.
95. Varro. R. R. iii. 7.
96. Hippocrat. De Inter. Affect. ; Galen. De Rat. Vict.
97. Apicius, vi. 9.
98. Varro. R. R. iii. 9.
99. Martial. sub Lemmat. Numidicæ.
100. Plin. xix. 4.
101. Apicius, vi. 9.
102. Athen. i. 10.
103. Sophocl. ap. Plin. xxxvii. 2.
104. Aristot. Hist. Animal. vi. 2.
105. Apud Athen. xiv. 9.
106. Ibid. ix. 8.
107. Varro. R. R.
108. Sueton. In Caligul. 22.
109. Hesych. Lexic. Suidas. In Verb. Meleagrides.
110. Volteran. De Urbe.
111. Beckmann ; Diction. des Découvertes.
112. Hurtaut, Dict. Historiq. de la Ville de Paris, tom. iv. p. 417.
113. Apicius, vi. 9.
114. Hurtaut. loc. cit.
115. Aldrovand. xiii. 1 ; Nonnius, ii. 24.
116. Ælian. xiii. 18.
117. Diodor. Sicul.

118. Ælian. xi. 33.
119. Varro. R. R. iii. 6 ; Athen. xiv. 9, 25.
120. Aul. Gell. vii. 16.
121. Ælian. v. 21 ; Aldrovand. xiii. 1.
122. Athen. xiv. 25.
123. Id. Ibid.
124. Macrob. Saturn. iii. 13.
125. Juvenal.
126. Varro. R. R. iii. 6 ; Ælian. v. 21 ;
     Plin. x. 20.
127. Horat. lib. ii. Sat. ii.
128. Varro. R. R.
129. Alexand. ab Alexandr. Genial. Dier.
     ii. 13.
130. Galen. De Aliment. Facult. iii.
131. S. Augustin. De Civit. Dei, xxii. 4.
132. Apicius, vi. 5.

XVIII.

MILK, BUTTER, CHEESE, AND EGGS.

1. Genes. xviii. 8.
2. Exod. iii. 8 ; Levitic. xx. 24 ; Numer.
     xiii. 28 ; et passim.
3. Proverb. xxvii. 27.
4. Ovid. Metam. i. 3 ; Fast. iv.
5. Homer.
6. Herodot. iv.
7. Strabo.
8. Cæsar ; Tacit.
9. Longus. iii.
10. Rosin. Antiq. Roman. p. 237.
11. Varro. R. R. ii. 11.
12. Hippocrat. Aphorism. v. 64.
13. Galen. De Ration. Vict.
14. Nonnius, ii. 15.
15. Sueton. In Othon. xii.
16. Martial. x. 68.
17. Juvenal. Sat. vi.
18. Plin. xxviii. 12 : xxxiii. 11.
19. Nonnius, ii. 15.
20. Apicius, iv. 2.
21. Beckmann.
22. Rabbi Salom.
23. Job, xxix. 6.
24. Aristot. Hist. Animal. iii. 20.
25. Id. Ibid.
26. Hippocrat. De Morbis, iv.
27. Hecat. Abderan. apud Athen. x. 14.
28. Galen. De Aliment ; Id. Simpl. Medi-
     cam. x. ; Plin. xxviii. 9.

29. Plin. Ibid.
30. Id. xi. 41.
31. Galen. De Aliment. Facult.
32. Dioscorid. ii. 81.
33. Herodot. iv. 2.
34. Plin. xxviii. 9.
35. Règlement du 20 Mars, 1635.
36. Antiquitat. Ecclesiast.
37. Dictionnaire de la France.
38. Parmentier : Beurre.
39. Justin. xiii.
40. Apollodor. ii. ; Pausan. viii.
41. Homer. Iliad.
42. i. Reg. xvii. 18 ; Judith, x. 5 ; Job, x. 10.
43. Aristot. Hist. Animal. iii. 20.
44. Hippocrat. De Morbis. iv. ; Aristot. loc.
     cit.
45. Plin. xi. 41 ; xxviii. 9.
46. Ulpian. in L. viii. sicut. § Aristo.
47. Onuphr. Panvini.
48. Athen. i. 30 ; Plin. xi. 42.
49. Plin. xi. 41.
50. Stuckius, Antiq. Convival. i. 21.
51. Pausan. vi.
52. Varro. De Ling. Lat. iv. 22.
53. Cic. Epist. xiv. 16 ; Famil. xi. 16, 17, 20.
54. Athen.
55. Strabo. xii.
56. Sueton. In August. 76.
57. Grégoire, Essai Historiq. sur l'Agricult.
58. Ovid. Fast. iv. 371.
59. Columell. vii. 8.
60. Id. Ibid.
61. Apicius, iv. 1.
62. Id. i. 33.
63. Parmentier : Fromage.
64. Plutarch. Sympos.
65. Alexand. Ab Alexandr. ; Villichius, De
     Arte Magiricâ, 10.
66. Lucian. De Deâ Syr.
67. Tit. Liv. xli. ; Varro. R. R. i. 2.
68. Suidas ; Juvenal. ; Macrob. vii. 16.
69. Plin. x. 55.
70. Cic. De Divinat.
71. Plutarch. Sympos. ; Macrob. Saturnal.
     vii. 16.
72. Suidas ; Cœl. Rhodig.
73. Triph. apud Athen. ii.
74. Horat. Sat. i. 3.
75. Id. Sat. ii. 4.
76. Galen. De Aliment. Facult.
77. Macrob. Sat. iii. 13.
78. Plin. x. 53.
79. Apud Athen. ii. 16.
80. Plin. x. 20.

81. Galen. De Dynamidiis; Plin. xxix. 3.
82. Apicius, vii. 17.
83. Id. Ibid.
84. Id. Ibid.
85. Id. ii. 3.
86. Id. iv. 1.
87. Id. iv. 2.
88. Court de Gebelin, Monde Primitif, tom. xiv. p. 251.
89. Brand's Popular Antiquities, vol. i. p. 147.
90. Diction. des Origines.

XIX.

HUNTING.

1. Genes. x. 9.
2. Ibid. xxi. 20.
3. I. Reg. xvii. 34, et seqq.
4. Ovid. lib. ix. Fab. 3.
5. Artemidor. ii. Oneirocrit. 35.
6. Xenophon.
7. Natalis Comes. Mythol.
8. Homer.
9. Aristot. De Republ. cap. 4.
10. Plato, De Legibus, Dialog. viii.
11. Horat. Epist. i. 18.
12. Jul. Poll.
13. Homer. Iliad. v.; Odyss. iv.
14. Plut. In Pelopid.
15. Id. In Alexandr.
16. Id. In Philopœm.
17. Xenoph. De Venatione, passim.
18. Symmach. Epist. v. 66.
19. Xenoph. loc. cit.
20. Id. Ibid.
21. Claudian. De Laud. Stilich. iii.; Symmach. Epist. ii. 17.
22. Montfaucon, Antiq. Expl.
23. Id. Ibid.
24. Apul. Milesiar. viii.
25. Prob. Grammatic. ad lib. iii. Georgic.
26. Sidon. Apollinar. Carm. vii. 198; Ovid. Metam. viii.
27. Strab. Geograph.
28. Lucret.
29. Martial.
30. Pollux, Onomast. v. 4.
31. Jul. Firmic. Maternus.
32. Dio Chrysost.
33. Varro. R. R. ii. 3; Plin. viii. 52.
34. Instit. Justinian. De Rer. Division. L. i. De Acquir. Doman. § 11.

35. L. iii. Quod enim. De Acquir. &c.
36. Genes. xxvii. 3, 4.
37. III. Reg. iv. 23.
38. Xenoph. Exped. Cyri, i.
39. Id. De Republ. Lacedæm.; Herodot. Hist. vii.; Athen. iv. passim; Petron. Sat.
40. Asserius, Vita Ælfredi.
41. W. Malmsbur. Hist. Reg. Anglor. ii. 6.
42. Id. Ibid. cap. 8.
43. Id. Ibid. cap. 13.
44. Ducarrel's Anglo-Norman Antiquities.
45. Johan. Sarisburiensis, De Nugis Curialium, i. 4.
46. Strutt's Sports and Pastimes, edit. 1801, p. 6.
47. Aristot. Hist. Animal. ix. 6.
48. Plin. viii. 32.
49. Galen. De Rat. Vict.
50. Deuteron. xii. 15, 22.
51. III. Reg. iv. 23.
52. Stuckius.
53. Nonnius, ii. 10.
54. Apicius, viii. 2.
55. Id. Ibid.
56. Id. Ibid.
57. Galen. loc. cit.; De Alim. Facult.
58. Athen. i. 4.
59. Xenoph. Exped. Cyri. i.; Athen. ii; Plin. viii. 53.
60. Apicius viii. 2.
61. Id. Ibid.
62. Id. Ibid.
63. Plin. loc cit.; Nonnius, ii. 10.
64. Apicius, loc. cit.
65. Athen. xii.
66. Petron. Sat.
67. Virgil. Æneid. ii. 1.
68. Macrob. Saturnal. iii. 13.
69. Plin. viii. 51.
70. Athen. iv. 1.
71. Hippocrat. De Diœt. ii.; Plin. viii. 51,52.
72. Juvenal. Sat. i. 141.
73. Plin. viii. 51; Mercurial. ii. 23.
74. Caton. Censor. Orat.; Plin. loc. cit.
75. Eubul. apud Athen. vii. 24.
76. Varro. R. R. iii. 13.
77. Senec. Epist. 90.
78. Varro. loc. cit.
79. Senec. De Providentiâ. cap. 4.
80. Apicius, viii. 1.
81. Id. Ibid.
82. Id. Ibid.
83. Id. Ibid.
84. Id. Ibid.

85. Apicius, viii. 1.
86. Plutarch. Sympos. iv. 5.
87. Joseph. contra Apion.
88. Levitic. xi. 6.
89. Cæsar, De Bell. Gall. v.
90. Xenoph. Exped. Cyri.
91. Herodot. vii.; Athen. iii. 1.
92. Apud. Athen. ix. 12.
93. Archestrat. ap. Athen. ix.
94. Athen. xiv.
95. Stuckius. ii. 8.
96. Hippocrat. De Diœt. ii.
97. Galen. De Aliment. Facult. et passim.
98. Lamprid. In Sever.
99. Martial. ad Gelliam.
100. Horat. Sat. lib. ii. 4.
101. Proverb. xxx. 26.
102. Martial. xiii. 60; Varro. R. R. iii. 12.
103. Plin.; Varro.
104. Bochart, De Animal. Sacr. Script. iii. 31.
105. Strabo. Geograph. iii.
106. Galen. De Alim. Facul. iii.; Varro. R. R. iii. 12; Plin. viii. 29.
107. Varro. R. R.
108. Plin. vii. 55.
109. Galen. De Alim. Facult. iii.
110. Athen. iv. 4.
111. Martial.
112. Aristot. Hist. Animal. vi. 26.
113. Athen. iv. 6.
114. Strabo. Geograph.
115. Photin. Biblioth. p. 1355.
116. Le Vaillant, Voyages, tom. ii. p. 27. edit. 18mo.
117. Id. Ibid. pp. 27 to 29.
118. Senec. Epist. 85, sub fin.
119. Id. De Brevit. Vitæ, cap. 13.

XX.

FEATHERED GAME.

1. Levitic. xi. 13 to 19.
2. Clem. Alexandr. Stromat. vii. fol. 718. Lutet. 1629.
3. Aristophan. In Avib. 532, et 1578.
4. Plin. x. 51.
5. Belon. Histoire des Oiseaux. anno 1555.
6. Aristophan. In Avib.; Martial xiii. 72.
7. Manilius, 370.
8. Isidor. xii. 7.
9. Calixen. apud Athen. xix. 8.
10. Ptolem. Everget. Comment. xii.
11. Aristophan. in Nubib. 109; Philoxen. ap. Athen. iv. 2.
12. Athen. xiv. 9.
13. Plin. x. 22; xi. 33, 37; xix. 4.
14. Sueton. In Vespasian.
15. Id.
16. Lamprid. xxxvii.
17. Sueton. In Caligul. 22.
18. Id. Ibid. 30.
19. Petrarca, De Remed. Dialog. xviii.
20. Galen. De Aliment. Facult. et passim.
21. Athen. ii. 12, et passim.
22. Plin. iv. 48.
23. Ælian. De Animal. Nat. ii. 1.
24. Lamprid. In Sever.
25. Aldrovand. Ornithol. xiii. 17.
26. Athen. i. 6.
27. Id. ix. 11.
28. Bochart. De Animal. Script. part. ii. lib. i. cap. 19.
29. Galen. De Part. Facili. cap. 155.
30. Athen. loc. cit.
31. Exod. xvi. 13.
32. Athen. ii. 12; iv. 1.
33. Aristophan. apud Athen. ix. 11.
34. Aristot. Hist. Animal. ix. 8.
35. Varro. R. R. iii. 5.
36. Plin. ix. 23, 72.
37. Galen. Epidemior. v. comm. 5, text. 45.
38. Apud Athen. xi.
39. Aristot. Hist. Animal. ix. 8.
40. Lucian. In Dialog. de Gymnasiis.
41. Aldrovand. Ornith. xiii. 22.
42. Quintilian. Institut. Orat. v. 9.
43. Athen. ii. 12.
44. Id. xiv. 6; Aristophan. In Avibus.
45. Athen. iv. 1, et passim.
46. Clem. Alexandr. Pædagog. ii. 1.
47. Varro. R. R. iii. 2, 3.
48. Id. i. 38.
49. Id. iii. 5; Nonnius, ii. 29.
50. Varro. loc. cit.
51. Pers. Sat. vi.
52. Martial. iii. 51.
53. Plaut. Triummo. act ii. sc. 4.
54. Lamprid. Elogabal.
55. Horat. Epist. xv. 41; Martial. xiii. 92.
56. Plutarch. In Pompeio.
57. Athen. ii. 12, et passim.
58. Varro. R. R. i. 38; Horat. Epist. ii.
59. Galen. De Cibis Boni et Mali Succi. i.
60. Chroniq. Scandal. de Louis XI.
61. Plin. x. 42.
62. Athen. ii. 12.
63. Galen. De Sanit. Tuendâ. xi. 16.

64. Apicius, x. 48.
65. Latinus Latinius ; Bayle.
66. Molière; Amphitryon.
67. Kiranides. c. 7.
68. Martial. xiii. 66.
69. Sueton. ; Lamprid.; Plin. x. 48.
70. Histoire Générale des Voyages, tom. i. p. 269.
71. Petron. c. 33.
72. Aristot. Hist. Animal. ix. 49 ; Plin. x. 29.
73. Athen. xiv.
74. Martial. xiii. 48.
75. Juvenal. xiv. 7.
76. Varro. R. R. iii. 5.
77. Id. Ib.
78. Strabo. xvi.
79. Marmol. Africa.
80. Lamprid. In Elogab.
81. Rosin. Antiquit. Roman. p. 207.
82. Horat. Sat. lib. i. 2, 49.
83. Nepot. Fragm. x. 1.
84. Aristot. Hist. Animal. ix. 26.
85. Varro. R. R. iii. 9.
86. Athen. i. 28.
87. Plin. x. 22.
88. Martial. xiii. 76.
89. Antiphan. apud Athen. ii. 12.
90. Ambros. In cap. i. Epist. ad Rom.
91. Martial. xiii. 85.
92. Aristot. Hist. Animal.
93. Banier. Mytholog. tom. i. p. 354.
94. Martial. v.
95. Galen. De Simplic. Medic. Facultat. xi. 33.
96. Suidas In Vitell.
97. Nicolas, Etudes sur le Christianisme. tom. i. 254.
98. Horat. Sat. i. 3.
99. Plutarch. Vita Caton.
100. Id. Vita Flamin.
101. Tacit.
102. Nicolas, loc. cit.
103. Plin. xxxii. 8 ; Cels. v. 6, 18 ; Dioscorid.
104. Diction. d' Hist. Nat.

XXI.

FISH.

1. Columell. R. R.
2. Levitic. xi. 10.
3. Strab. xvii. 1.
4. Clem. Alexandr. Strom. vii. fol. 718 ; Lutet. 1619.
5. Athen. viii. 4.
6. Odyss. xii. 332.
7. Plat. De Republ. iii.
8. Athen. i.
9. Id. viii.
10. Lucian. Bion Praxis.
11. Athen. vii. 20.
12. Id. vi. 2.
13. Xenarch. Comic. Apud Athen.
14. Plutarch. Sympos. iv. 4.
15. Plin. xviii. 3.
16. Senec. Quæst. Natural. iii. 17, 18.
17. Juvenal. iv. 11.
18. Plin. ix.
19. Cic. Epist. xx. ad Atticum. 1.
20. Plin. loc. cit.; Dio Cassius, L. iv.; Senec. De Clement. i. 18.
21. Senec. De Irà. iii. 40.
22. Id. Ib.
23. Dio In Sever. xxi.
24. Règlements de St. Louis.
25. Edit sans date.
26. Lettres Patentes du 19 Mars, 1543.
27. Ib. du 16 Septembre, 1606.
28. The Popish Kingdome, fol. 55.
29. Delamarre.
30. Poésies des Troubadours.
31. Athen. vii. 6, 12 ; Macrob. Saturnal. iii. 16.
32. Athen. loc. cit.
33. Id. Ib.
34. Plin. ix. 17.
35. Martial. xiii. 91.
36. Dio liii.
37. Statutum de Prærogativa Regis ; anno 17, Edward. ii. c. 11.
38. Sonnini, Poissons. tom. iv. p. 351.
39. Id. Ib. p. 341.
40. Id. Ib.
41. Diction. de la Conversation. tom. ii. 533.
42. Diction. d' Histoire Naturel. tom. x. p. 485.
43. Ib.
44. Athen. i. 11.
45. Senec. Quæst. Natur. iii. 17, 18.
46. Plin. ix. 30.
47. Horat. Sat. ii.
48. Martial. x. 31.
49. Juvenal. iv. 11.
50. Sueton. In Tiber. 34.
51. Senec. Epist. 95.
52. Galen. De Aliment. Facultat.
53. Plin. ix. 31.

54. Lamprid. Elogab. 20.
55. Apicius, ix. 13.
56. Id. Ib.
57. Athen. vii. 22.
58. Macrob. Sat. iii. 15 ; Ælian. Var. Hist. c. 173 ; Porphyr. De Abstin. ab Animal.
59. Id. Ib.
60. Plin. x. 70 ; Lucian. De Deâ Syr. ; Martial. x. 30.
61. Varro. R. R. iii. 2, 17.
62. Id. viii. 16.
63. Tertullian. De Pallio.
64. Geoponic. xx.
65. Varro. iii. 3 ; Platina, De Tuendâ Valetudin.
66. Sueton. In Vitel.
67. Lamprid. In Elogab.
68. Athen. i. 6.
69. Horat. Sat. ii. ult.
70. Apicius, x. 8.
71. Galen. De Aliment. Facul. iii.
72. Herodot. ii.
73. Sonnini, Poissons, tom. vi. p. 51.
74. Id. Ib. p. 6o.
75. Macrob. Saturnal. ii. 2.
76. Gessner, De Aquatilibus, iii.
77. Oppian. Halieuticon, x.
78. Pennant, British Zoology, vol. iii. p. 78.
79. Bloch. Ichtyologie : Lamproie.
80. Paolo Giovio.
81. Platina.
82. Id.
83. Athen. vii.
84. Id. Ib.
85. Plin. ix. 17.
86. Id. Ib.
87. Marlianus, Topographia, v.
88. Plato. apud. Athen. vii. 8.
89. Horat. Epod. ii. v. 49.
90. Athen. vii. ; Martial. xiii. 84.
91. Plin. ix. 17.
92. Aristot. ii. 17.
93. Ælian. i. 2.
94. Oppian. Halieut. iv, 78.
95. Horat.
96. Plin. ix. 42.
97. Juvenal. Sat. iv.
98. Id. Ib.
99. Berchoux, Gastronomie.
100. Clem. Alexandr. Pædagog.
101. Athen. i. 6.
102. Plat. apud Athen. vii. 8.
103. Strab.

104. Encyclop. Méthod. Antiquités.
105. Nonnius, Ichthyophagia, p. 9.
106. Aristot. Hist. Animal. viii. 13.
107. Plin. ix. 15.
108. Apicius, ix. 12.
109. Athen.
110. Id.
111. Plin. ix. 3.
112. Cetti, Pesce di Sardegna, p. 134.
113. Aldrovand. De Piscibus ; Gessner, De Piscibus.
114. Eudox. apud Athen. vii.
115. Archestrat. apud Athen. Ib.
116. Philœmon. apud Athen. Ib.
117. Galen. De Aliment. Facult.
118. Plat. apud Athen. vii. 8.
119. Apicius, x. 2.
120. Paw.
121. Herodot. Hist.
122. Apollodor. In Chronic. ; Plutarch. De Solert. Animal. ; Ælian. De Piscibus.
123. Athen. vii.
124. Agathiocid. apud Athen.
125. Macrob. Saturnal. ii.
126. Aristophan. In Lysistrat. 36.
127. Bulenger. De Conviviis. xi. 30.
128. Athen. vii. 12, 13.
129. Hippocrat. De Internis Affect.
130. Apud Athen.
131. Juvenal. Sat. v. ; Nonnius, iii. 5.
132. Apicius, x. 14.
133. Bloch. Ichtyolog. Anguille.
134. Plin. ix. 2.
135. Auson. Mosella.
136. Bloch. Ichtyolog.
137. Aristot. iv. 8 ; vi. 14 ; Athen. vii. ; Plin. xxxii. 11.
138. Alexand. apud Athen. vii.
139. Apicius, iv. 2.
140. Bloch.
141. Id.
142. Plin. ix. 29.
143. Athen. vii.
144. Ælian. Hist. Animal. xvii. 1.
145. Varro. iii. 3. ; Plin. ix. 17, 54.
146. Athen.
147. Macrob. Saturnal. iii. 15.
148. Plin. xxxii. 5.
149. Martial. xiii. 90.
150. Festus.
151. Apicius, x. 12.
152. Rondelet. Poissons.
153. Athen.
154. Apicius, ix. 9.

155. Plin. ix. 17.
156. Athen. vii. 20.
157. Galen. De Aliment. Facult. iii.
158. Bloch.; Sonnini.
159. Aristot. vi. 14.
160. Athen.
161. Id.
162. Auson. In Mosel.
163. Apicius, x. 6.
164. Lacépède, Poissons, tom iii. p. 131, note.
165. Plato apud Athen. vii. 8.
166. Dorion. apud Athen. vii.
167. Arist. Hist. Animal. ii. 5.
168. Plin. ix. 42.
169. Lacépède, Poissons, tom. iii.
170. Id. Ib. p. 117.
171. Salmo à Saltu; Olaus Magnus, xx. 3.
172. Auson. In Mosel. 97.
173. Plin. ix. 18.
174. Id. Ib.
175. Sir W. Scott, The Covenanters, vol. i. chap. viii.
176. Plin. ix. 29.
177. Apicius, ix. 4.
178. Athen. vii. 7; Aldrovand. iii.
179. Scholiast. Aristophan. In Equit. 768.
180. Auson. Mosel. 827.
181. Horat. Sat. ii. 2.
182. Apicius, x. 1.
183. Juvenal. xv. 317.
184. Apicius, ix. 11.
185. Athen. i. 6.
186. Vid. Ælian. Hist. Animal. xiv. 1.
187. Athen. i. 49.
188. Horat. Sat. ii. 8.
189. Plin. xxii. 11.
190. Id. Ib.
191. Auson. Mosel. 125.
192. Id. Ib.
193. Mnesim. apud Athen. ix. 15; Aldrovand. De Piscibus, ii.
194. Apicius, ix. 3.
195. Athen. vii. 22.
196. Galen. De Cib. Boni et Mali Succi.
197. Sonnini, Poissons, tom. iv. p. 143.
198. Aldrovand. De Piscibus, iii. 66.
199. Columell. viii.
200. Plin xxxii. 11.
201. Athen. vii. 8; Aldrovand. ii.
202. Galen. De Aliment. Facult. iii.
203. Apicius, ix. 10.
204. Id. Ib.
205. Athen. i. 6.
206. Plutarch. De Superstit.
207. Apicius, iv. 2.

208. Anaximand. apud Athen. vii.
209. Martial. xiii. 88.
210. Plin. ix. 17.
211. Bosc. Hareng.
212. Sonnini, Anchois.
213. Dio. Caligul.
214. Athen. iii. 12.
215. Horat. Epod. ii. 49.
216. Athen. i. 6.
217. Apicius, ix. 14.
218. Id. ix. 7.
219. Macrob. Saturnal.
220. Lucilius, Sat. xiii.
221. Plutarch. Sympos. ix.; Senec. Epist 108.
222. Athen. iv.; Clem. Alex. Pædag. ii.
223. Athen. loc. cit.
224. Senec. Epist. 88.
225. Plin. xxxii. 6.
226. Juvenal. vi. 302.
227. Plin. loc. cit.
228. Athen. iv.; Macrob. iii.
229. Nonnius, iii. 36.
230. Plin. loc. cit.
231. Id. ix. 54.
232. Plin. loc. cit.; Varro. R. R. iii.
233. Plin. loc. cit.
234. Athen. i. xiii.
235. Senec.
236. Dio.; Sueton.
237. Athen. i. 6.
238. Id. Ib.
239. Auson. Epist. xiii.
240. Id. Ib.; Sidon. Apollinar.
241. Apicius, ix. 6.
242. Id. i. 12.
243. Athen. iii. 23.
244. Id. Ib.
245. Id. Ib.
246. Trallian. De Epilepsiâ.
247. Apicius, ix. 8.
248. Id. iii. 5.
249. Id. i. 29.
250. Athen. loc. cit.
251. Horat. Sat. lib. ii. 4.
252. Isidor. Origin. xii. 6.
253. Strabo. vii.; Plin. ix. 19.
254. Plin. Ib.
255. Ælian. De Animal. xii. 41.
256. Chiliad.
257. Plin. xxxii. 2.
258. Apicius, ix. 2.
259. Id. Ib.
260. Athen. i. 12.
261. Plin. ix. 2.

262. Juvenal.
263. Apicius, ix. 1.
264. Id. Ib.
265. Maton. Parog. apud Athen.
266. Ib.
267. Apicius, loc. cit.
268. Id. Ib.
269. Id. Ib.
270. Id. Ib.
271. Athen. i. 8.
272. Apicius, ix. 5.
273. Isai. xix. 8; Jerem. xvi. 16; Ezech. xlvii. 10.
274. Homer. Odyss. xxii. 384.
275. 944 years B.C.
276. Hesiod. Scut. Hercul. v. 212.
277. Plutarch. Sympos.
278. Ercolano. 1757, tom. i. Tavola, 36.
279. Varro.
280. Cic. Epist. lib. ii. ad Atticum.
281. Senec. Controv. v. 5.
282. Id. Epist. 100.
283. Id. Nat. Quæst. iii. 17.
284. Apicius, i. 2.
285. Galen. De Cib. &c. 15.

XXII.

THE COOK.

1. Medicus ad Palatum.
2. Anton. Liberal. Fab. ii.
3. Senec. Epist. 95.
4. Dio In Neron.
5. Alexand. ab Alexandr. Genial. Dier.
6. Lex Fannia; L. Orchia; L. Cornelia, &c.
7. Martial. Domini debet habere gulam.
8. Athen. i. 31.
9. Homer. Iliad.
10. Evemer. apud Athen. xiv. 22.
11. Athen. vii.
12. Id. i. 8.
13. Id. Ib.
14. Id. Ib.
15. Plato. In Gorg.
16. Athen. i. 7.
17. Id. i. 9.
18. Id. i. 10.
19. Senec. Oculorum Gula.
20. Athen. xii.
21. Id. Ib.
22. Ælian. Var. Hist. i. 27.
23. Plutarch. Præcept. San.

24. Sueton. In Claud. 32.
25. Id. In Vitell.; Dio.
26. Id. Ib.
27. Sueton. In Tiber. 42.
28. Id. In Galba. 22.
29. Spartian. In Vero. 5.
30. Id. In Getâ.
31. Taillevant.
32. Id.
33. Id,
34. Histoire du Dauphiné.
35. Froissart, tom. iv. chap. 2.
36. Ecole de Salerne, &c.
37. Monteil, Histoire des Français, tom. ii p. 68.
38. Mémoires de Lamarche.
39. Onuphr. Panvini.
40. Martial. vii. 30.
41. Varro. R. R. i. 2.
42. Petron. edit. Nodot. tom. i. p. 116.
43. Donat. In Adelph. act iv. sc. 2.
44. Juvenal. vii. 184.
45. Senec. Epist. 47.
46. Varro. De Vitâ Popul. Roman. i.
47. Vid. Lips. Saturn. ii. 2; Juvenal. v. 121.
48. Petron. c. 36; Senec. Epist. 47.
49. Sidon. Apollin. ii. Epist. 9.
50. Ercolano.
51. Petron. c. 47.
52. Stephan. v. Foculus.
53. Horat. Od. i. 9, v. 5.
54. Juvenal. Sat. ii. 262.
55. Rosin. Antiquit. Roman. p. 237.
56. Aristophan. Vesp. act i. sc. 2.
57. Appian. Bell. Civil. iv.
58. Athen. i. 49.
59. Virg. Æneid. iii. 466.
60. Athen. i. viii.; Plin. xvi. 11.
61. Ercolano.
62. Ib.
63. Ib.
64. Lamprid. Elogab. 19; Cic. Pro Rosc. Amer. 133.
65. Encyclopéd. Méthod. Antiquités.
66. Galen. De Compos. Medicam. iii. 5.
67. Apicius, passim.
68. Ercolano; Varro. De L. L. iv. 27.
69. Encyclopéd. loc. cit.
70. Columell. xiî. 46.
71. Apud Siracidem. xiii. 3.
72. Senec. Epist. 85.
73. Caylus, Antiquit. Romain. tom. i.
74. Plin. xxiii. 2.
75. Cato. R. R. 84.
76. Varro. De L. L. iv.; Plin. xxxiii. 4.

77. Ercolano; Winckelmann.
78. Petron. c. 33; Martial. xiv. 121.
79. Athen. i. 6.
80. Caylus, Recueil d'Antiquités, tom. iii. pl. 84, no. 5.
81. Ercolano.
82. Ib.
83. Coel. Rhodig. xiii. 32.
84. Aristophan. In Avibus. 361.
85. Mat. Régnier, Sat. x.
86. Cic. Tuscul. v. 21; Martial. xii. 67; Tit. Liv. xxxix. 6.
87. Athen. ii. 9.
88. Petron. Satyr.
89. Beyerlink. Theatr. Vitæ Human.
90. Cato. c. 74.
91. Plin. xviii. 11.
92. Pers. Sat.; Plin. loc. cit.
93. Plin. Ib.
94. Athen. iv.
95. Varro. R. R. iii. 14.
96. Plin. xviii. 24.
97. Id. Ib.; Veget. De Arte Vet. i. 52.

XXIII.

SEASONINGS.

1. Euseb. Præpar. Evang. i.; Polydor. Virgil. De Rerum. Invent. iii. 5.
2. Levitic. ii. 3.
3. Diodor. Sicul. ii. 48.
4. Galen. De Simplic. Medicam.
5. Festus.
6. Arnob. ii.
7. Sallust. Bell. Tugurt.
8. Athen. iii. 1.
9. Tit. Liv. xi. 9.
10. Plin. xxxi. 7.
11. Lib. vi. F. F. De Captiv. et Post.
12. Delamarre.
13. Plaut. Pœnul. i. 2, 32.
14. Columell. xii. 6.
15. Plin. xxxi. 8.
16. Vid. Scaliger.; Auson. Lect. ii. 28, p. 165.
17. Pollux. vi. 9; Athen. x.
18. Apicius. i. 27.
19. Plin. xxxi. 3, 7.; xxxii. 11.
20. Isidor. Origin. xx. 3.
21. Plin. loc. cit.
22. Id. xxxi. 43.
23. Id. Ib.
24. Martial. xiii. 102.
25. Plin. xxxi. 8.
26. Plin. à Lemaire. tom. viii. p. 439, note.
27. Stephan. Thesaur. Ling. Græc. v. Garon.
28. Id. Ib.; Geoponic. xx.
29. Apicius; Plin. à Lemaire. tom. viii. p. 435, note.
30. Plin. ix. 17.
31. Id. viii. 31.; Nonnius. iii. 44.; Columell. vi. 9.
32. Geoponic. xx.
33. Ib.
34. Ib.
35. Dioscord.; Stephan. loc. cit.
36. Stephan. Ib.; Martial. viii. 26.
37. Stephan. Ib.
38. Galen. De Simplic. Medici. ii.
39. Lamprid. Elogab. 29.; Apicius, i. 31.
40. Apicius, i. 34.
41. Id. i. 33.
42. Id. i. 35.
43. Judic. xiv. 18.
44. Plin. xxii. 24.
45. Geoponic. xv. 7.
46. Ib.
47. Plin. loc. cit.
48. Apollod. ii.; Pausan. viii.; Plin. vii. 56.
49. Genes. xliii. 11.
50. Justin. xiii.
51. Plin. xi. 13.; xxi. 10.
52. Athen. iii. 25.
53. Diog. Laert. Vitæ Philosophor. viii.
54. Athen. ii. 6.
55. Fulgentius, De Obscuris Vocibus.; Arnob.
56. Theophrast. De Melle.
57. Virgil. Georg. iv.
58. Plin. x. 5, 12.
59. Galen. De Aliment. Facult. iii.
60. Varro.
61. Aristot. Hist. Animal. iii. 10.
62. Dioscorid. ii. 75.
63. Id. Ib.; Plin.xxii. 24.
64. Apicius, i. 1.
65. Id. i. 32.
66. Id. Ib.
67. Theophrast. loc. cit.
68. Dioscorid. ii. 75.
69. Plin. xii. 8.
70. Strabo. xv.; Senec. Epist. 64; Galen. De Simpl. Medic. vii.
71. Paul. Æginet. De Ling. Asperitate, c. 2.
72. Pancirol. Rerum Mirabilium, &c. ii. 5.
73. Theophrast. Hist. Plant. iv. 6; ix. 4, 5, 7.

74. Herodot. Hist. ; Aristot. Hist. Animal. ix. 14.
75. Plin. xii. 19.
76. Galen. De Antidotis.
77. Id. De Simplic. Medic. vii.
78. Mathiol. In Dioscorid. i. 13; anno 1570.
79. Saint-Foix, Essais sur Paris.
80. Plin. xii. 7.
81. Theophrast. ix. 22.
82. Dioscorid. ii. 153 ; Plin. xii. 27.
83. Dioscorid. v. 6 , et ibi Mathiol.
84. Galen. De Simplic. Medicam. iv. v.
85. Ruth ii. 12.
86. Athen. ii. 26.
87. Juvenal xiii. 85 ; Martial. xiii. 122.
88. Columell. xii. 17 ; Plin. xiv. 20.
89. Dioscorid. v. 17 ; Galen. Simpl. Medic. i. ; Æginet. De Simpl. p. 51.
90. Spartian. In Hadrian.
91. Columell. xii. 4.
92. Salmas. Exercitat Plinianæ, p. 898 ; Plin. xx. 20.
93. Amelot de la Houssaye, Mémoires Historiques.
94. Athen. ii. 21.
95. Plin. xix. 2.
96. Id. xix. 3.
97. Id. xix. 2.
98. Dioscorides.
99. Id.
100. Athen.
101. Philoxen. apud Athen.
102. Athen. ii. 21.
103. Martial. xiii. 50.
104. Apicius, i. 31.
105. Id. Ib.
106. Platina, De Honestâ Voluptate.
107. Avicenn.
108. Plin. xix. 2.
109. Apicius, i. 25.
110. Dio. In Claud. sub. fin.
111. Id. Ib.
112. Id. Ib.
113. Senec. Epist. xcv.
114. Id. Epist. cviii.
115. Horat. ii. Sat. iv.
116. Senec. Nat. Quæst. iv. 13, sub fin.
117. Martial. xiii. 47.
118. Athen. ii. 19.
119. Id. Ib.
120. Id. Ib.
121. Id. Ib.

XXIV.

PASTRY.

1. Dictionnaire de la Conversation, tom. xlii. p. 344.
2. Genes. xl. 17.
3. Calmet. Bible, tom. vi. p. 257, fol. ; Levit. ii.
4. Athen. iii. 25.
5. Id. Ib.
6. Hesychius ; Plin. viii. 2.
7. Athen. iv. 14.
8. Cic. Familiar. ix. 20.
9. Levitic. ii. 5.
10. Athen. xiv. 14.
11. Id. Ib.
12. Id. Ib.
13. Lamprid. In Elogab. c. 27.
14. Athen.
15. Id. xiv.
16. Juvenal. vi. 202.
17. Cato. R. R. c. 84.
18. Pers. vi. 50.
19. Spartian. In Vero. 5.
20. Cato. R. R.
21. Fabri Thesaurus v. Placenta.
22. Horat. Epist. i. 10, 11 ; Plin. vii. 53 ; Athen. ii.
23. Plin. xviii. 11.
24. Cato. R. R.
25. Id. Ib. c. 80.
26. Plin. xviii. 11.
27. Apicius, vii. 11.
28. Id. Id.
29. Id. Ib.
30. Id. Ib.
31. Taillevant.
32. Id.
33. Id.
34. Plutarch. Vita. Coriolan. ; Plin. xxxvii. cap. ultimo.
35. Polydor. Virgil. v. 2 ; Nouvelles Ephémérides : 6 Janvier.
36. Tertullian. De Idolol. c. 14 ; S. Cyprian. Epist. 103 ; Concil. Trull. can. lxii.
37. Brand's Popul. Antiquit. vol. i. p. 132, 133.
38. Stuckius ; Platina.
39. Fontanon, Ordonnances.
40. Delamarre.
41. Taillevant.
42. Id.
43. Platina, De Honest. Volupt.

XXV.

WATER.

1. Aristot. Metaphys. i. 3; Senec. Nat. Quæst. iii. 13.
2. Herodot.; Cyrill. adv. Jul.
3. Strabo.
4. Jul. Firmicus, De Profan. Relig.; Athanas. orat. contra. Gent.
5. Banier, Mythologie, tom. iv. p. 279.
6. Id. Ib.
7. Virgil. Æneid. viii. 72.
8. Psalm. xciii. 4.
9. Pausan.
10. Tolosanus, In Syntag. Juris. i. 4; Sigonius, De Republ. Athen. iv.
11. Plato. De Legib. vi.
12. 460 years B.C.
13. Plin. xxxi. 3.
14. Frontin. De Aquæduct. i.; Lips. De Magnitud. Rom. iii.
15. Eutrop. ii. 9.
16. Plin. iii. 15; Cassiodor. vii. ep. 6.
17. Plin. xxxi. 6.
18. In Tit. Liv. i.
19. Rosinus, Antiquit. Rom. p. 60.
20. Frontin.
21. Id.
22. Sueton. In. Aug. cap. 13.
23. Ingeniosa Sitis. Martial. xiv. 117.
24. Senec. Nat. Quæst. iv. 13.
25. Ant. Marc. Salvin. in Lect. Acad. Furfur.
26. Senec. loc. cit.
27. Rosin. Ant. Rom. p. 403.
28. Gell. xix. 5; Plin. xix. 4.
29. Martial. xiv. 117.
30. Montfaucon. Antiquit. Expliq.
31. Sueton. In Domit. 21.
32. Id. Ib.
33. Martial. xii.; Juvenal. Sat. v. 60.
34. Athen. i. ii.
35. Dio. In Claud.
36. Antich. Ercolan.
37. Hippocrat. De Diæt.
38. Id. Ib.
39. Ib.
40. Cels. iv. 19.
41. Sueton. In August.
42. Plin. xix. 1.
43. Id. Ib.
44. Mémoires du Sire de Joinville.
45. Plin. xxi. 37.
46. Bory St. Vincent, Essai sur les Iles Fortunées, pp. 220 et seqq.

XXVI.

BEVERAGES,

OF WHICH WATER IS THE FOUNDATION.

1. Diodor. Sicul. iv.
2. Herodot. ii. 77.
3. Plin. xxii. 25; Columell. x. 116; Dioscorid. ii. 79, &c.
4. Plin. loc. cit.
5. Paw.
6. Strab.
7. Plin.; Strab.; Paw.
8. Plin.
9. Aristot. De Ebrietate.
10. Eschyl. In Lycurgo.
11. Sophocl. In Triptolemo.
12. Antholog. Græc.
13. Plin. xxii.
14. Meibom. De Cerevisia, 6, 7; In Thesaur. Gronovii, tom. ix.
15. Tacit. De Morib. German. c. 23; Plin. xiv. 22.
16. Plin. Ib.
17. Dioscorid. ii. 80, 81.
18. Mallet, Northern Antiquities, 6.
19. Cæsar. De Bell. Gall.
20. British Cyclopedia.
21. Ibid.
22. Beckmann. Invent. tom. iv.
23. Vol. xv. p. 201, Edinburgh, 1795.
24. From a Manuscript, quoted by Strutt, Manners, &c. vol., iii. pp. 72, 73.
25. Stow's Chronicles, p. 218.
26. Holinshed, Descript. Brit. 94.
27. Monteil, Histoire des Français, tom. ii. pp. 49, 50.
28. Plin.
29. Hippocrat. De Dentitione; Cels. iii. 7.
30. Mercurial. Observ. iii.; Cœlius, xxx. 21.
31. Spartian. In Hadrian.
32. Plin. xiv.; Q. Curt. lib. xxiii. Hort. c. 16, ex Palladio.
33. Dictionnaire des Origines.
34. Plin. xiv. 16.
35. Deuteron. xiv. 26; xxix. 6; et Bibl. Sacr. passim; Ambrosius, De Helia et Jejun. c. 15; Hieron. ad Nepotian.
36. Plin. xiv. 17.
37. Id. Ib.
38. Isidor. xx. 3.
39. Id.; Paul. Æginet.
40. Paul. Æginet.
41. Dioscorid. v. 22; Pallad. August. 13.
42. Columell. xii. 37; Pallad. xiii. 2.

43. Discorid. v. 34; Plin. xiv. 16.
44. Plin. Ib.
45. Id. Ib.
46. Id. Ib.
47. Cœl. Rhodig. vii. 26 ; xxi. 7.
48. Sueton. In Neron. c. 48.

XXVII.

DRINKING CUPS.

1. Clem. Alexandr. Pædagog, ii. 2.
2. Homer.
3. Eumen. Cardian. et Diodot. Erythræus, In Diariis Rerum ab Alexandro Gestarum.
4. Theopomp. Hist. 26.
5. Aristot. In Syracusan. Polit.
6. Sueton. In Tiber. 42.
7. Id. Ib.
8. Athen. i. 30.
9. Homer. Odyss.
10. Hippocrat. De Diœt. iii. sub. fin.
11. Senec. De Tranquillitate Animæ, sub fin.
12. Plat. De Republ. ii.
13. Athen. i. 21, 23.
14. Id. xi. 14.
15. Musonius, De Luxu Græcor. c. 2.
16. Id. Ib.
17. Strab.
18. Cæsar.
19. Id.
20. Valer. iv. 3 ; Senec. Epist. 95.
21. Ovid. Fast. iii.; Tibull. i. 10.
22. Plin. xvi. 35.
23. Id. Ib.
24. Apul. Milesiar. ii.
25. Plin. xxxvi. 26.
26. Cœl. Rhodig. Antiq. Lection. xx. 30 ; Crinitus. Honest. Disciplin. xxiii. 4 ; Douza. Comment. In Petron.
27. Petron. à Nodot. tom. 1. pp. 198, 200.
28. Plin. Præfat. ad libr. xxxiii.
29. Rosin. Antiq. Roman. p. 398.
30. 61 years B.C.
31. Plin. xxxvii. 2.
32. Id. Ib.
33. Martial. xiv. 113.
34. Scaliger. Exercitat. 92.
35. Cardan. De Subtilit. v. f. 143.
36. Mme. Dacier, Eutrop. Delphin. p. 104.
37. Mariette ; Caylus, &c.

38. Propert. lib. 4, eleg. 5.
39. Christius, De Murrinis, &c. Lips. 1743.
40. Mongez.
41. Montfaucon, Antiquit. Expliq. tom. ii. pl. 78
42. Apuleius; Sidon. Apollinar. carm. 24 in fine.
43. Martial. viii. 51.
44. Plin. xxxiii. 12.
45. Id. Præfat. ad lib. xxxiii.
46. Athen. xi.
47. Montfaucon. Antiq. Expliq.

XXVIII.

WINE.

1. Herod. ii. ; Plutarch. De Isid. et Osirid. ; Diodor. iii.
2. Cic. De Natur. Deor. iii.
3. Theopomp.
4. Plutarch.
5. Aurel. Victor.
6. Eutrop. ix. 17.
7. Genes. ix. 20.
8. Plin. xiv.
9. Deuteron. xxii. 9.
10. Ib. xxii. 6.
11. Osee. xiv. 8.
12. Ezech. xxvii. 18.
13. Genes. xlix. 11 ; Jerem. ii. 21.
14. Psalm ciii. 15.
15. Calmet. Commentaire sur Esther. v. 6.
16. Cantic. viii. 2.
17. Herodot. i.
18. Id. Ib.
19. Banier, Mythologie, tom. i. p. 464.
20. Plutarch. De Isid. et Osirid.
21. Athen. xv.
22. Tit. Liv.
23. Horat. Epist. lib. ii. ad Torquat.
24. Serenus Sammonicus.
25. Euseb. In Chron.
26. Plin. vii. 56.
27. Diodor. Sicul. v.
28. Plutarch. De Legend Poet.
29. Plutarch. Sympos. iii. 10.
30. Hippocrat. De Diætet.
31. Id. Ib.
32. Herodot. iv.
33. Martial. viii. 26.
34. Horat. Od. ii. 11, 17.
35. S. Augustin. De Civ. Dei. xviii. 13.

36. Ovid. Fast. iv. 861, et seqq.
37. Plin. xviii. 19.
38. Banier, Mythol. tom. i. p. 548.
39. Columell. xi. 2 ; iv. 28.
40. Leg. Duod. Tabul. L. lxii. ; Plin. xviii. 3.
41. Ulpian.
42. Apicius, i. 17.
43. Id. Ib.
44. Geoponic. vi. 11.
45. Ib.; Virgil. Georg. ii. 241.
46. Georg. ii. 7.
47. Athen. v.; Anacr. Od. xvii.
48. Columell. xii. 41.
49. Plin. xiv. 11 ; Athen. i.
50. Vitruv. xi. 9.
51. Longus. ii. 1, 2.
52. Cato. R. R. 12, 13, 18 ; Vitruv. vi. 6.
53. Le Pitture Antiche d'Ercolano, Napoli, 1757, tom. i ; Tavola, 35.
54. Varro. i. 54 ; Cato. 23.
55. Cic. De Clar. Orat. c. 83.
56. Nonnius, xvii. 13.
57. Geoponic. vi. 15.
58. Le Pitture, &c. loc. cit.; Athen. i. 31 ; Dioscor. v. 9.
59. Pallad. xi. 18.
60. Plin. xiv. 9.
61. Id. Ib.
62. Ib. ix. 57.
63. Id. xviii. 74.
64. Id. Ib.
65. Ovid. Fast. iv. 782 ; Festus, Burranica.
66. Geoponic. vi. 16 ; Plutarch. Quæst. Nat. 26 ; Plin. xiv. 11.
67. Geoponic. vi. 12.
68. Varro. R. R. i. 13 ; Geoponic. vi. 2, 12.
69. Le Pitture, &c.
70. Antiq. de Pomp.
71. Sponii, Miscell. Erud. Antiq. p. 125.
72. Id. Ib.; Juvenal. xiv. 311.
73. Plin. xiv. 21.
74. Geoponic. vi. 2 ; Varro. R. R. i. 13 ; Cato. R. R. 23.
75. Columell. xii. 25, 80 ; Cato. 107 ; Varro. i. 65 ; Geoponic. iv. 12.
76. Id.
77. Id.
78. Geoponic. vii. 15 ; Columell. xii. 38.
79. Geoponic. vii. 22.
80. Ib. vii. 37.
81. Pollux. vi. 19 ; x. 75.

82. Geoponic. vii. 5, 6.
83. Horat. Art. Poet. v. 21.
84. Id. Od. i. 20.
85. Petron. 34.
86. Senec. Epist. 115 ; Columell. xii. 41.
87. Columell. i 6 ; Horat. Od. iii. 8.
88. Plin. xiv. 4.
89. Id. xiv. 6, 29.
90. Id. xiv. 13.
91. Virgil. Georgic. ii. 91.
92. Horat. Epod. ix. 34
93. Id. Sat. i. 10, 24.
94. Geopon. passim.
95. Plin. xiv. 6.
96. Id. Ib.
97. Id. Ib.
98. Id. Ib.
99. Id. xiv. et xxiii.
100. Athen. i. et ix.
101. Aristot.
102. Galen.
103. Petron. c. 34.
104. Plin. xiv. 4.
105 Martial. xi. 60.
106. Apul. Milesiar. ii.
107. Senec. Epist. 64.
108. Lucan. Pharsal. x. 164.
109. Athen. i. 47.
110. Id. Ib.
111. Id. Ib.
112. Id. Ib.
113. Apicius, i. 6.
114. Athen. i.
115. Plin. xiv.
116. Cato. R. R.
117. Plin. xiv. 8.
118. Id. Ib.
119. Museum Borbonicum. tom. iii. ; Ta. vol. 28.
120. Plin. xiv. 9.
121. Varro. De Vitâ Pop. Rom.; Columell. R. R. ; Martial. xiii. 106 ; Juvenal. xiv. 270.
122. Columell. xii. 27.
123. Dio. Commod.
124. Macrob. vii. 12 ; Plin. xxii.
125. Leclerc, Histoire de la p. 479.
126. Geoponic. viii.
127. Ibid.
128. Apicius, i. 4.
129. Id. Ib.
130. Id. Ib.
131. Plin. xiv. 13.
132. Ercolano.

133. Plin. xxiii. 1.
134. Columell. iii. 3.
135. Bœkh, Public Economy of Athens, vol. i. p. 133.
136. Valer Max. ii. 1.
137. Plin. xiv. 13.
138. Fab. Pictor. apud Plin. Ib.
139. Plin. Ib.
140. Id. xiv. 6.
141. Id. xiv. 28.
142. Athen. v.
143. Dio. Trajan.
144. Id. In Sever.
145. Sueton. In Claud.
146. Dio. Domitian.
147. Id. In Caligul.
148. Athen. i. 47.
149. Tibull. iii. eleg. 6 ; Martial. v. 65.
150. Athen. i. 48.
151. Plin. xiv. 16.
152. Plutarch. Sympos. viii. 6.
153. Festus.
154. Plin. loc. cit.
155. Id. Ib.
156. Id. Ib. Columell. xii. 35.
157. Plin. loc cit. ; Columell. xii. 37.
158. Dioscorid. v. 13 ; Plin. loc. cit.
159. Meursius.
160. Plin. loc. cit.
161. Strutt, Manners and Customs of the Ancient Britons, vol. 1. p. 7.
162. W. Malmsbur. De Pont. lib. iv.
163. Delamarre, Traité de la Police.
164. Id. Ib.
165. Id. Ib.
166. Mélanges Tirés d'une Grande Bibliothèque.
167. Ménage.
168. Arnaud de Villeneuve ; Traité du Régime de la Santé.
169. Les Bigarrures du Seigneur des Accords.
170. Baluze. Capitul. Reg. Franc. passim.
171. Fontanon. Conf. des Ordon. tom. ii. p. 822.
172. Strutt, Manners and Customs, &c.
173. Id. Ib.
174. Id. Ib.

XXIX.

REPASTS.

1. Athen. i. 16.
2. Id. i. 15.

3. Homer. Iliad.
4. Athen. i. 16.
5. Aristot. Probl. xxvi. 45.
6. Posidippus. In Epigr.
7. Hierap. Theodor. de Certam.
8. Ætol. Alexand.
9. Theodorus.
10. Xanthus, In Lydiacis.
11. Theopomp.
12. Clearch.
13. Mnesimach, In Philippo.
14. Crates Theban. In Lamia.
15. Hecatæus apud Athen.
16. Sueton, In Claud. 33.
17. Id. Ib.
18. Id. In Galba. 22.
19. Id. In Vitell. 13.
20. Virgil. Æneid. iii.
21. Sueton. loc. cit.
22. Id. In Vitell. 17.
23. Fuller's Worthies.
24. Berchoux, Gastronomie, note.
25. Athen. i. 19.
26. Herodot. i. 63 ; Theophrast. Charact. c. 3.
27. Plat. Epist. 7.
28. Athen. i. 9.
29. Id. Ib.
30. Id. v.
31. Plutarch. Sympos. viii. 6.
32. Ecclesiast. x. 16.
33. Mercurial. Variar. lect. iv. 17, In Arte Gymnast. i. 11.
34. Homer. Odyss.
35. Athen. i. 19 ; Aristophan. In Avib. 1286.
36. Id. Ib. ; Schrevelius ; Plutarch. Sympos. viii. 6.
37. Apuleius, Metam. i.
38. Martial. xiv. 233.
39. Apul. loc. cit.
40. Sueton. In August. 76.
41. Genes. xliii. 16.
42. Act. x. 9, 10.
43. Athen. i. 9. Plutarch. Sympos. viii. 6.
44. Cic. Tusculan. Quæst. 5.
45. Sueton. In Caligul. 58.
46. Horat. Sat. i. 6.
47. Senec. Epist. 84, 87.
48. Sueton. In Claud. 32.
49. Berchoux, Gastronomie, notes.
50. Isidor. Origin. xx.
51. Joseph. De Bello Jud. vii.
52. Jud. xx. 26 ; II. Reg. i. 12 ; Ib. iii. 25.
53. Biblia Sacra, passim ; Iliad. ix. 206, 218 ; Odyss. xv. 322.

54. Homer. Iliad. xxi. 363.
55. Id. Ib. ix. 217.
56. Id. Odyss. xvii. 455.
57. Id. Iliad. vii. 480.
58. Id. Ib. xii. 311.
59. Id. Ib. ix. 225.
60. Id. Odyss. i. 226 ; Terent. Eunuch. iii. 4 ; Athen. viii.
61. Aristophan. Eccl. 652.
62. Macrob. Saturnal. ii. 13 ; Val. Max. ii. 1.
63. Biblia Sacra, passim.
64. II. Reg. xix. 35.
65. See La Farce de Pathelin.
66. Mémoires de Dangeau.
67. Plato. De Republ. iii. 13.
68. Pollux, vi. 83.
69. Martial. iv. 8.
70. Juvenal. i. 95.
71. Liv. ix.
72. Sueton. in Vitell. 13.
73. Nicolas, Etudes sur le Christianisme, tom. i. p. 254.
74. Strabo ; Diodor. Sicul. ; Cæsar.
75. Strutt, Manners, &c. vol. i. p. 48.
76. Id. Ib.
77. Id. Ib. p. 49.
78. Plutarch. Sympos. i. ; Xenoph. Respubl. Laced. ; Plat. De Conviviis.
79. Exod. xxxii. 6 ; I. Reg. ix. 22, et passim.
80. Philo. De Vitâ Contempl.
81. S. Paul. I. Corinth. xi. 20, et seqq. ; Chrysostom. Homil. 27 ; Tertull. Apologet. c. 39 ; Augustin. Epist. 64 ; Baron. Annal. sub an. 57, 377, 384.
82. Plat. De Conviviis ; Aristot. Polit. ii. 8 ; vii. 10.
83. Xenoph. De Repub. Lac. ; Plutarch. In Vita Lycurg.
84. Plutarch. Ib.
85. Diogen. Laert. ; Plutarch. Vita Solon.
86. Flor. i. 1 ; Liv. i. 6 ; Dionys. Halicarn. Ant. Rom. i. ; Plutarch. Vita Romuli.
87. Plutarch. Vita Sullæ.
88. Sueton. In J. Cæsar.
89. Bulenger, De Conviviis.
90. Id. Ib.
91. Vid. Sueton. ; Lamprid. ; Dio. &c.
92. Id.
93. Apud Strutt, Manners, &c. vol. iii. p. 111.
94. Monteil, Histoire des Français, tom. ii. p. 126.
95. Id. Ib. tom. vii. p. 338, et seqq.

96. See Piganiol, Description de la France.
97. Holinshed, p. 969.
98. Stow, Chron. p. 267.
99. Id. Survey of London, p. 521.
100. Strutt, Manners, &c. vol. ii. p. 104.
101. Holinshed. Descrip. Brit. 94.
102. Massinger, The City Madam.
103. Id. Ib.
104. Killigrew, The Parson's Wedding.
105. Strutt, Manners, &c. vol. ii. p. 19.
106. Mathieu Paris, anno 1243.
107. Stow's Survey of London ; apud Strutt, vol. ii. p. 19.
108. Monteil, Histoire des Français, tom. i. p. 106, et seqq.
109. L'Isle des Hermaphrodites.
110. Contes d' Eutrapel.
111. Ibid.
112. Des Accords, Les Bigarrures. ch. 6.
113. Aventures de Foeneste, liv. iv. ch. 2.

XXX.

VARIETY OF REPASTS.

1. Biblia Sacra, passim.
2. Levitic. iii. 16.
3. Isai. xxv. 6.
4. Prov. xxi. 17.
5. III. Reg. iv. 22, 23.
6. Biblia Sacra, passim.
7. Ap. Ulric. Rasium, In Catal. Legg. Antiquar. ad Leg. Jul. de Annonâ.
8. Plato. De Leg. vi. xxxiv. ; Aristot. de Republ. iv. 4, 15 ; vi. 8 ; Postel. De Magistrat. Athen.
9. Gorræi. Annal.
10. Accurs.
11. Rosin. Antiquit. Roman. p. 533.
12. Athen. i. 4.
13. Philostrat.
14. Athen. i. 5.
15. Id. v. ; Homer. Virgil. passim ; Banier ; Stuckius.
16. Arnob. iii.
17. Varro.
18. Columell.
19. Senec. De Vitâ Beatâ, c. 11.
20. Liv. xxiv.
21. Plaut. Menech. i. 1, 25.
22. Tibull. i. 3,
23. Macrob. Saturnal. i. 7.
24. Horat. Od. ii. 14.

25. Varro. R. R. iii. 6.
26. Apul. Metam. iv. 152.
27. Sueton. ; Lamprid. ; Dio.
28. Plin, ix. 55.
29. Possidon. ii.
30. Crinit. De Honest. Discipl. xxiv. 5.
31. Spartian. ; Stuckius.
32. Lucian. In Lapith.
33. Sueton. In Vitell. 13.
34. Plaut. Bacch. i. 1, 61.
35. Vatin. c. 12 ; Varro. apud Nonnium. i. 234.
36. Barthélemy, Anacharsis.
37. Pererius, Comment. In Daniel.
38. Athen. iv.
39. Polyæn. Strateg. vi.
40. Athen. ii. ix.
41. Id. iv.
42. Aristoph. Acharn.
43. Monteil. Histoire des Français, tom. i. p. 203.
44. Id. Ib. iii. p. 489.
45. Strutt. Manners, &c. vol. iii. p. 113.
46. From a Manuscript in the Harleian Library, quoted by Strutt, Manners, &c. vol. iii. p. 114.
47. Taillevant. Le Viandier.
48. Id. Ib.
49. Id. Ib.
50. Id. Ib.
51. Id. Ib.
52. Id. Ib.

XXXI.

THE DINING-ROOM.

1. Valla. iv.
2. Fest. Pomp. iii.
3. Vid. Fabr. v. Solarium.
4. Petron. Satyric.
5. Ercolano, &c. ; Gell's Pompeiana, passim ; Senec. Epist. 90.
6. Sueton. In Neron. 31.
7. Id. Ib.
8. Id. Ib.
9. Senec. De Tranquill. Anim. c. 9.
10. Cornel. Nepos.
11. Juvenal. Sat. ii.
12. Athen. iii. 21 ; Gell.iii. 19.
13. Athen. Lys. Frag. 46.
14. Athen. Pollux. x. 122 ; Plat. Repub. iii. ; Theophr. Charact. 22.
15. Juvenal. iii. 204.

16. Encyclop. Méthod. Antiquit.
17. Ib.
18. Ib.
19. Virgil. Æn. vii. 528.
20. Monstrelet, Chroniques.
21. Mélanges Tirés d'une Grande Bibliothèque.
22. Ib.
23. Chroniques de St. Denis.
24. Vigiles de Charles VII.
25. L'Isle des Hermaphrodites.
26. Jerem. xxxvi. 22.
27. Ercolano, &c.
28. Plin. Epist. ii. 17.
29. Apul. Metam. iv.
30. Columell. ii. 22.
31. Sil. Italic. Punicor. vi.
32. Petron. à Nodot. tom. i. p. 116.
33. Paulinus, Episcop. Nolæ. D. Felicis Natali, 6.
34. Mercure Galant. Mars, 1681.

XXXII.

THE TABLE.

1. Athen. i. 20.
2. Tibull. ii. 6 ; Valer. Flac. Argonaut. i.
3. Plin. xxxiii. 11.
4. Hom. Odyss. iii. 138.
5. Athen. xi. 78.
6. Athen. ix. 75.
7. Homer. Odyss. iii. 354 et seqq. ; 361 et seqq.
8. Athen. xi. 27.
9. Potter, ii. p. 377.
10. Liv. ix. Decad. 4.
11. Id. Ib.
12. Plin. xvi. 27.
13. Id. xiii. 15.
14. Id. Ib.
15. Id. Ib. ; Senec. De Tranquil. Anim. c. i. ; Id. De Beneficiis, vii. 9.
16. Plin. ix. 11.
17. Id. Ib.
18. Id. xvi.
19. Fest. v.
20. Varro. L. L. iv.
21. Sidon. Apollin. Epist. ii. 2.
22. Id. Ib. i. 11.
23. Rosin. Ant. Rom. p. 377.
24. Servius. Æn. i. ad finem.
25. Homer. Odyss. i. 259 ; Pind. Olymp. i. 26.

26. Martial.
27. Apul. Milesiar. ii. ; Basil. Magnus Orat. ad Divites.
28. Plin. xiii. 15.
29. Id. Ib.
30. Id. Ib.
31. Id. Ib.
32. Stuckius.
33. Id.; Calmet.
34. Gregor. Tur.
35. Eginhard.
36. Polydor. Virgil. p. 257 ; Rapin De Thoiras.
37. Varro. L. L. iv. 26.
38. Printed A.D. 1508

THE TABLE SEATS.

39. Calmet.
40. i. Reg. ix. 22. ; xx. 25.
41. Calmet. tom. v. fol. 256.
42. Diodor. Sicul.
43. Ercolano, tom. i. tav. 29 ; Athen. xi. 72.
44. Athen. i. 31.
45. Id. Ib.
46. Id. Ib.
47. Isidor. xx. 11.
48. Valer. Maxim. ii. 1.
49. Rosinus ; Stuckius.
50. Scholiast. Juvenal. Sat. v. 17.
51. Rosin. p. 380.
52. Athen. ii. 9.
53. Martial. ii. 46.
54. Id. iii. 49.
55. Rosinus.
56. Horat. Serm. ii. 3, 253.
57. Stuckius ; Rosinus ; Ercolano, passim.
58. Lambin. In Sat. iv. lib. ii.; Horat.; Mercurial. De Art. Gymnast.
59. Xenoph. De Pæd. Cyri, viii.
60. Plutarch. Sympos.
61. Lamprid. In Elogab.
62. Spartian. In Vero.
63. Lamprid. loc. cit.
64. Id. Ib.
65. Possidonius.
66. Strabo.
67. Diodor.
68. Le Moine de St. Gal.
69. Ménage.
70. L'Isle des Hermaphrodites.
71. Vie de St. Arnould.
72. Mélanges Tirés d'une Grande Biblio-thèque.
73. Vita S. Berlandæ.

74. Martial. xii. 29.
75. Alain Chartier.
76. L'Isle des Hermaphr.
77. Martial. loc. cit.
78. Plin. xxxv. 15 ; xxxvi. 19.
79. Id. Ibid.

XXXIII.

THE SERVANTS.

1. Gruterus, pp. 260, 966, 973.
2. Kipping. Antiquitat.
3. Dionys. Halicarnass. ii.
4. Exod. xxi. 6 ; Deuteron. xv. 17.
5. Juvenal. Sat. i.
6. Cœl. Rhodig. Antiquit. viii. 11.
7. Zachar. xiii. 6.
8. Plaut. Casin. act ii. sc. 6.
9. Gruterus, p. 596.
10. Petron. Satyric.
11. Columell. i. ; Tibull. i. 7.
12. Vid. Pignorium, De Servis.
13. Id. Ib. ; Petron. loc. cit.
14. Senec. Epist. 47.
15. Plin. xxxv. 10 ; Senec. De Irâ. iii. 37.
16. Pignor. loc. cit.
17. Sueton. In Domit. 16; Capitol. Pertin. 4.
18. Hildebrand. Compend. Antiquit. Rom.
19. Plin. xxxii. 6 ; Petron. c. 47.
20. Petron. c. 35.
21. Id. c. 36.
22. Philo. De Vitâ Contemplativâ.
23. Plaut. Trin. ii. 1, 22.
24. Propert. ii. 25, 11.
25. Terent. Eunuch. iii. 5, 47 ; Fulv. Ursin. In Appendic. ad Ciaccon.
26. Plaut. Most. iv. 1, 24 ; Terent. Adelphi. 12.
27. Pignorius ; Sueton. In Claud. 44.
28. Petron. c. 22 ; Pignorius.
29. Senec. Epist. 29 ; Lips. Elector. i. 19.
30. Ulpian. L. i. § 5, Dig. De Naut. Caupon. et Stabular.
31. Id. Dig. xxxviii. t. 7, L. viii. Fin. § 1.
32. Stuckius.

XXXIV.

THE GUESTS.

1. Genes. xliii. et passim.
2. Schol. Theocrit. In Idyll. vii. 24 ; Plut. Sympos. viii. 6.

3. Athen. i. 21.
4. Id. i. 23.
5. Homer.
6. Athen. i. 19.
7. Id. i. 7.
8. Xenoph. De Republ. Laced. ; Plut. Vita Lycurg.
9. Athen. i.
10. Plutarch. Sympos.
11. Apul. Milesiar. x.
12. Macrob. Saturnal. iii. 17.
13. Gell. xiii. 11 ; De Num. Conviv.
14. Macrob. loc. cit.
15. Sammonic. Severus ; Macrob. loc. cit.
16. Plaut. ; Horat.
17. Plaut.
18. Athen. vi. 5 ; Terent. Eunuch. ii. 2, 13, et 16.
19. Virg. Æn. i. ; Plaut. Pers. v. 2 ; Athen. xiv.
20. Genes. xviii. 4 ; xix. 2 ; Judic. xix. 21 ; Luc. vii. 44 ; 1 Timoth. v. 10, et passim.
21. Tibull. Eleg. iv. 6.
22. Marc. xiv. 3.
23. Horat. Od. iii. 14 ; Anacr. passim.
24. Plin. xiv. 22 ; Plut. Sympos. ; Athen. x.
25. Strutt, Anglo-Saxons, vol. i. p. 49.
26. Id. Ib. p. 48.
27. Froissard.
28. Saint-Foix, Essais sur Paris.
29. Laneham, Sports exhibited at Kenilworth.
30. Johan. Sarisburiensis, i. 8, p. 34.
31. Saint-Foix, Essais, tom. iv. p. 135.
32. Herodot. ii.
33. Sapient. iii. 4.

XXXV.

A ROMAN SUPPER.

1. Genes. xviii. ; Esther, v. ; Matth. xxii.
2. Plin. xxxv. 10.
3. Mercurial. De Arte Gymnast. p. 94, edit. Frisii ; Apul. Metamorph. v. In Principio ; Id. lib. iv. Asini.
4. Apul. loc. cit.
5. Leclerc, Histoire de la Médecine, p. 573.
6. Apul. lib. i. Apologiæ Suæ, ex Catull.
7. Sammonic. Seren. De Medicinâ, c. 15.
8. Plaut. In Captivis, act i. sc. 2, v. 84.
9. Martial. v. 44.
10. Plin. vii. 60.

11. Id. xxxvi. 10.
12. Turneb. Adversar. xxiii. 19 ; xxvii. 18.
13. Theophrast. Charact. 20.
14. Virgil. Æn. i. v. 729.
15. Montfaucon. Antiq. Expl.
16. Petron. à Nodot. tom. i. p. 122.
17. Plutarch. Problem. Romanor. 76.
18. Petron. loc. cit.
19. Terent. Heautontimor. act i. sc. 1.
20. Octav. Ferrarius, De Re Vestiariâ, i. 31.
21. Le Pitture Antiche d'Ercolano, tom. i. tav. 14.
22. Dio. lxix.
23. Senec. De Vitâ Beatâ ; Tibull. iv. 6 ; Psalm. passim.
24. Sil. Ital. Punicor. vi.
25. Petron. Conviv. Trimalcion.
26. Just. Lips.
27. Juvenal. Sat. xi.
28. Pacatus.
29. Vitruv. Architect. v. 8.
30. Quintilian. Institut. Orator. i. 14.
31. Valer. Maxim. ii. 1.
32. Arnob. ii.
33. Id. Ib.
34. Quintilian. Declamat. 301.
35. Juvenal. Sat. v. 32 ; vi. 154.
36. Terent. Eunuch. act. i. sc. 2, v. 85.
37. Virgil. Æn. v.
38. Cic. ad Familiar. ix. 20.
39. Horat. Sat. ix. 8, 9.
40. Petron. à Nodot. tom. i. p. 124.
41. Id. Ib.
42. Id. Ib.
43. Apicius, ii. 1.
44. Id. Ib.
45. Id. Ib.
46. Petron. p. 128.
47. Athen. iv.
48. Id. Ib.
49. Id. Ib.
50. Petron. tom. i. p. 130.
51. Alex. Trallian. lib. Problem 1.
52. Aul. Gell. xv. 2.
53. Plutarch. Sympos. i. Quæst. 4.
54. Martial. vi. 89.
55. Id. iii. 8.
56. Lucan. Pharsal. lib. iii. carm. 14.
57. Athen. iii. 21.
58. Virgil. Georg. ii. 528.
58 A Macrob. Saturnal. ii. 9.
59. Martial. xiii. 52.
60. Plin.
61. Martial. iii. 5.
62. Id. xiii. 71.

63. Juvenal. i. 141,
64. Petron. à Nodot, tom. i. p. 136.
65. Martial. xiii. 44.
66. Id. xiii. 56.
67. Id. xiii. 55.
68. Petron. tom. i. p. 130.
69. Id. p. 136.
70. Martial. iii. 82.
71. Id. Ib.
72. Horat. Sat. ii. 8, 86.
73. Petron. p. 138.
74. Martial. i. 62.
75. Petron. p. 132.
76. Id. Ib.
77. Virgil. Æn. ii. 49.
78. Plaut. Cur. i. 3, 15.
79. Encyclop. Méthod. Antiquités.
80. Plaut. In Sticho.
81. Sueton. In Galba.
82. Juvenal. Sat. xi.
83. Gell. xiii. 11.

84. Martial. v. 79.
85. Fest. Paniroll. tom. ii. tit. 2, De Porcellanis.
86. Nicephor. Gregoras; Manilius; Nicetas; Vopiscus.
87. Casaub. In Athen. i. 15.
88. Xenoph. In Conviv.
89. Herodot. vi. 129.
90. Xenoph. loc. cit.; Caylus. Recueil d'Antiquités. tom. i. p. 202.
91. Caylus, Ib. ; Athen. iv.
92. Socrat. In Conviv. Xenoph.
93. Horat. Sat. lib. ii. 7, v. 82.
94. Caylus, tom. iv. pl. 80, No. 1 ; tom. vi. pl. 90, No. 3 ; tom. vii. p. 164.
95. Vet. Scholiast. Juvenal. ad v. 162, sat. 11.
96. Rosinus, Antiquit. Roman. p. 391.
97. Macrob. Saturnal. ii. 1.
98. Rosinus, Ib.
99. Id. p. 410.

TABLE OF RECIPES

OF

Ancient Cookery, and for the making of various Dishes.

———

FISH.

SAUCE AND SEASONING.

WATER.

BEVERAGES.

TEA.

COFFEE.

INDEX.

Page 16, *line* 19, *for* which great and the, *read* which the great and glorious. *P.* 19, *l.* 16, *for* Picardy to make bread, *read* in Picardy. To make bread. *P.* 19, *l.* 16, *for* of leaven and, *read* of leaven is required, and. *P.* 26, *l.* 6, *for* Flamine, *read* Flamen. *P.* 26, *l.* 25, *for* leaves *read* loaves. *P.* 27, *l.* 20, *for* Cabire *read* Cabira. *P.* 28, *l.* 28, *for* hand-mill ; by the Britons, *read* hand-mill, by the Britons. *P.* 32, *l.* 11, *for* Megalarte and Megalomar, *read* Megalartus and Megalomazus. *P.* 33. *l.* 2, *for* escarites, *read* escharites. *P.* 33, *l.* 7, *for* melitutes, *read* melitates. *P.* 37, *l.* 8, *for* Septier, *read* Setier. *P.* 50, *l.* 25, *for* Ciens cheris, *read* lieux cheris. *P.* 63, *l.* 28, *for* chrysolacanon, *read* chrysolachanon. *P.* 65, *l.* 34, *for* has, *read* have. *P.* 67, *l.* 20, *for* Amitermes, *read* Amiternum. *P.* 68, *l.* 18, *for* possessed, *read* possesses. *P.* 79, *l.* 11, *for* Algidea, *read* Algidus. *P.* 84, *l.* 25, *for* dressed it in, *read* dressed in. *P.* 93, *l.* 32, *for* Corcyrus, *read* Corcyra. *P.* 98, *l.* 15, *for* Halmade, read Halmades. *P.* 99, *l.* 26, *for* Venafra, *read* Venafrum. *P.* 100, *l.* 31, *for* sechar, *read* schecar. *P.* 103, *l.* 11, *for* Cœcilian, *read* Cecilian. *P.* 106, *l.* 18, *for* fruit of, *read* fruit, the. *P.* 124, *l.* 31, *for* Hyberbius, *read* Hyperbius. *P.* 125, *l.* 2, *for* Erichtonius, *read* Erichthonius. *P.* 129, *l.* 1, *for* curators, *read* curator. *P.* 129, *l.* 25, *for* life, *read* life, the. *P.* 136, *l.* 16, *for* Chalies, *read* Chalcis. *P.* 139, *l.* 38, *for* à la Bœotienne *read* à la Bèotienne. *P.* 143, *l.* 15, *for* Thasos, *read* Thasus. *P.* 149, *l.* 2, *for* Mœlos, *read* Melos. *P.* 153, *l.* 2, *for* Carniphobis, *read* Carniphobus. *P.* 150, *l.* 25, *for* Scipio, Metellus, and, *read* Scipio Metellus and. *P.* 170, *l.* 26, *for* philosopher, *read* philologist. *P.* 171, *l.* 17, *for* bouturos, *read* bouturon. *P.* 176, *l.* 7, *for* consort of Nero, *read* consort of Augustus. *P.* 189, *l.* 5, *for* consectuive, *read* consecutive. *P.* 203, *l.* 23, *for* Marmot, *read* Marmol. *P.* 213, *l.* 9, *for* scare, *read* scar. *P.* 216, *l.* 9, et passim, *for* accipenser, *read* acipenser. *P.* 225, *l.* 8, *for* Pachynum, *read* Pachynus. *P.* 296, *l.* 13, *for* Sicyona, *read* Sicyon. *P.* 230, *l.* 23, *for* pèsant, *read* pèsent. *P.* 235, *l.* 21, *for* of Scyathus, *read* of Sciathos. *P.* 236, *l.* 29, *for* the Mostella, *read* the Mosella. *P.* 237, *l.* 17, *for* the Bulistes, *read* the Balistes. *P.* 238, *l.* 2, of Phaleres, *read* of Phalera. *P.* 242, *l.* 9, *for* of Polareo, *read* of Pelorus. *P.* 247, *l.* 6, *for* Minturnus, *read* Minturnæ. *P.* 250, *l.* 12, *for* a hook, *read* to hook. *P.* 251. *l.* 24, *for* Pandarea, *read* Pandarus. *P.* 253, *l.* 12, *for* the act of eating, *read* the art of eating. *P.* 378, *l.* 3, *for* Cnide *read* Cnidus. *P.* 270, *l.* 12, *for* Acarnidea, Alopecomesia, *read* Acarne, Alopeconnesus. *P.* 291, *l.* 26, *for* eleven hundred, *read* eleven. *P.* 293, *l.* 25, *for* he prayed it might be, *read* he prayed that the Tiber might be. *P.* 309, *l.* 27, *for* Simon introduced Pauli, *read* Simon Pauli introduced. *P.* 317, *l.* 25, *for* we have spoken, *read* we will soon speak. *P.* 323, *l.* 1, *for* Helbon, *read* Hebron. *P.* 325, *l.* 39, *for* Plate III., *read* Plate I. *P.* 366, *l.* 30, *for* minutalim, *read* minutatim. *P.* 378, *l.* 15 and 36, *for* Procillatores, *read* Procillator.

DESCRIPTION OF PLATE No. XXVI. A, Page 365.

No. 1.   Terra-Cotta Drinking-Vase, in the shape of a Bird.
No. 2.   Drinking-Vase in the shape of a Tea-pot.
No. 3.   Drinking-Cup, with Jupiter's Head.